3 **M**agilumiere
MAGICAL GIRLS INC.

STORY BY **Sekka Iwata**   *ART BY* **Yu Aoki**

KANA SAKURAGI

Kana is struggling to find a job when Magical Girl Koshigaya entices her to come work for Magimuliere Magical Girls Inc.! Kana has an incredible memory and is very hardworking, preparing thoroughly for every job.

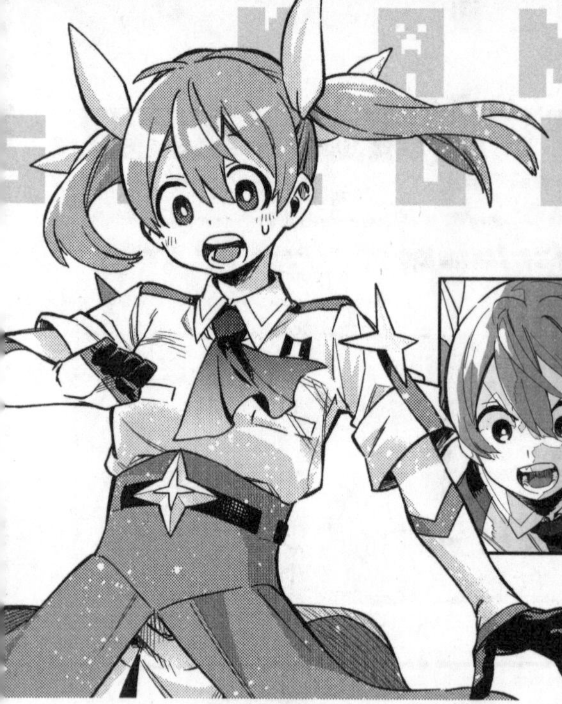

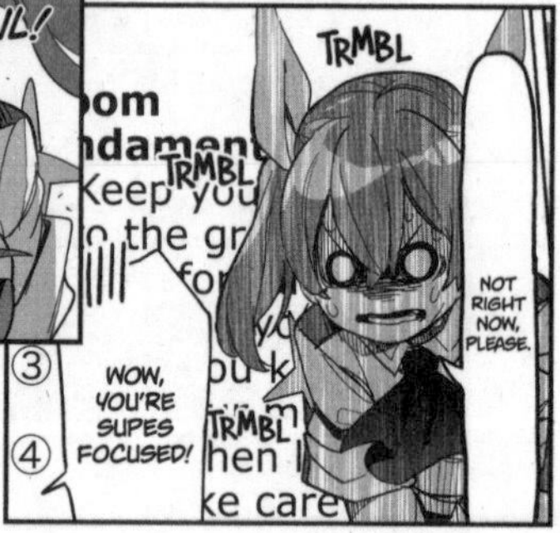
TRMBL
TRMBL
NOT RIGHT NOW, PLEASE.
TRMBL
WOW, YOU'RE SUPES FOCUSED!

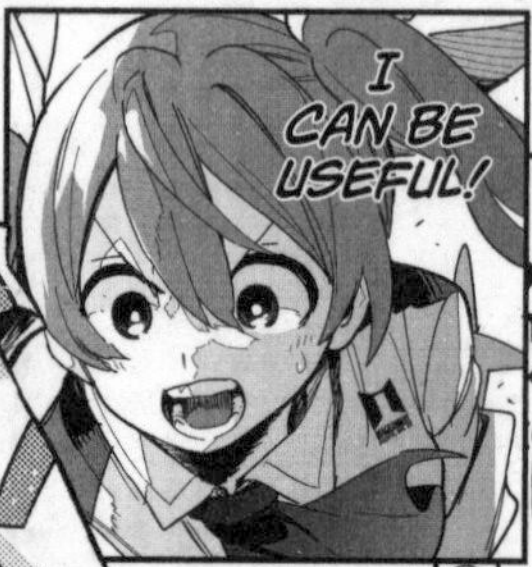
I CAN BE USEFUL!

KOSHIGAYA

Magical girl at Magilumiere Magical Girls Inc. She always wears track-suits and uses slang, but she's a magical girl prodigy.

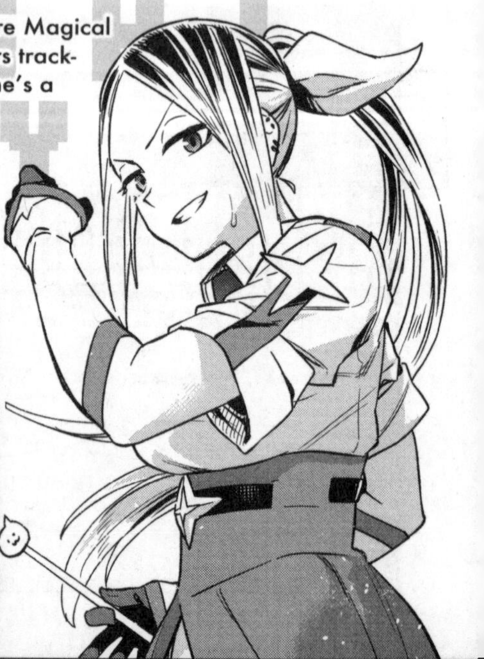

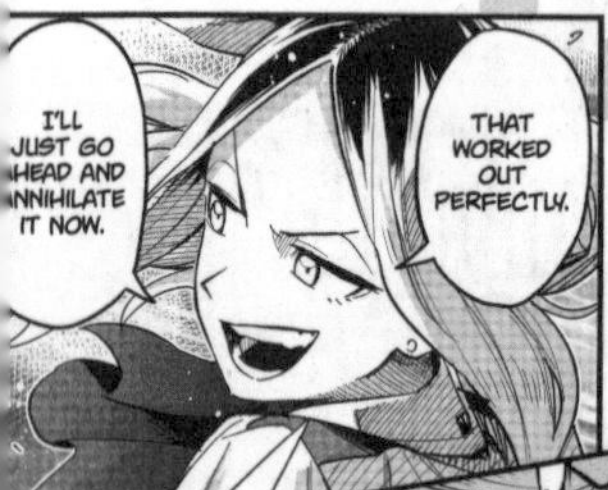
THAT WORKED OUT PERFECTLY.
I'LL JUST GO HEAD AND NNIHILATE IT NOW.

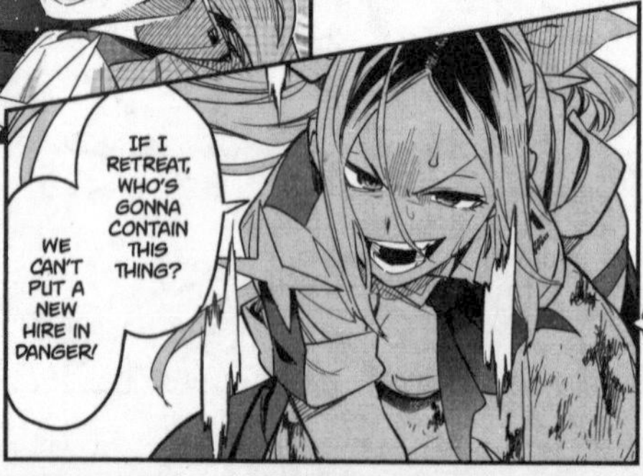
IF I RETREAT, WHO'S GONNA CONTAIN THIS THING?
WE CAN'T PUT A NEW HIRE IN DANGER!

SHIGEMOTO

CEO of Magilumiere Magical Girls Inc. He's a hard-core supporter of magical girls and always wears magical girl cosplay at the office.

I'M SHIGE-MOTO, THE PRESIDENT OF THIS COMPANY.
SO, YOU'RE THE NEW GRAD.

What Are Magical Girls?

Magical girls are exterminators responsible for containing monsters known as kaii, which are a kind of spontaneous natural disaster. There are more than 500 magical girl companies, from big corporations to small, independent businesses. It's a sought-after, high-paying job.

NIKOYAMA

Magilumiere's magic engineer. He gets so intensely focused while he's working that he becomes oblivious to his surroundings.

MIDORIKAWA

Magilumiere Magical Girls Inc.'s entire sales department. He's mild mannered and detail oriented, and he supports the president.

LEAVE IT TO US!

LILY AOI

A magical girl at Miyakodo Cosmetics. She is the embodiment of elegance, strength, and beauty.

Kana Sakuragi is a recent grad trying to find a job, but it's not going well, and she's losing confidence. Then one day, at a job interview, she gets sucked into a kaii incident! Kana puts her astonishing memory to work and ends up assisting Magical Girl Koshigaya in suppressing the kaii! The experience gives Kana a taste of the joy that comes from being useful. And Magilumiere Magical Girls Inc., the start-up where Koshigaya works, just happens to be hiring!

Before she knows it, Kana is getting sent out on jobs—even though she's barely settled into her new position! When a local shopping district has a kaii outbreak, Kana proposes an efficient extermination method, but the boss rejects a by-the-book approach. Kana learns the importance of conducting a thorough on-site investigation, and the entire company works together to defeat the kaii with a new kind of magic!

Later, Kana is given her next assignment—a joint operation with a cosmetics company, where she'll be working with Magical Girl Lily Aoi. What will it be like working with a whole new magical girl?!

STORY

CONTENTS

✦ **CHAPTER 14** ✦
SMILE!
005

✦ **CHAPTER 15** ✦
AESTHETIC VS. RESULTS
025

✦ **CHAPTER 16** ✦
CLASSIFIED INFORMATION
045

✦ **CHAPTER 17** ✦
MAGIC INDUSTRY EXPO
065

✦ **CHAPTER 18** ✦
WORKING WITHOUT A CONTRACT
085

✦ **CHAPTER 19** ✦
THE SHIVERS
105

✦ **CHAPTER 20** ✦
FRIENDS
125

✦ **CHAPTER 21** ✦
COOPERATION
145

✦ **CHAPTER 22** ✦
A MERE VENTURE COMPANY
165

✦ **BRAND-NEW BONUS COMIC** ✦
184

Magilumiere
MAGICAL GIRLS INC.

Chapter 14: Smile!

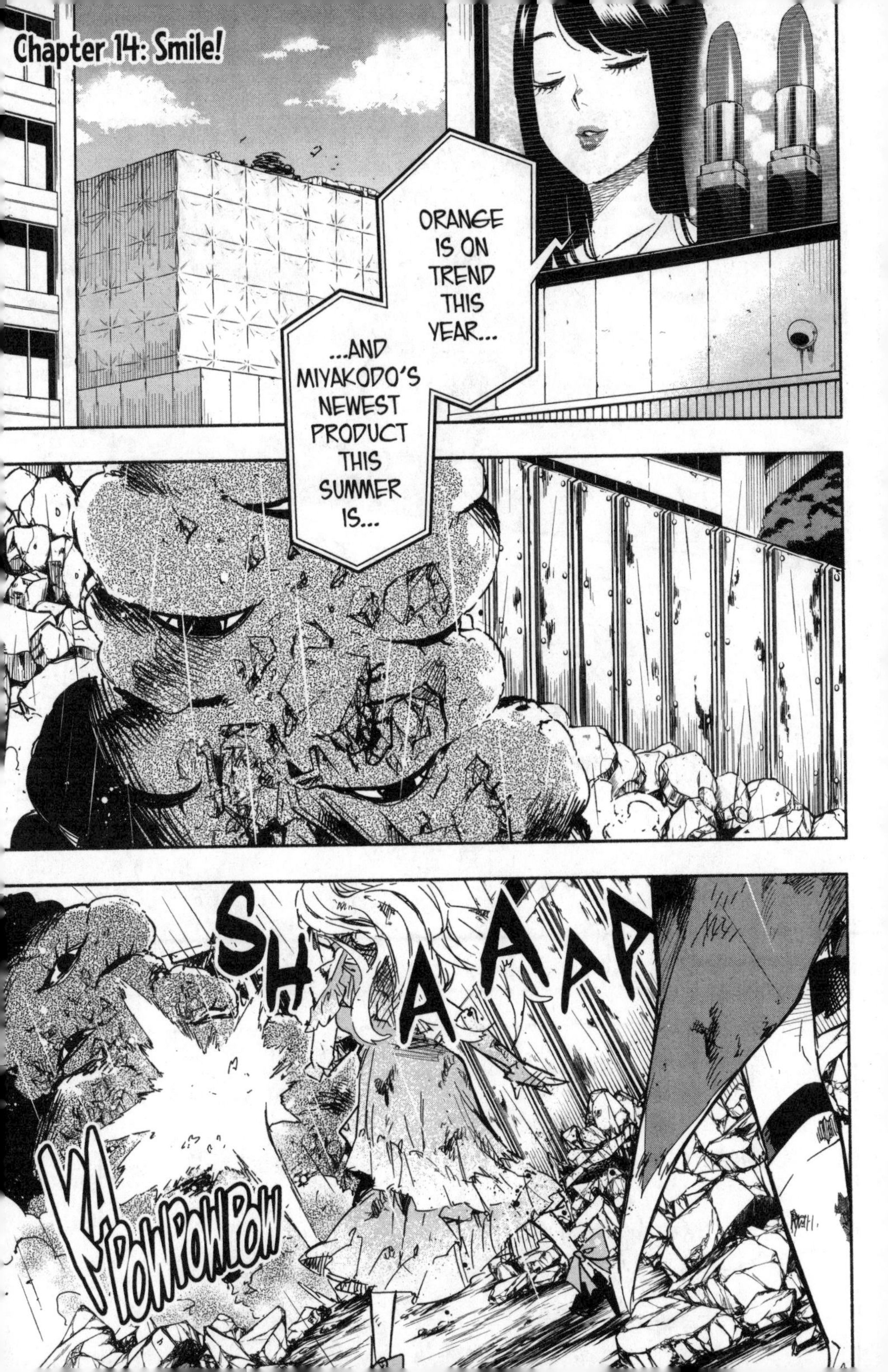
ORANGE IS ON TREND THIS YEAR...
...AND MIYAKODO'S NEWEST PRODUCT THIS SUMMER IS...
SHAAAAP
KA POWPOWPOW

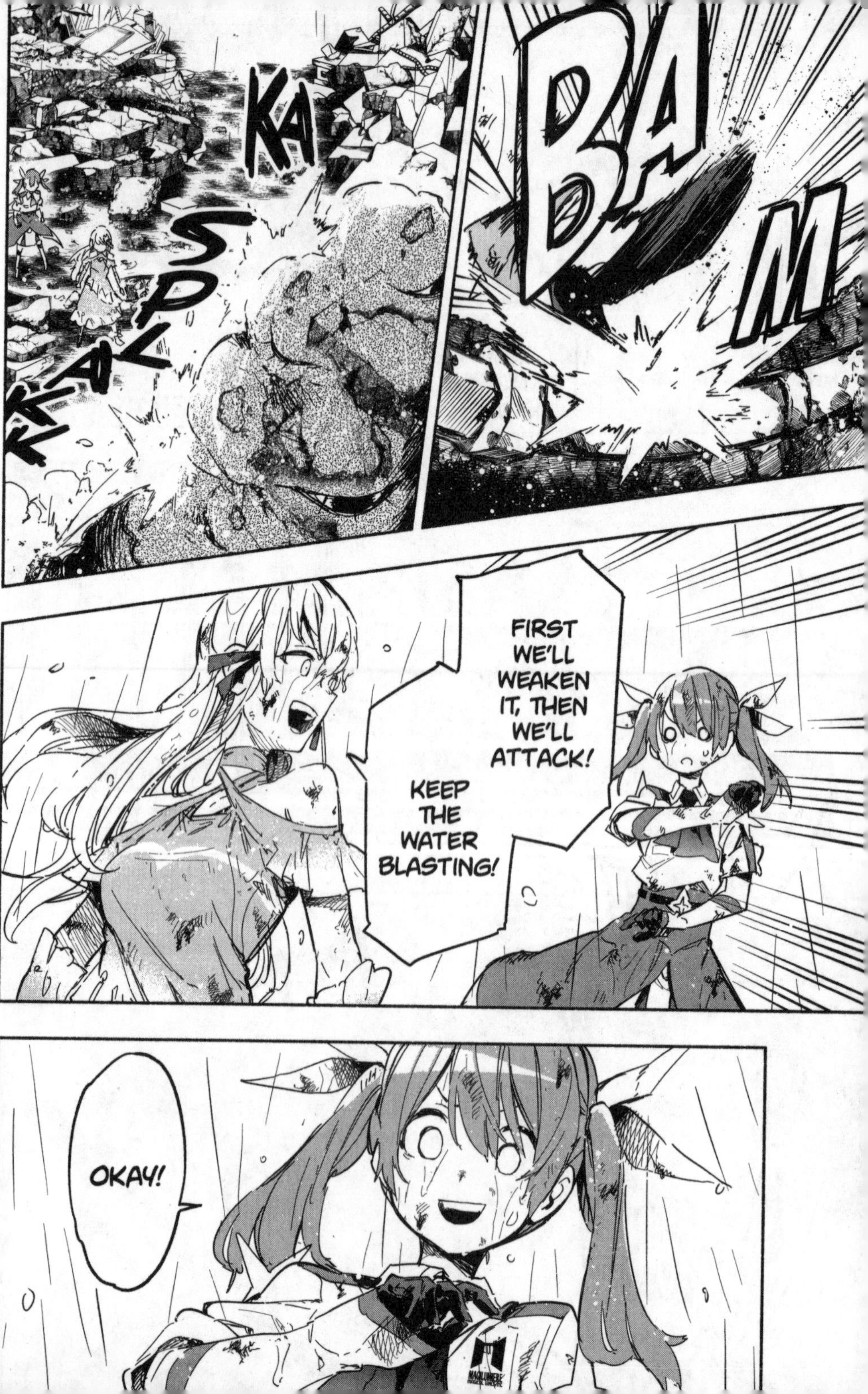
DAM
KA
SPLAT
FIRST WE'LL WEAKEN IT, THEN WE'LL ATTACK!
KEEP THE WATER BLASTING!
OKAY!

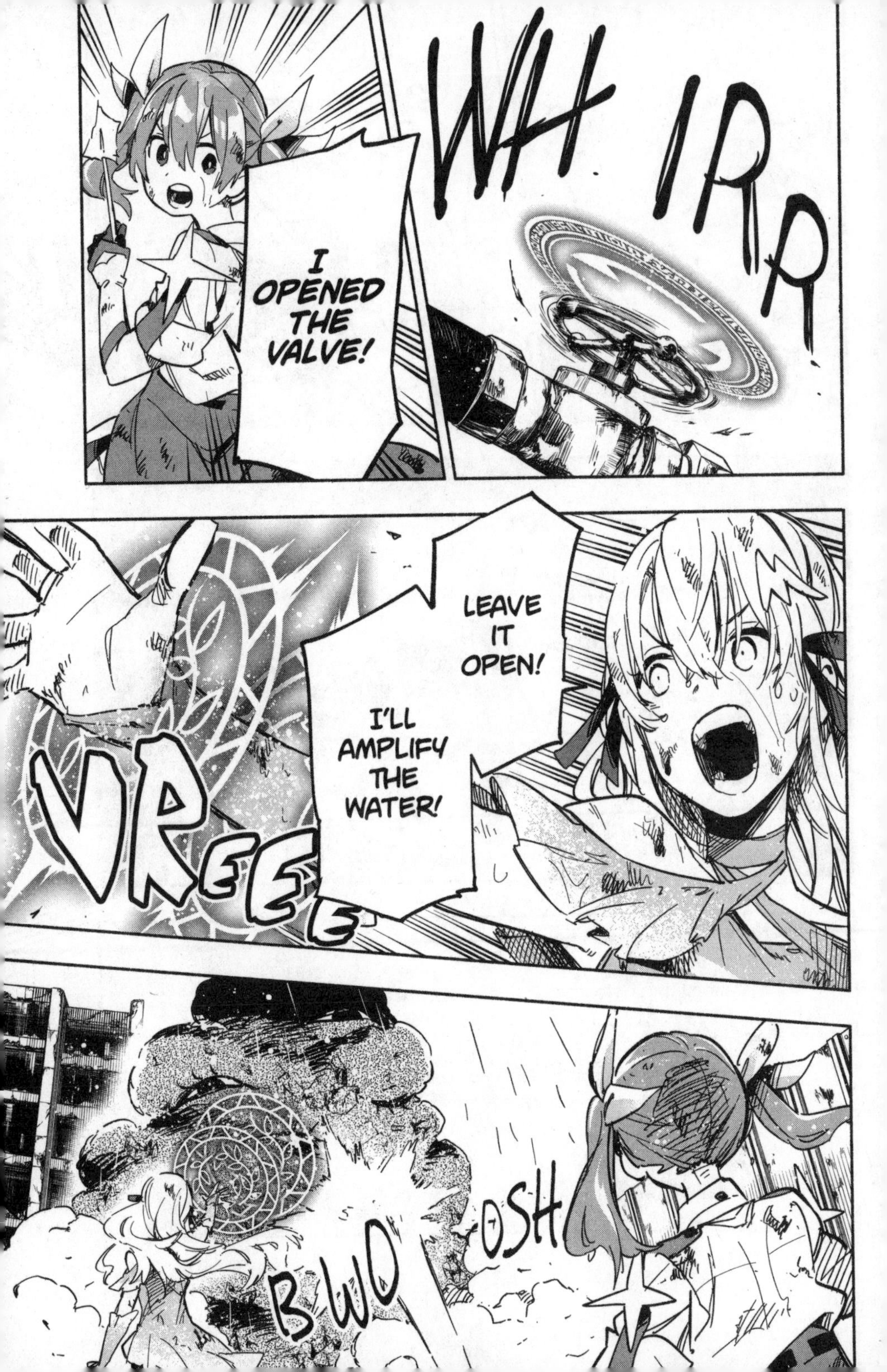
WHIRR
I OPENED THE VALVE!
LEAVE IT OPEN!
I'LL AMPLIFY THE WATER!
VREEE
BWOOSH

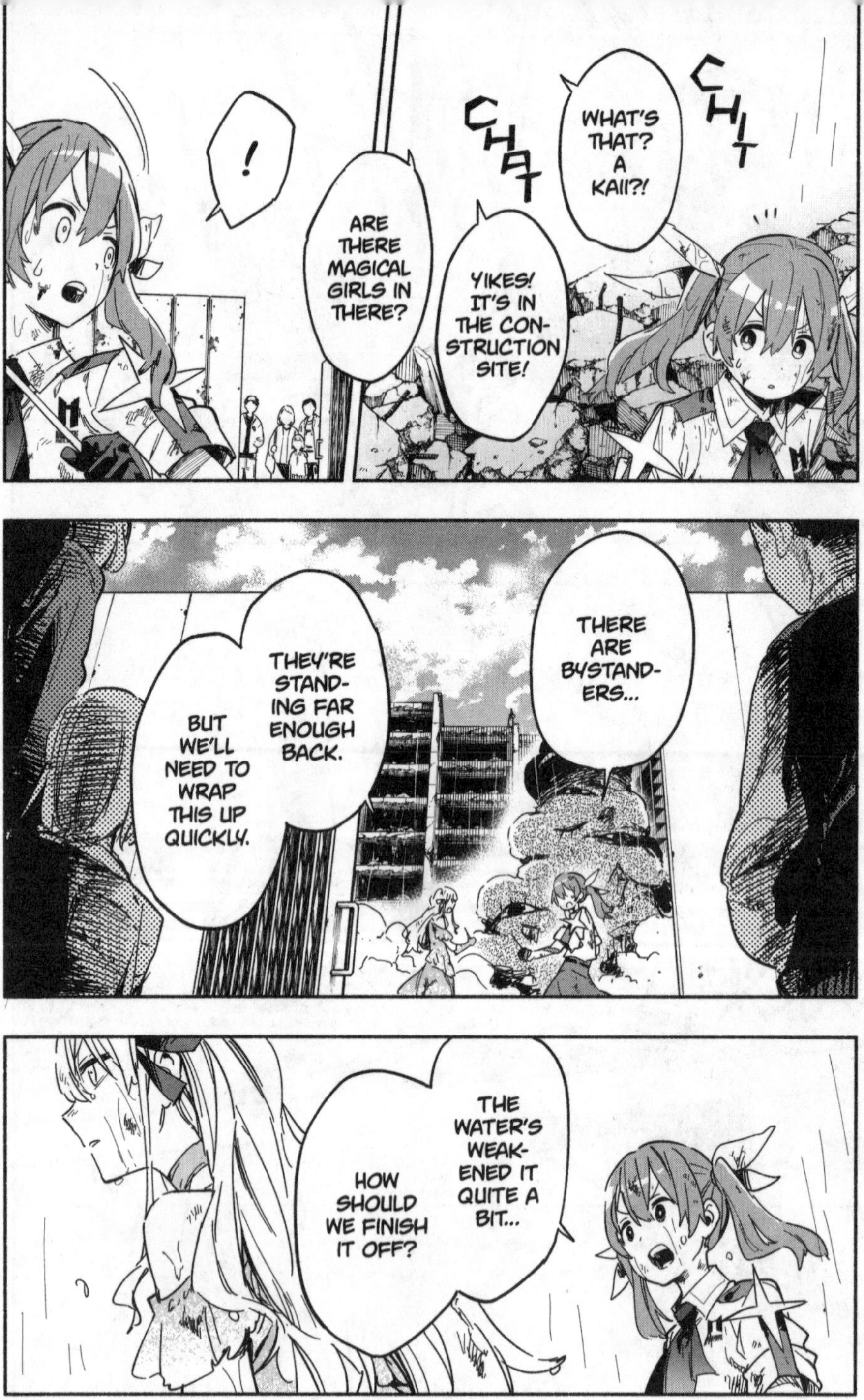
CHIT
WHAT'S THAT? A KAII?!
CHAT
YIKES! IT'S IN THE CONSTRUCTION SITE!
ARE THERE MAGICAL GIRLS IN THERE?
!
THERE ARE BYSTANDERS...
THEY'RE STANDING FAR ENOUGH BACK.
BUT WE'LL NEED TO WRAP THIS UP QUICKLY.
THE WATER'S WEAKENED IT QUITE A BIT...
HOW SHOULD WE FINISH IT OFF?

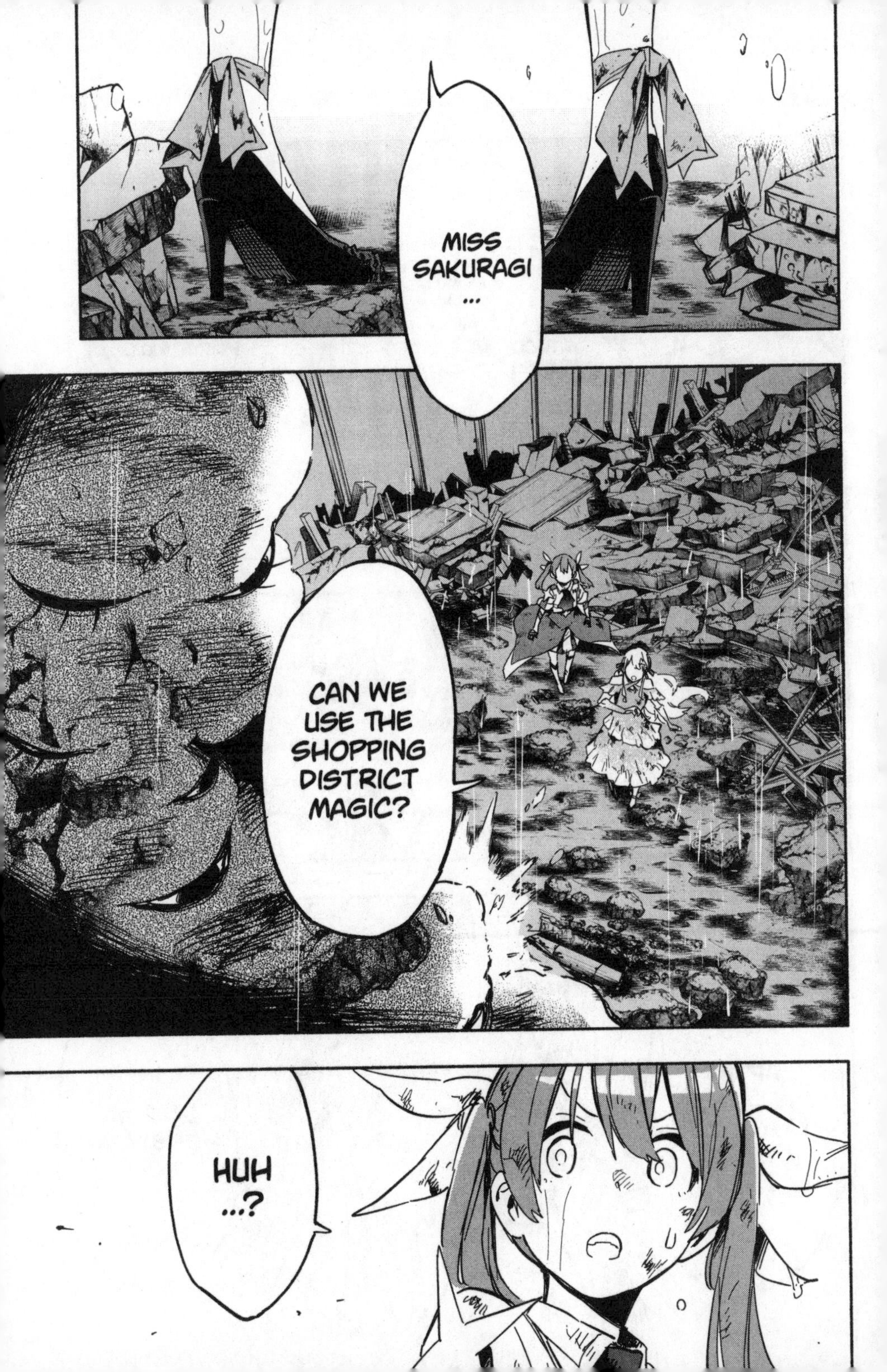
MISS SAKURAGI ...
CAN WE USE THE SHOPPING DISTRICT MAGIC?
HUH ...?

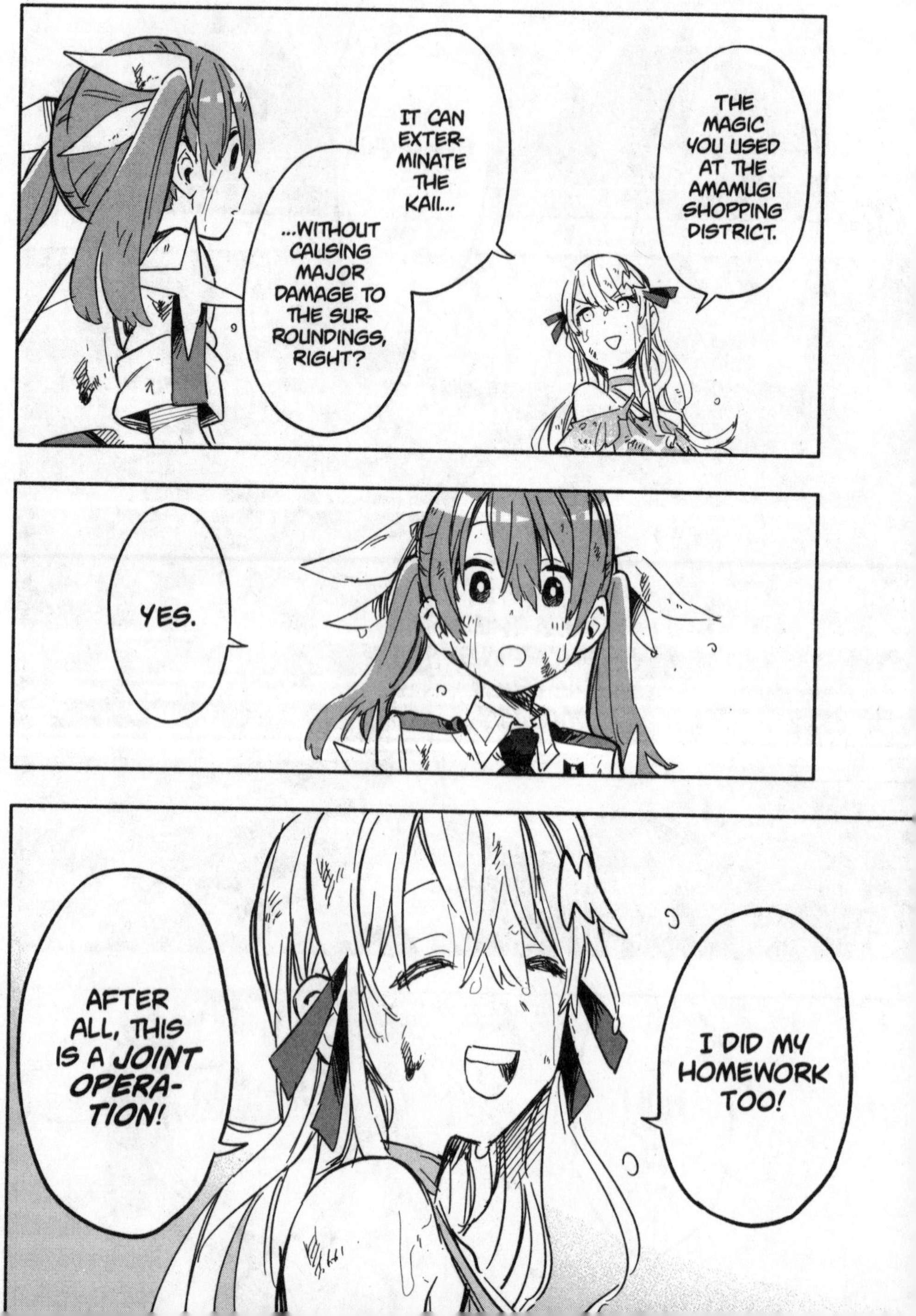
THE MAGIC YOU USED AT THE AMAMUGI SHOPPING DISTRICT.
IT CAN EXTERMINATE THE KAII...
...WITHOUT CAUSING MAJOR DAMAGE TO THE SURROUNDINGS, RIGHT?
YES.
I DID MY HOMEWORK TOO!
AFTER ALL, THIS IS A *JOINT OPERATION!*

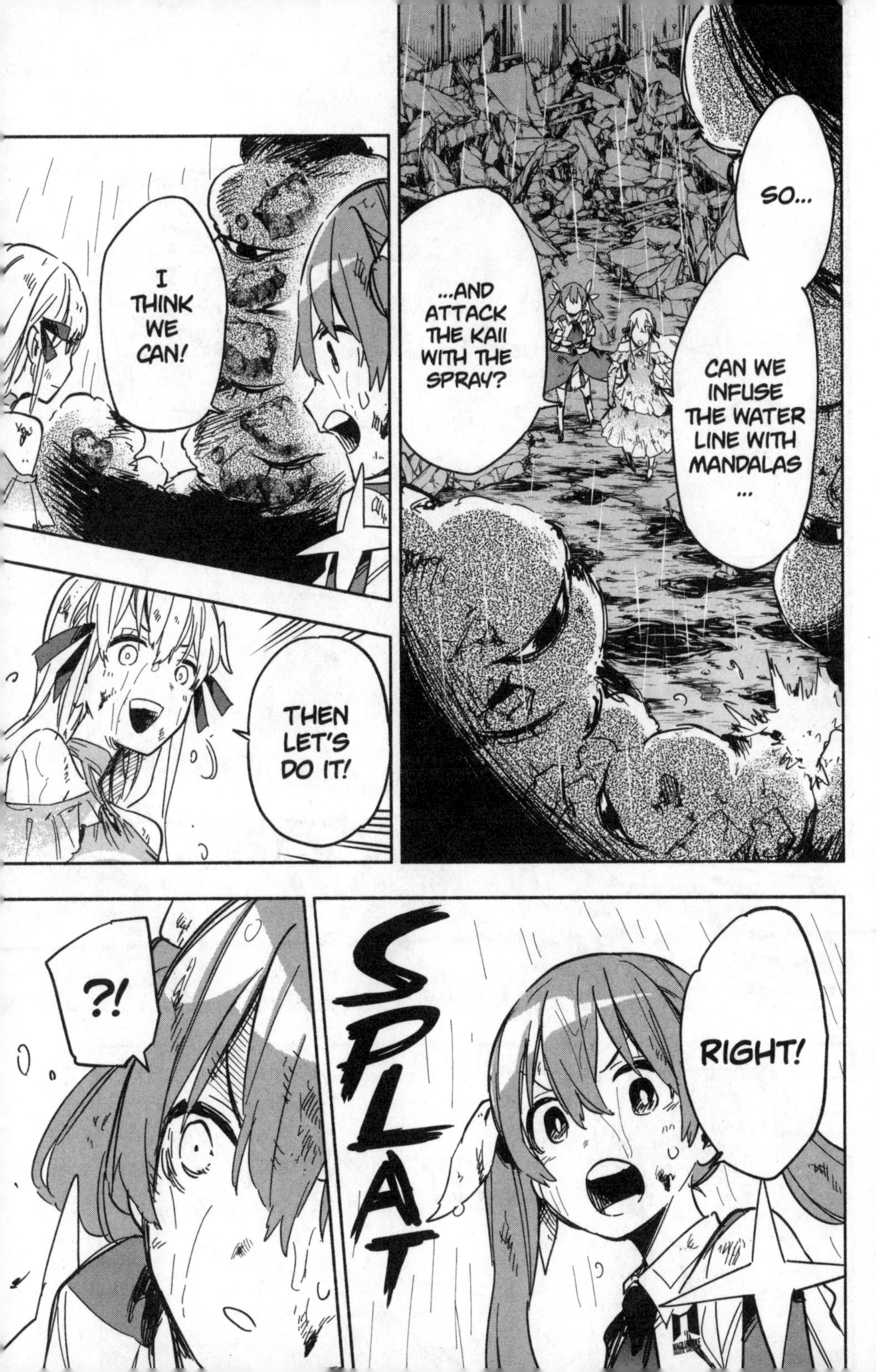

SO...
CAN WE INFUSE THE WATER LINE WITH MANDALAS ...
...AND ATTACK THE KAII WITH THE SPRAY?
I THINK WE CAN!
THEN LET'S DO IT!
RIGHT!
SPLAT
?!

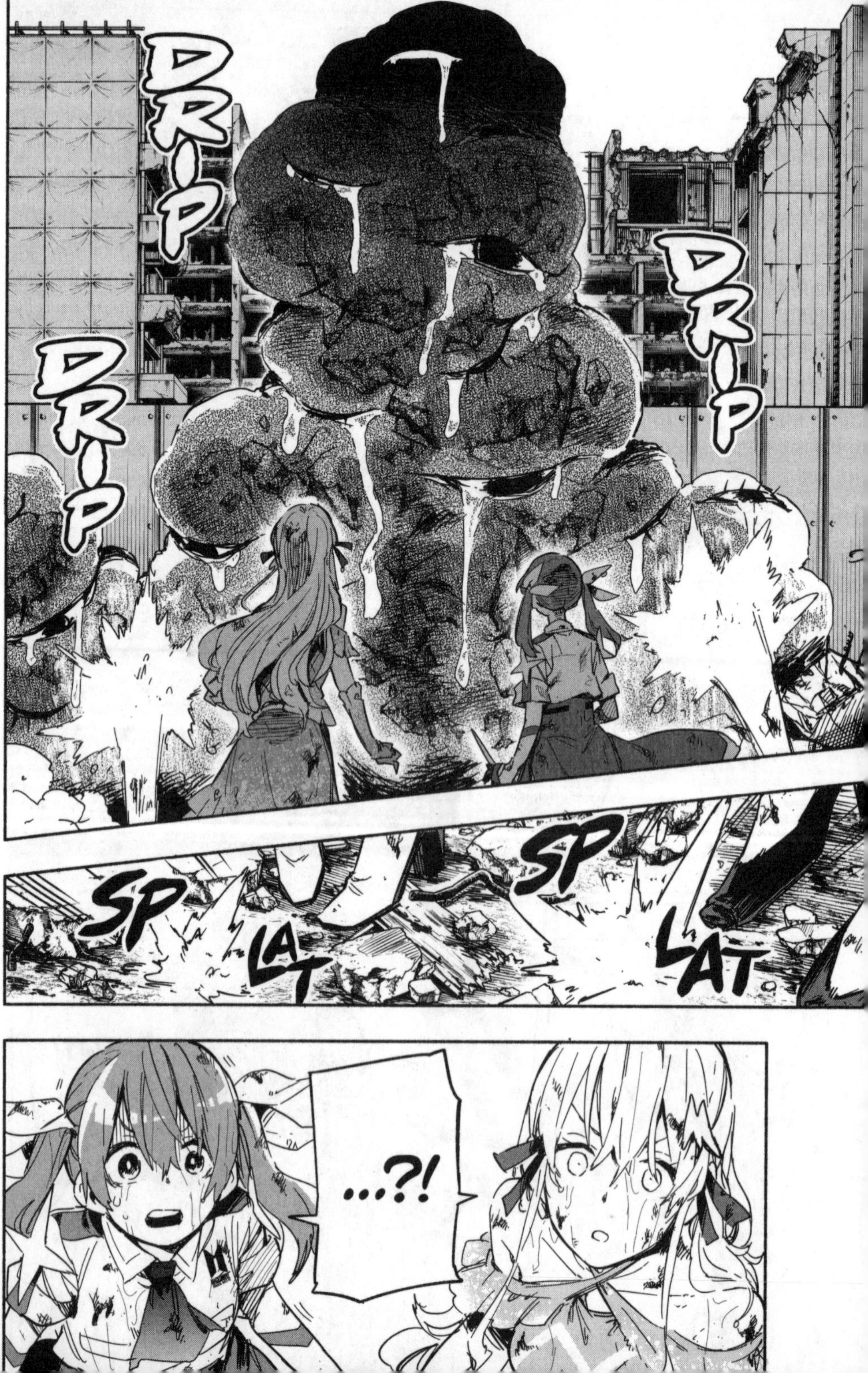
DRIP
DRIP
DRIP
SPLAT
SPLAT
...?!

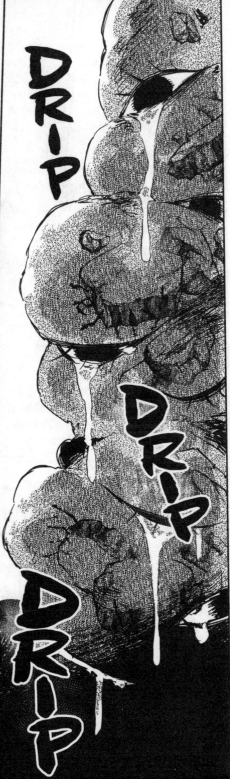

IS IT... CRYING?

IS THAT THE WATER WE SPRAYED AT IT?

IT DOESN'T LOOK LIKE IT...

COULD IT BE...?

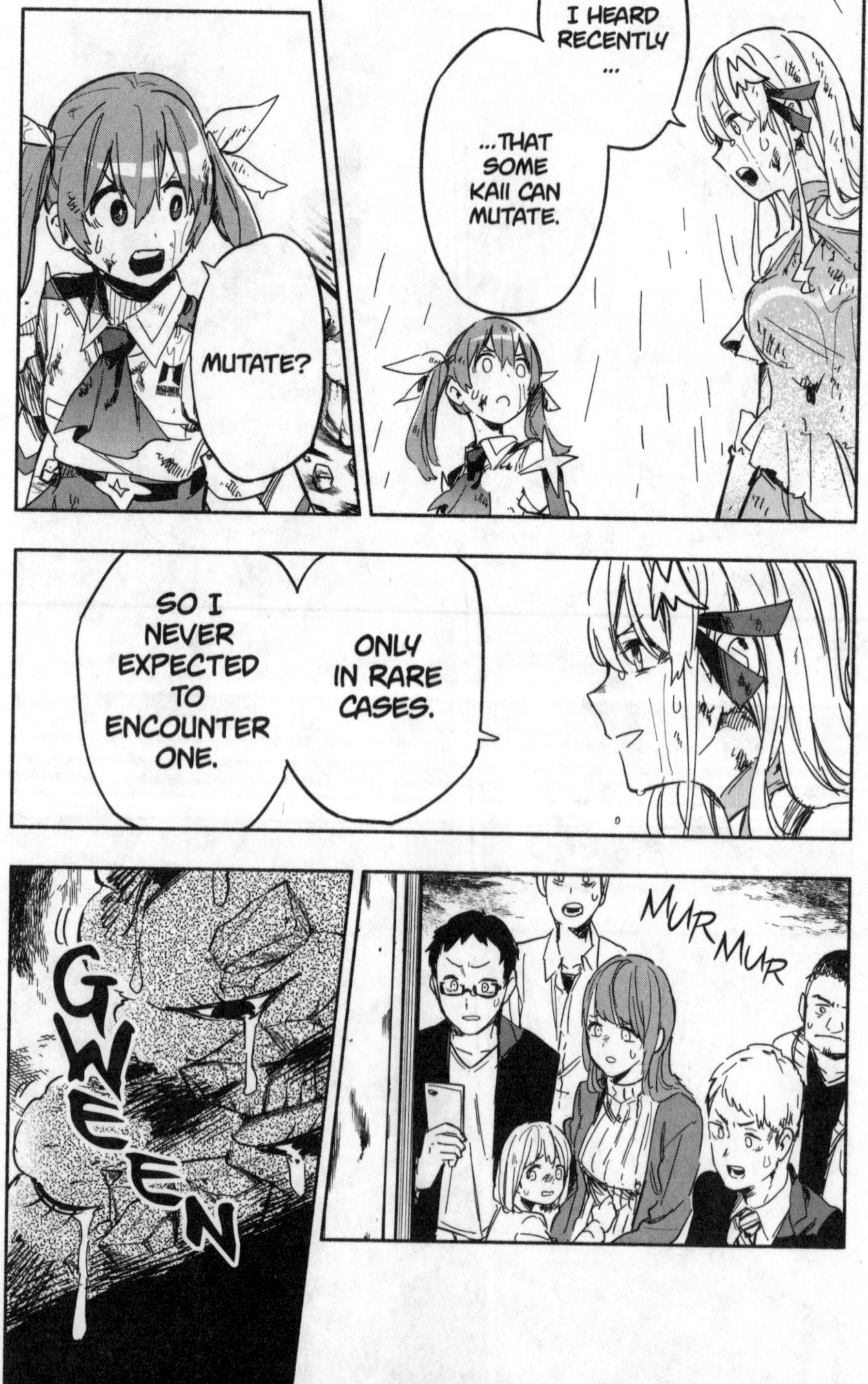
I HEARD RECENTLY ...
...THAT SOME KAII CAN MUTATE.
MUTATE?
ONLY IN RARE CASES.
SO I NEVER EXPECTED TO ENCOUNTER ONE.
MUR MUR
GWEEN

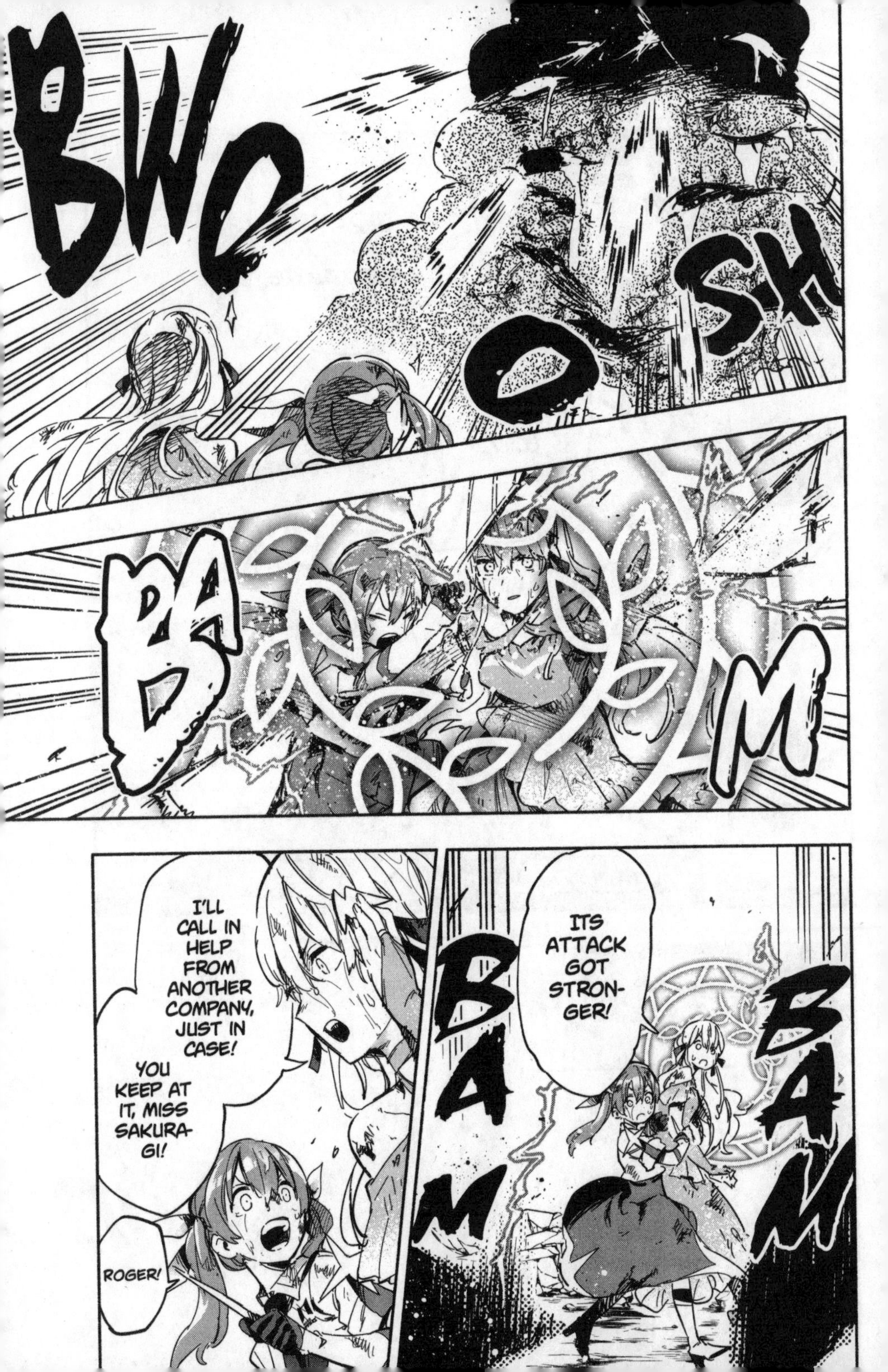
BWO
O
SH
BAB
M
BAM
ITS ATTACK GOT STRONGER!
BAM
I'LL CALL IN HELP FROM ANOTHER COMPANY, JUST IN CASE!
YOU KEEP AT IT, MISS SAKURAGI!
ROGER!

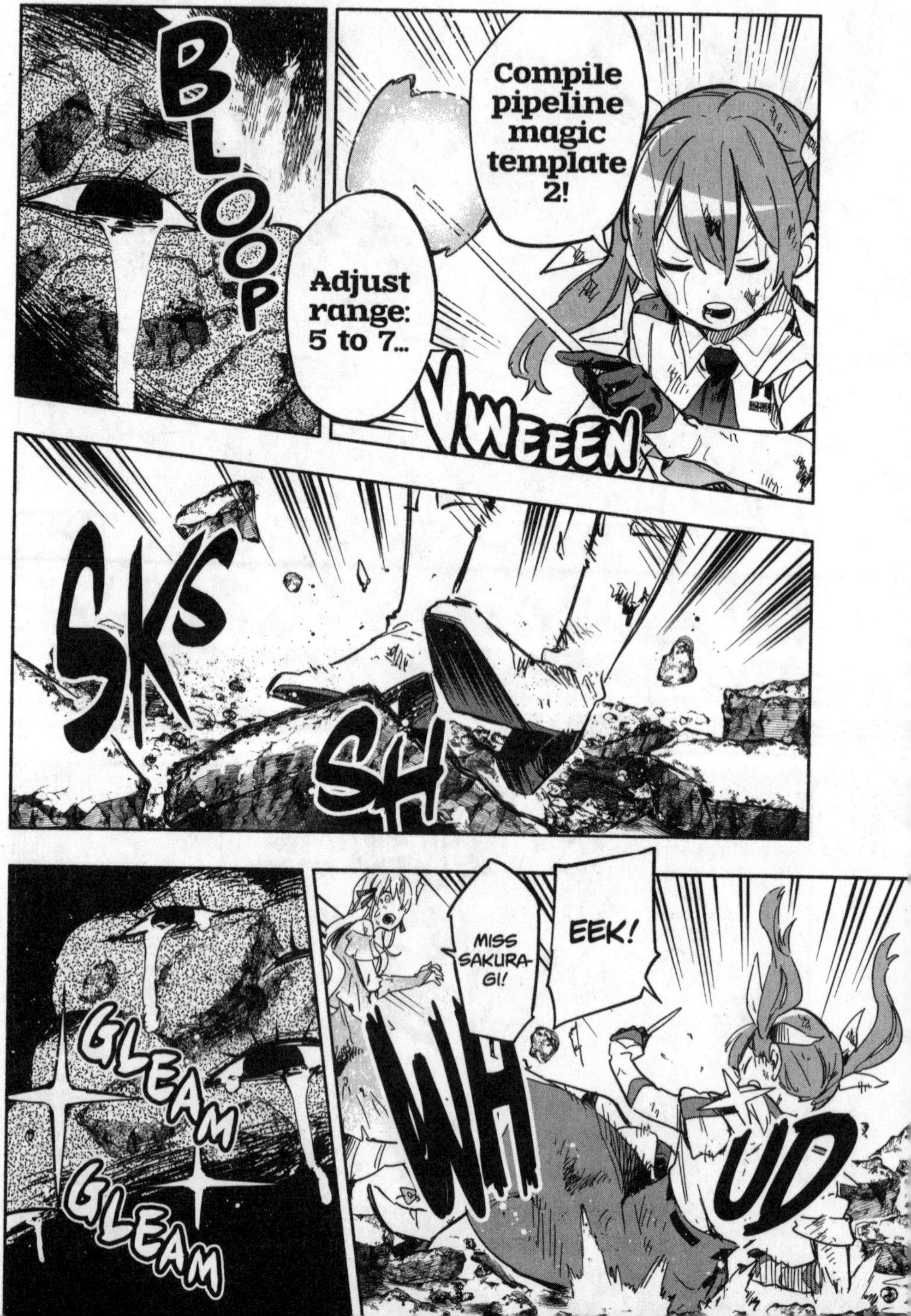
Compile pipeline magic template 2!
Adjust range: 5 to 7...
VWEEEN
BLOOP
SKS
SH
EEK!
MISS SAKURA-GI!
WH
UD
GLEAM
GLEAM

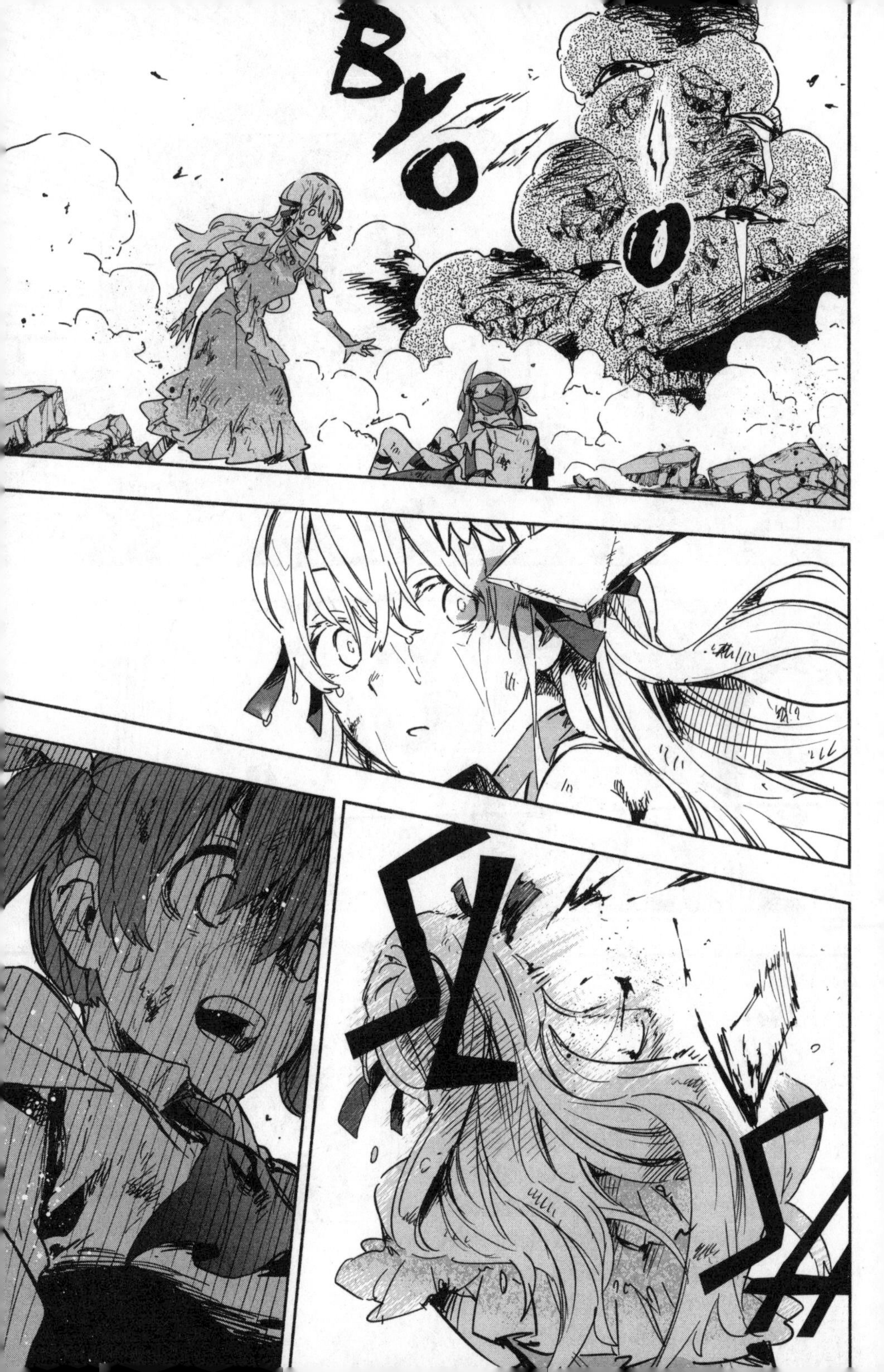
BYOOO

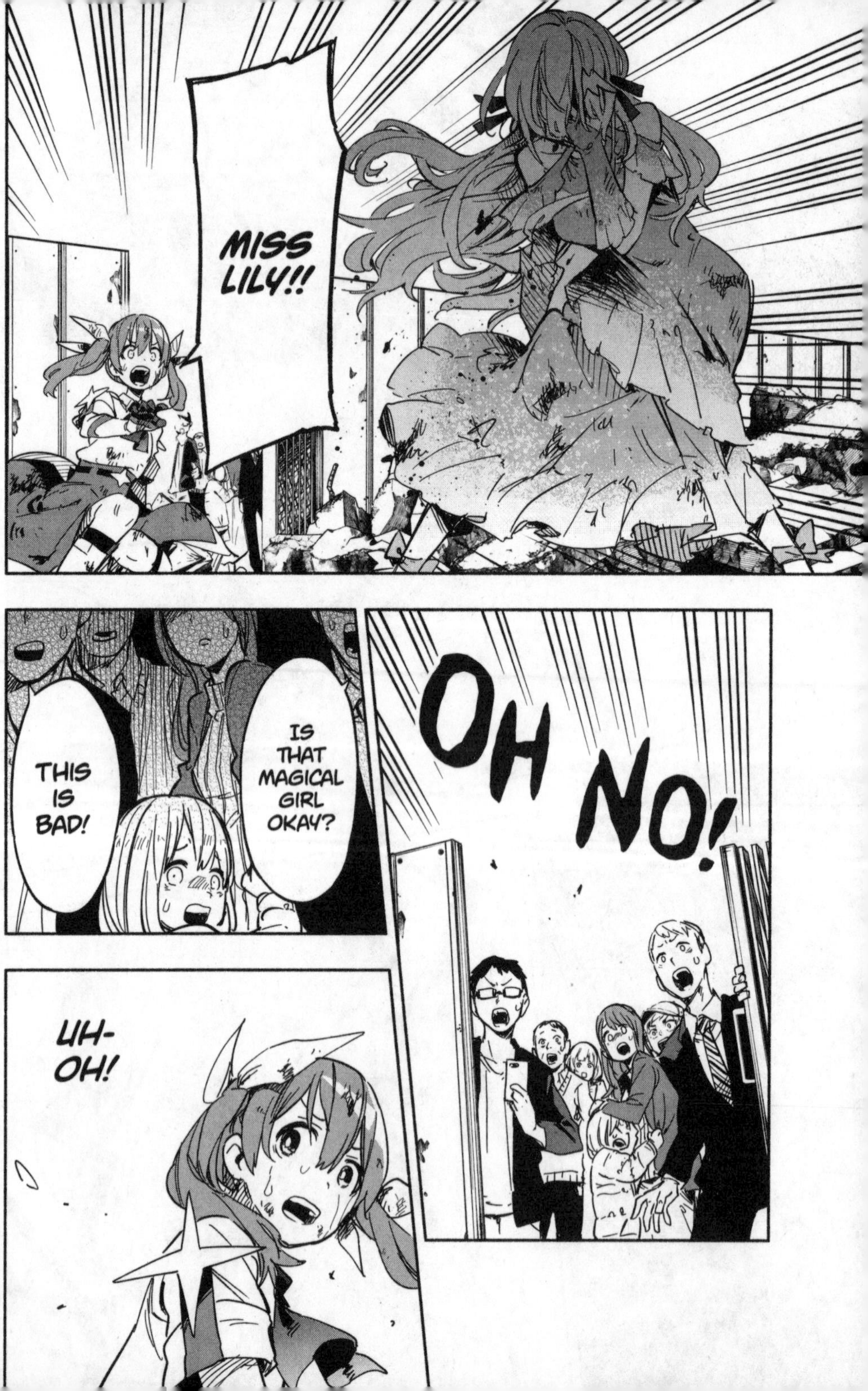
MISS LILY!!
OH NO!
IS THAT MAGICAL GIRL OKAY?
THIS IS BAD!
UH-OH!

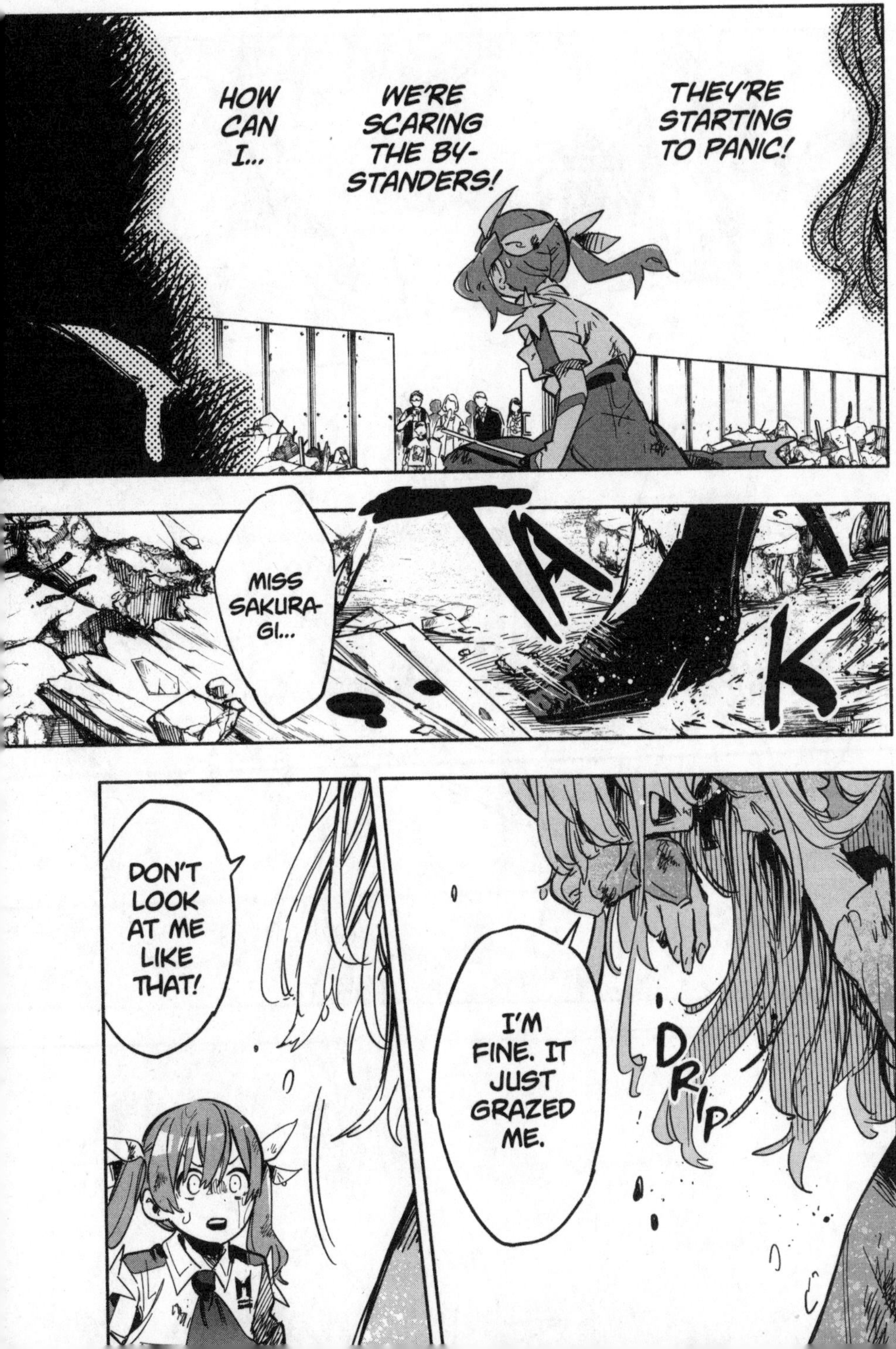
THEY'RE STARTING TO PANIC!
WE'RE SCARING THE BY-STANDERS!
HOW CAN I...
TAK
MISS SAKURA-GI...
I'M FINE. IT JUST GRAZED ME.
DRIP
DON'T LOOK AT ME LIKE THAT!

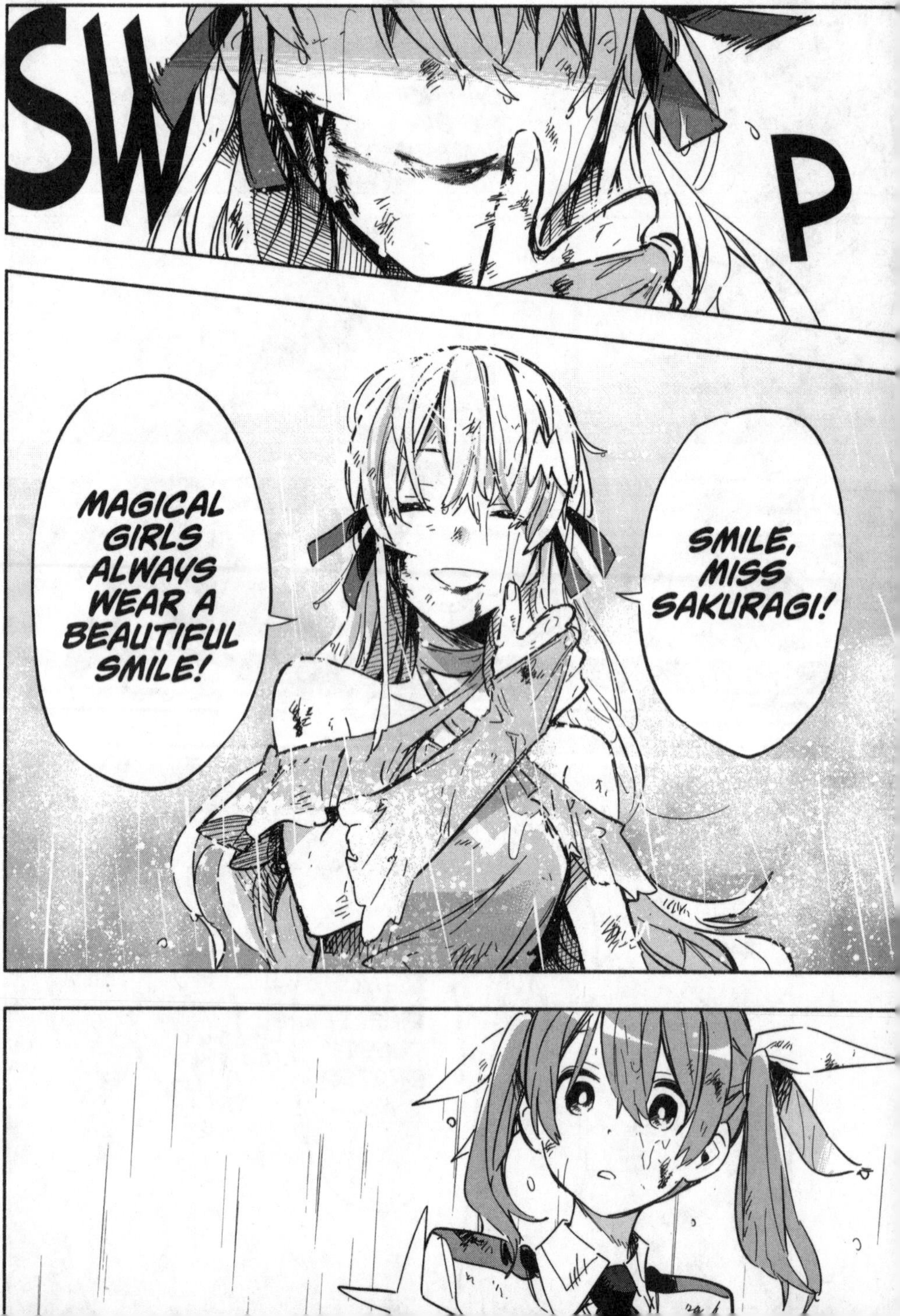
SW P
SMILE, MISS SAKURAGI!
MAGICAL GIRLS ALWAYS WEAR A BEAUTIFUL SMILE!

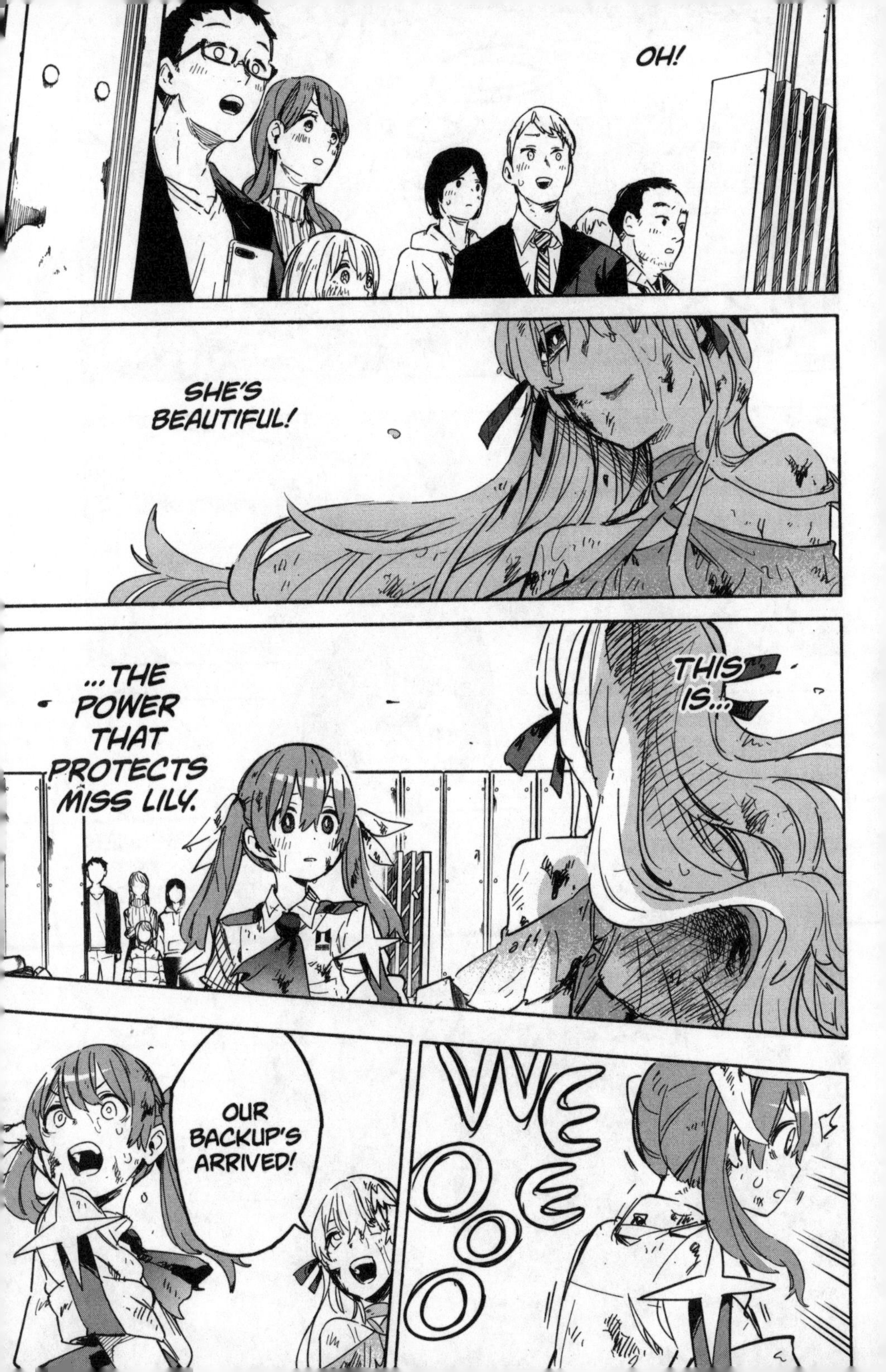
OH!
SHE'S BEAUTIFUL!
THIS IS...
...THE POWER THAT PROTECTS MISS LILY.
WEEOOOO
OUR BACKUP'S ARRIVED!

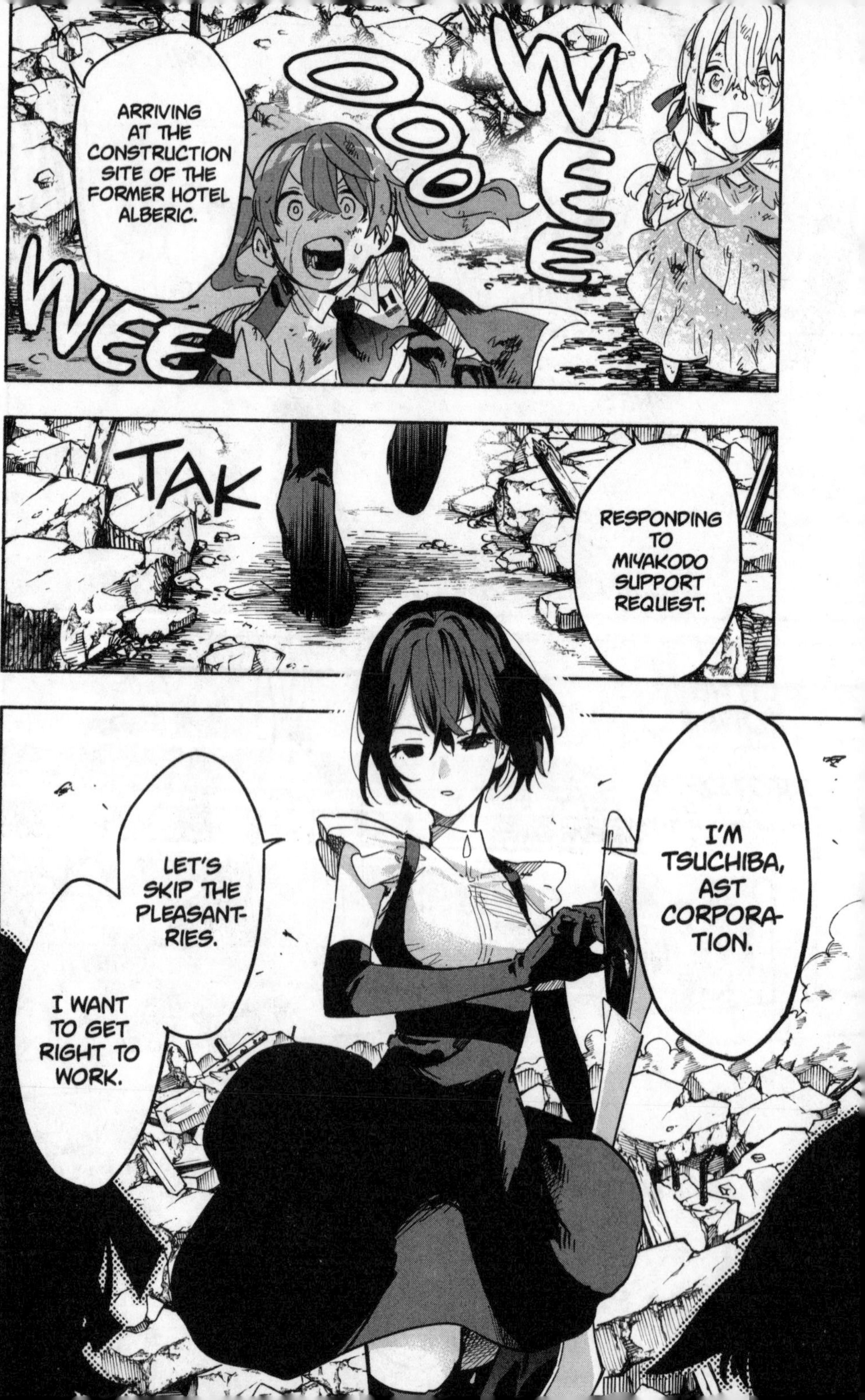
WEE
OOO
ARRIVING AT THE CONSTRUCTION SITE OF THE FORMER HOTEL ALBERIC.
WEE
RESPONDING TO MIYAKODO SUPPORT REQUEST.
TAK
I'M TSUCHIBA, AST CORPORATION.
LET'S SKIP THE PLEASANT-RIES.
I WANT TO GET RIGHT TO WORK.

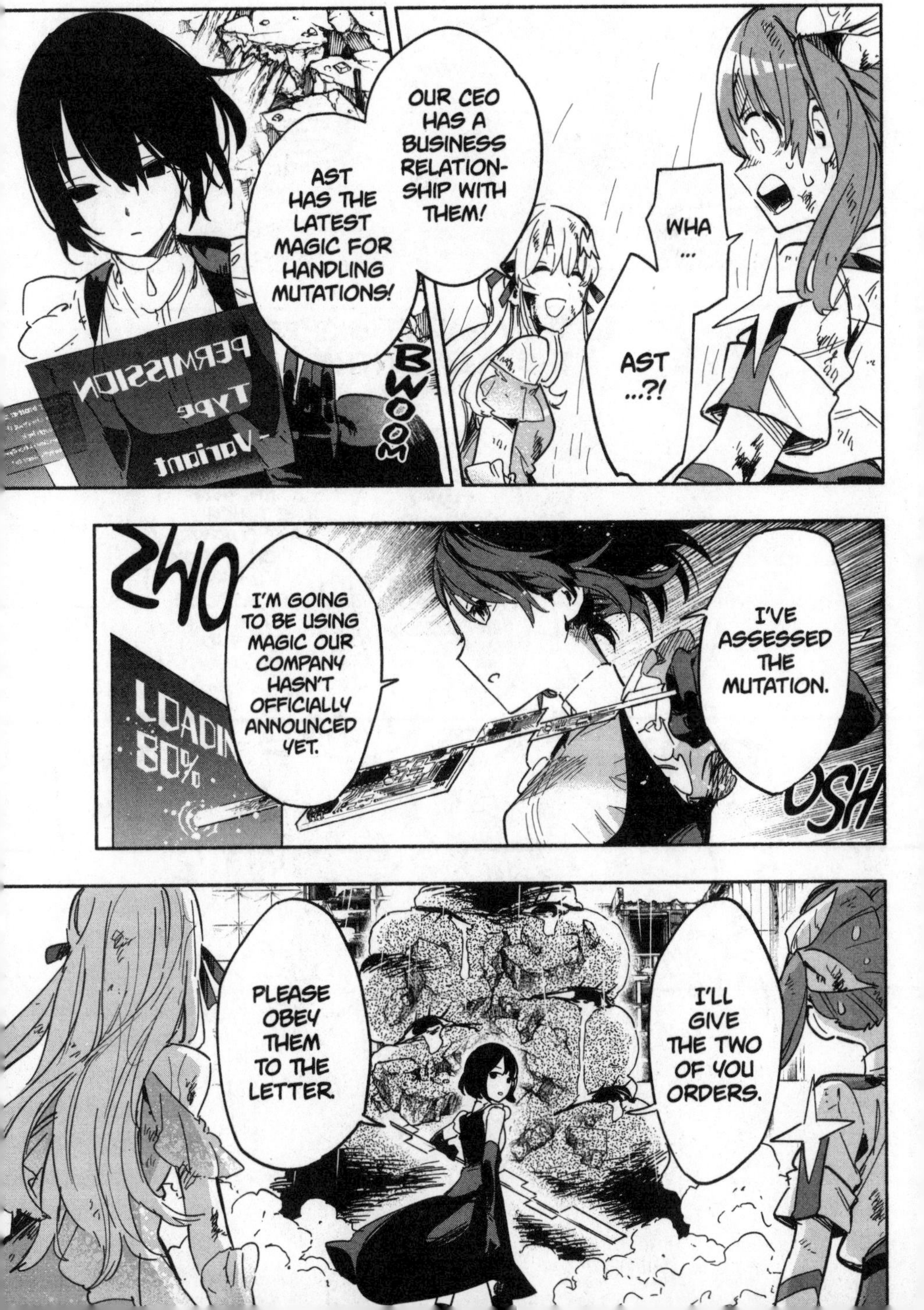
WHA ...
AST ...?!
OUR CEO HAS A BUSINESS RELATION-SHIP WITH THEM!
AST HAS THE LATEST MAGIC FOR HANDLING MUTATIONS!
BWOOM
PERMISSION
Type
Variant
I'VE ASSESSED THE MUTATION.
OSH
I'M GOING TO BE USING MAGIC OUR COMPANY HASN'T OFFICIALLY ANNOUNCED YET.
I'LL GIVE THE TWO OF YOU ORDERS.
PLEASE OBEY THEM TO THE LETTER.

IF THEY HADN'T SKIPPED THE PLEASANTRIES

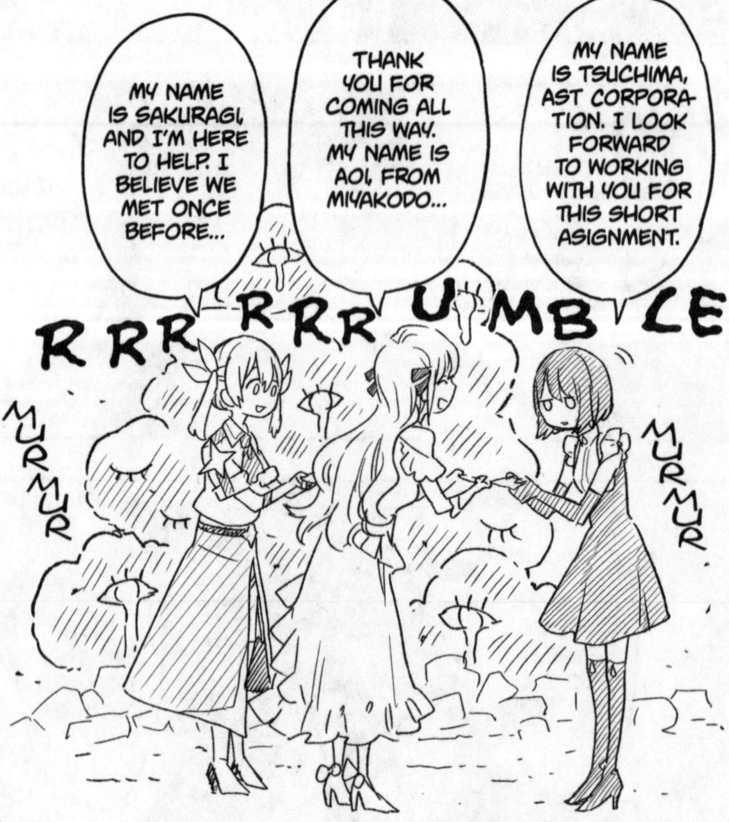
MY NAME IS TSUCHIMA, AST CORPORATION. I LOOK FORWARD TO WORKING WITH YOU FOR THIS SHORT ASIGNMENT.
THANK YOU FOR COMING ALL THIS WAY. MY NAME IS AOI, FROM MIYAKODO...
MY NAME IS SAKURAGI, AND I'M HERE TO HELP. I BELIEVE WE MET ONCE BEFORE...
RRRRRRUMBLE
MURMUR
MURMUR

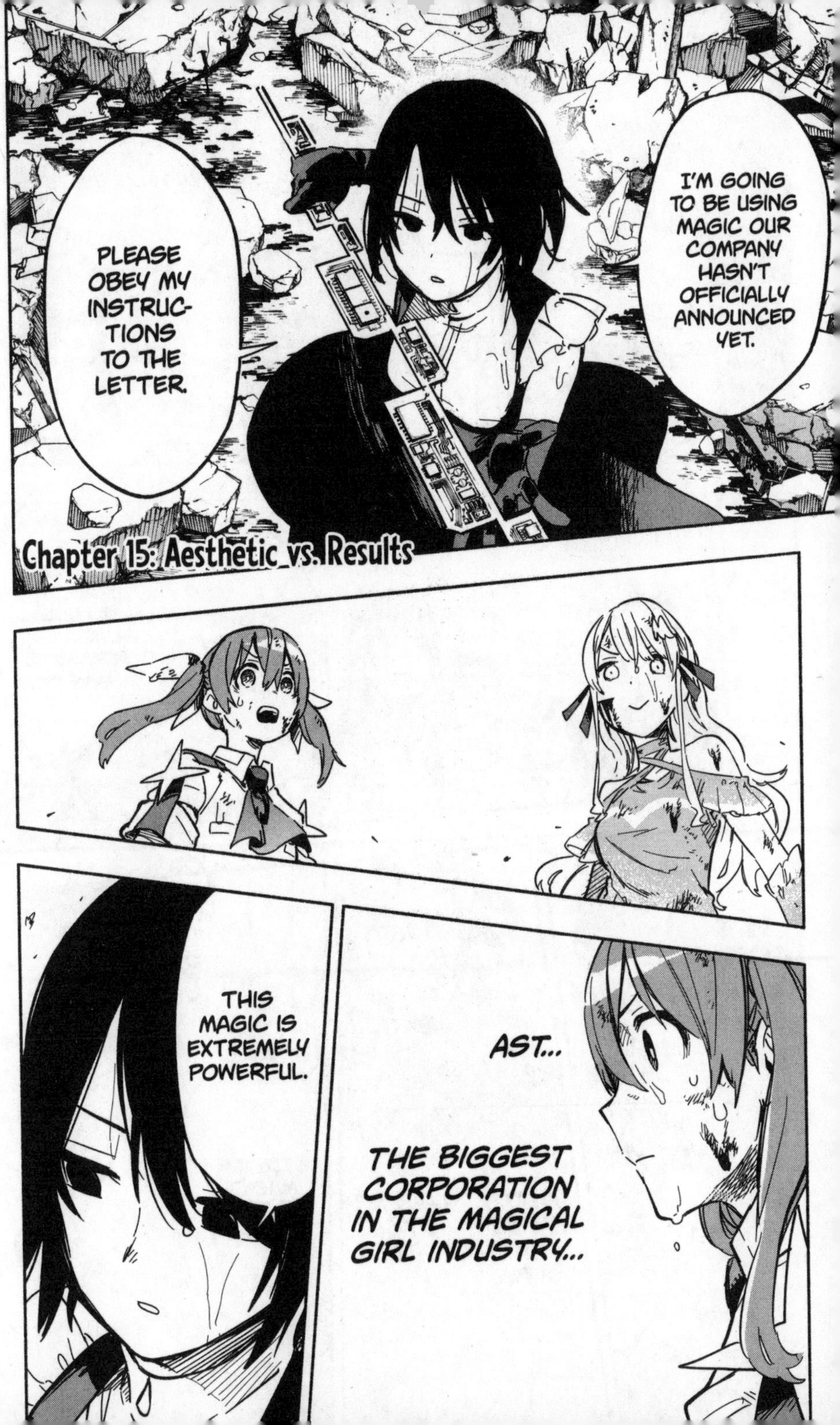
I'M GOING TO BE USING MAGIC OUR COMPANY HASN'T OFFICIALLY ANNOUNCED YET.
PLEASE OBEY MY INSTRUCTIONS TO THE LETTER.
Chapter 15: Aesthetic vs. Results
AST...
THE BIGGEST CORPORATION IN THE MAGICAL GIRL INDUSTRY...
THIS MAGIC IS EXTREMELY POWERFUL.

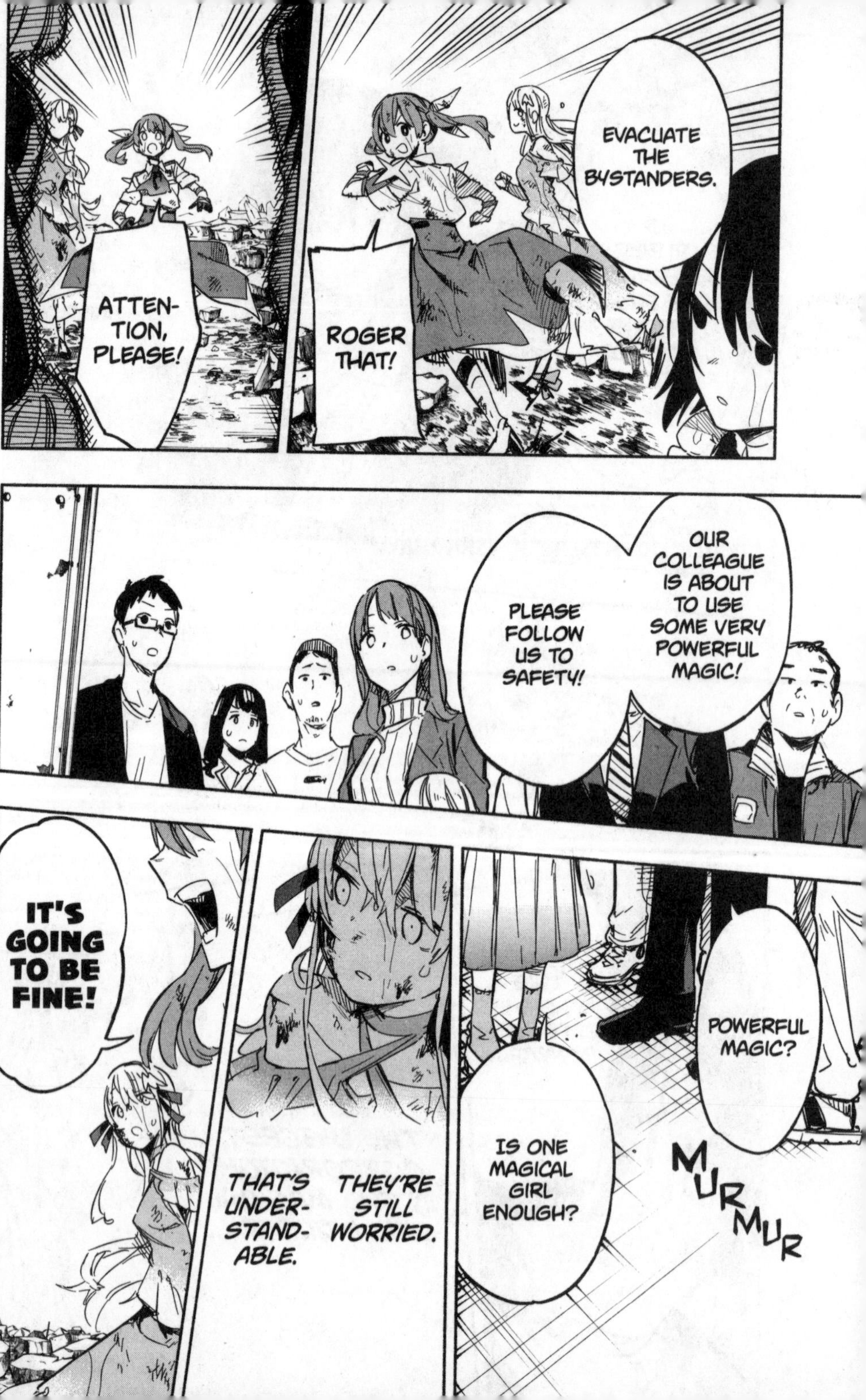
EVACUATE THE BYSTANDERS.
ROGER THAT!
ATTEN-TION, PLEASE!
OUR COLLEAGUE IS ABOUT TO USE SOME VERY POWERFUL MAGIC!
PLEASE FOLLOW US TO SAFETY!
MURMUR
POWERFUL MAGIC?
IS ONE MAGICAL GIRL ENOUGH?
THEY'RE STILL WORRIED.
THAT'S UNDER-STAND-ABLE.
IT'S GOING TO BE FINE!

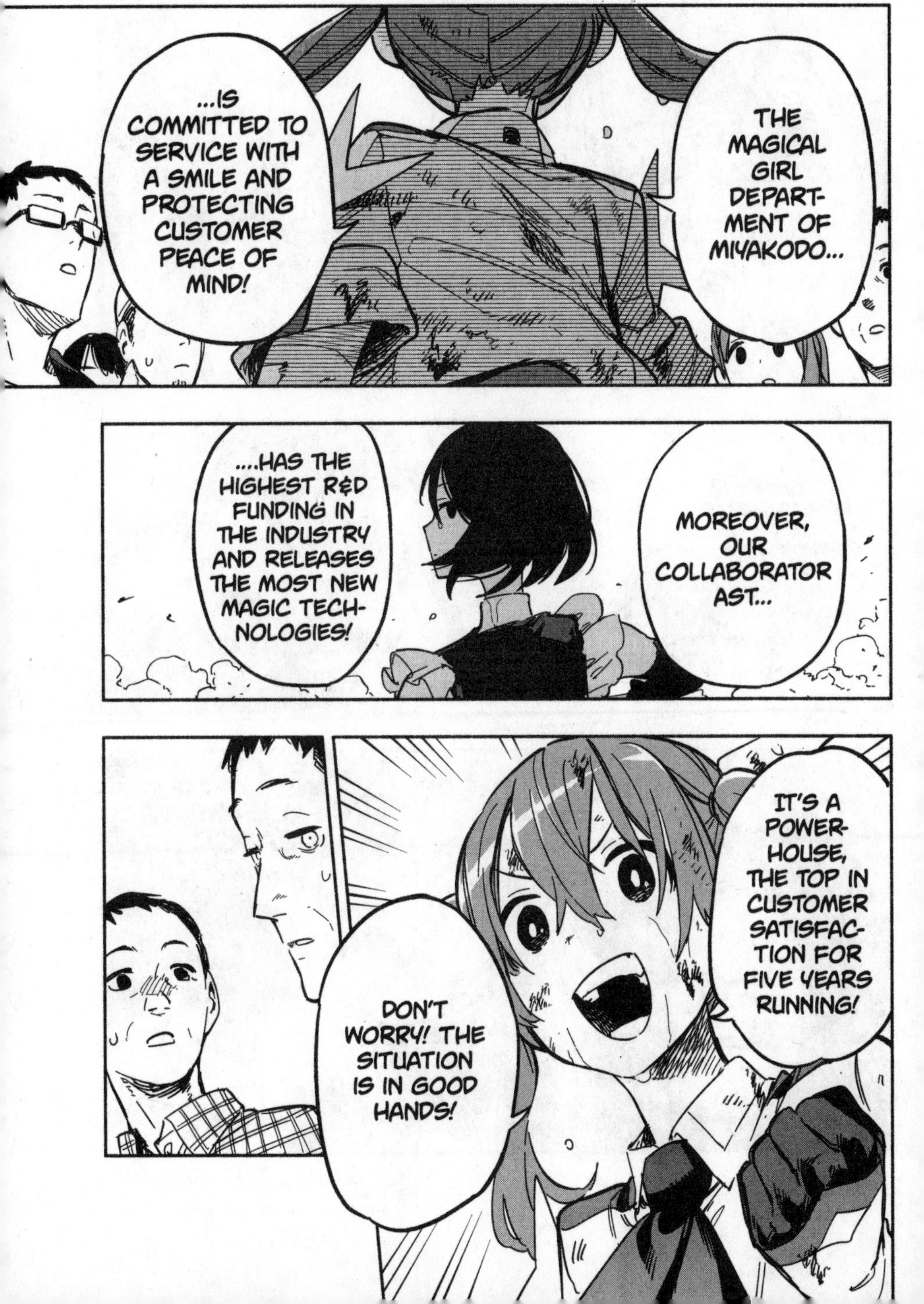
THE MAGICAL GIRL DEPART-MENT OF MIYAKODO...
...IS COMMITTED TO SERVICE WITH A SMILE AND PROTECTING CUSTOMER PEACE OF MIND!
MOREOVER, OUR COLLABORATOR AST...
....HAS THE HIGHEST R&D FUNDING IN THE INDUSTRY AND RELEASES THE MOST NEW MAGIC TECH-NOLOGIES!
IT'S A POWER-HOUSE, THE TOP IN CUSTOMER SATISFAC-TION FOR FIVE YEARS RUNNING!
DON'T WORRY! THE SITUATION IS IN GOOD HANDS!

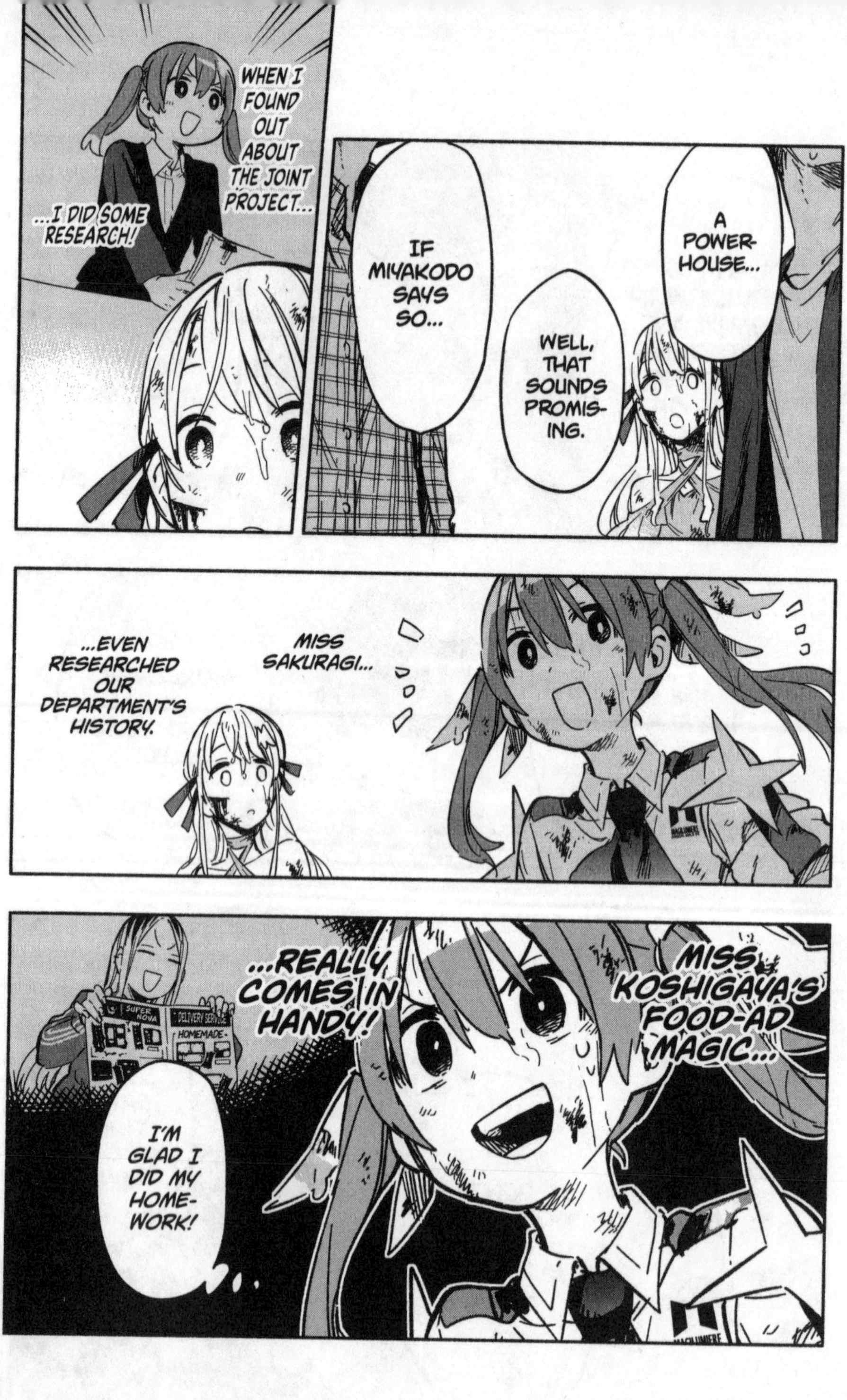
A POWER-HOUSE...
IF MIYAKODO SAYS SO...
WELL, THAT SOUNDS PROMIS-ING.
WHEN I FOUND OUT ABOUT THE JOINT PROJECT...
...I DID SOME RESEARCH!
MISS SAKURAGI...
...EVEN RESEARCHED OUR DEPARTMENT'S HISTORY.
MISS KOSHIGAYA'S FOOD-AD MAGIC...
...REALLY COMES IN HANDY!
SUPER NOVA
DELIVERY SERVICE
HOMEMADE
I'M GLAD I DID MY HOME-WORK!

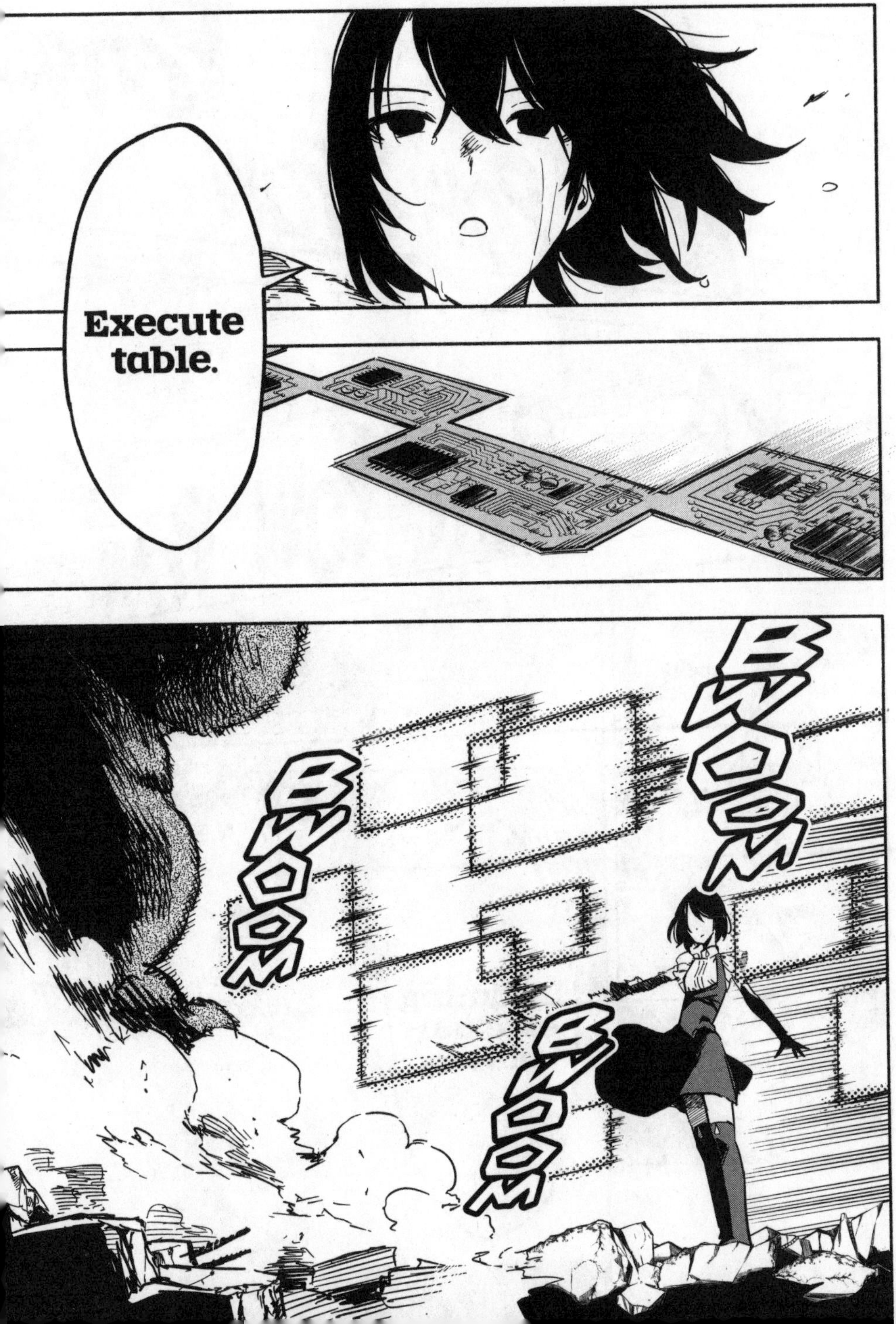
Execute table.
BWOOM
BWOOM
BWOOM

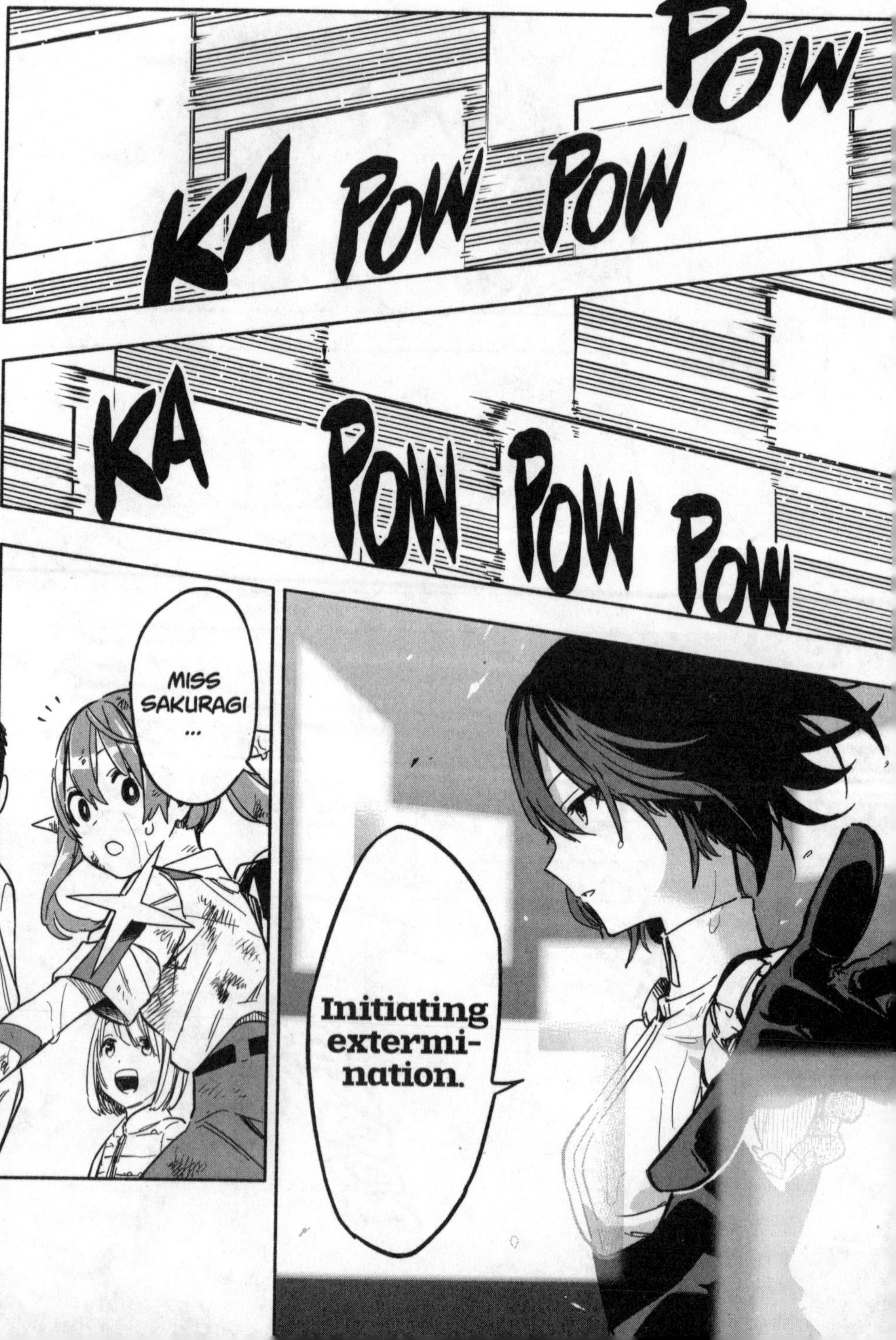
KA POW POW POW
KA POW POW POW
Initiating extermi-nation.
MISS SAKURAGI ...

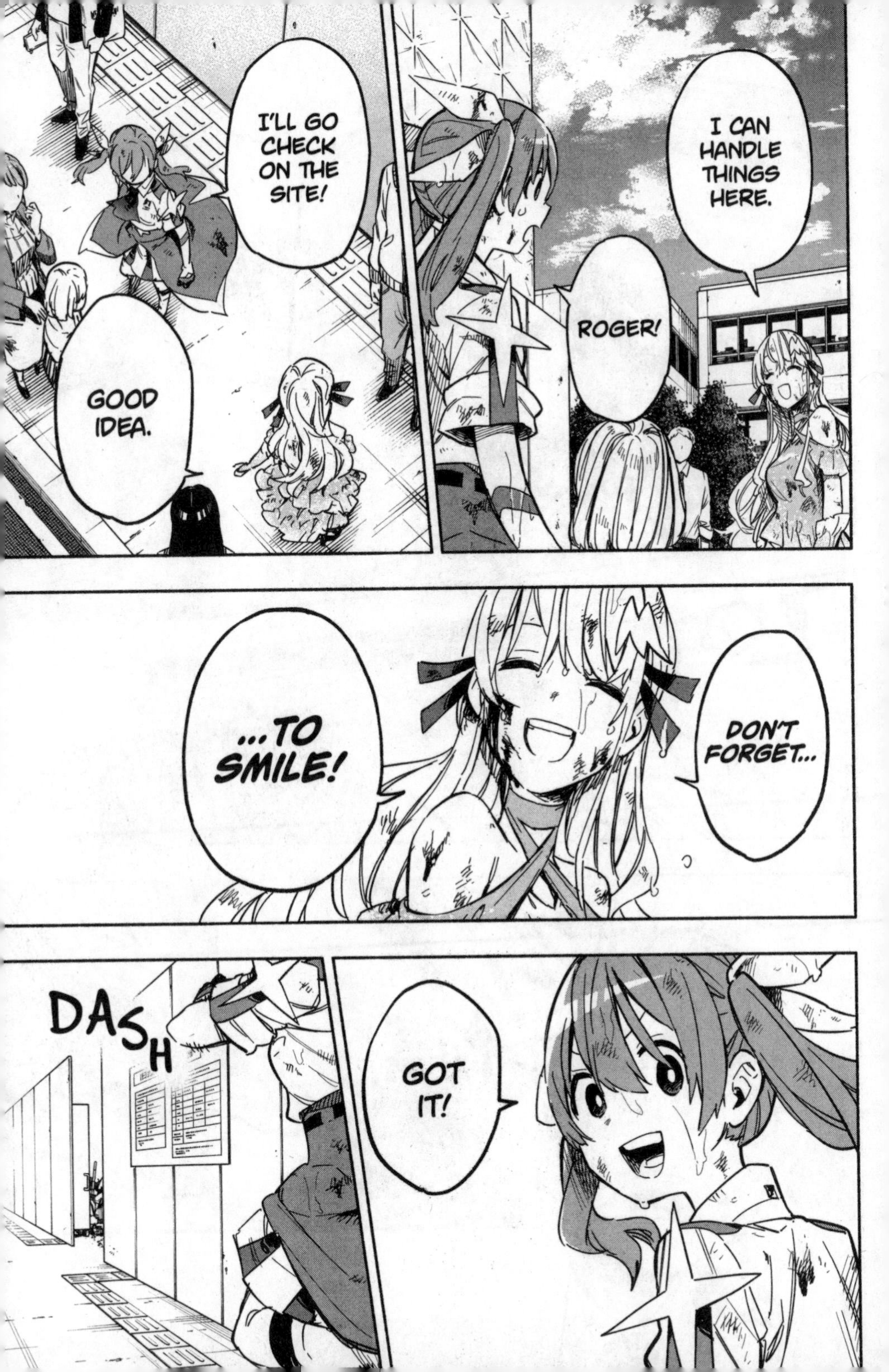
I CAN HANDLE THINGS HERE.
ROGER!
I'LL GO CHECK ON THE SITE!
GOOD IDEA.
DON'T FORGET...
...TO SMILE!
GOT IT!
DASH

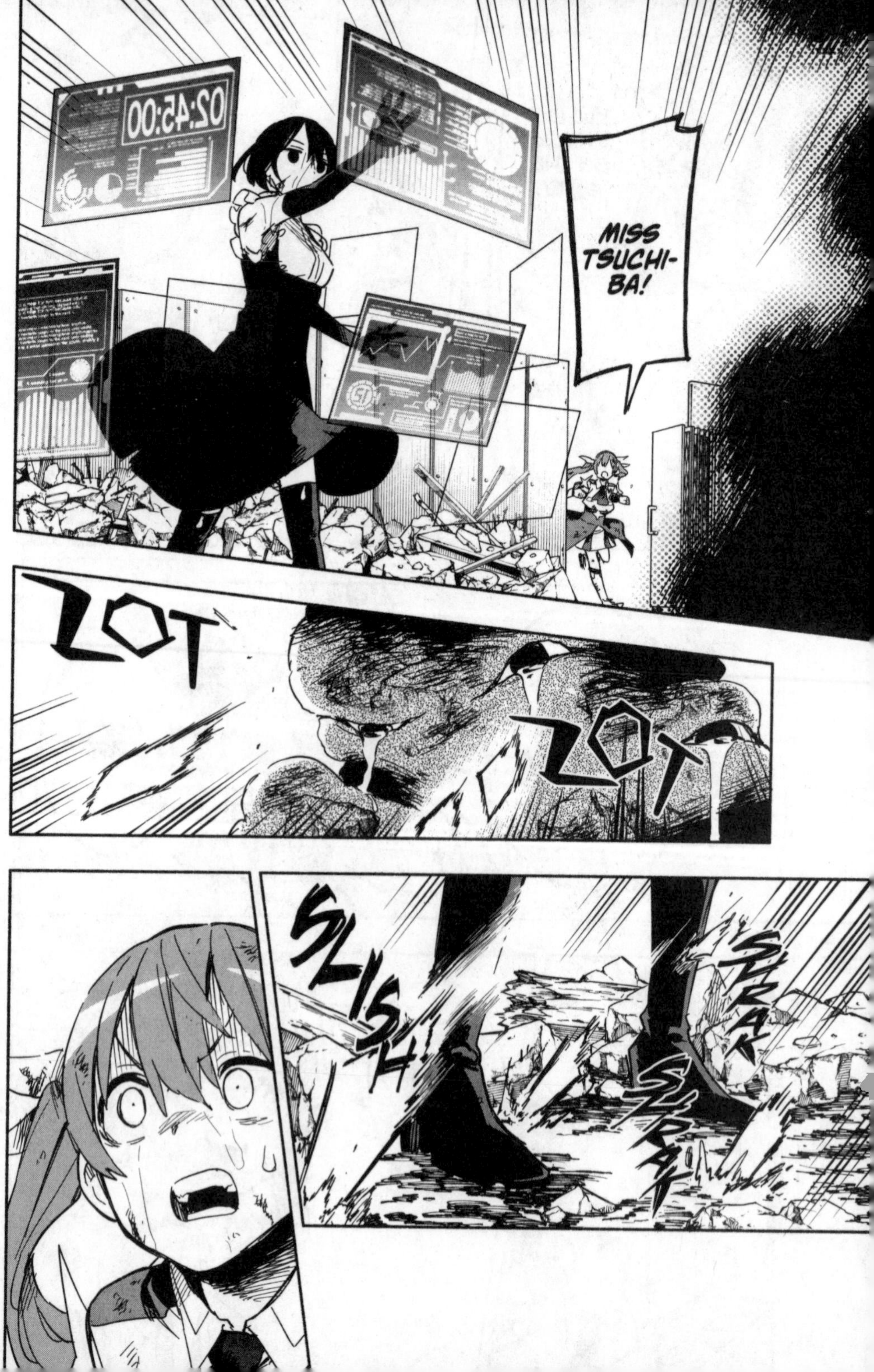
MISS TSUCHI-BA!
ZOT
ZOT
SPRAK
SPRAK
SLISH

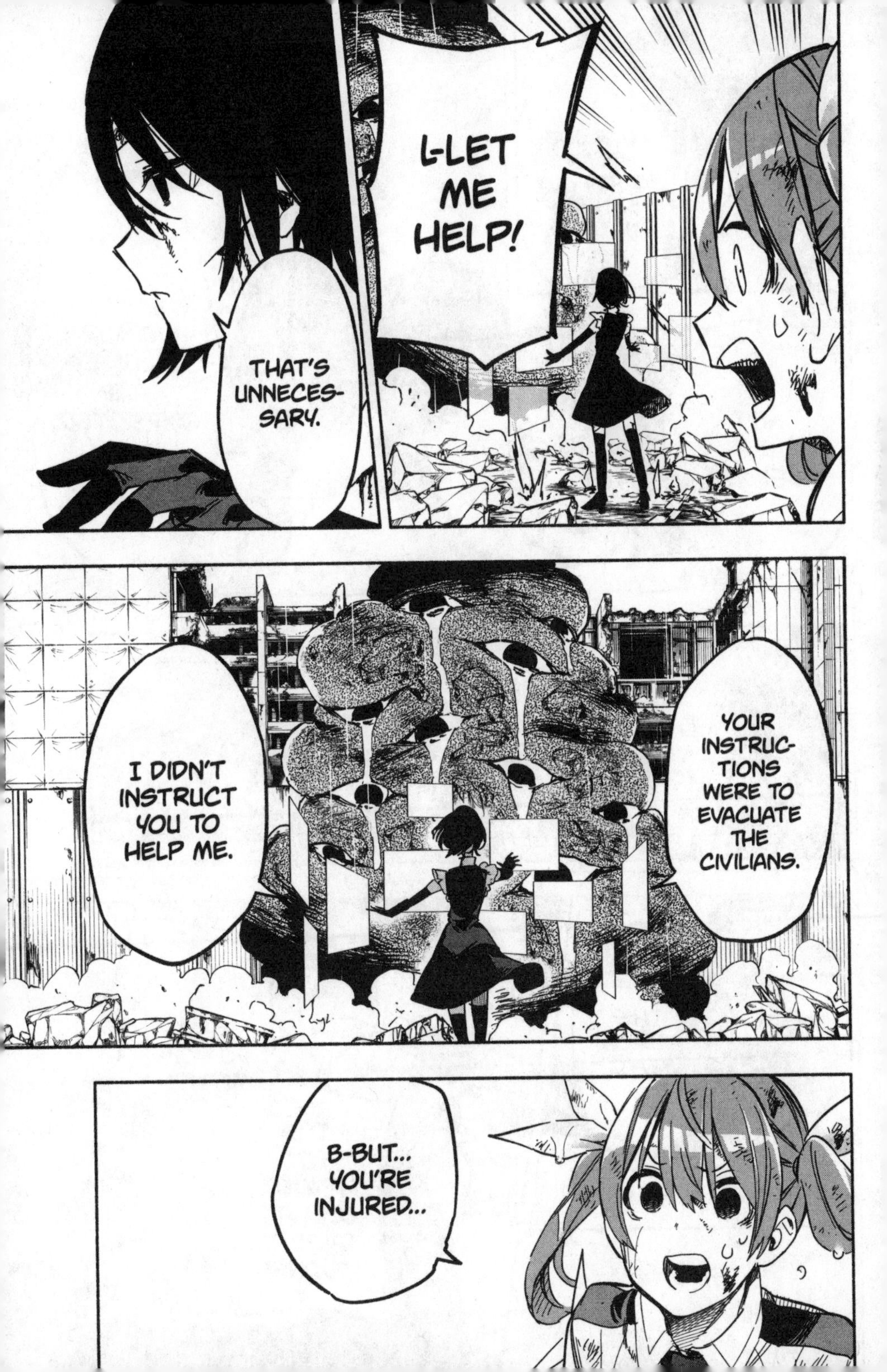
L-LET ME HELP!
THAT'S UNNECES-SARY.
YOUR INSTRUC-TIONS WERE TO EVACUATE THE CIVILIANS.
I DIDN'T INSTRUCT YOU TO HELP ME.
B-BUT... YOU'RE INJURED...

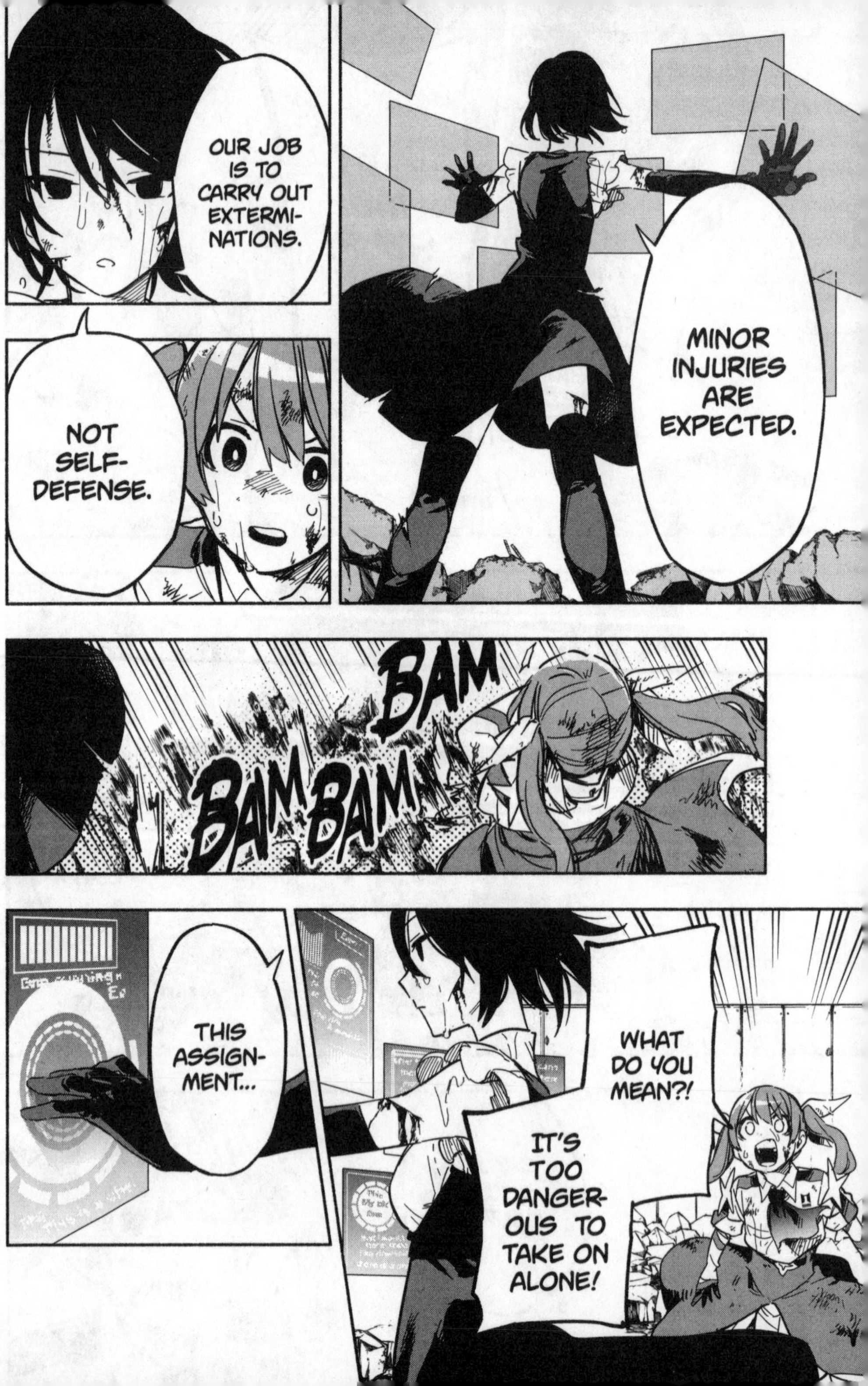
MINOR INJURIES ARE EXPECTED.
OUR JOB IS TO CARRY OUT EXTERMINATIONS.
NOT SELF-DEFENSE.
BAM
BAM BAM
WHAT DO YOU MEAN?!
IT'S TOO DANGEROUS TO TAKE ON ALONE!
THIS ASSIGNMENT...

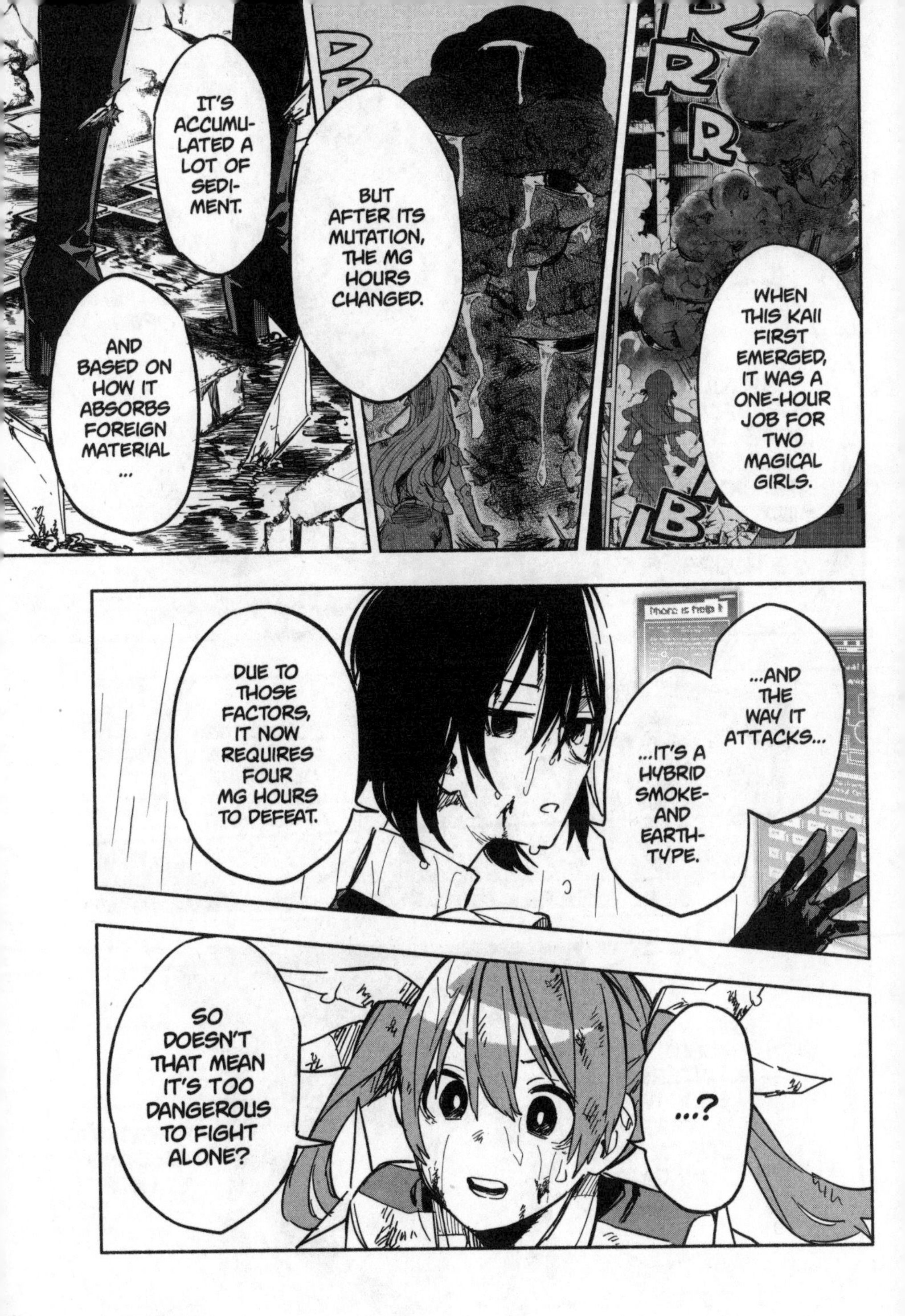
RRR
WHEN THIS KAII FIRST EMERGED, IT WAS A ONE-HOUR JOB FOR TWO MAGICAL GIRLS.
BUT AFTER ITS MUTATION, THE MG HOURS CHANGED.
IT'S ACCUMULATED A LOT OF SEDIMENT.
AND BASED ON HOW IT ABSORBS FOREIGN MATERIAL...
...AND THE WAY IT ATTACKS...
...IT'S A HYBRID SMOKE-AND EARTH-TYPE.
DUE TO THOSE FACTORS, IT NOW REQUIRES FOUR MG HOURS TO DEFEAT.
...?
SO DOESN'T THAT MEAN IT'S TOO DANGEROUS TO FIGHT ALONE?

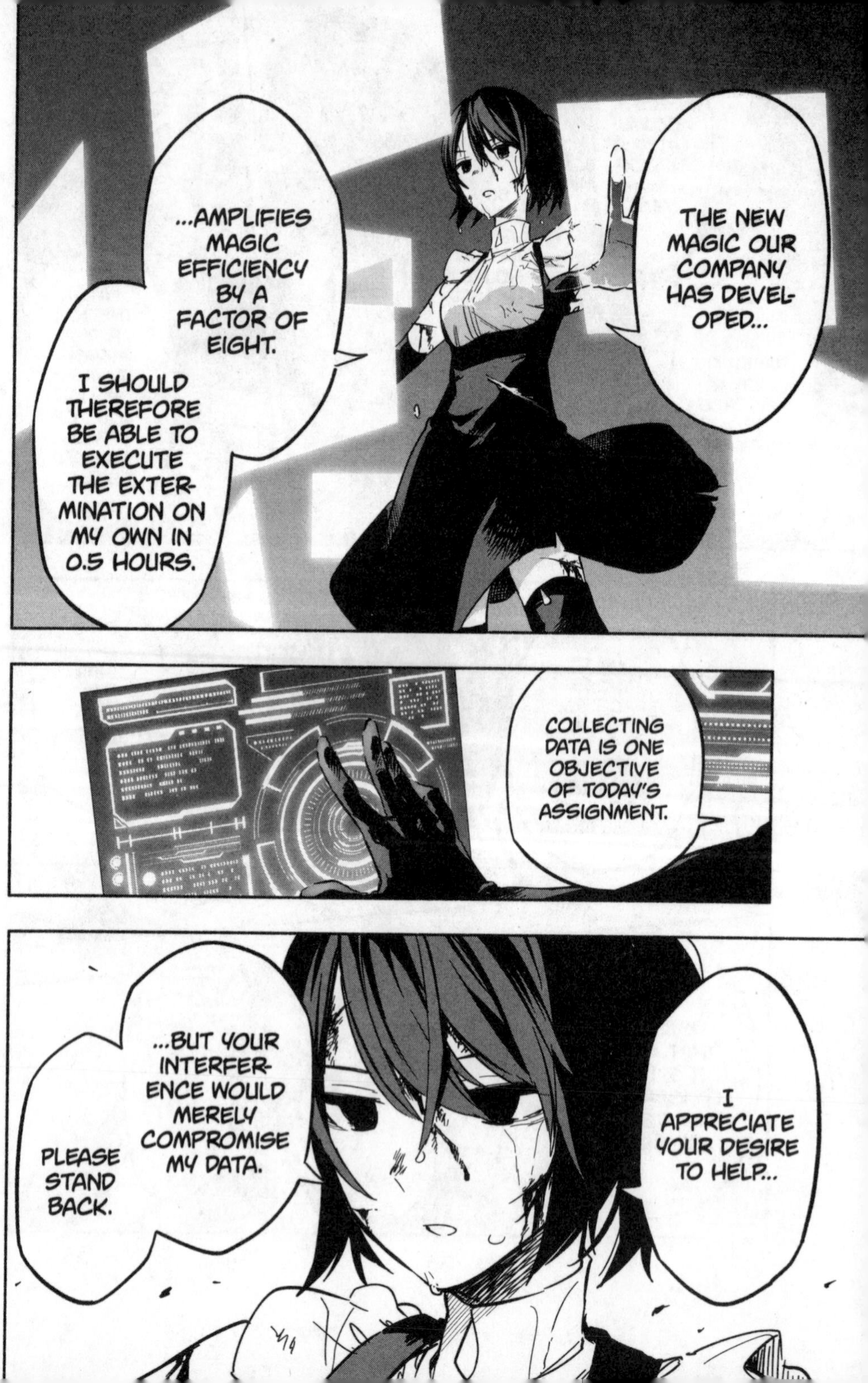
THE NEW MAGIC OUR COMPANY HAS DEVELOPED...
...AMPLIFIES MAGIC EFFICIENCY BY A FACTOR OF EIGHT.
I SHOULD THEREFORE BE ABLE TO EXECUTE THE EXTERMINATION ON MY OWN IN 0.5 HOURS.
COLLECTING DATA IS ONE OBJECTIVE OF TODAY'S ASSIGNMENT.
I APPRECIATE YOUR DESIRE TO HELP...
...BUT YOUR INTERFERENCE WOULD MERELY COMPROMISE MY DATA.
PLEASE STAND BACK.

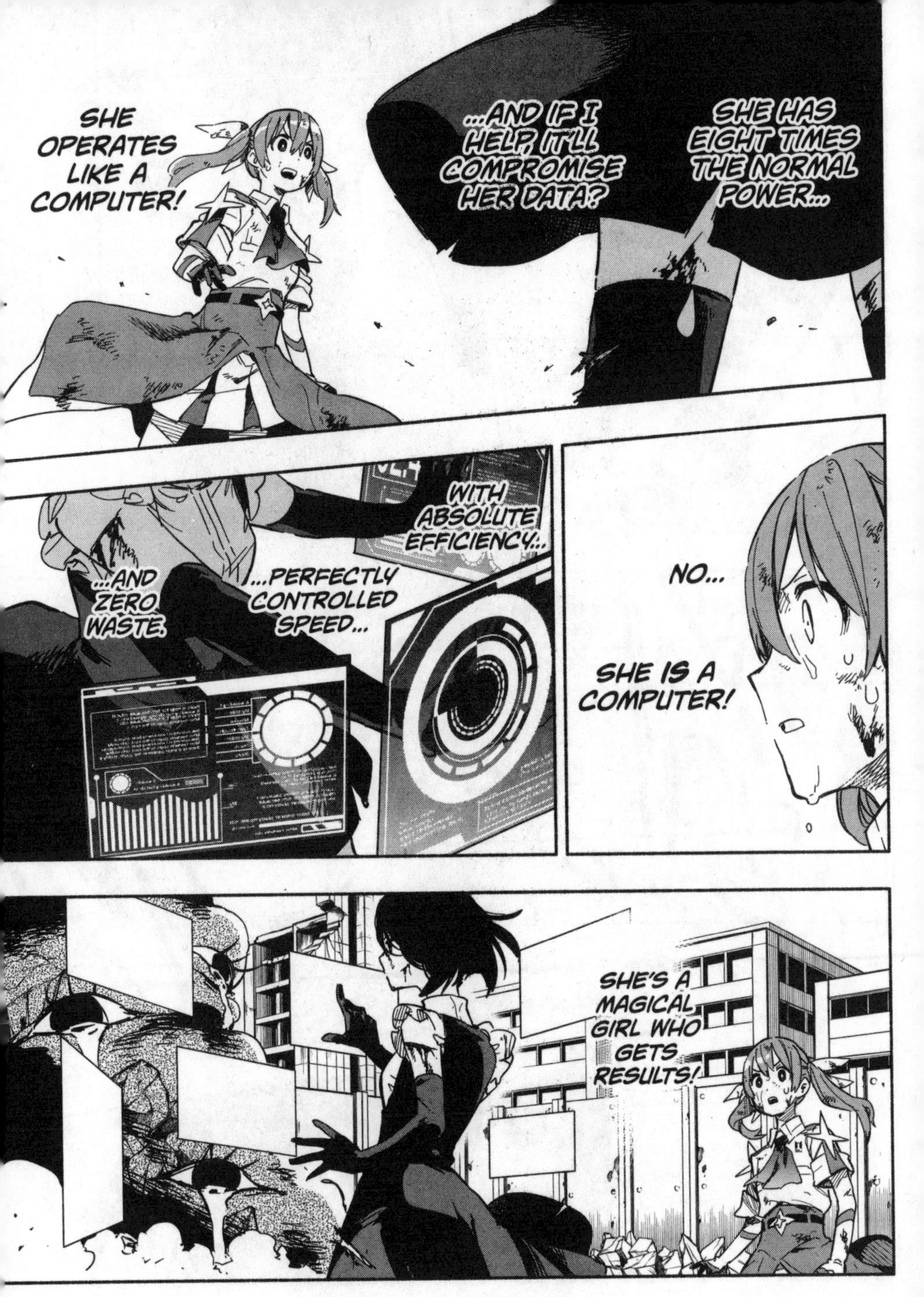
SHE HAS EIGHT TIMES THE NORMAL POWER...
...AND IF I HELP, IT'LL COMPROMISE HER DATA?
SHE OPERATES LIKE A COMPUTER!
NO...
SHE IS A COMPUTER!
WITH ABSOLUTE EFFICIENCY...
...PERFECTLY CONTROLLED SPEED...
...AND ZERO WASTE.
SHE'S A MAGICAL GIRL WHO GETS RESULTS!

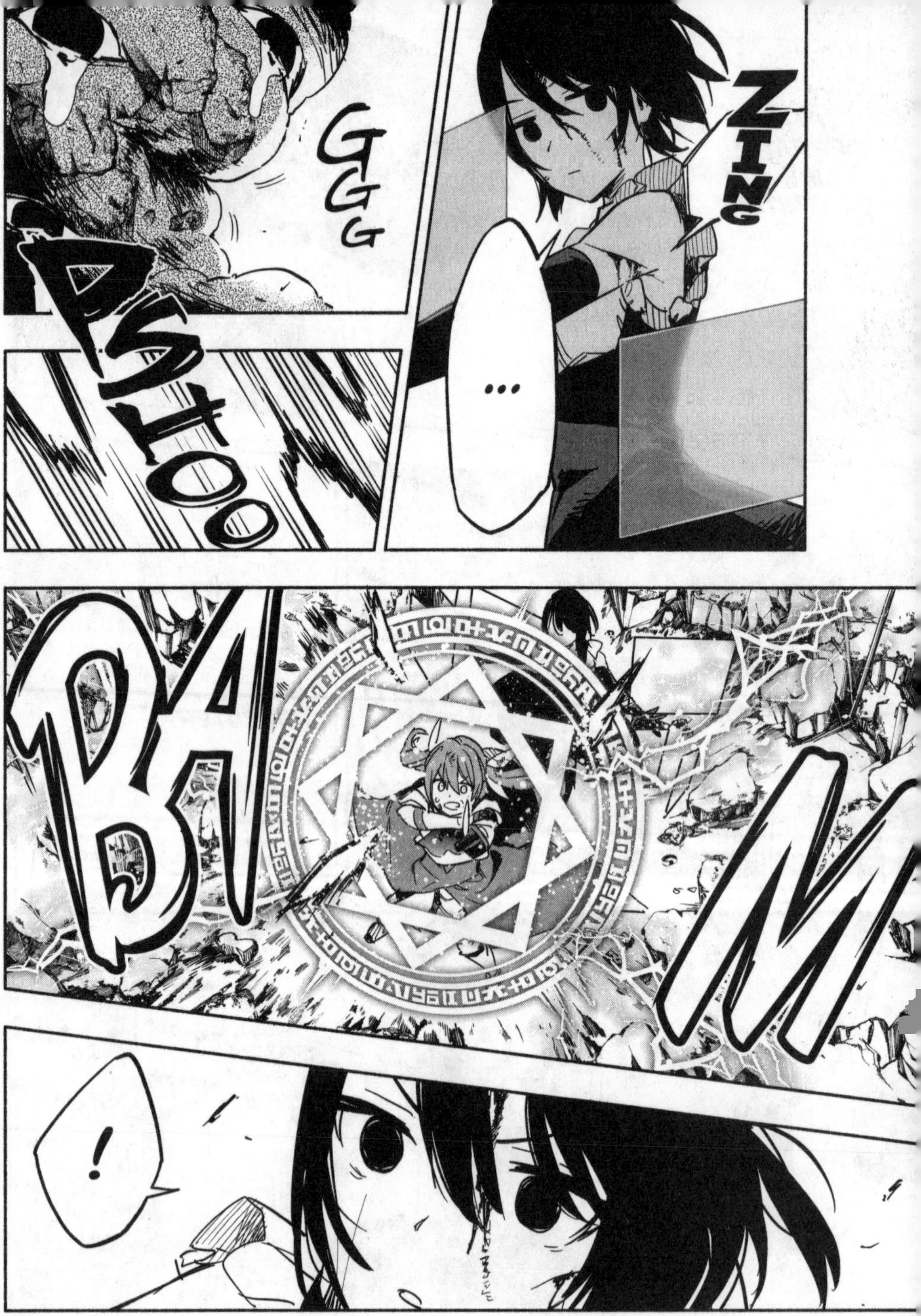
ZING
...
GGG
PASHOOO
BAM
!

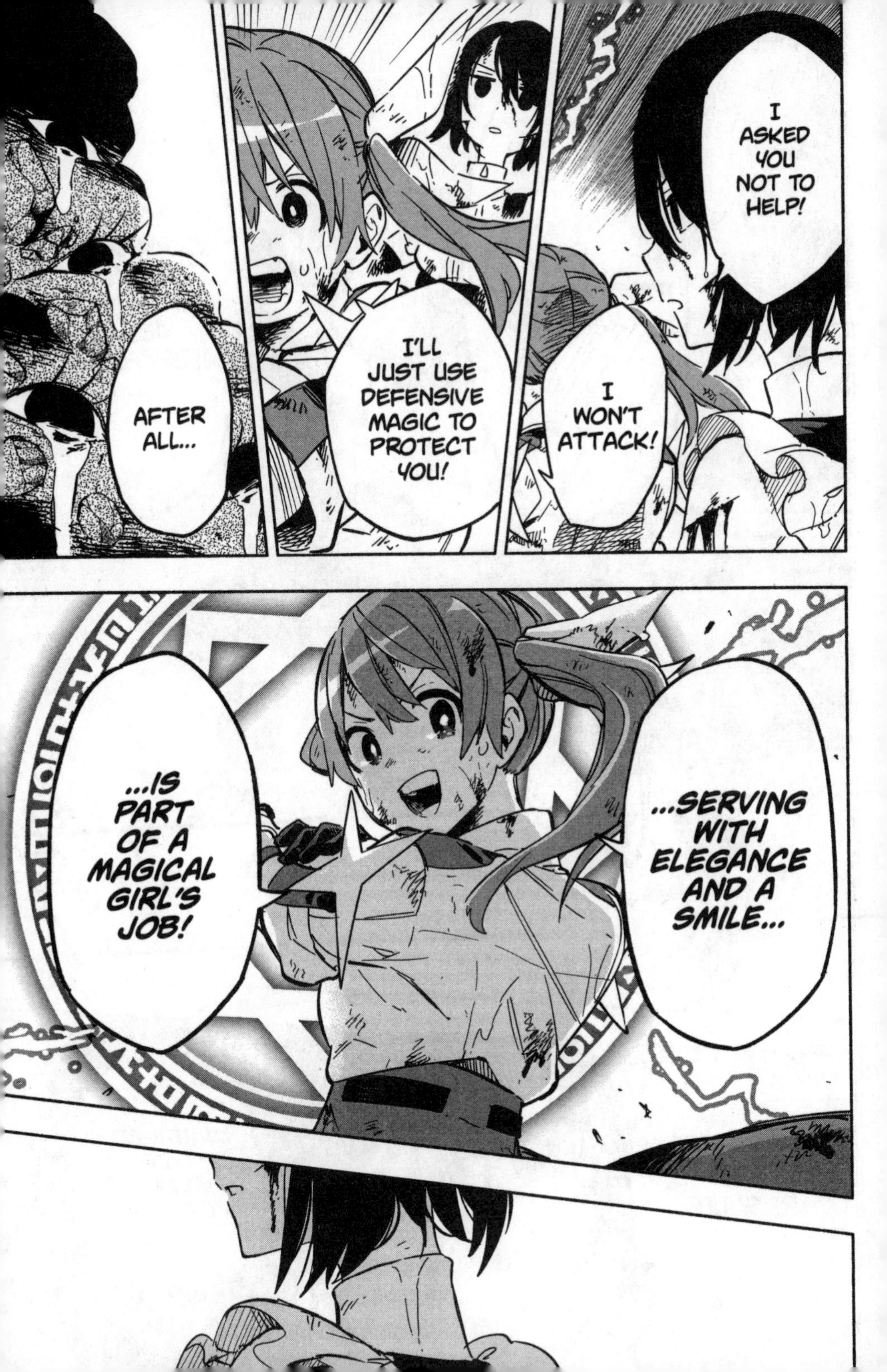
I ASKED YOU NOT TO HELP!
I WON'T ATTACK!
I'LL JUST USE DEFENSIVE MAGIC TO PROTECT YOU!
AFTER ALL...
...SERVING WITH ELEGANCE AND A SMILE...
...IS PART OF A MAGICAL GIRL'S JOB!

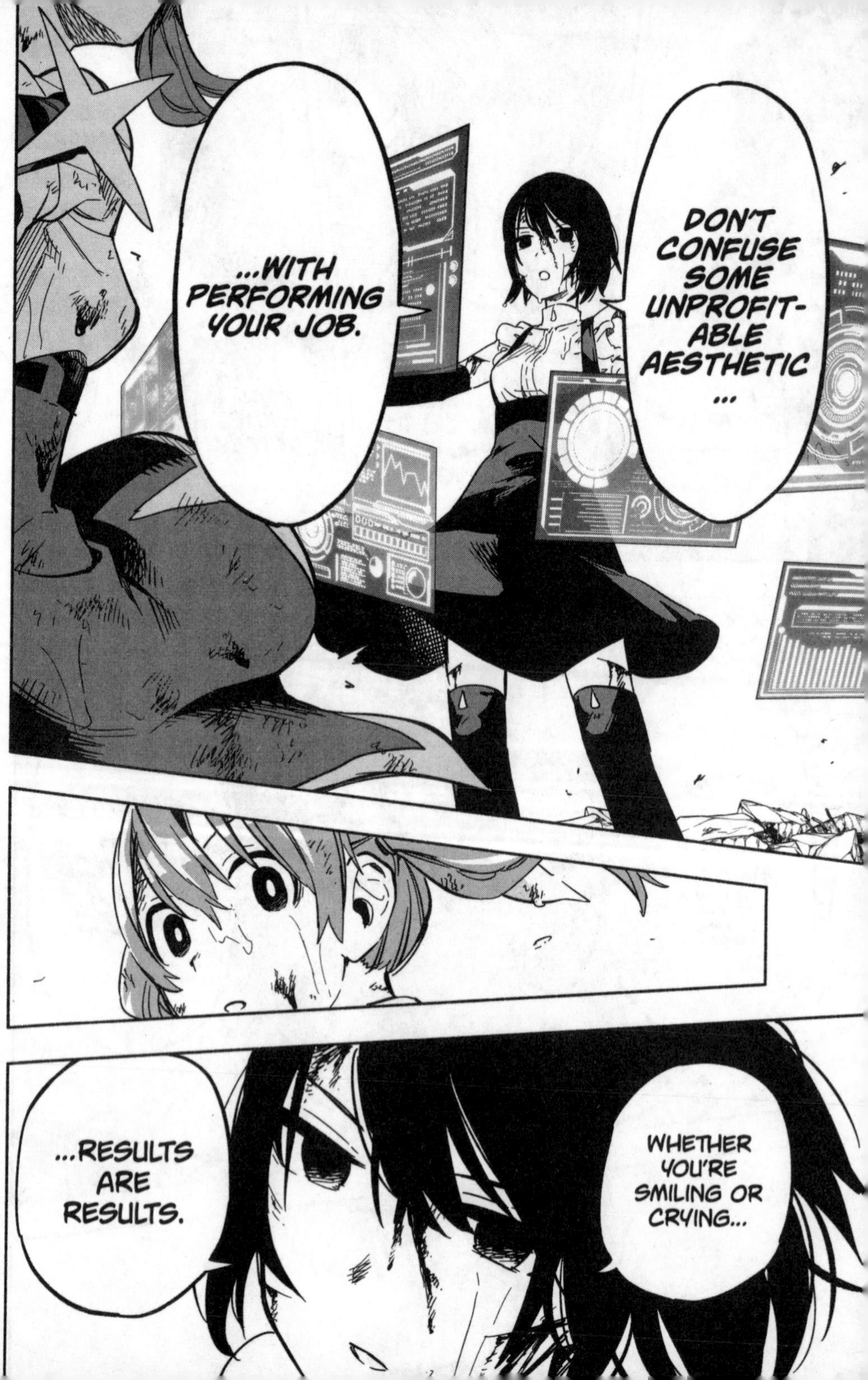
DON'T CONFUSE SOME UNPROFIT-ABLE AESTHETIC ...
...WITH PERFORMING YOUR JOB.
WHETHER YOU'RE SMILING OR CRYING...
...RESULTS ARE RESULTS.

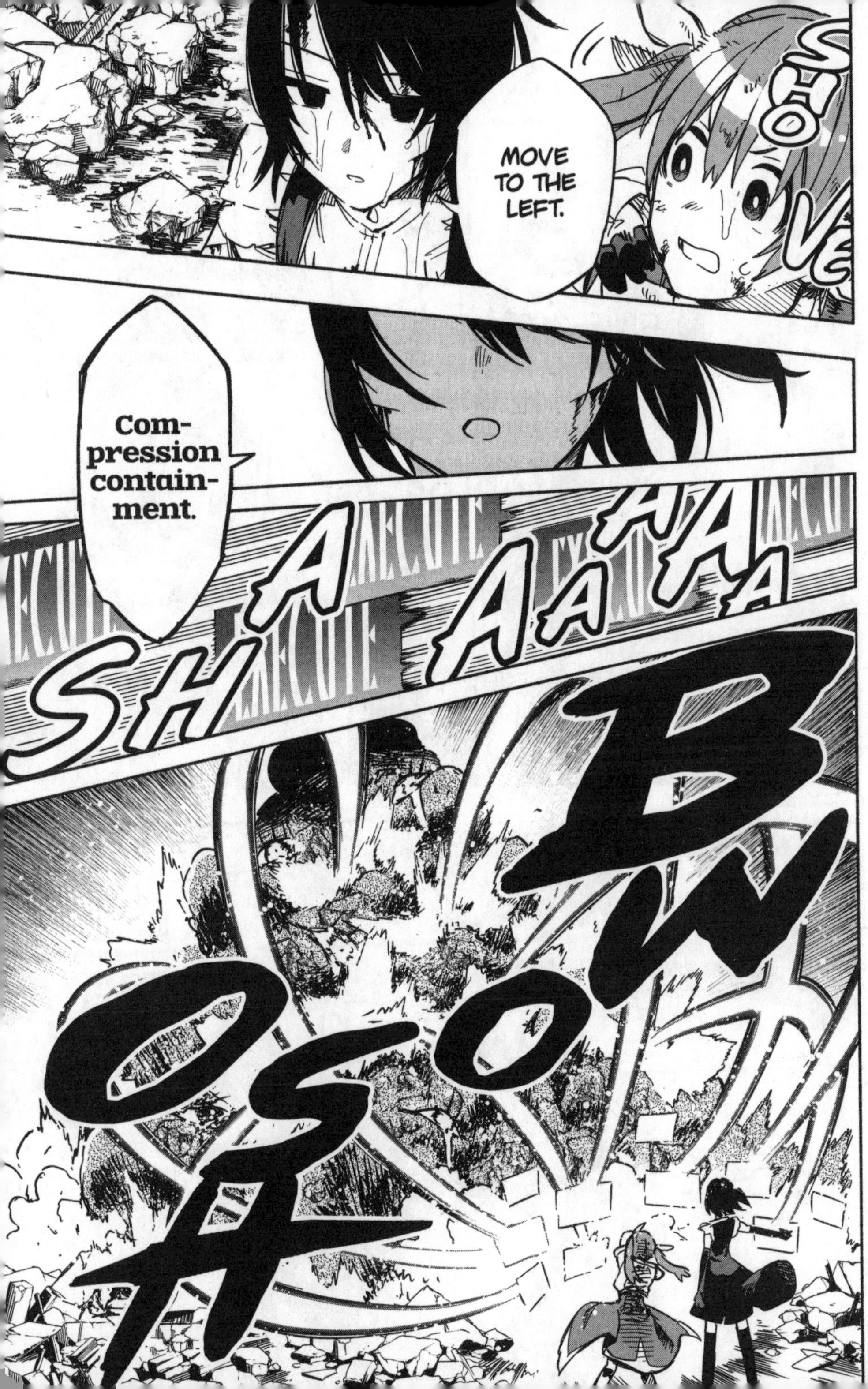
SHOVE
MOVE TO THE LEFT.
Compression containment.
SHAAAAAAA
BWOOSH

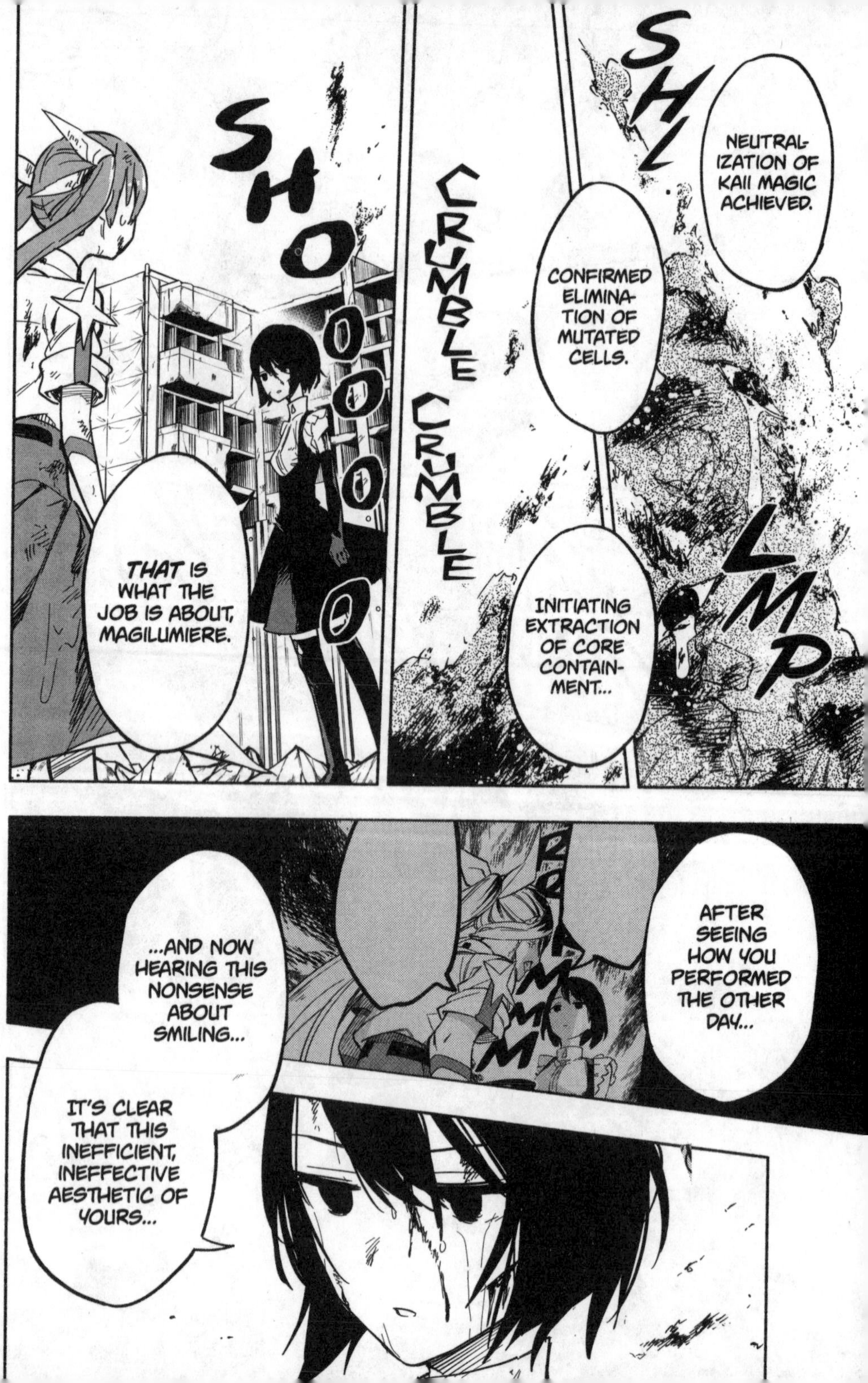
SHL
NEUTRALIZATION OF KAII MAGIC ACHIEVED.
CONFIRMED ELIMINATION OF MUTATED CELLS.
INITIATING EXTRACTION OF CORE CONTAINMENT...
LMP
CRUMBLE CRUMBLE
SHOOOOOO
THAT IS WHAT THE JOB IS ABOUT, MAGILUMIERE.
AFTER SEEING HOW YOU PERFORMED THE OTHER DAY...
...AND NOW HEARING THIS NONSENSE ABOUT SMILING...
IT'S CLEAR THAT THIS INEFFICIENT, INEFFECTIVE AESTHETIC OF YOURS...

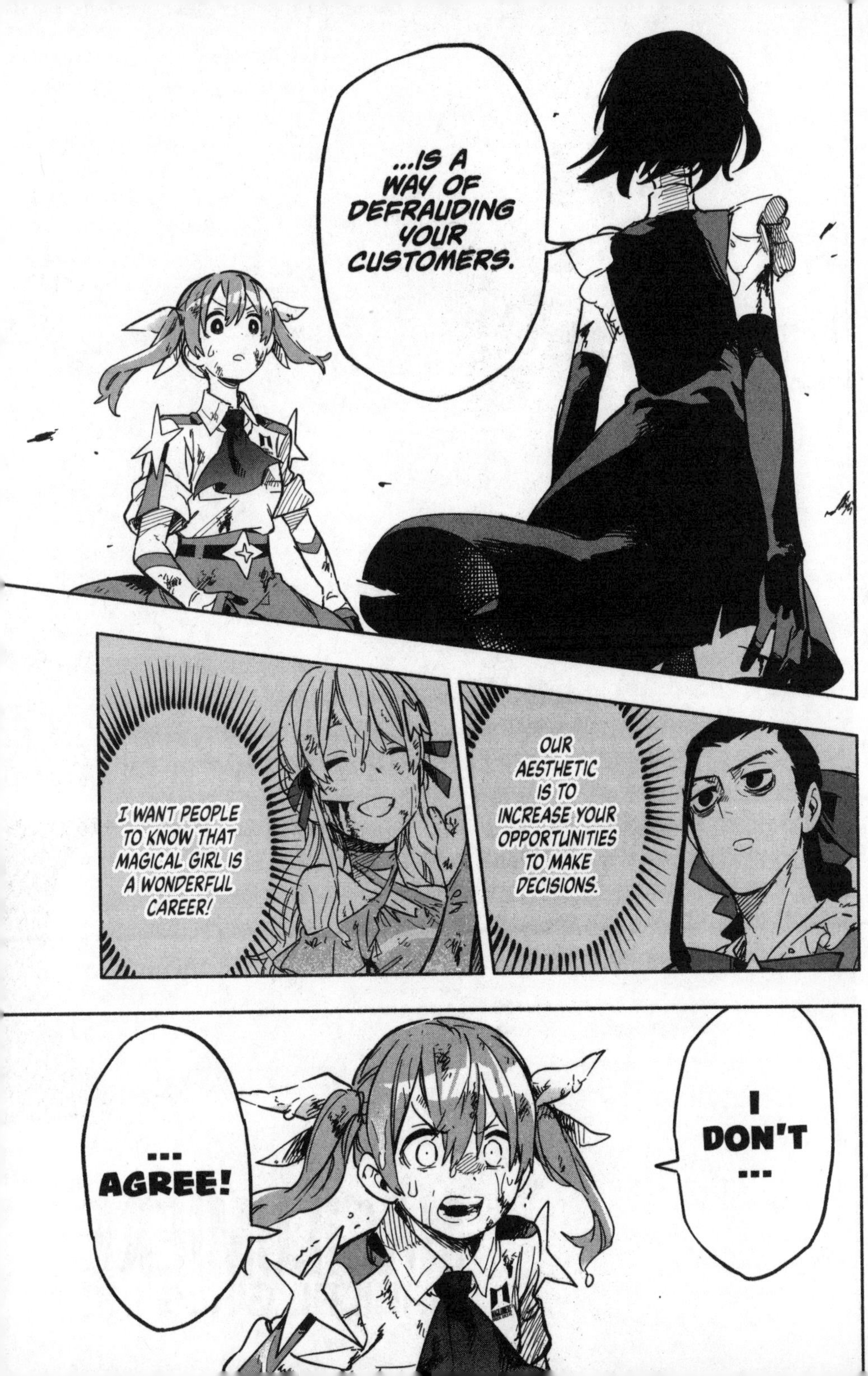
...IS A WAY OF DEFRAUDING YOUR CUSTOMERS.
OUR AESTHETIC IS TO INCREASE YOUR OPPORTUNITIES TO MAKE DECISIONS.
I WANT PEOPLE TO KNOW THAT MAGICAL GIRL IS A WONDERFUL CAREER!
I DON'T ...
... AGREE!

MAGILUMIERE
MAGICAL GIRLS INC

Chapter 16: Classified Information

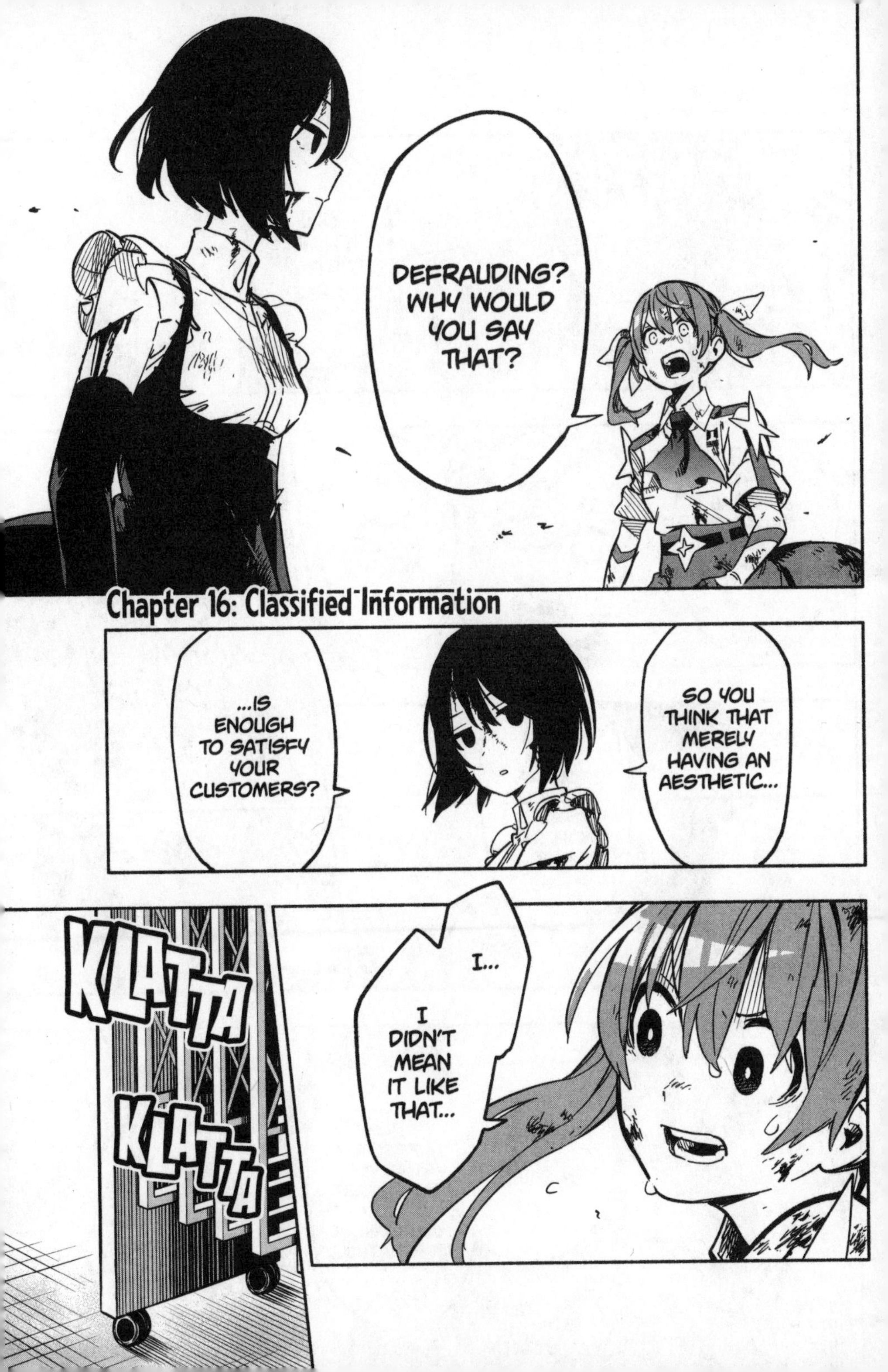
DEFRAUDING? WHY WOULD YOU SAY THAT?
SO YOU THINK THAT MERELY HAVING AN AESTHETIC...
...IS ENOUGH TO SATISFY YOUR CUSTOMERS?
I...
I DIDN'T MEAN IT LIKE THAT...
KLATTA
KLATTA

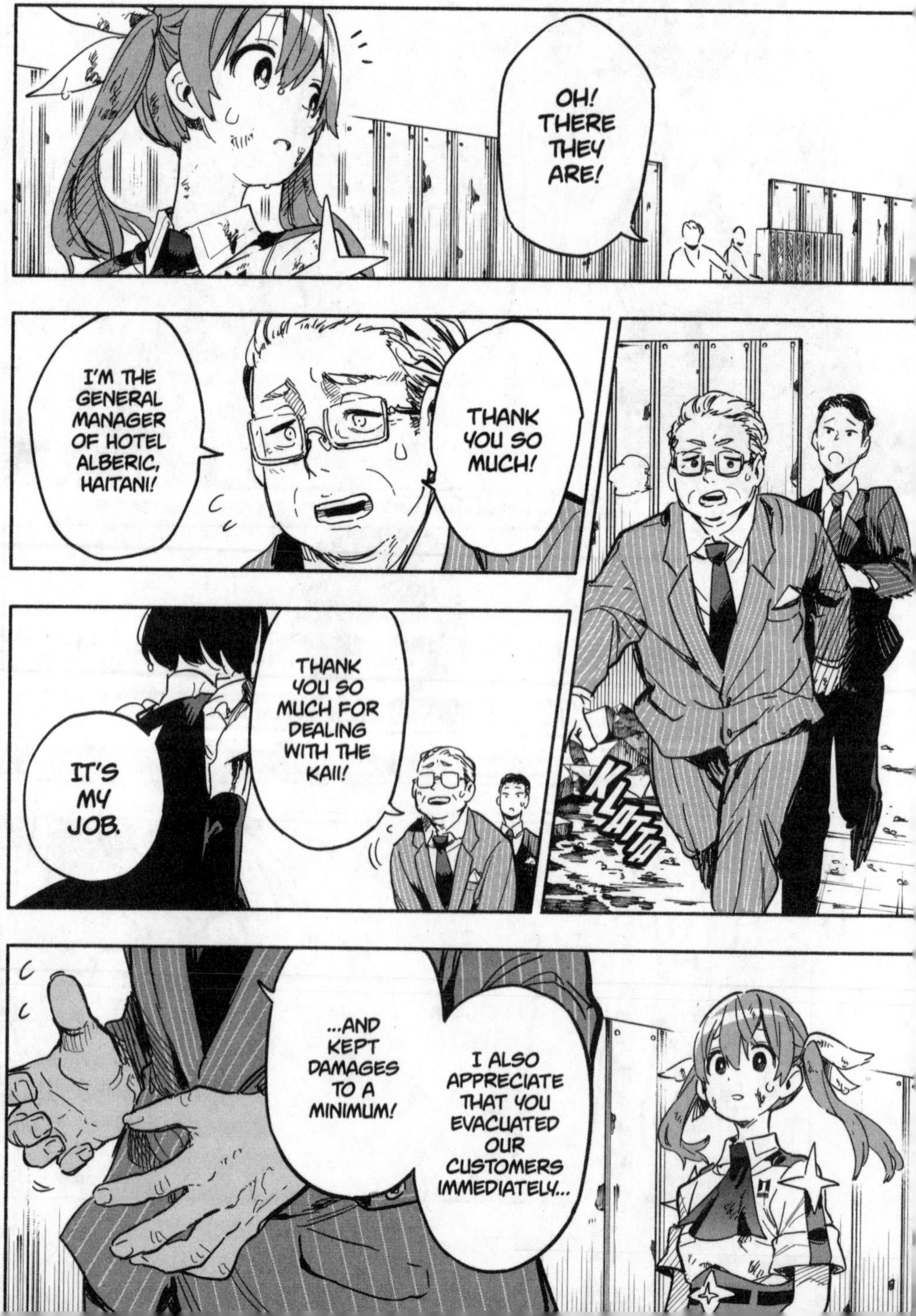
OH! THERE THEY ARE!
KLATTA
THANK YOU SO MUCH!
I'M THE GENERAL MANAGER OF HOTEL ALBERIC, HAITANI!
THANK YOU SO MUCH FOR DEALING WITH THE KAII!
IT'S MY JOB.
I ALSO APPRECIATE THAT YOU EVACUATED OUR CUSTOMERS IMMEDIATELY...
...AND KEPT DAMAGES TO A MINIMUM!

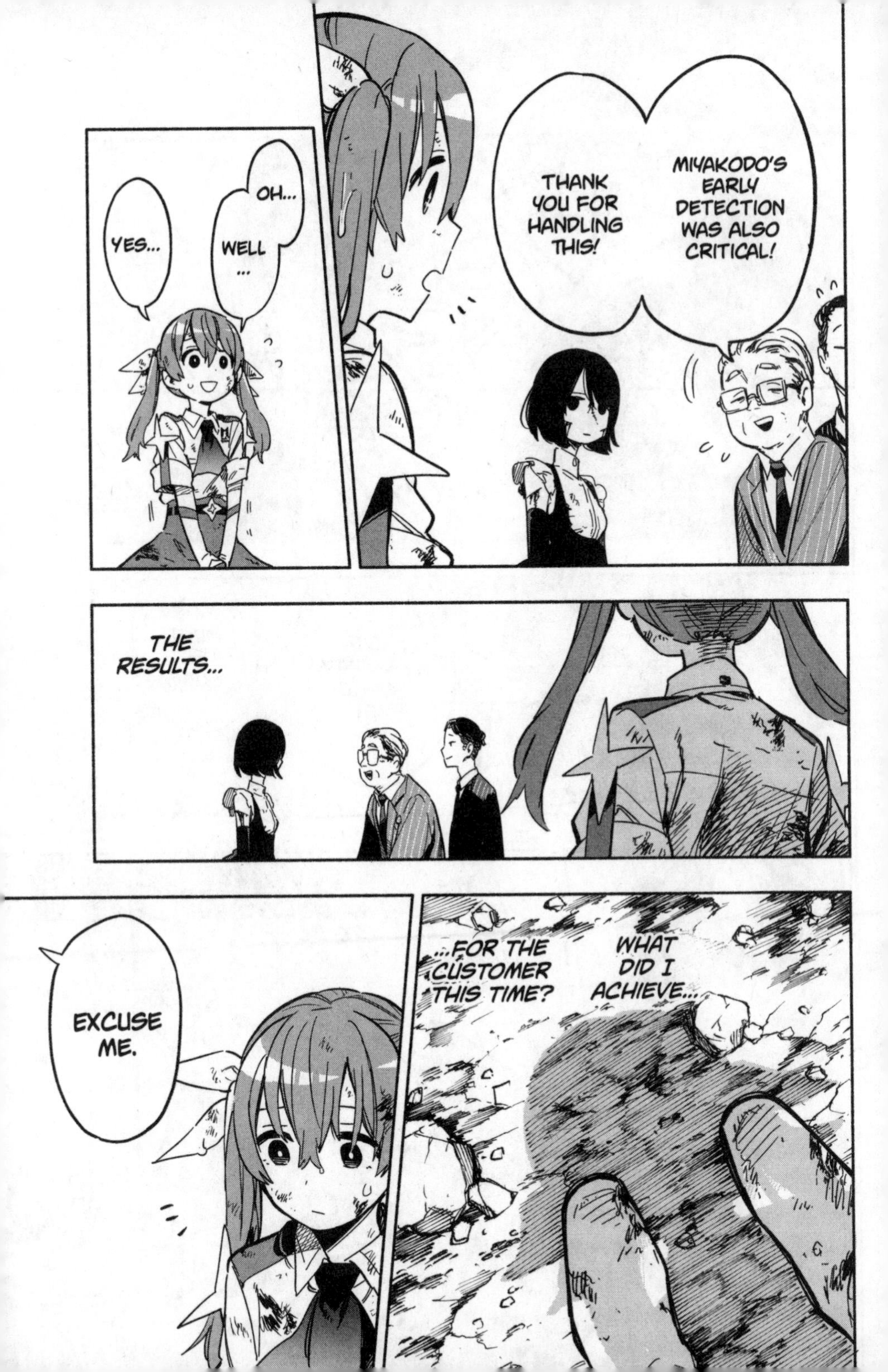
THANK YOU FOR HANDLING THIS!
MIYAKODO'S EARLY DETECTION WAS ALSO CRITICAL!
OH... WELL...
YES...
THE RESULTS...
WHAT DID I ACHIEVE...
...FOR THE CUSTOMER THIS TIME?
EXCUSE ME.

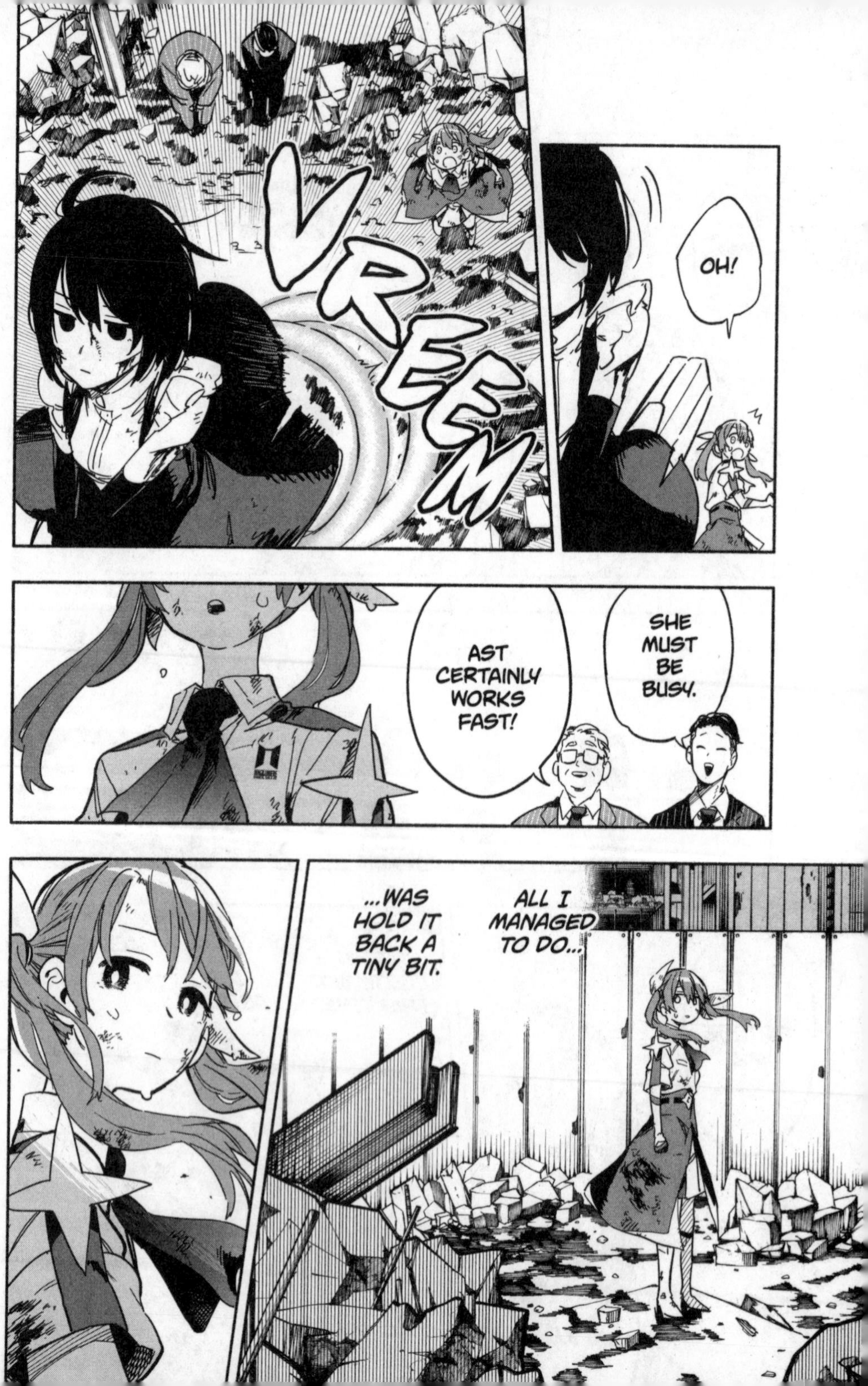
VREEM
OH!
SHE MUST BE BUSY.
AST CERTAINLY WORKS FAST!
ALL I MANAGED TO DO...
...WAS HOLD IT BACK A TINY BIT.

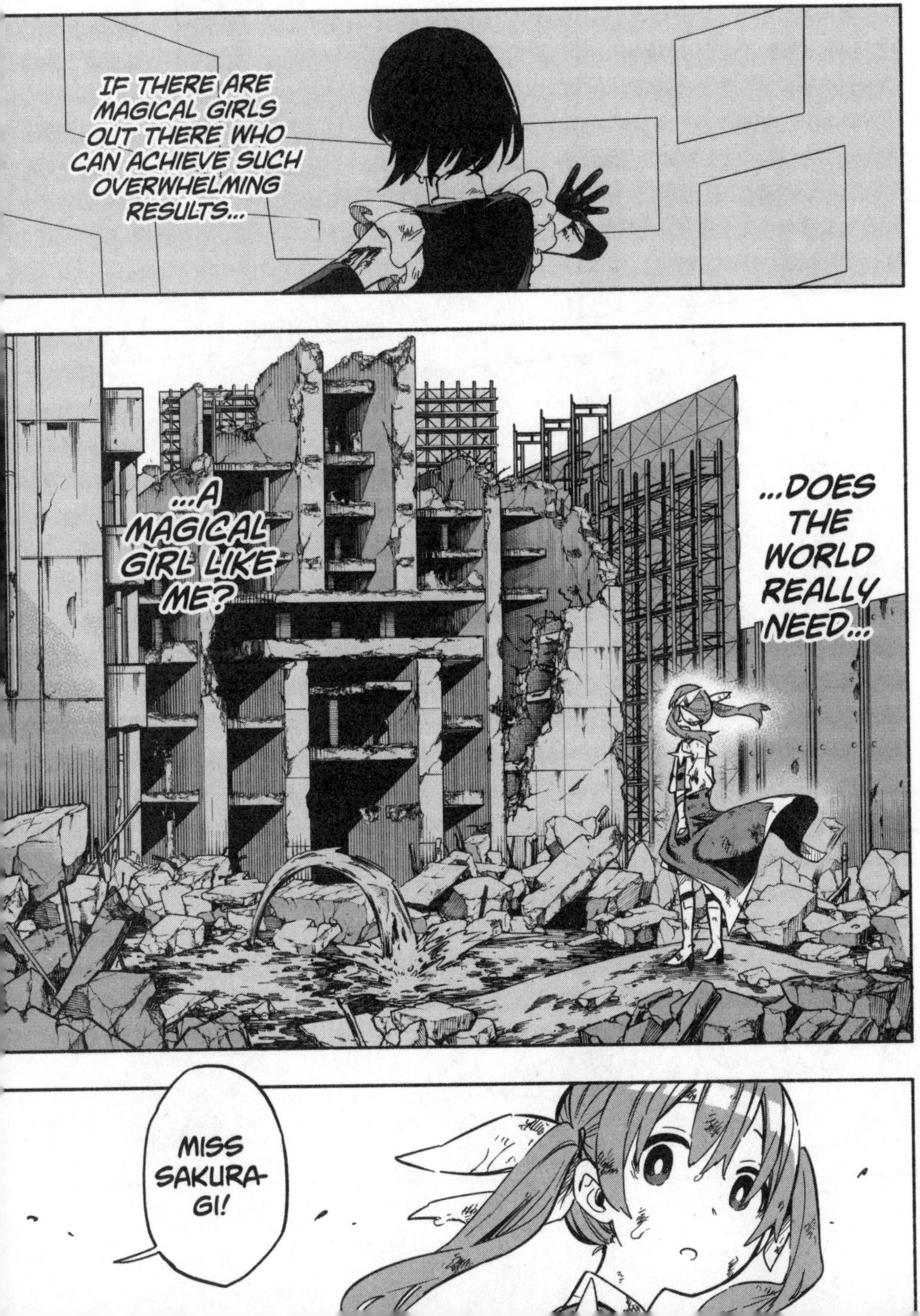
IF THERE ARE MAGICAL GIRLS OUT THERE WHO CAN ACHIEVE SUCH OVERWHELMING RESULTS...
...DOES THE WORLD REALLY NEED...
...A MAGICAL GIRL LIKE ME?
MISS SAKURA-GI!

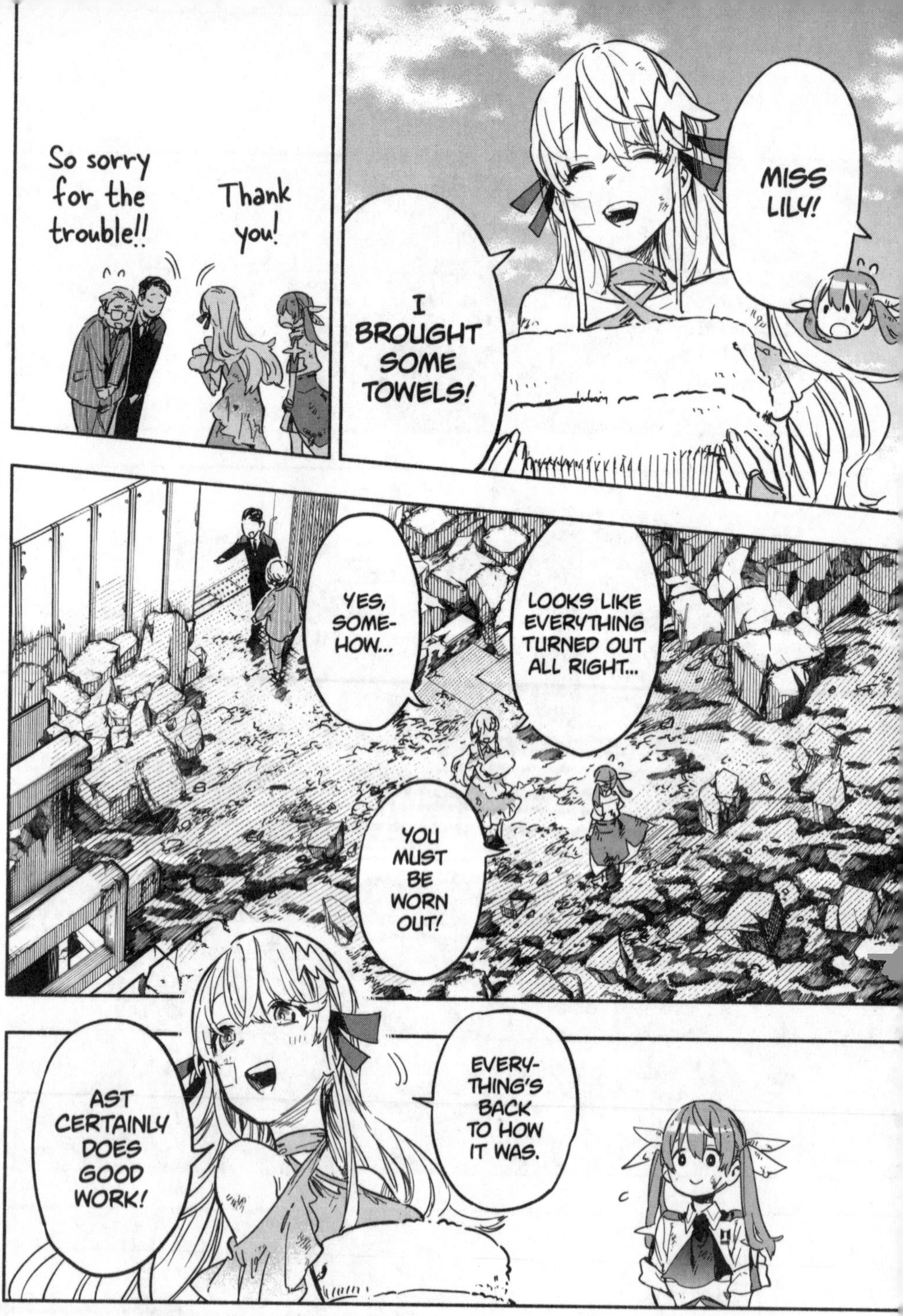
MISS LILY!
I BROUGHT SOME TOWELS!
Thank you!
So sorry for the trouble!!
LOOKS LIKE EVERYTHING TURNED OUT ALL RIGHT...
YES, SOME-HOW...
YOU MUST BE WORN OUT!
EVERY-THING'S BACK TO HOW IT WAS.
AST CERTAINLY DOES GOOD WORK!

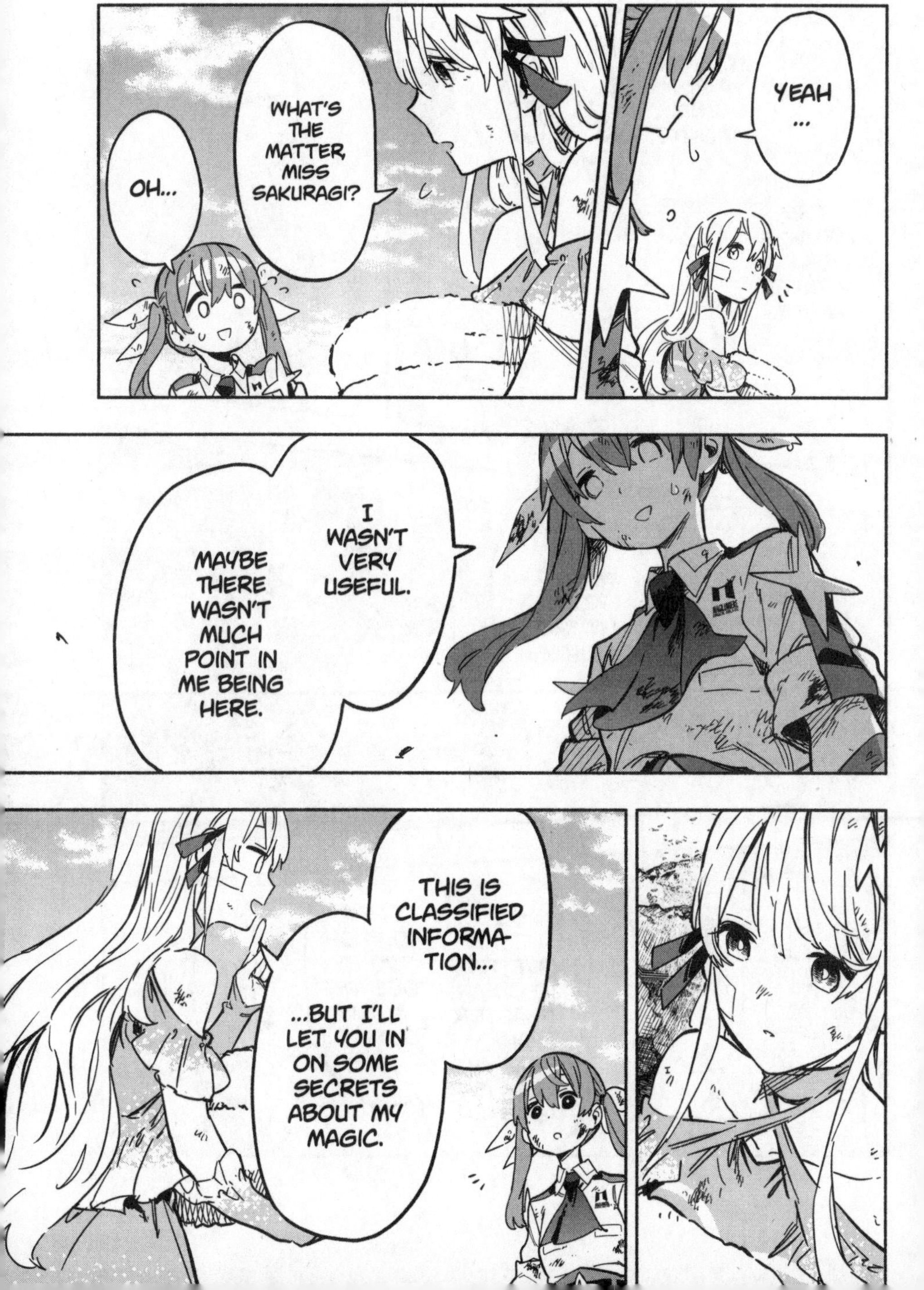
YEAH...
WHAT'S THE MATTER, MISS SAKURAGI?
OH...
I WASN'T VERY USEFUL.
MAYBE THERE WASN'T MUCH POINT IN ME BEING HERE.
THIS IS CLASSIFIED INFORMATION...
...BUT I'LL LET YOU IN ON SOME SECRETS ABOUT MY MAGIC.

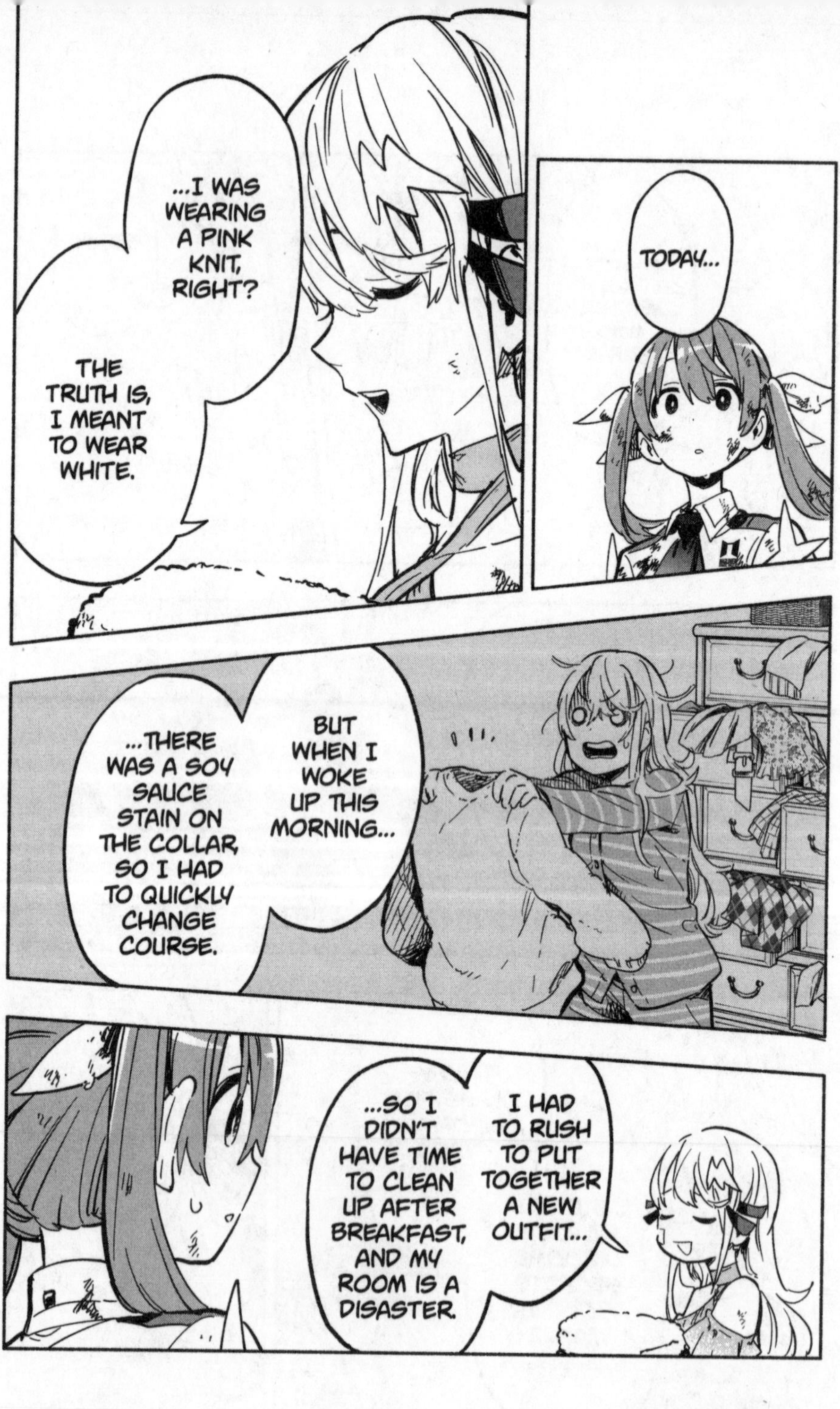
TODAY...
...I WAS WEARING A PINK KNIT, RIGHT?
THE TRUTH IS, I MEANT TO WEAR WHITE.
BUT WHEN I WOKE UP THIS MORNING...
...THERE WAS A SOY SAUCE STAIN ON THE COLLAR, SO I HAD TO QUICKLY CHANGE COURSE.
I HAD TO RUSH TO PUT TOGETHER A NEW OUTFIT...
...SO I DIDN'T HAVE TIME TO CLEAN UP AFTER BREAKFAST, AND MY ROOM IS A DISASTER.

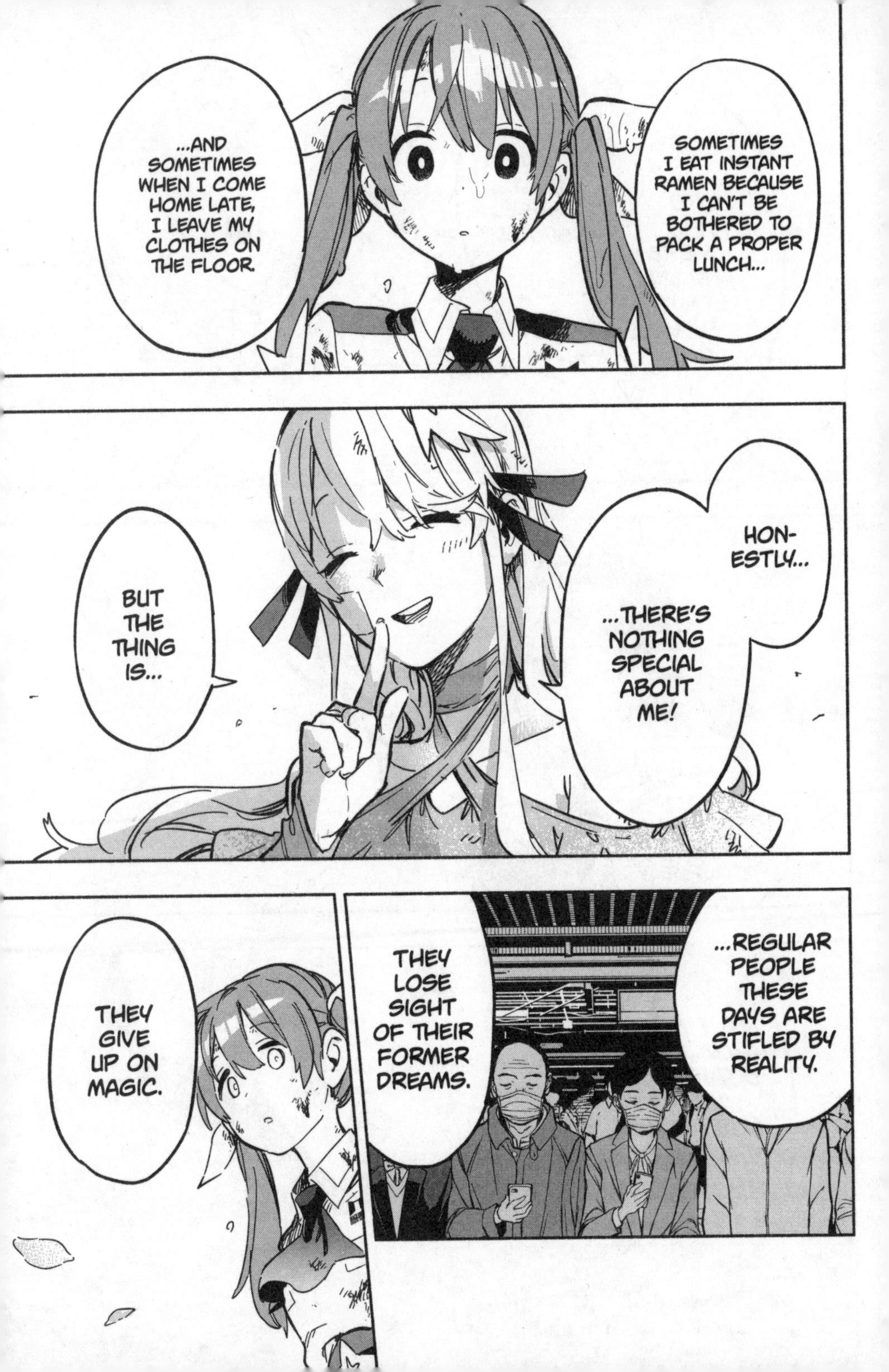
SOMETIMES I EAT INSTANT RAMEN BECAUSE I CAN'T BE BOTHERED TO PACK A PROPER LUNCH...
...AND SOMETIMES WHEN I COME HOME LATE, I LEAVE MY CLOTHES ON THE FLOOR.
HON-ESTLY...
...THERE'S NOTHING SPECIAL ABOUT ME!
BUT THE THING IS...
...REGULAR PEOPLE THESE DAYS ARE STIFLED BY REALITY.
THEY LOSE SIGHT OF THEIR FORMER DREAMS.
THEY GIVE UP ON MAGIC.

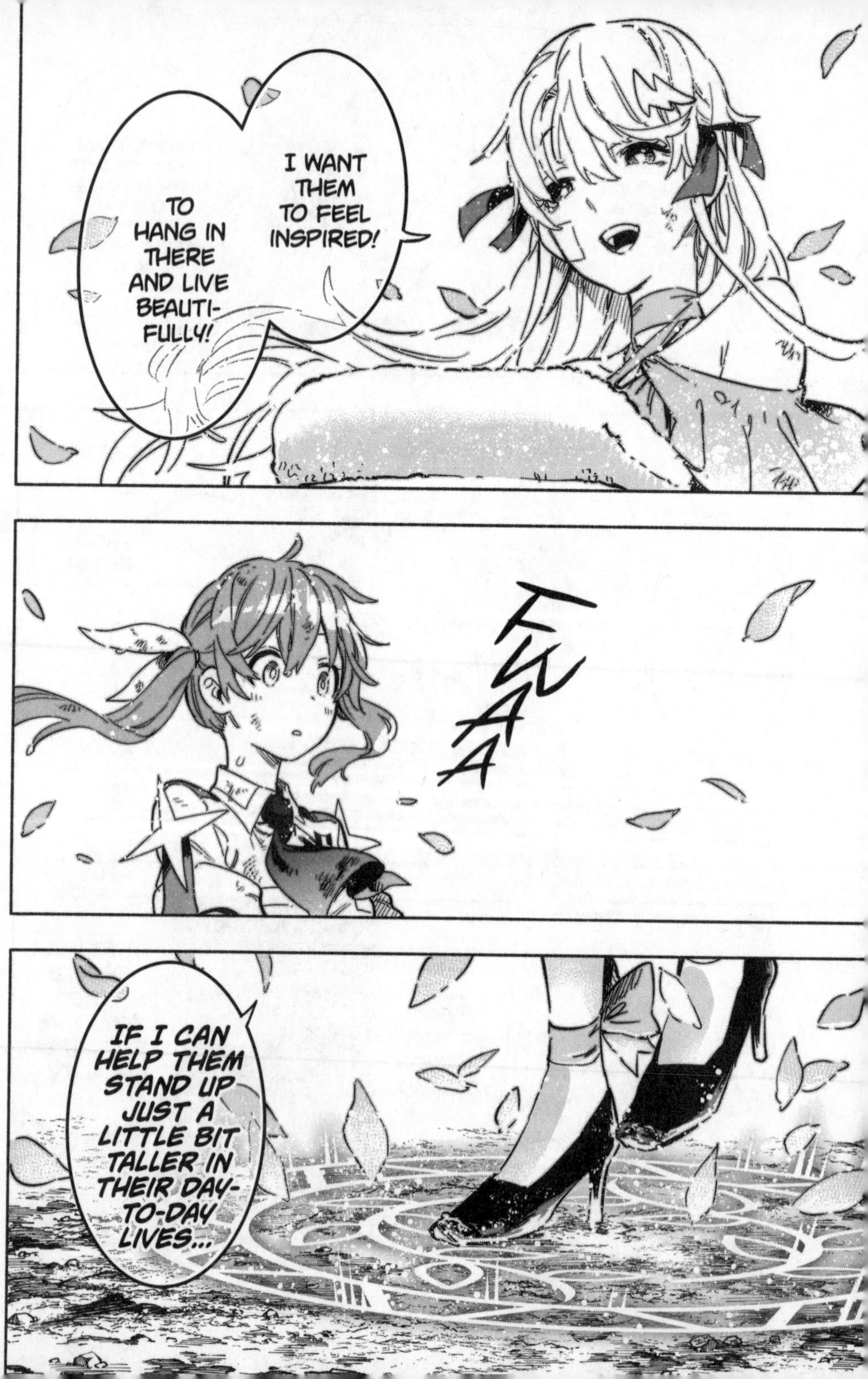
I WANT THEM TO FEEL INSPIRED!
TO HANG IN THERE AND LIVE BEAUTI-FULLY!
FWAA
IF I CAN HELP THEM STAND UP JUST A LITTLE BIT TALLER IN THEIR DAY-TO-DAY LIVES...

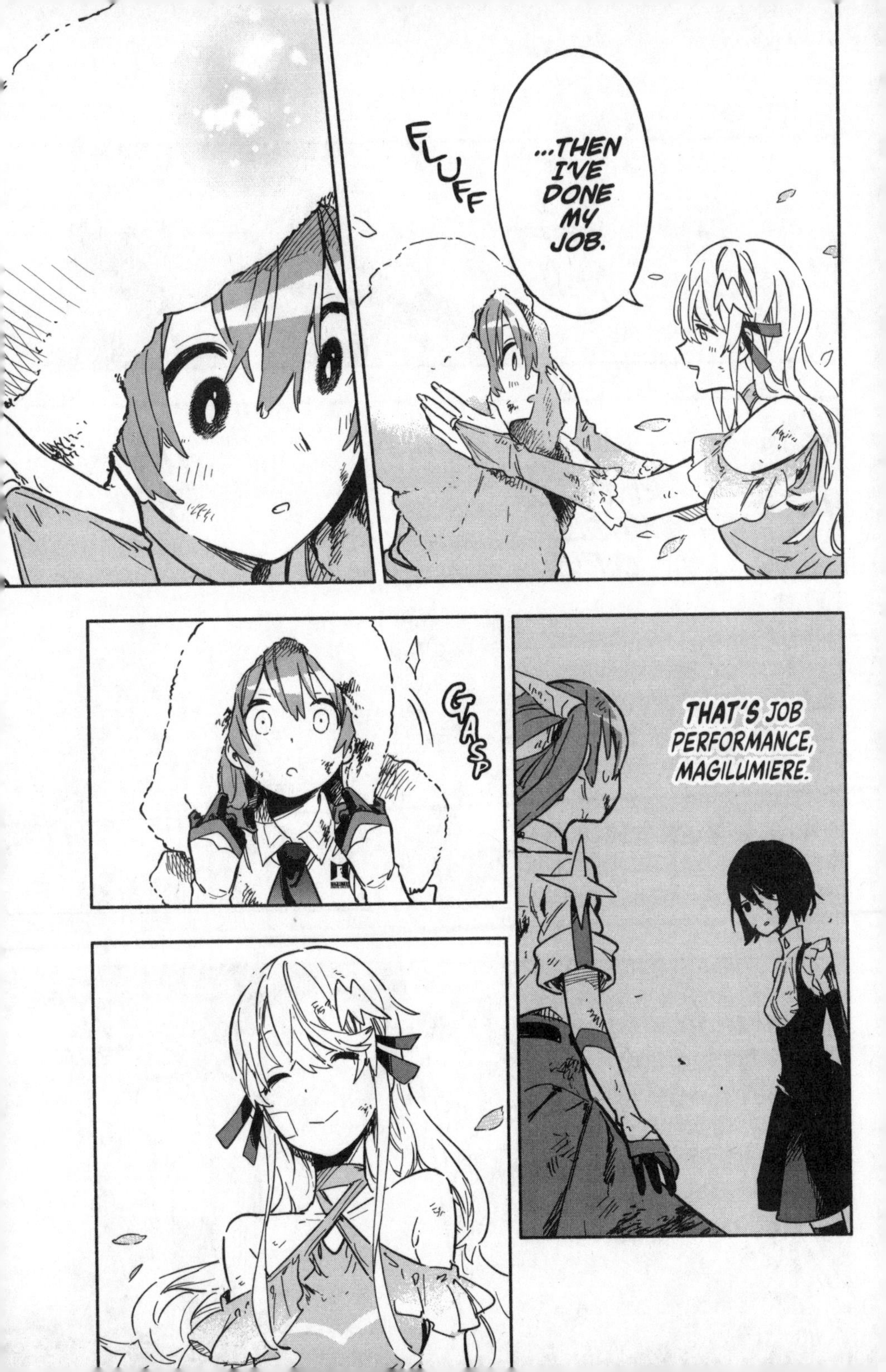
...THEN I'VE DONE MY JOB.
FLUFF
THAT'S JOB PERFORMANCE, MAGILUMIERE.
GASP

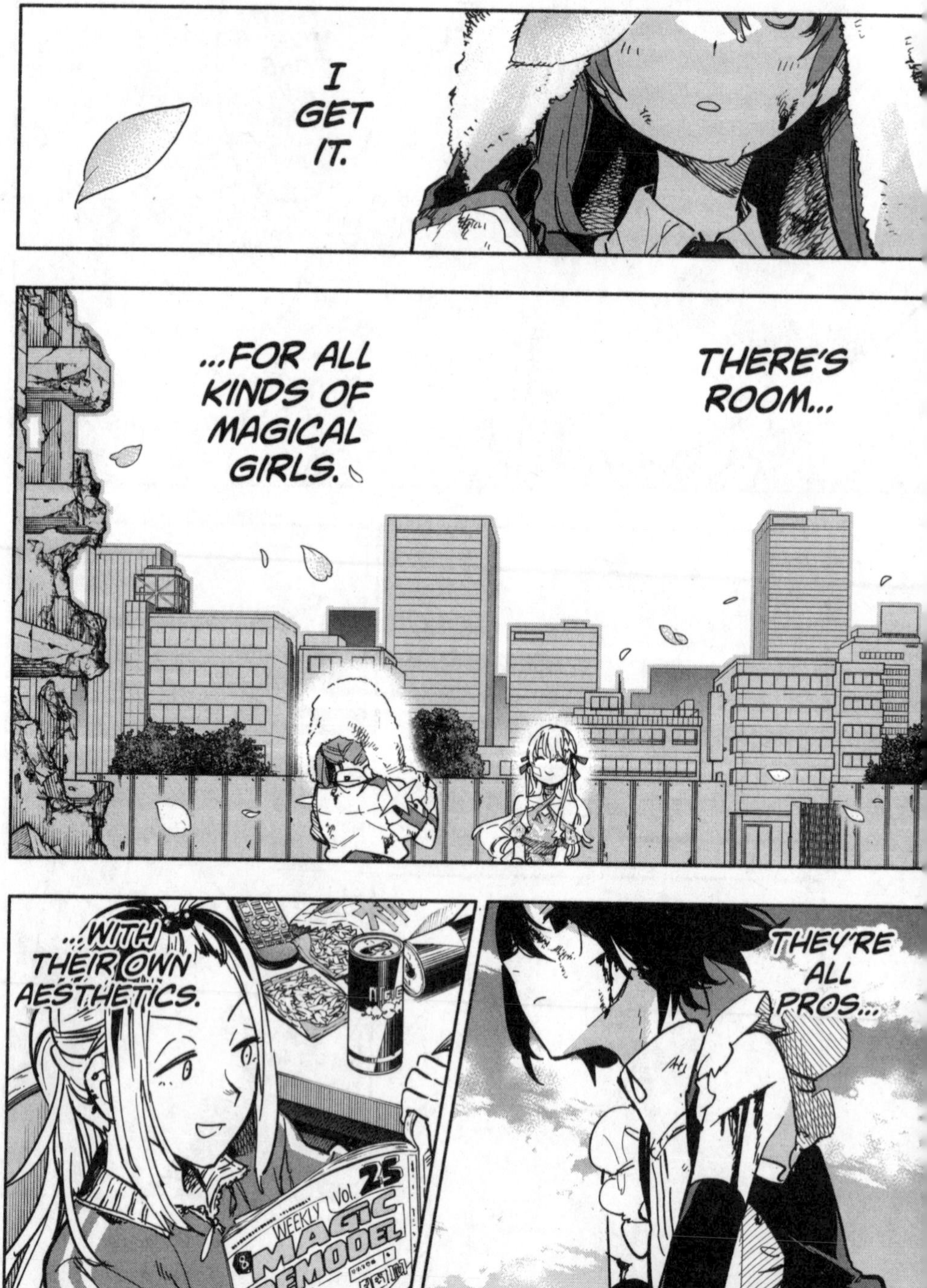
I GET IT.
THERE'S ROOM...
...FOR ALL KINDS OF MAGICAL GIRLS.
THEY'RE ALL PROS...
...WITH THEIR OWN AESTHETICS.
WEEKLY Vol. 25
MAGIC REMODEL

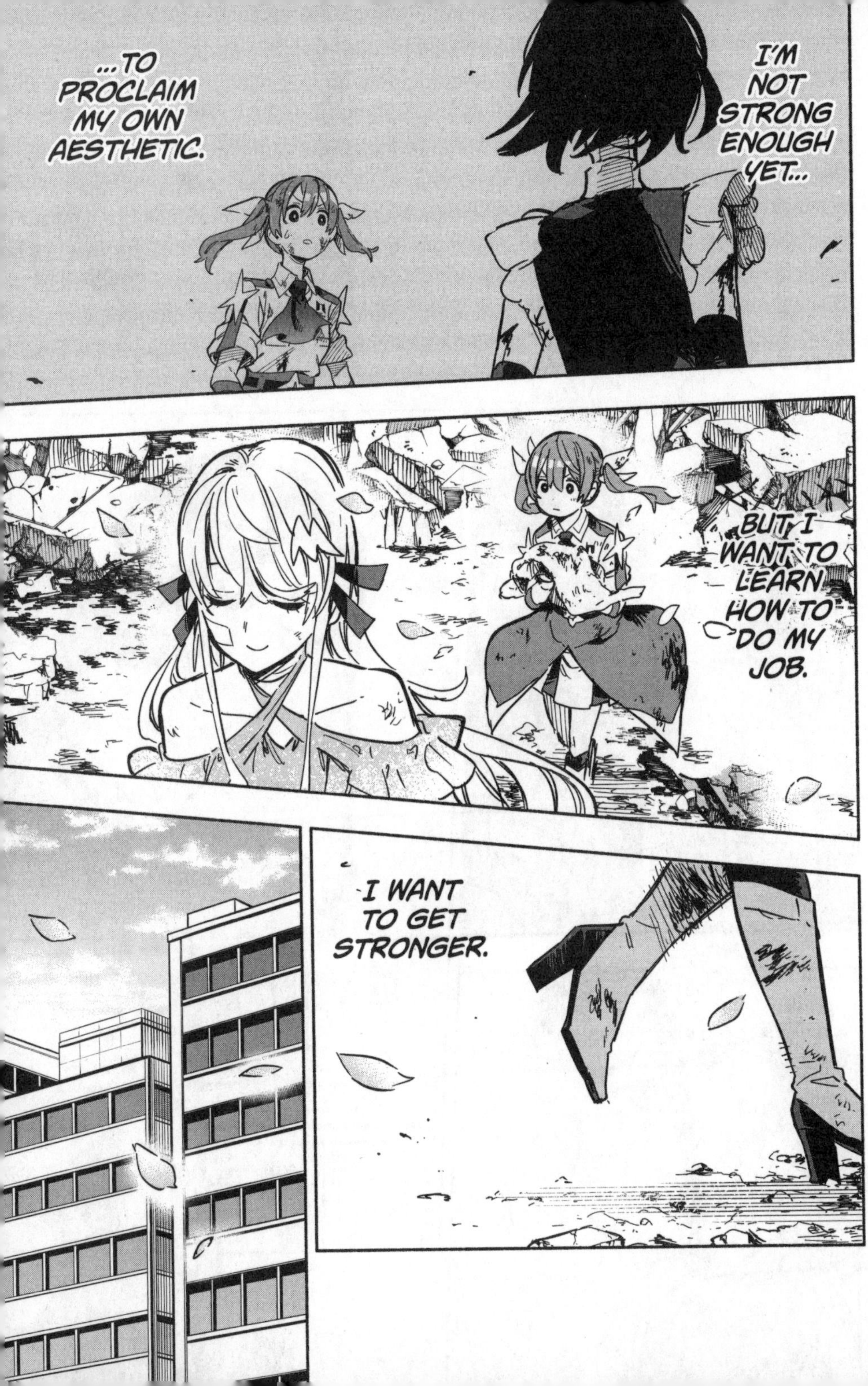
I'M NOT STRONG ENOUGH YET...
...TO PROCLAIM MY OWN AESTHETIC.
BUT I WANT TO LEARN HOW TO DO MY JOB.
I WANT TO GET STRONGER.

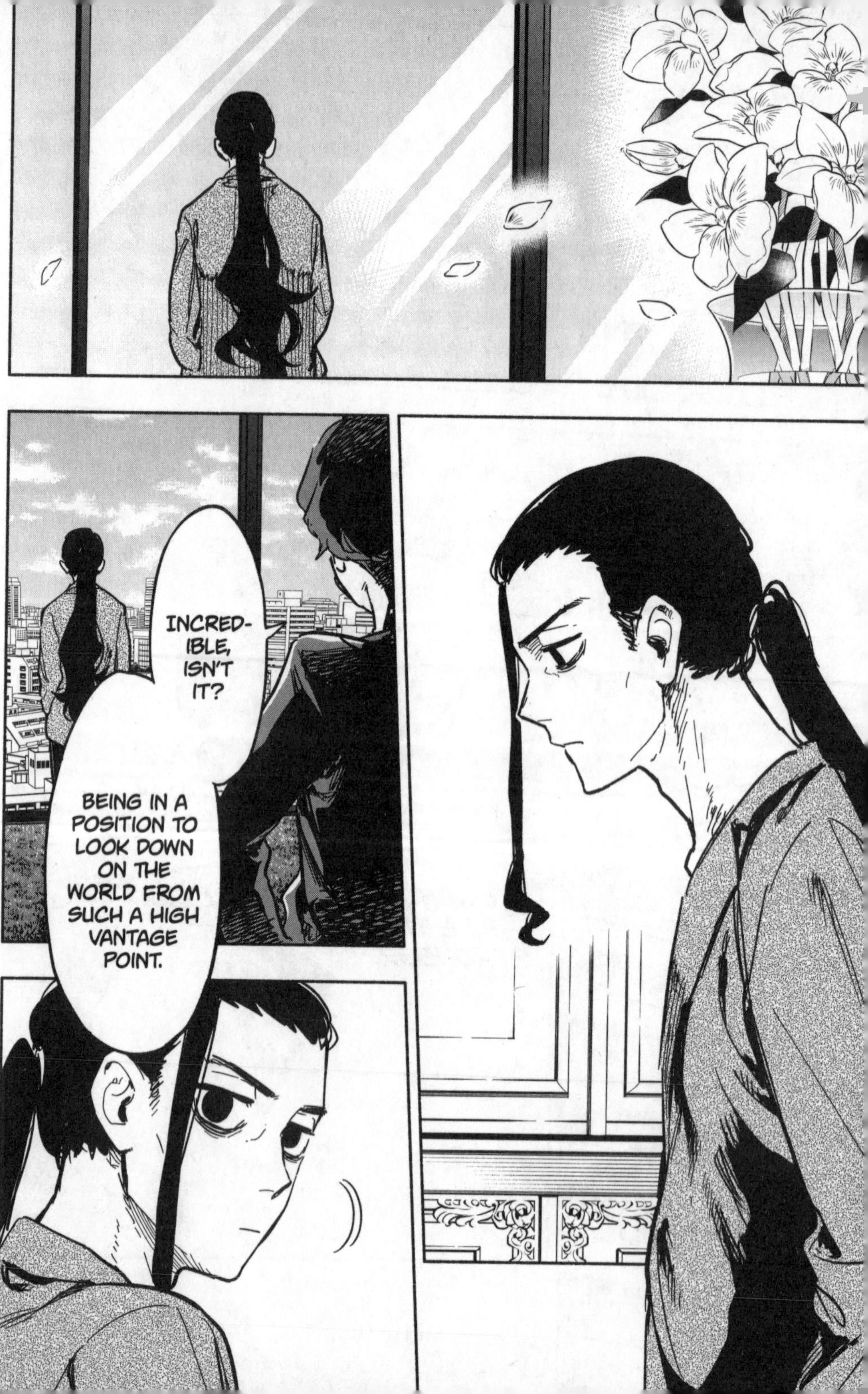
INCREDIBLE, ISN'T IT?
BEING IN A POSITION TO LOOK DOWN ON THE WORLD FROM SUCH A HIGH VANTAGE POINT.

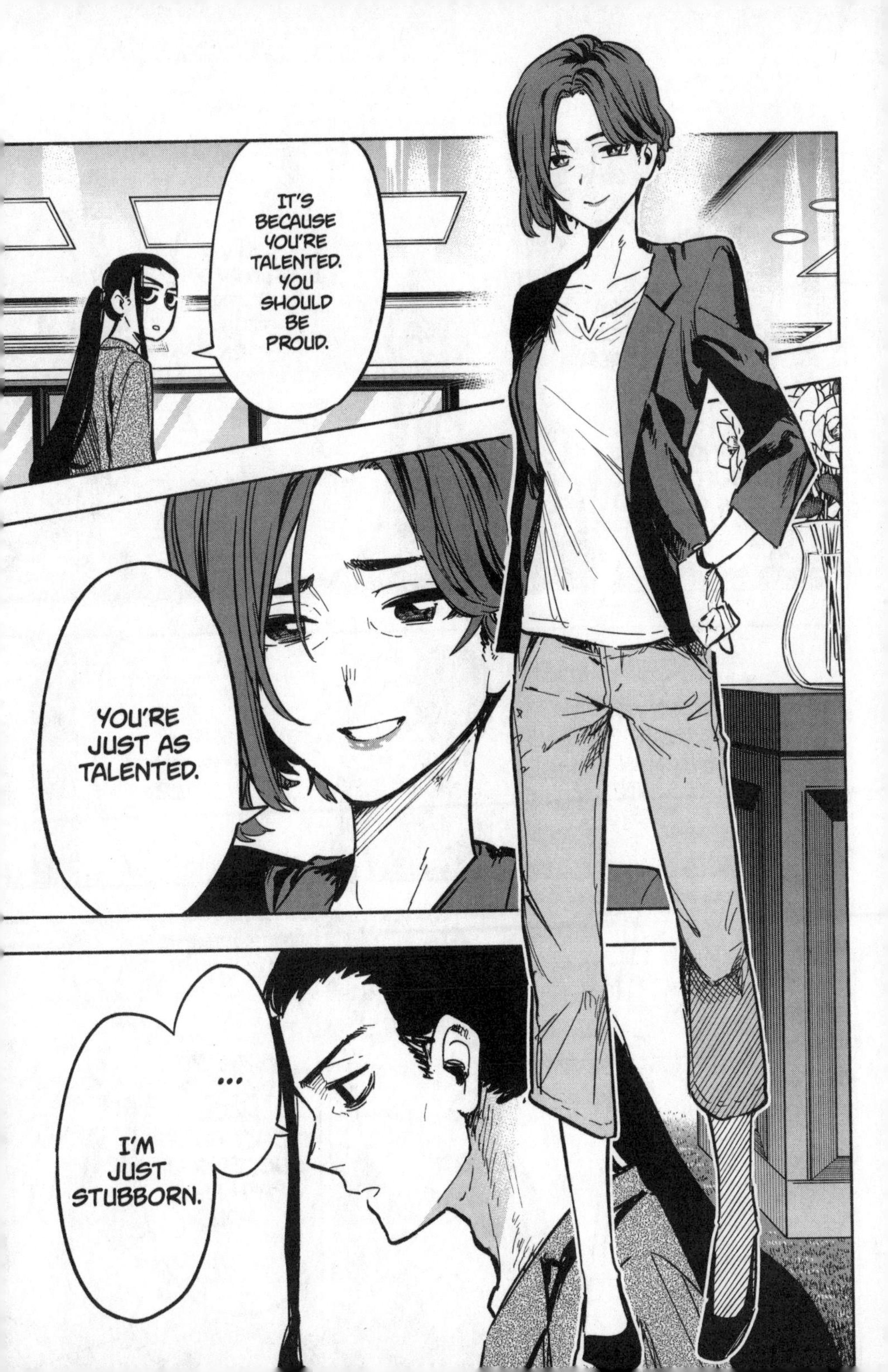
IT'S BECAUSE YOU'RE TALENTED. YOU SHOULD BE PROUD.
YOU'RE JUST AS TALENTED.
...
I'M JUST STUBBORN.

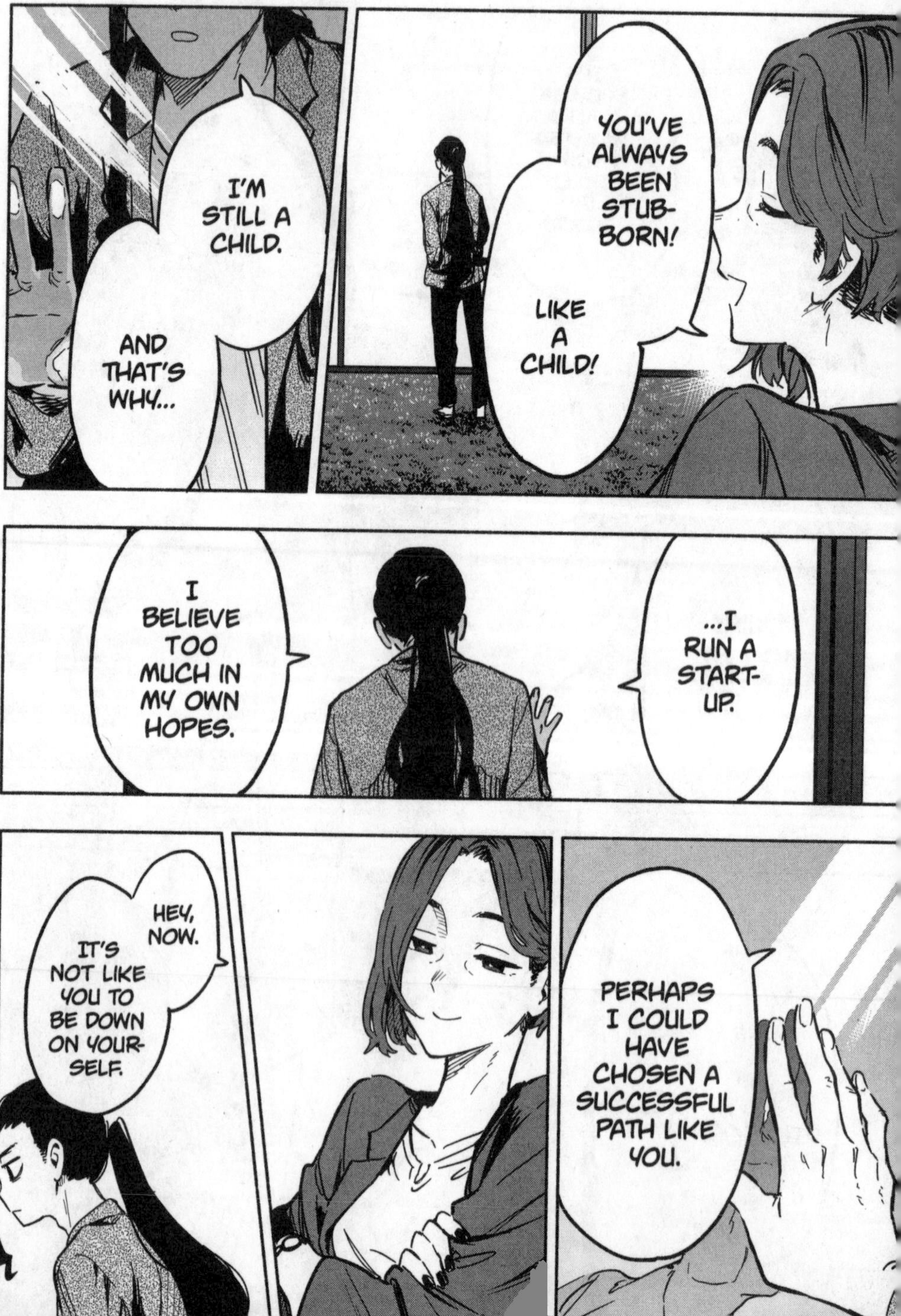
YOU'VE ALWAYS BEEN STUB-BORN!
LIKE A CHILD!
I'M STILL A CHILD.
AND THAT'S WHY...
...I RUN A START-UP.
I BELIEVE TOO MUCH IN MY OWN HOPES.
PERHAPS I COULD HAVE CHOSEN A SUCCESSFUL PATH LIKE YOU.
HEY, NOW.
IT'S NOT LIKE YOU TO BE DOWN ON YOUR-SELF.

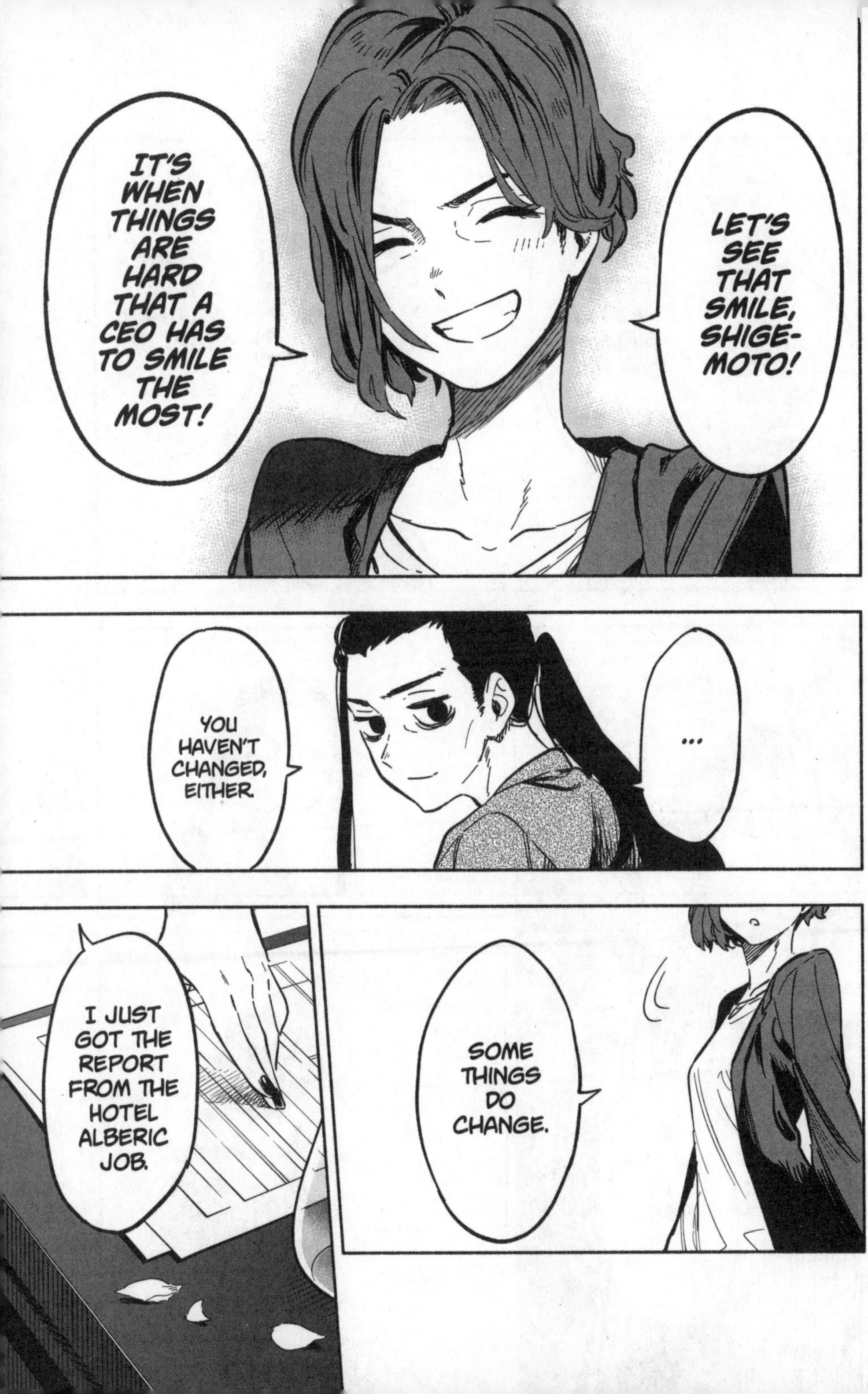
LET'S SEE THAT SMILE, SHIGE-MOTO!
IT'S WHEN THINGS ARE HARD THAT A CEO HAS TO SMILE THE MOST!
...
YOU HAVEN'T CHANGED, EITHER.
SOME THINGS DO CHANGE.
I JUST GOT THE REPORT FROM THE HOTEL ALBERIC JOB.

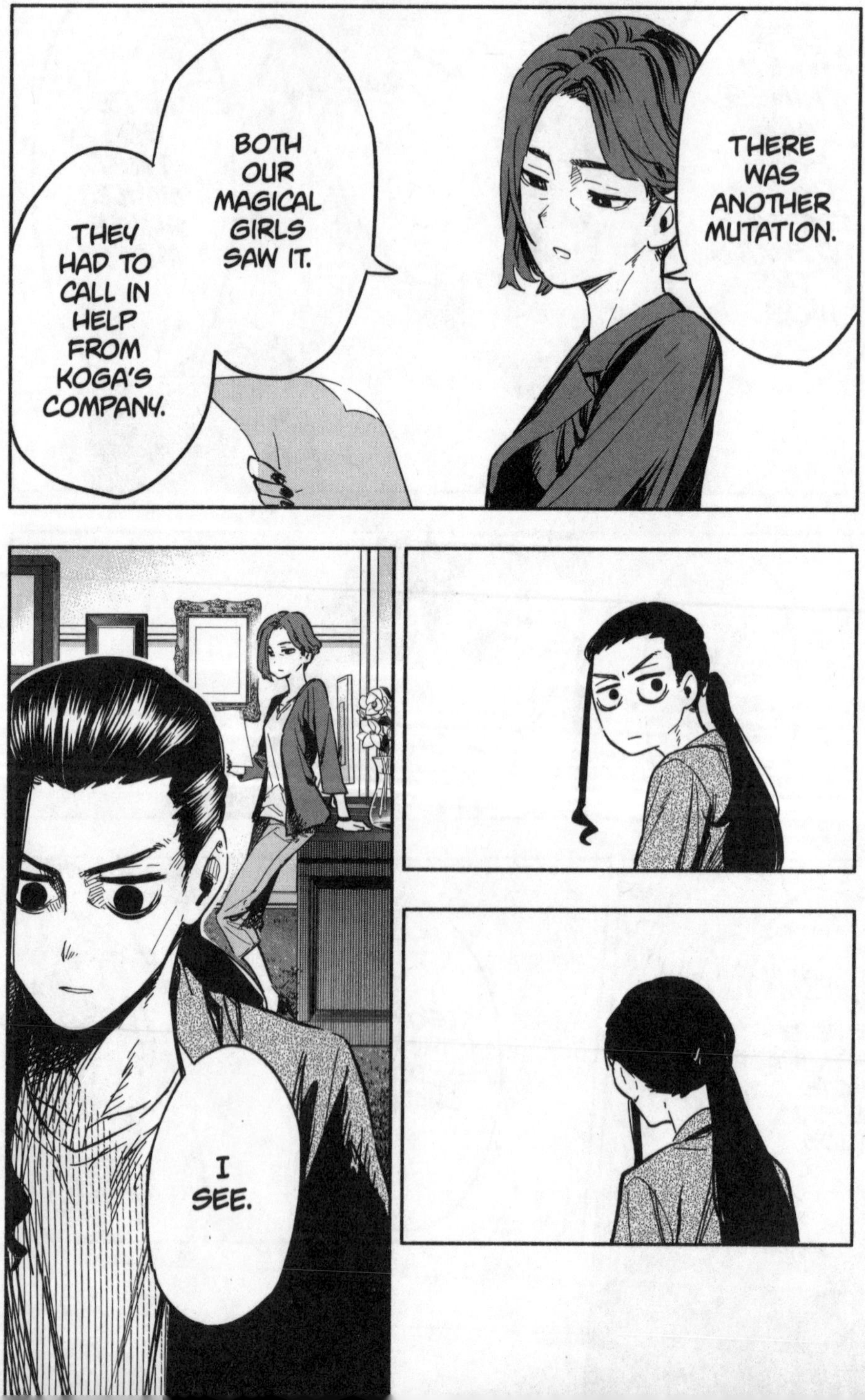
THERE WAS ANOTHER MUTATION.
BOTH OUR MAGICAL GIRLS SAW IT.
THEY HAD TO CALL IN HELP FROM KOGA'S COMPANY.
I SEE.

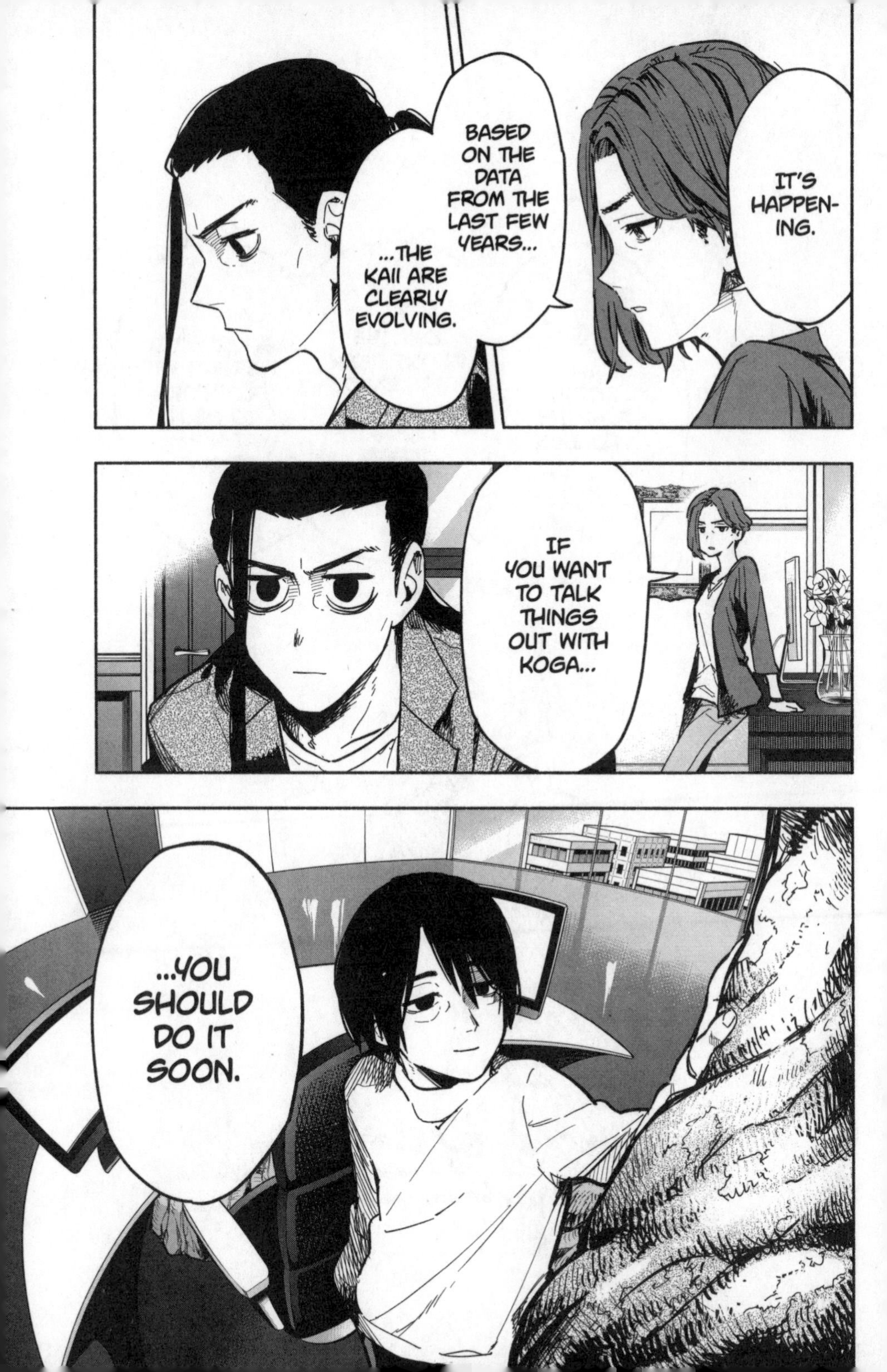
IT'S HAPPEN-ING.
BASED ON THE DATA FROM THE LAST FEW YEARS...
...THE KAII ARE CLEARLY EVOLVING.
IF YOU WANT TO TALK THINGS OUT WITH KOGA...
...YOU SHOULD DO IT SOON.

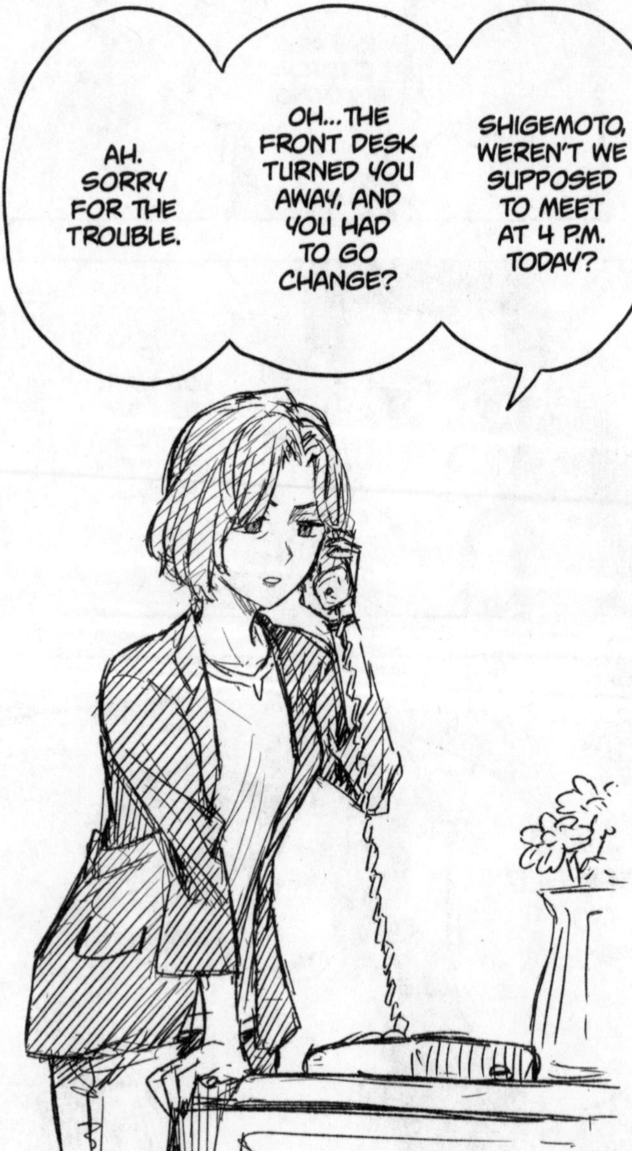
SHIGEMOTO, WEREN'T WE SUPPOSED TO MEET AT 4 P.M. TODAY?
OH...THE FRONT DESK TURNED YOU AWAY, AND YOU HAD TO GO CHANGE?
AH. SORRY FOR THE TROUBLE.

Chapter 17: Magic Industry Expo

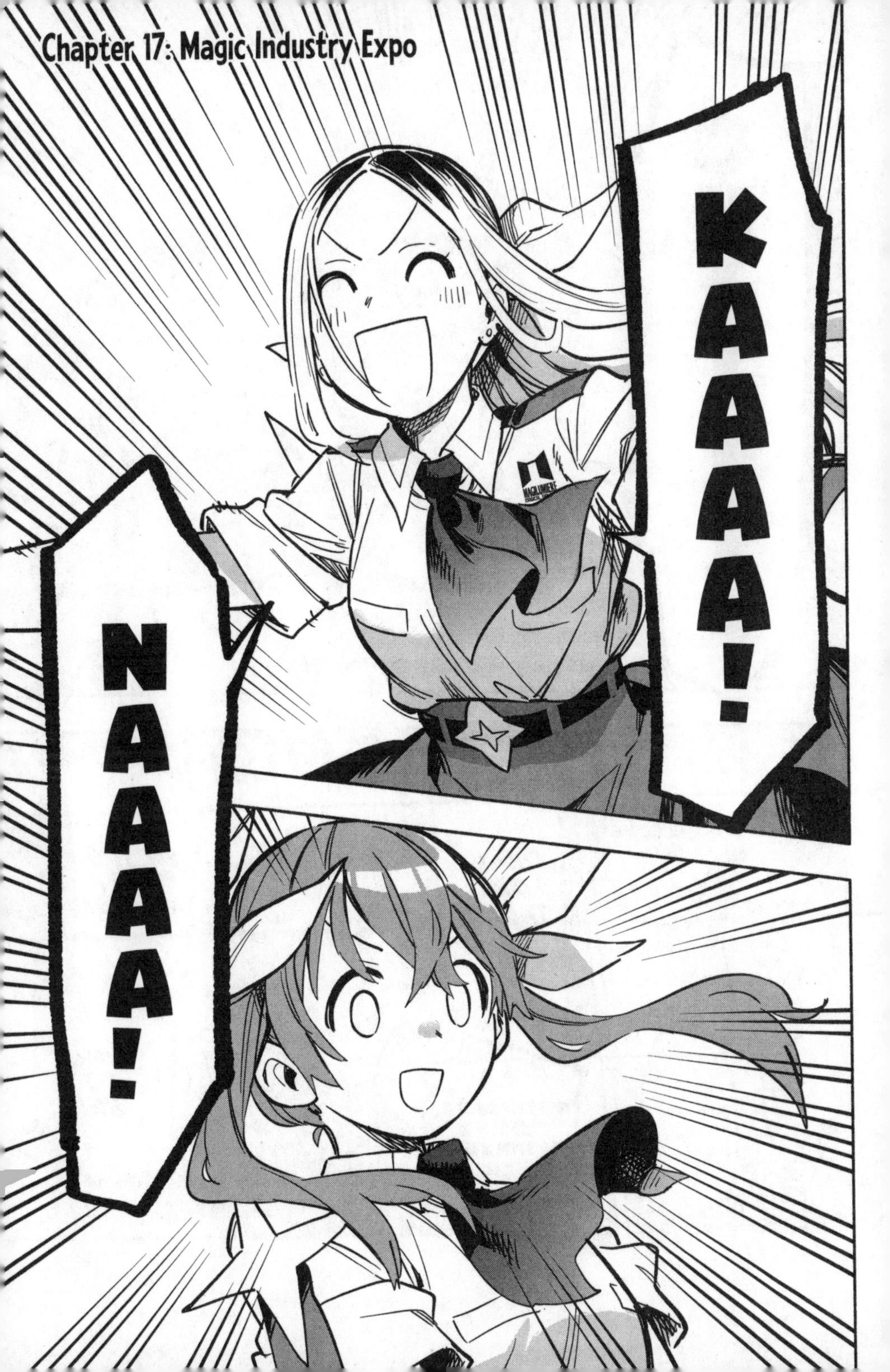
KAAAA!
NAAAA!

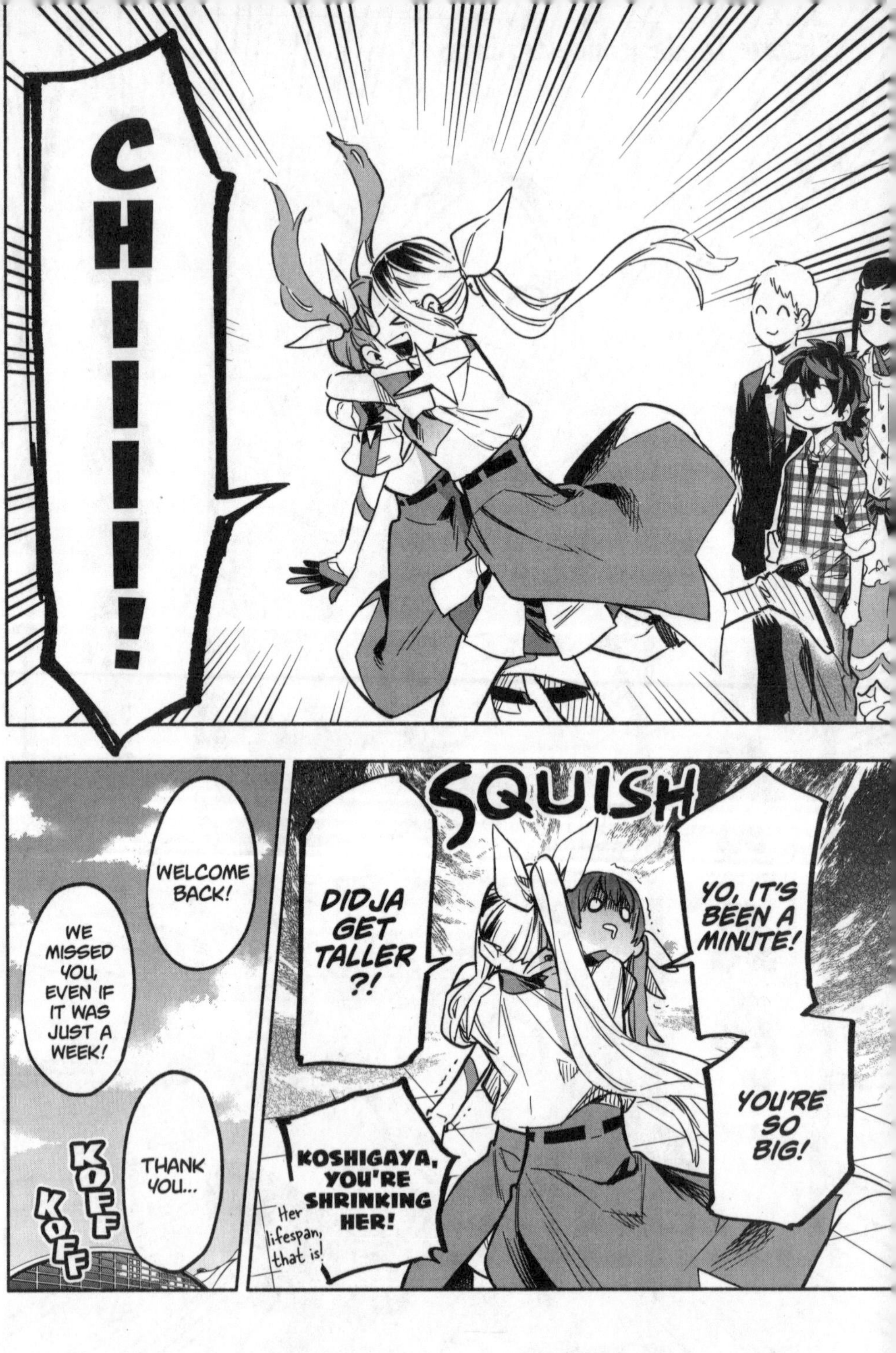
CHIIII!
SQUISH
YO, IT'S BEEN A MINUTE!
DIDJA GET TALLER?!
YOU'RE SO BIG!
KOSHIGAYA, YOU'RE SHRINKING HER!
Her lifespan, that is!
WELCOME BACK!
WE MISSED YOU, EVEN IF IT WAS JUST A WEEK!
THANK YOU...
KOFF KOFF

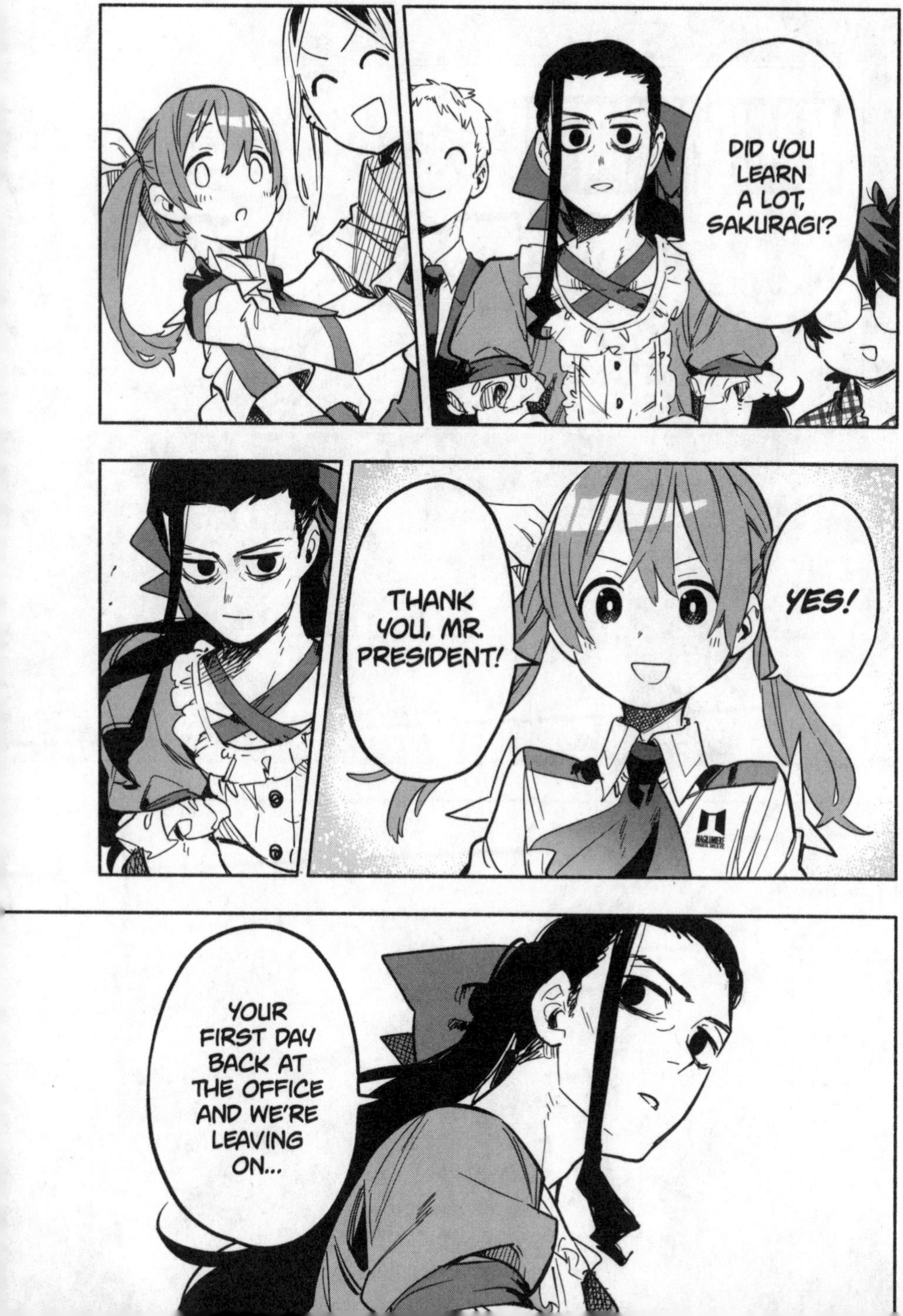
DID YOU LEARN A LOT, SAKURAGI?
YES!
THANK YOU, MR. PRESIDENT!
YOUR FIRST DAY BACK AT THE OFFICE AND WE'RE LEAVING ON...

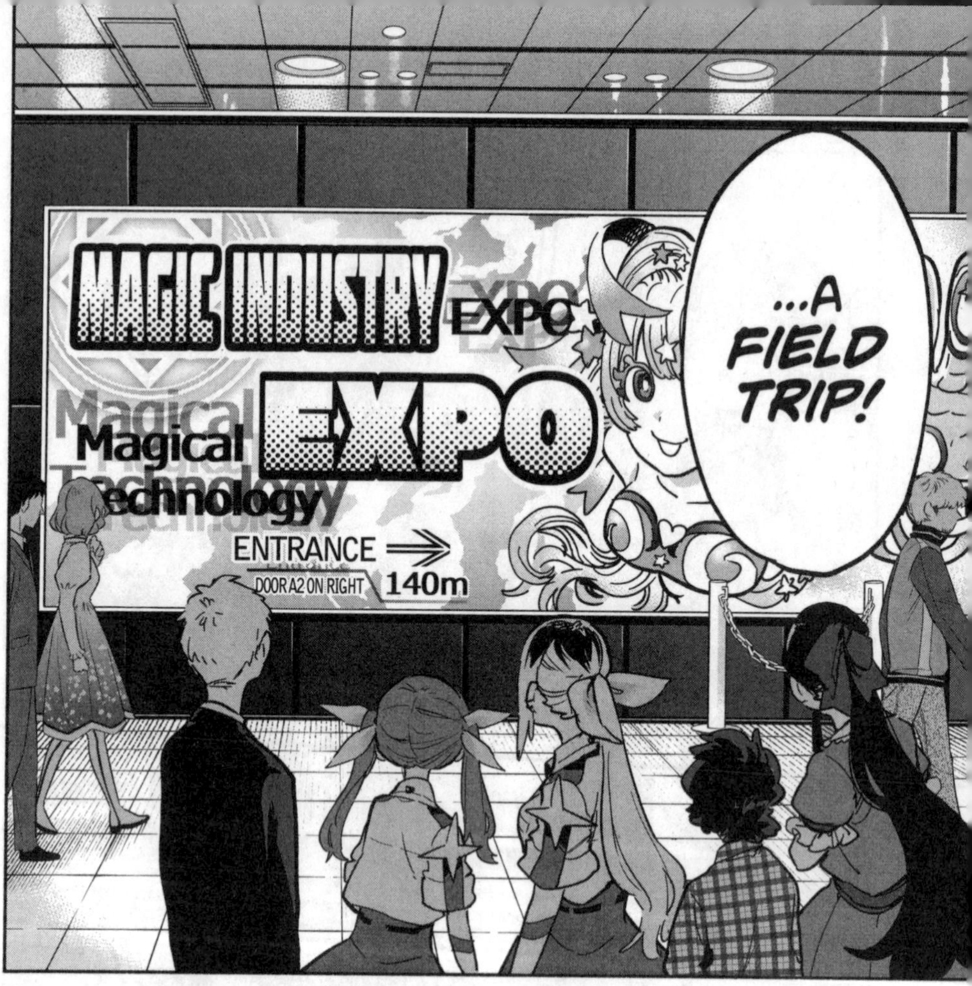
MAGIC INDUSTRY EXPO
Magical Technology EXPO
ENTRANCE
DOOR A2 ON RIGHT 140m
...A FIELD TRIP!

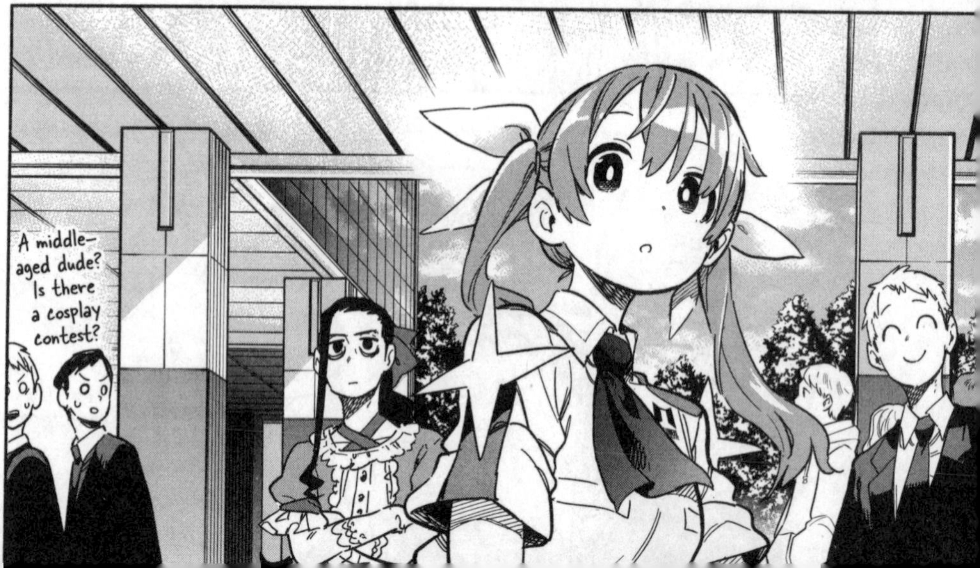
A middle-aged dude? Is there a cosplay contest?

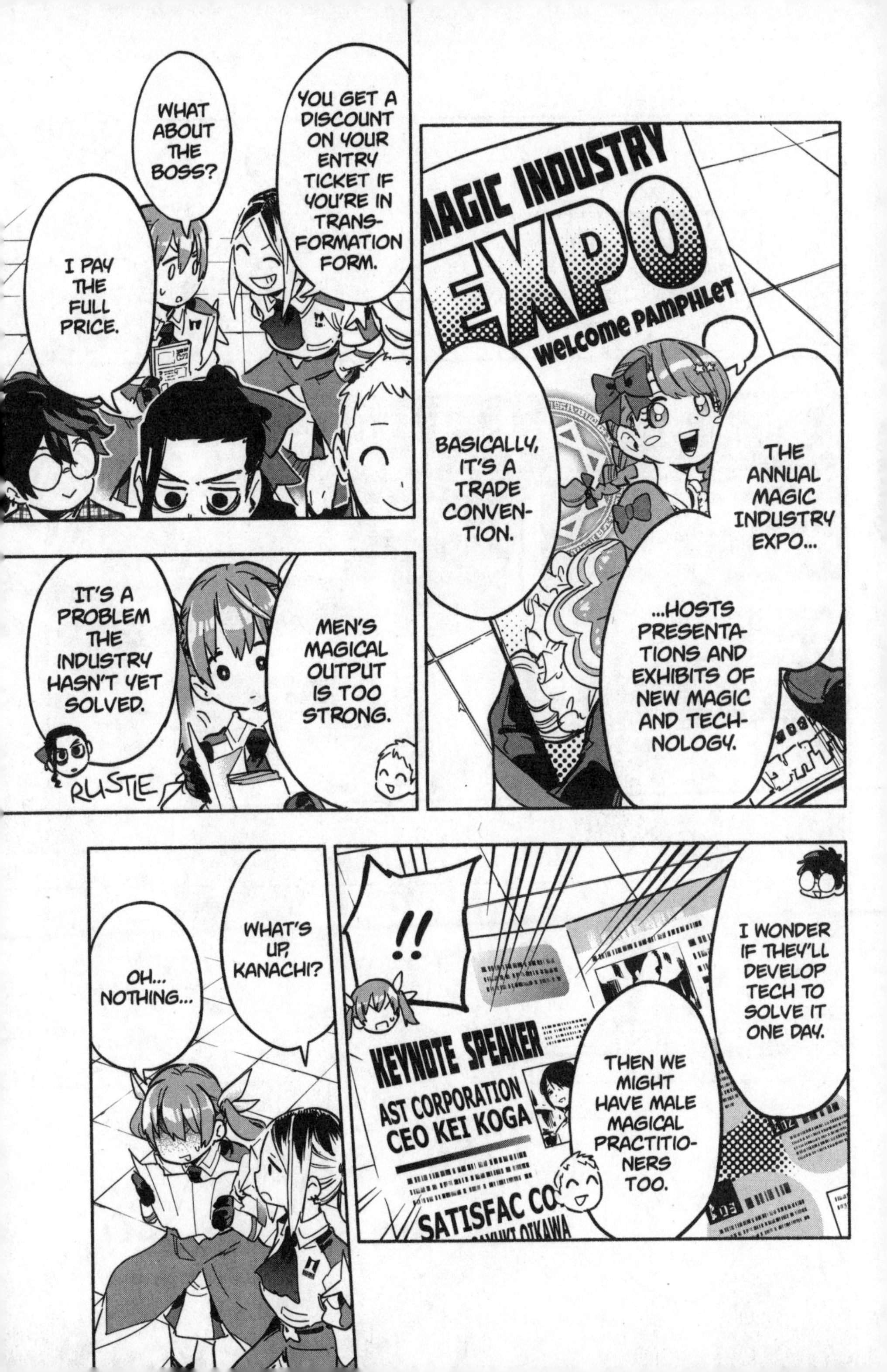
YOU GET A DISCOUNT ON YOUR ENTRY TICKET IF YOU'RE IN TRANS-FORMATION FORM.
WHAT ABOUT THE BOSS?
I PAY THE FULL PRICE.
MAGIC INDUSTRY EXPO
welcome PAMPHLET
THE ANNUAL MAGIC INDUSTRY EXPO...
...HOSTS PRESENTA-TIONS AND EXHIBITS OF NEW MAGIC AND TECH-NOLOGY.
BASICALLY, IT'S A TRADE CONVEN-TION.
MEN'S MAGICAL OUTPUT IS TOO STRONG.
IT'S A PROBLEM THE INDUSTRY HASN'T YET SOLVED.
RUSTLE
I WONDER IF THEY'LL DEVELOP TECH TO SOLVE IT ONE DAY.
THEN WE MIGHT HAVE MALE MAGICAL PRACTITIO-NERS TOO.
!!
KEYNOTE SPEAKER
AST CORPORATION CEO KEI KOGA
SATISFAC CO.
WHAT'S UP, KANACHI?
OH... NOTHING...

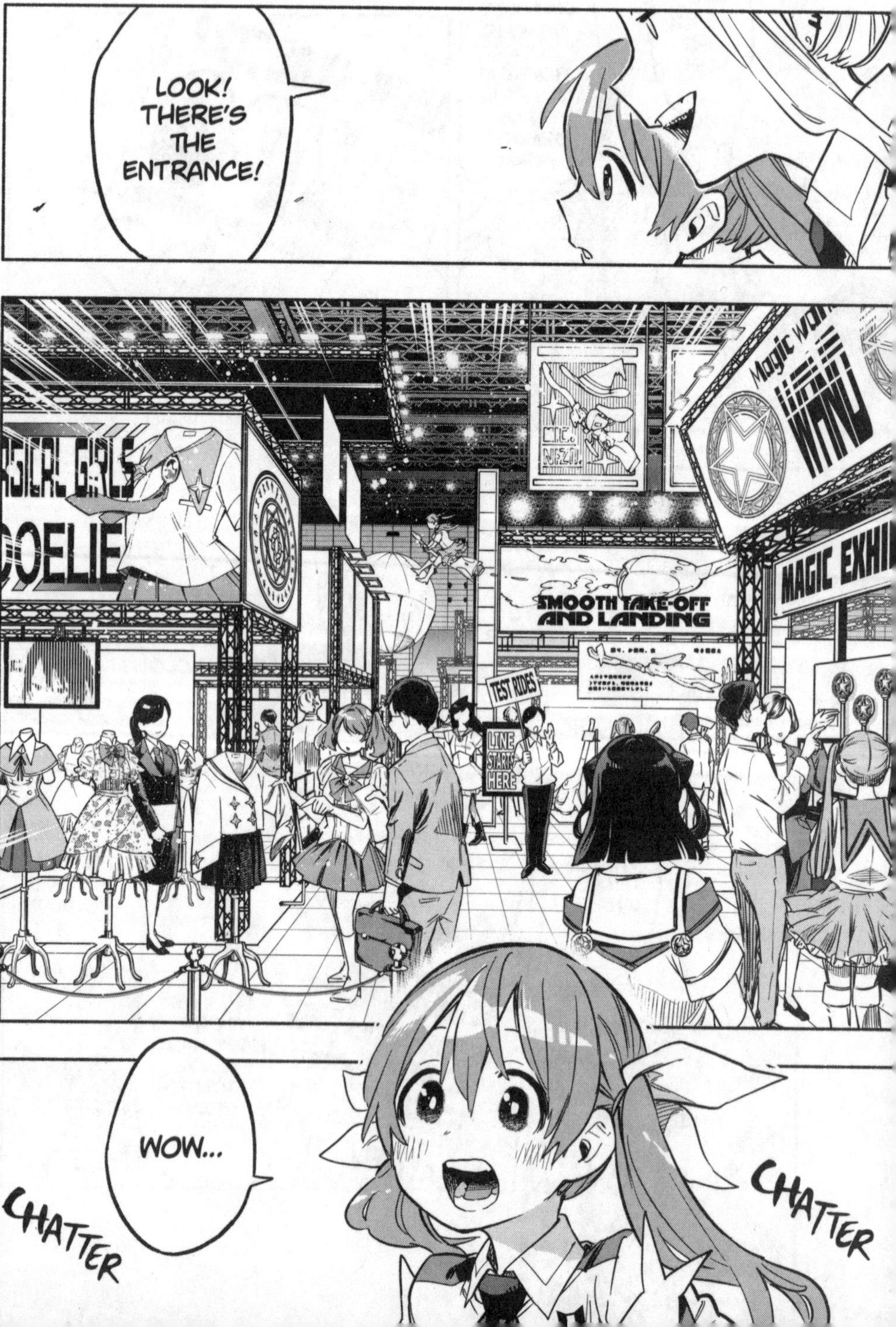
LOOK! THERE'S THE ENTRANCE!
SMOOTH TAKE-OFF AND LANDING
TEST RIDES
LINE STARTS HERE
CHATTER
WOW...
CHATTER

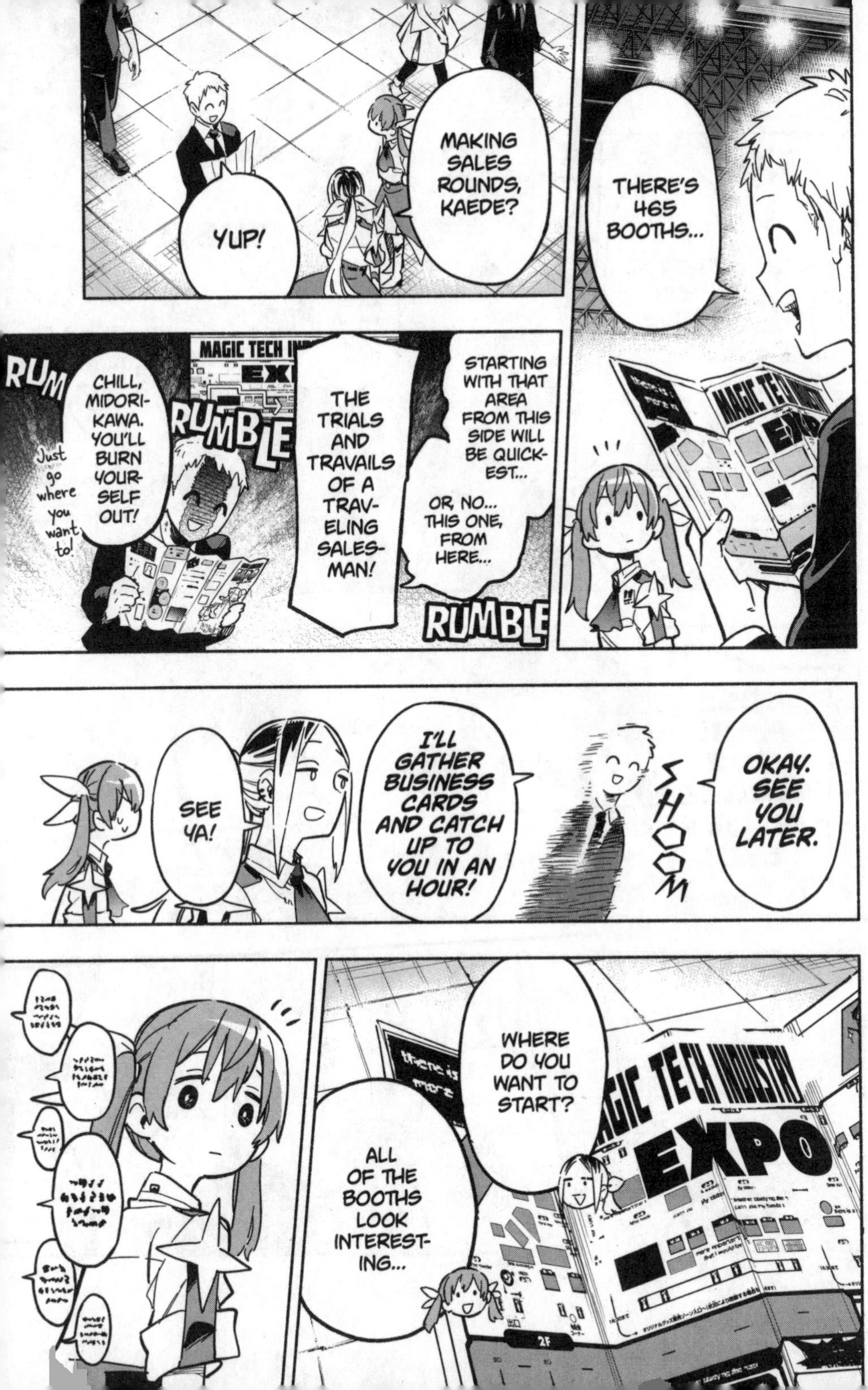
THERE'S 465 BOOTHS...
MAKING SALES ROUNDS, KAEDE?
YUP!
STARTING WITH THAT AREA FROM THIS SIDE WILL BE QUICK-EST...
OR, NO... THIS ONE, FROM HERE...
RUMBLE
THE TRIALS AND TRAVAILS OF A TRAV-ELING SALES-MAN!
MAGIC TECH IN
EX
RUMBLE
CHILL, MIDORI-KAWA. YOU'LL BURN YOUR-SELF OUT!
Just go where you want to!
RUM
OKAY. SEE YOU LATER.
SHOOM
I'LL GATHER BUSINESS CARDS AND CATCH UP TO YOU IN AN HOUR!
SEE YA!
WHERE DO YOU WANT TO START?
AGIC TECH INDUSTRY
EXPO
ALL OF THE BOOTHS LOOK INTEREST-ING...

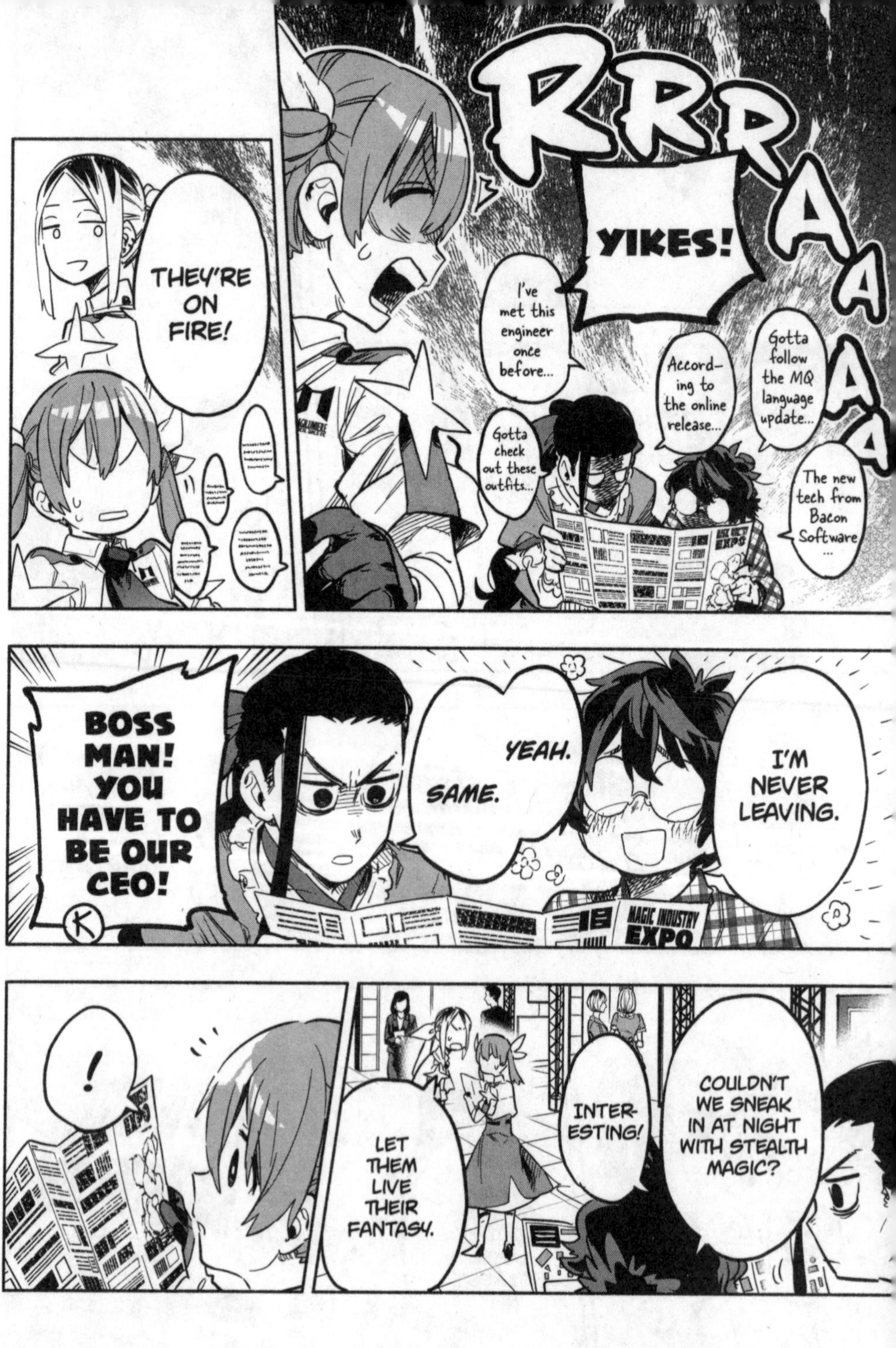
RRRAAAAA
YIKES!
Gotta follow the MQ language update...
I've met this engineer once before...
Accord-ing to the online release...
The new tech from Bacon Software ...
Gotta check out these outfits...
THEY'RE ON FIRE!
I'M NEVER LEAVING.
YEAH.
SAME.
BOSS MAN! YOU HAVE TO BE OUR CEO!
MAGIC INDUSTRY EXPO
COULDN'T WE SNEAK IN AT NIGHT WITH STEALTH MAGIC?
INTER-ESTING!
LET THEM LIVE THEIR FANTASY.
!

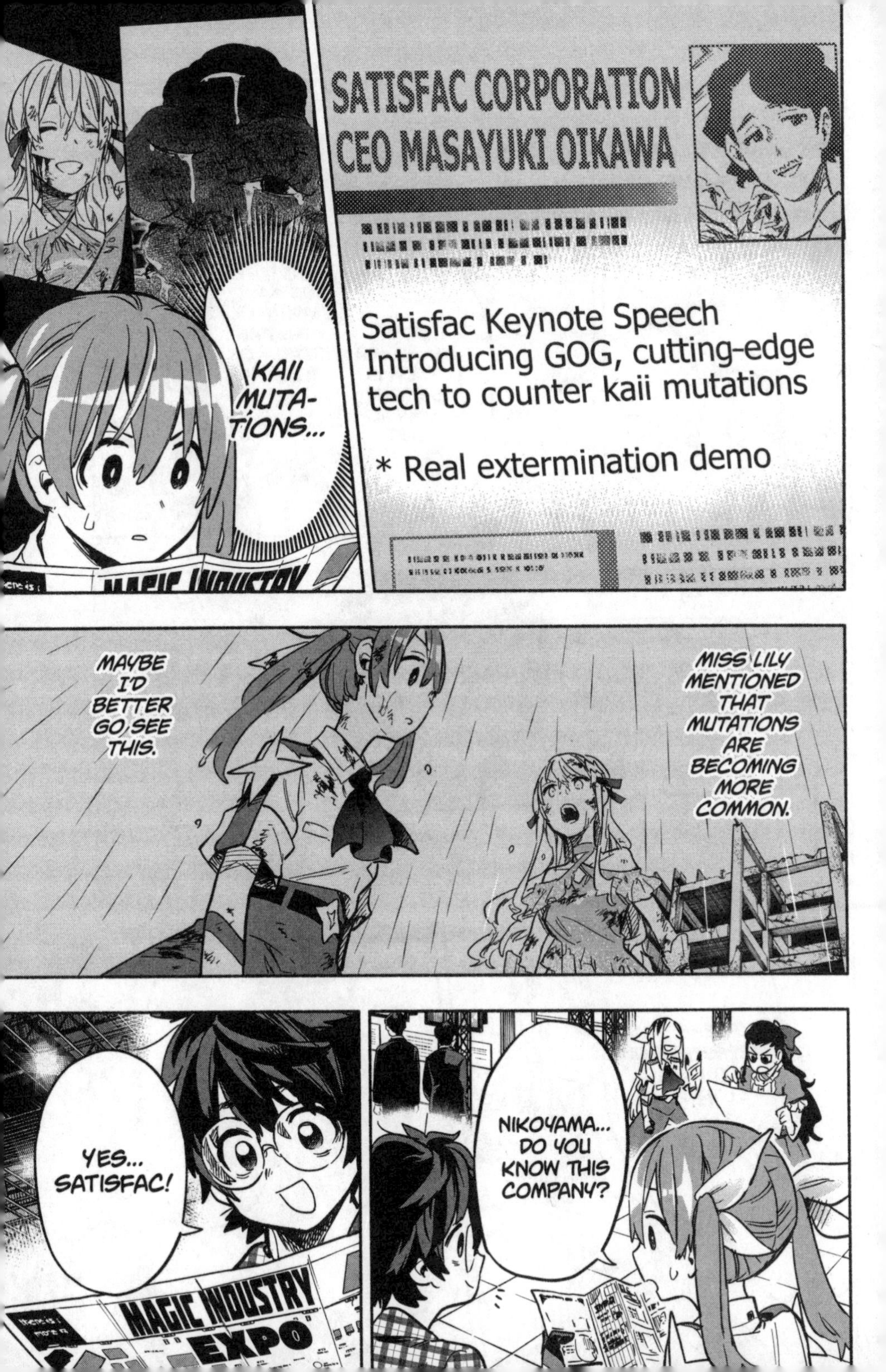
SATISFAC CORPORATION
CEO MASAYUKI OIKAWA
Satisfac Keynote Speech
Introducing GOG, cutting-edge tech to counter kaii mutations
* Real extermination demo
KAII MUTATIONS...
MISS LILY MENTIONED THAT MUTATIONS ARE BECOMING MORE COMMON.
MAYBE I'D BETTER GO SEE THIS.
NIKOYAMA... DO YOU KNOW THIS COMPANY?
YES... SATISFAC!
MAGIC INDUSTRY EXPO

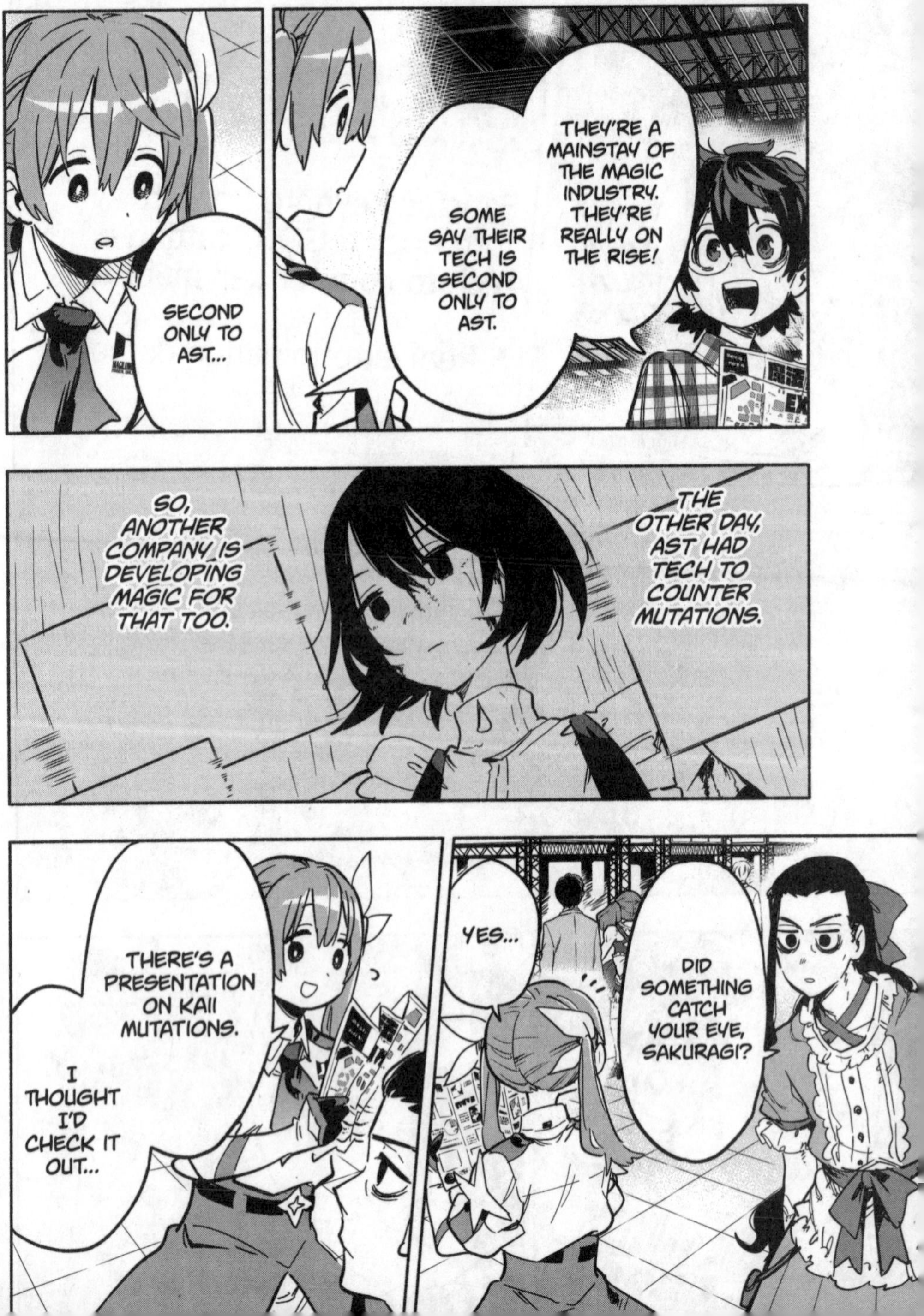
THEY'RE A MAINSTAY OF THE MAGIC INDUSTRY. THEY'RE REALLY ON THE RISE!
SOME SAY THEIR TECH IS SECOND ONLY TO AST.
SECOND ONLY TO AST...
THE OTHER DAY, AST HAD TECH TO COUNTER MUTATIONS.
SO, ANOTHER COMPANY IS DEVELOPING MAGIC FOR THAT TOO.
DID SOMETHING CATCH YOUR EYE, SAKURAGI?
YES...
THERE'S A PRESENTATION ON KAII MUTATIONS.
I THOUGHT I'D CHECK IT OUT...

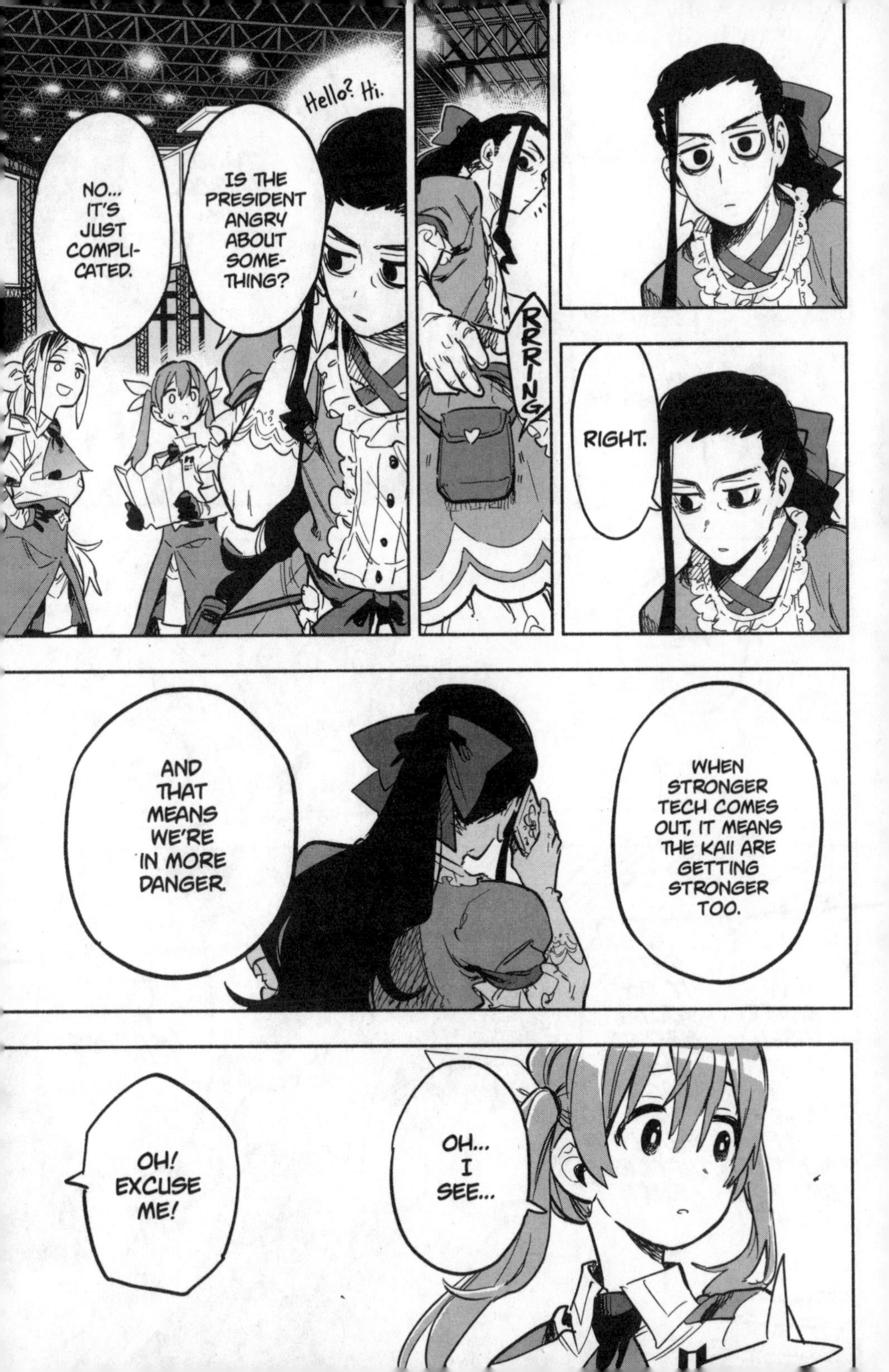
RIGHT.
RRRING
Hello? Hi.
IS THE PRESIDENT ANGRY ABOUT SOMETHING?
NO... IT'S JUST COMPLICATED.
WHEN STRONGER TECH COMES OUT, IT MEANS THE KAII ARE GETTING STRONGER TOO.
AND THAT MEANS WE'RE IN MORE DANGER.
OH... I SEE...
OH! EXCUSE ME!

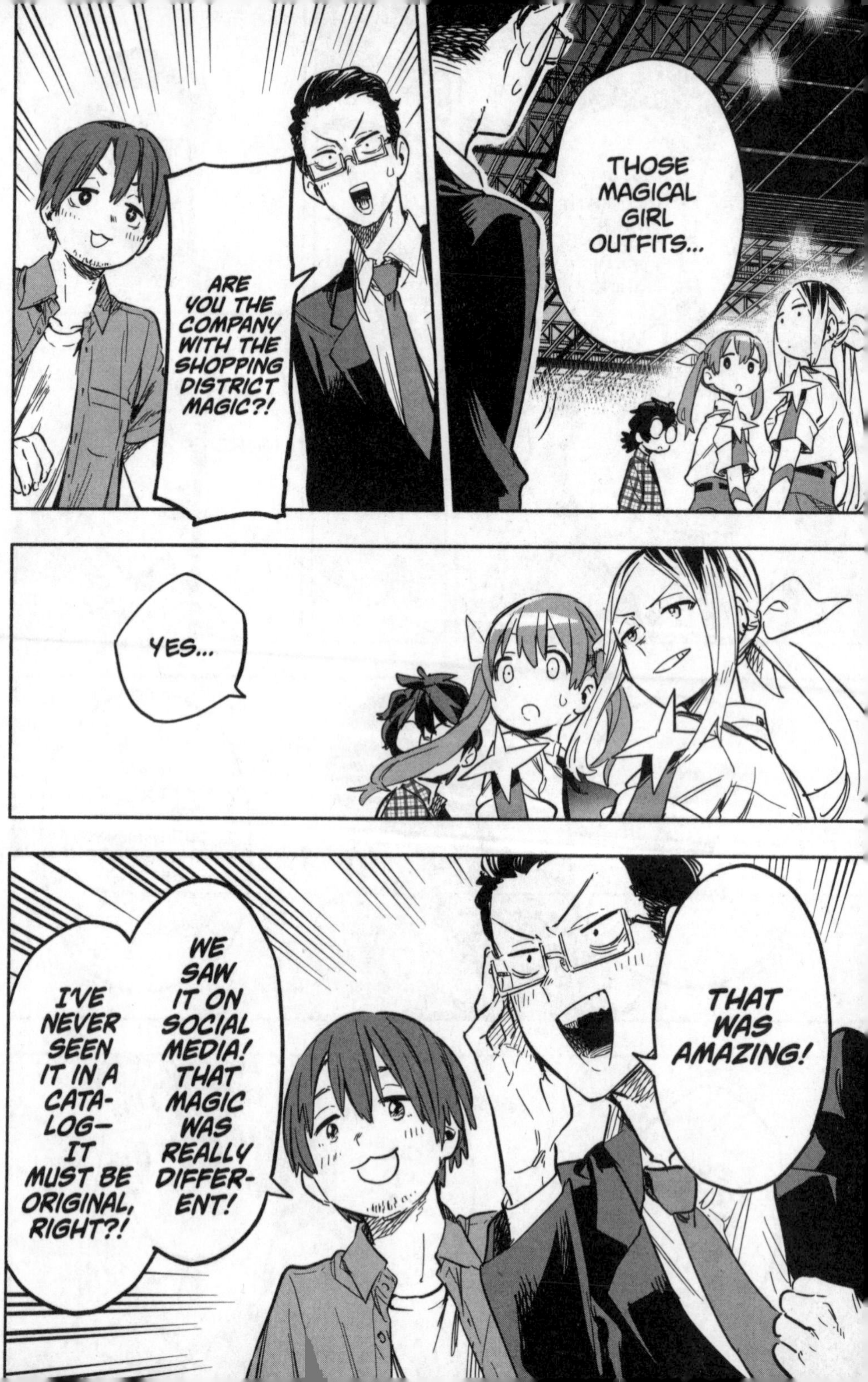
THOSE MAGICAL GIRL OUTFITS...
ARE YOU THE COMPANY WITH THE SHOPPING DISTRICT MAGIC?!
YES...
THAT WAS AMAZING!
WE SAW IT ON SOCIAL MEDIA! THAT MAGIC WAS REALLY DIFFERENT!
I'VE NEVER SEEN IT IN A CATALOG— IT MUST BE ORIGINAL, RIGHT?!

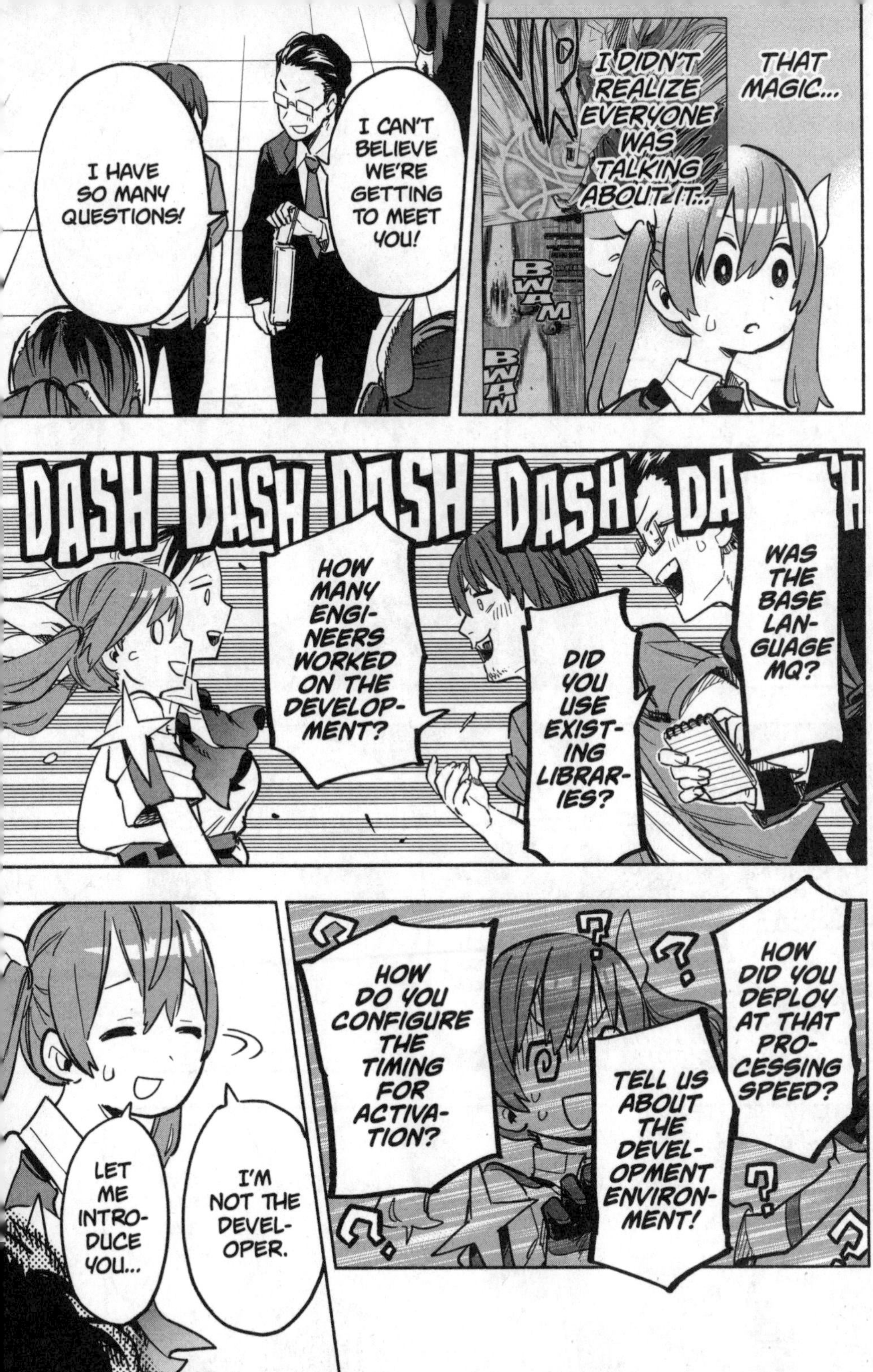
THAT MAGIC...
I DIDN'T REALIZE EVERYONE WAS TALKING ABOUT IT...
BWAM
BWAM
I CAN'T BELIEVE WE'RE GETTING TO MEET YOU!
I HAVE SO MANY QUESTIONS!
DASH DASH DASH DASH
WAS THE BASE LANGUAGE MQ?
DID YOU USE EXISTING LIBRARIES?
HOW MANY ENGINEERS WORKED ON THE DEVELOPMENT?
HOW DID YOU DEPLOY AT THAT PROCESSING SPEED?
TELL US ABOUT THE DEVELOPMENT ENVIRONMENT!
HOW DO YOU CONFIGURE THE TIMING FOR ACTIVATION?
I'M NOT THE DEVELOPER.
LET ME INTRODUCE YOU...

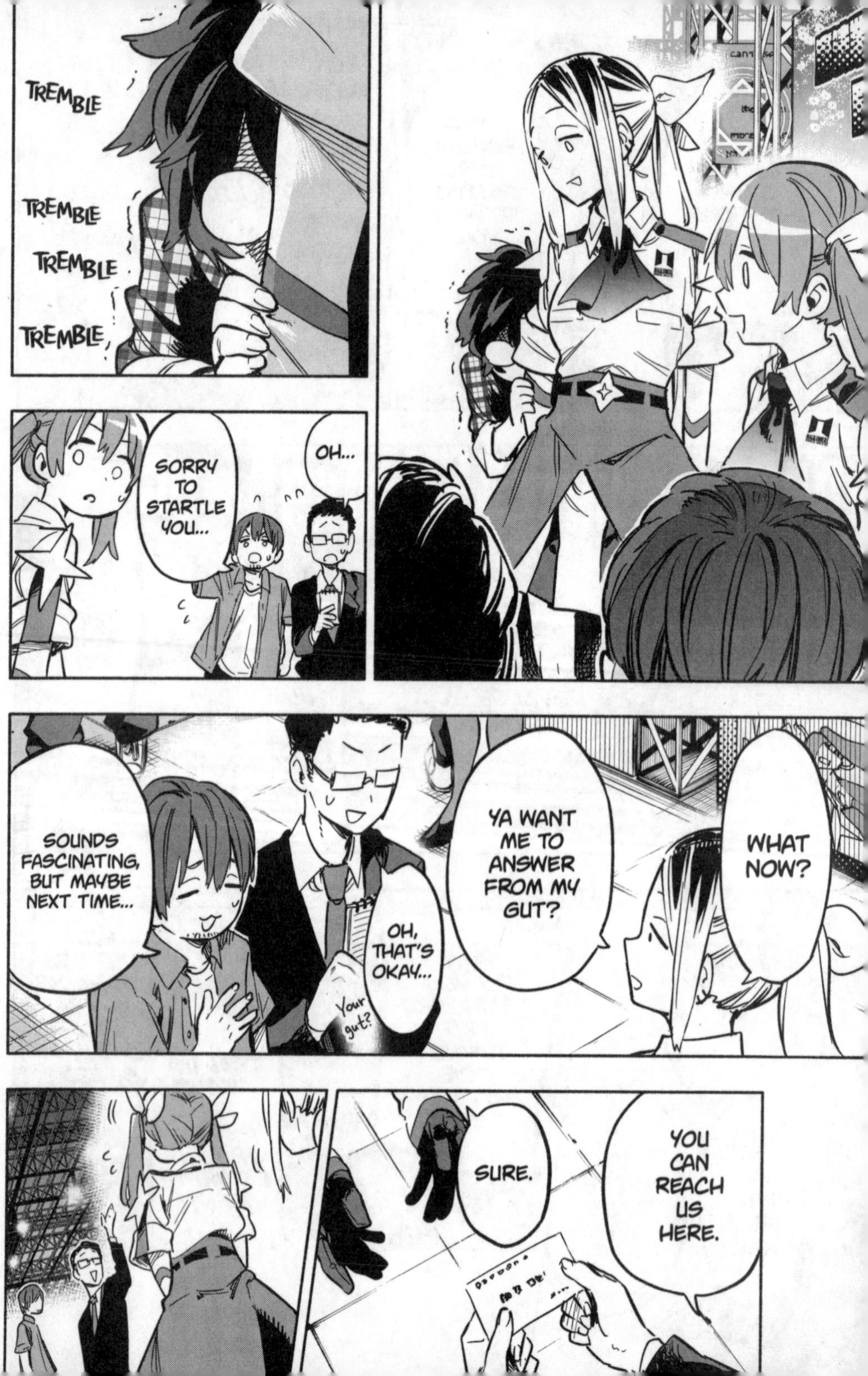
TREMBLE
TREMBLE
TREMBLE
TREMBLE
OH...
SORRY TO STARTLE YOU...
WHAT NOW?
YA WANT ME TO ANSWER FROM MY GUT?
OH, THAT'S OKAY...
Your gut?
SOUNDS FASCINATING, BUT MAYBE NEXT TIME...
YOU CAN REACH US HERE.
SURE.

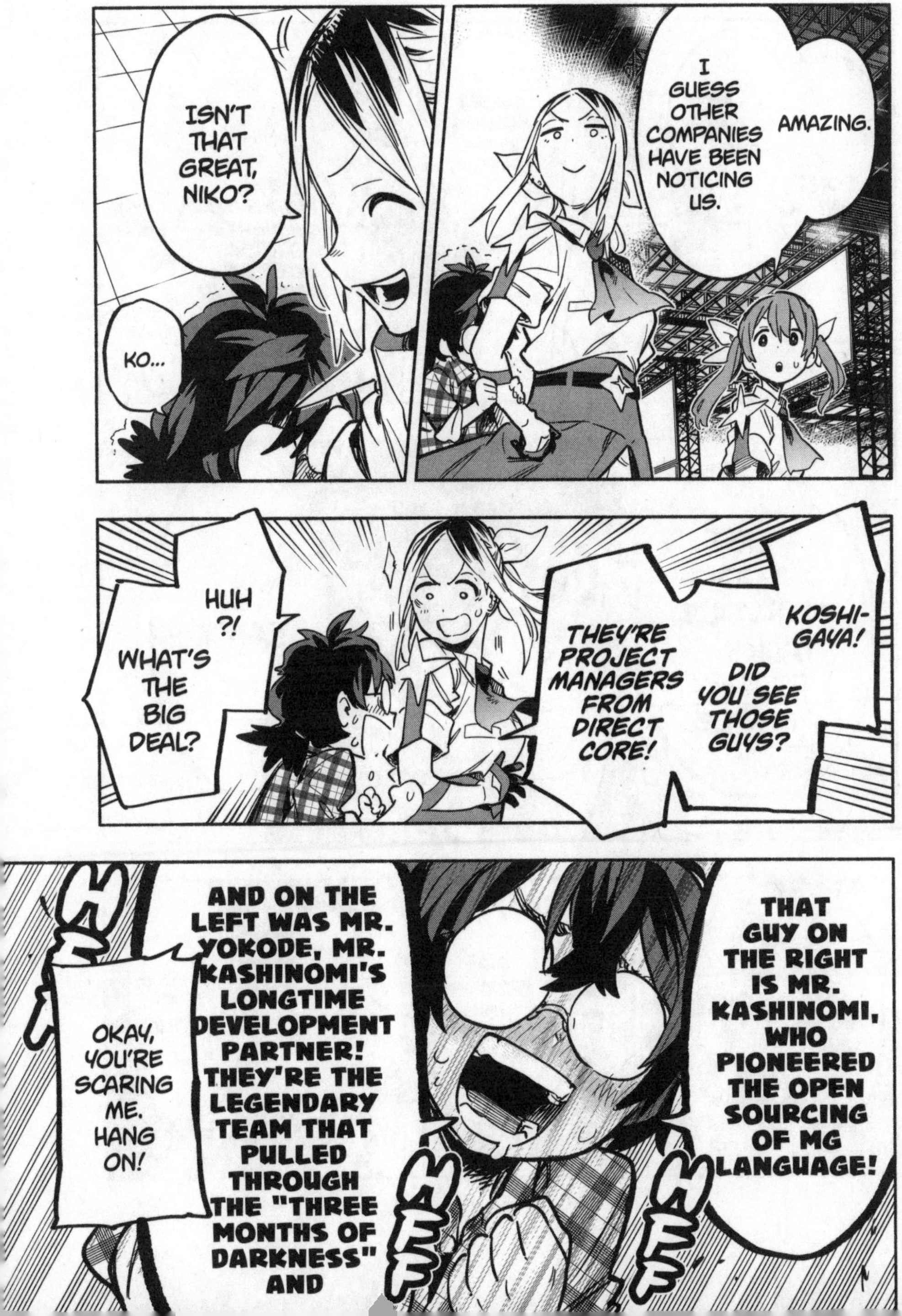
AMAZING.
I GUESS OTHER COMPANIES HAVE BEEN NOTICING US.
ISN'T THAT GREAT, NIKO?
KO...
KOSHI-GAYA! DID YOU SEE THOSE GUYS?
THEY'RE PROJECT MANAGERS FROM DIRECT CORE!
HUH?! WHAT'S THE BIG DEAL?
THAT GUY ON THE RIGHT IS MR. KASHINOMI, WHO PIONEERED THE OPEN SOURCING OF MG LANGUAGE!
HEFF
AND ON THE LEFT WAS MR. YOKODE, MR. KASHINOMI'S LONGTIME DEVELOPMENT PARTNER! THEY'RE THE LEGENDARY TEAM THAT PULLED THROUGH THE "THREE MONTHS OF DARKNESS" AND
HEFF
OKAY, YOU'RE SCARING ME. HANG ON!

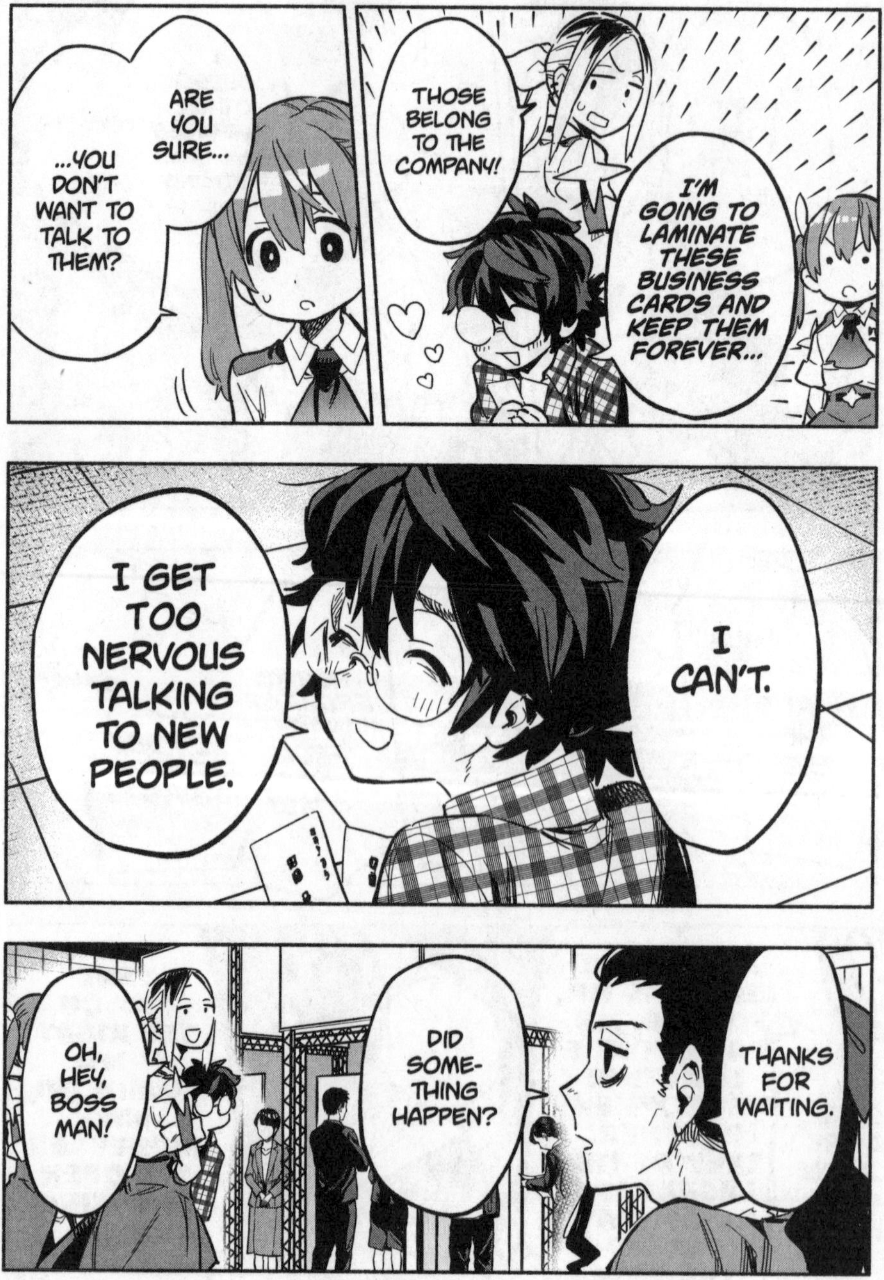
I'M GOING TO LAMINATE THESE BUSINESS CARDS AND KEEP THEM FOREVER...
THOSE BELONG TO THE COMPANY!
ARE YOU SURE...
...YOU DON'T WANT TO TALK TO THEM?
I CAN'T.
I GET TOO NERVOUS TALKING TO NEW PEOPLE.
THANKS FOR WAITING.
DID SOME-THING HAPPEN?
OH, HEY, BOSS MAN!

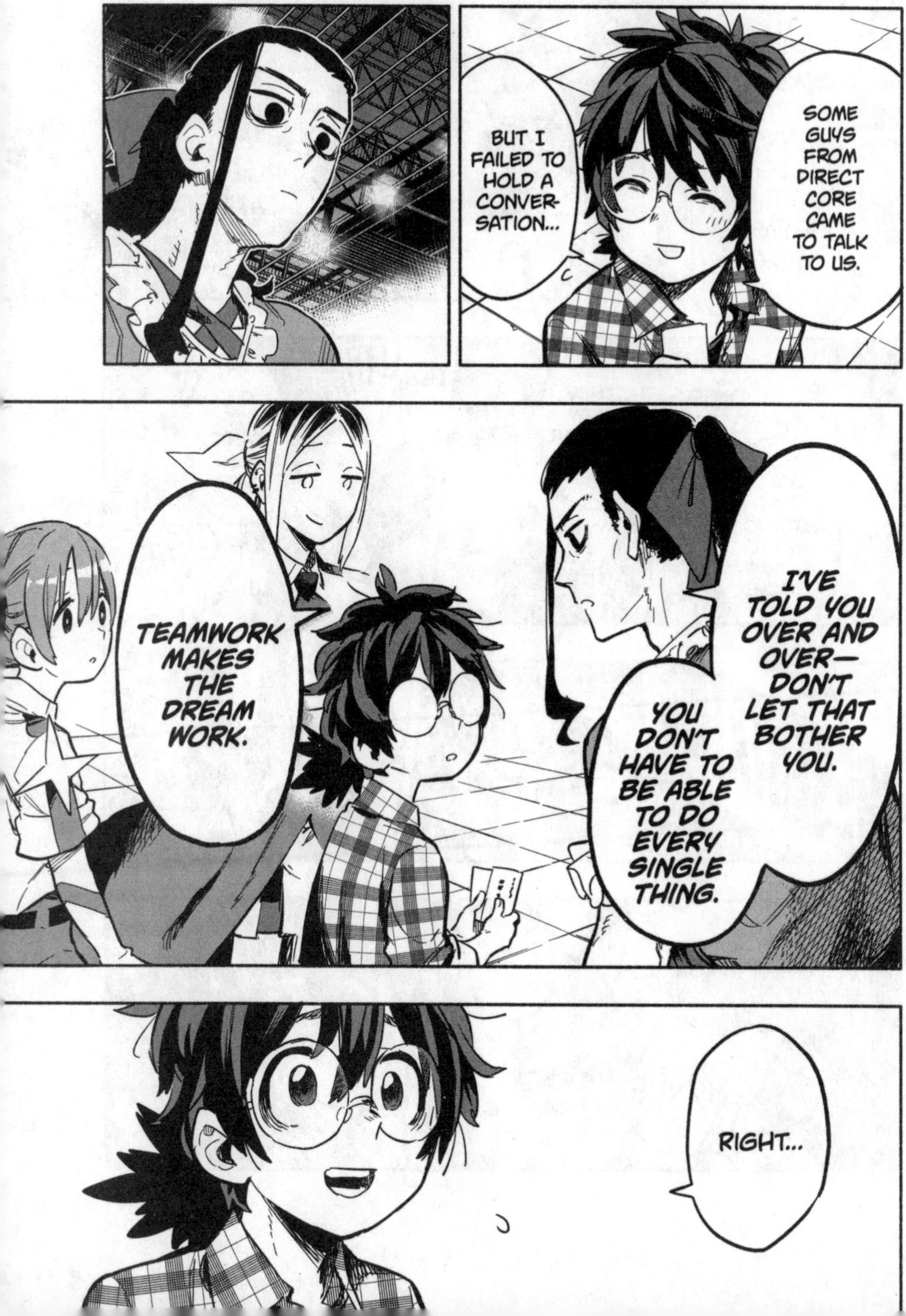
SOME GUYS FROM DIRECT CORE CAME TO TALK TO US.
BUT I FAILED TO HOLD A CONVERSATION...
I'VE TOLD YOU OVER AND OVER—DON'T LET THAT BOTHER YOU.
YOU DON'T HAVE TO BE ABLE TO DO EVERY SINGLE THING.
TEAMWORK MAKES THE DREAM WORK.
RIGHT...

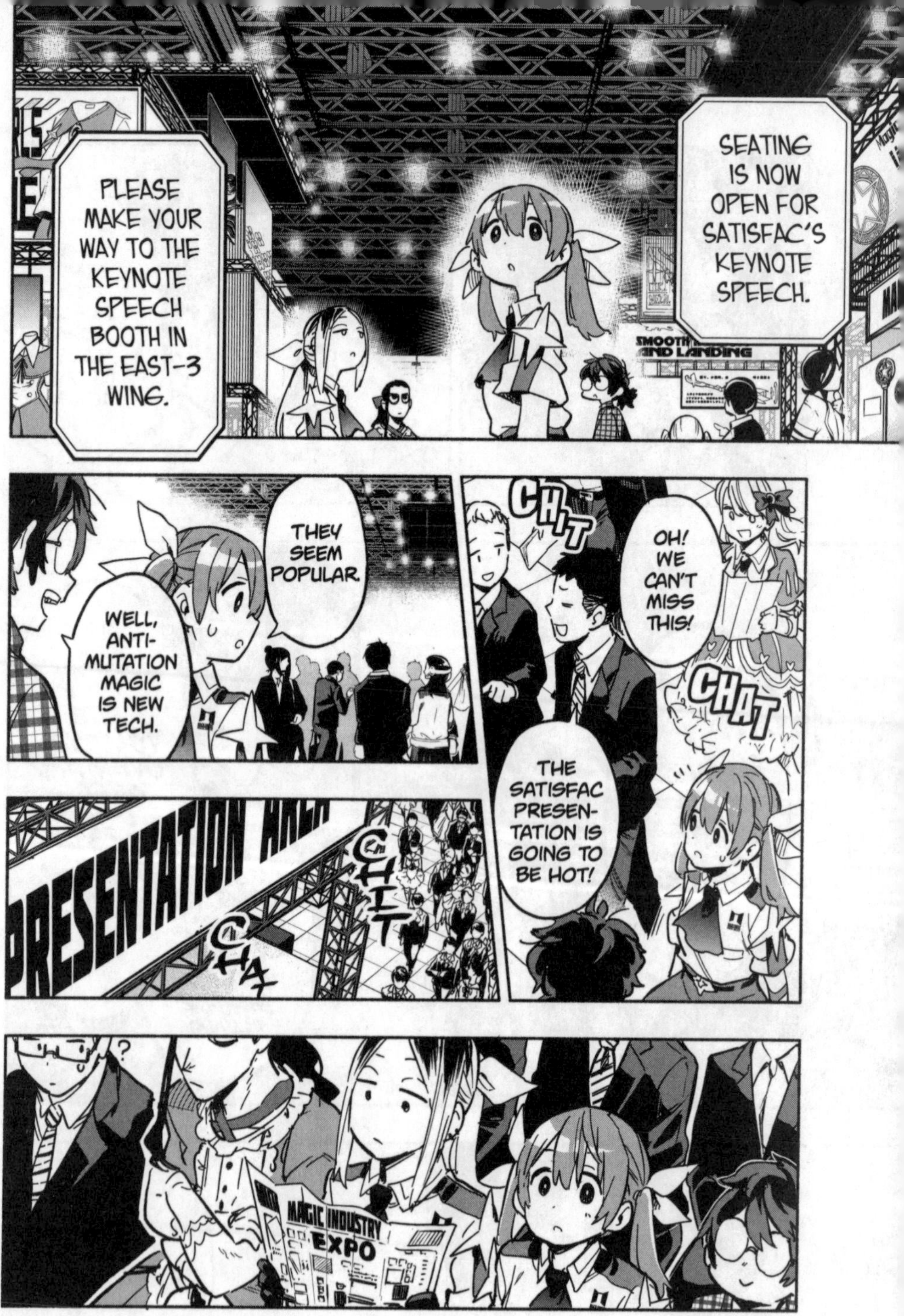
SEATING IS NOW OPEN FOR SATISFAC'S KEYNOTE SPEECH.
PLEASE MAKE YOUR WAY TO THE KEYNOTE SPEECH BOOTH IN THE EAST-3 WING.
CHIT
OH! WE CAN'T MISS THIS!
CHAT
THE SATISFAC PRESENTATION IS GOING TO BE HOT!
THEY SEEM POPULAR.
WELL, ANTI-MUTATION MAGIC IS NEW TECH.
PRESENTATION
CHIT
CHAT
?
MAGIC INDUSTRY EXPO

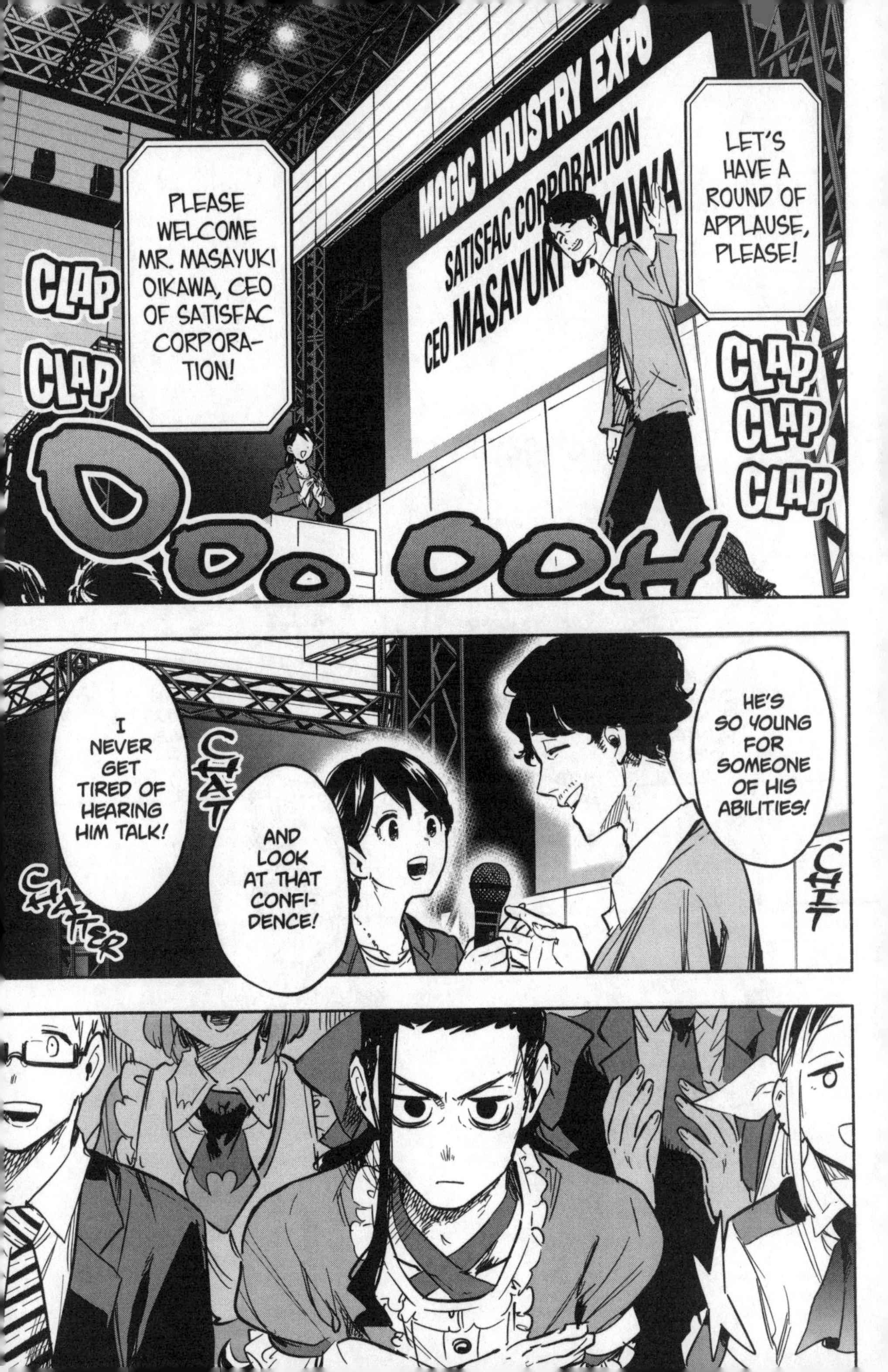
MAGIC INDUSTRY EXPO
LET'S HAVE A ROUND OF APPLAUSE, PLEASE!
CLAP CLAP CLAP
PLEASE WELCOME MR. MASAYUKI OIKAWA, CEO OF SATISFAC CORPORA-TION!
CLAP
CLAP
OOO OOOH
HE'S SO YOUNG FOR SOMEONE OF HIS ABILITIES!
CHIT
AND LOOK AT THAT CONFI-DENCE!
CHAT
I NEVER GET TIRED OF HEARING HIM TALK!
CHATTER

Koshigaya's gut answers

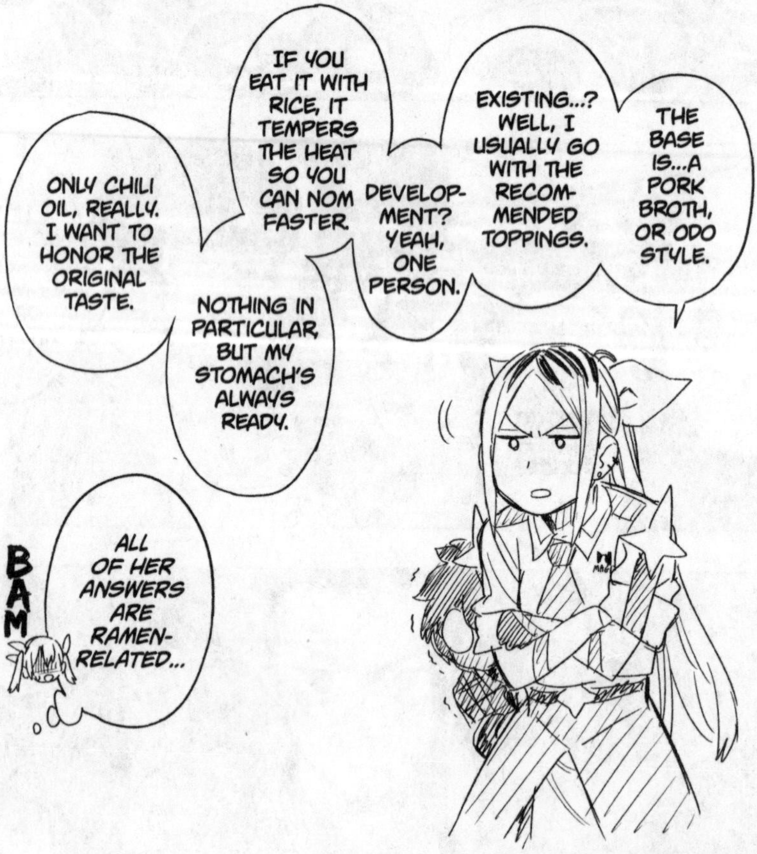
THE BASE IS...A PORK BROTH, OR ODO STYLE.
EXISTING...? WELL, I USUALLY GO WITH THE RECOMMENDED TOPPINGS.
DEVELOPMENT? YEAH, ONE PERSON.
IF YOU EAT IT WITH RICE, IT TEMPERS THE HEAT SO YOU CAN NOM FASTER.
NOTHING IN PARTICULAR, BUT MY STOMACH'S ALWAYS READY.
ONLY CHILI OIL, REALLY. I WANT TO HONOR THE ORIGINAL TASTE.
ALL OF HER ANSWERS ARE RAMEN-RELATED...
BAM

Chapter 18: Working Without a Contract

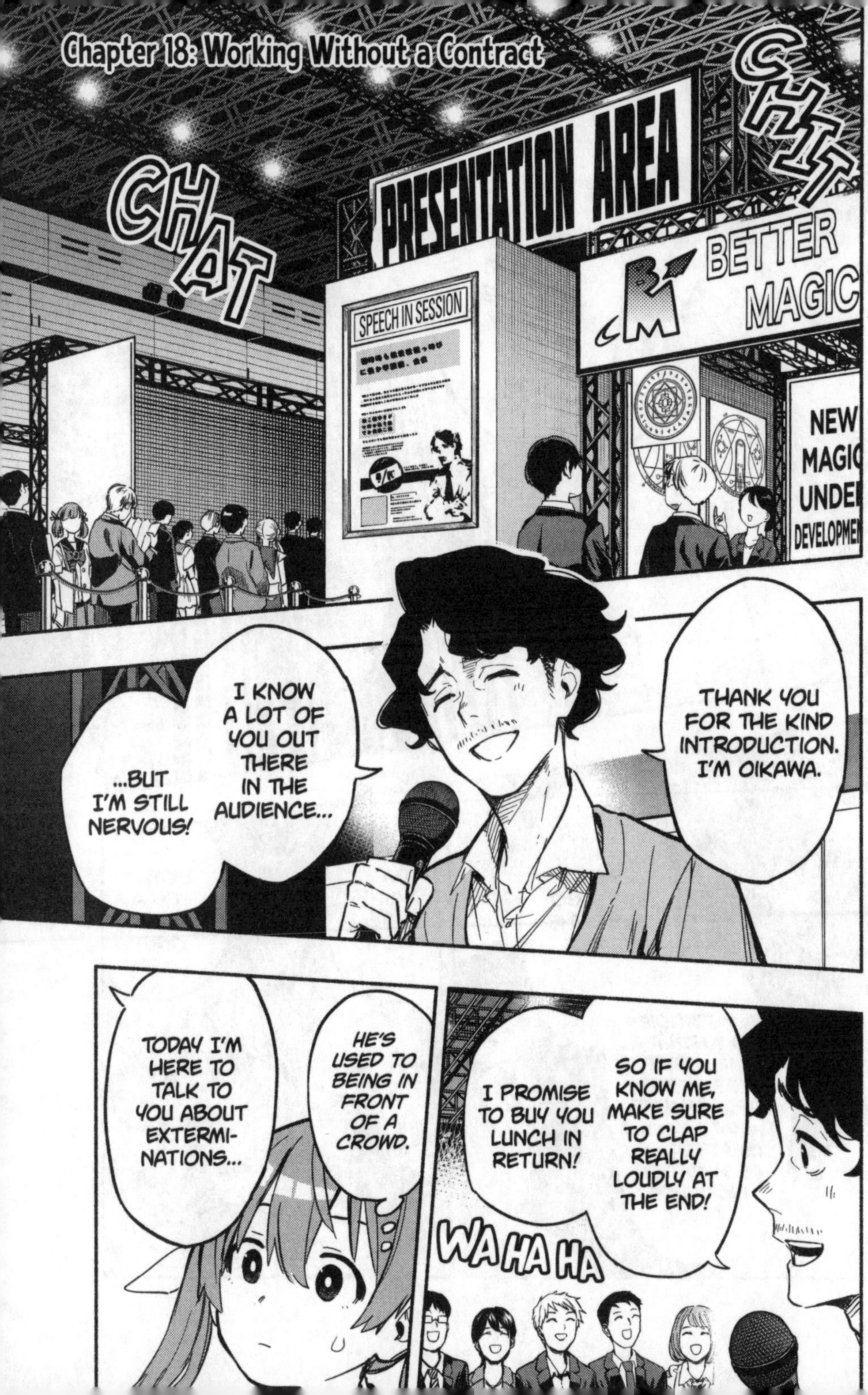
CHIT
PRESENTATION AREA
CHAT
BETTER MAGIC
NEW MAGIC UNDER DEVELOPMENT
SPEECH IN SESSION
THANK YOU FOR THE KIND INTRODUCTION. I'M OIKAWA.
I KNOW A LOT OF YOU OUT THERE IN THE AUDIENCE...
...BUT I'M STILL NERVOUS!
SO IF YOU KNOW ME, MAKE SURE TO CLAP REALLY LOUDLY AT THE END!
I PROMISE TO BUY YOU LUNCH IN RETURN!
WA HA HA
HE'S USED TO BEING IN FRONT OF A CROWD.
TODAY I'M HERE TO TALK TO YOU ABOUT EXTERMI-NATIONS...

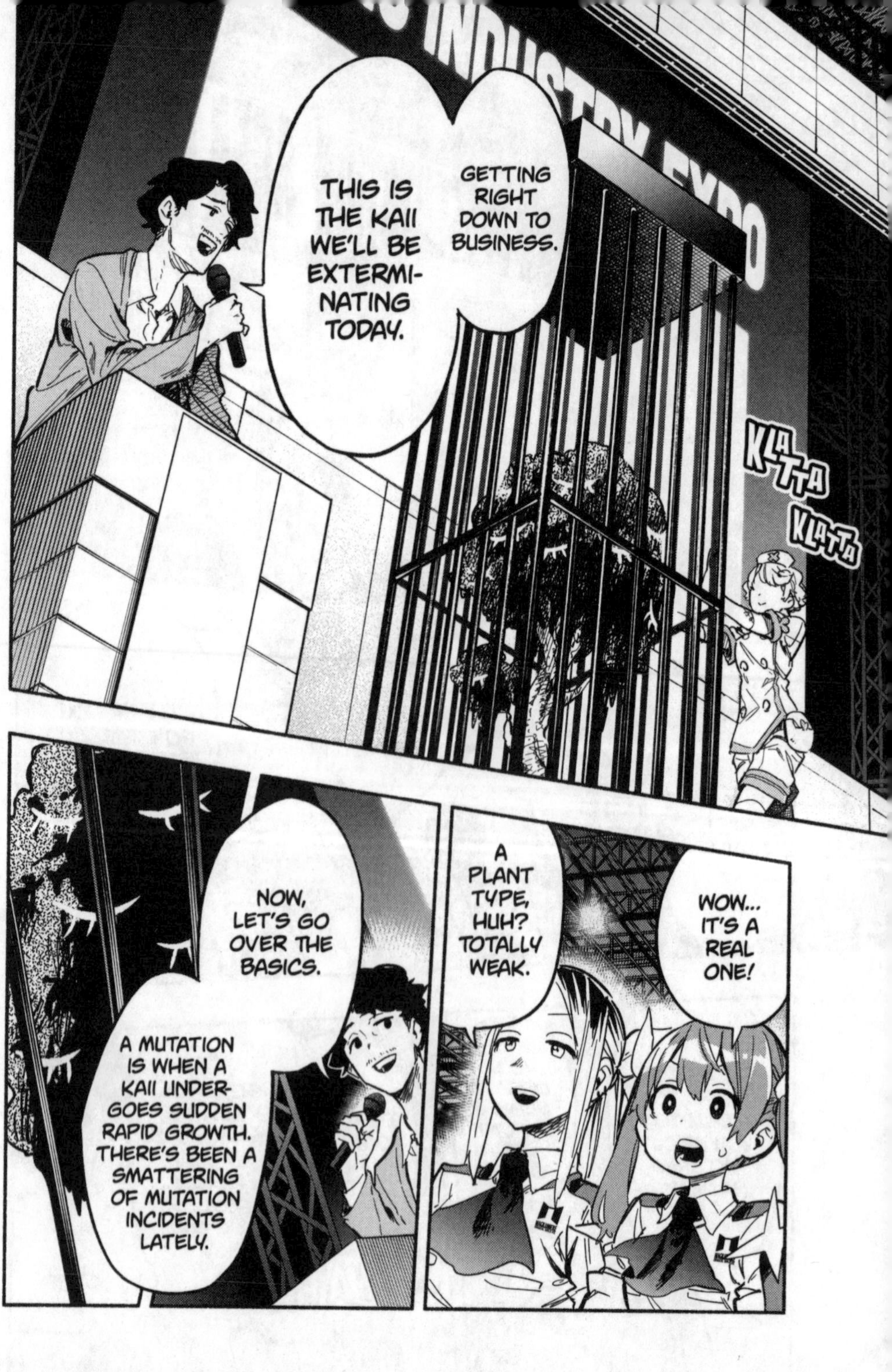
INDUSTRY EXPO
GETTING RIGHT DOWN TO BUSINESS.
THIS IS THE KAII WE'LL BE EXTERMI-NATING TODAY.
KLATTA KLATTA
WOW... IT'S A REAL ONE!
A PLANT TYPE, HUH? TOTALLY WEAK.
NOW, LET'S GO OVER THE BASICS.
A MUTATION IS WHEN A KAII UNDER-GOES SUDDEN RAPID GROWTH. THERE'S BEEN A SMATTERING OF MUTATION INCIDENTS LATELY.

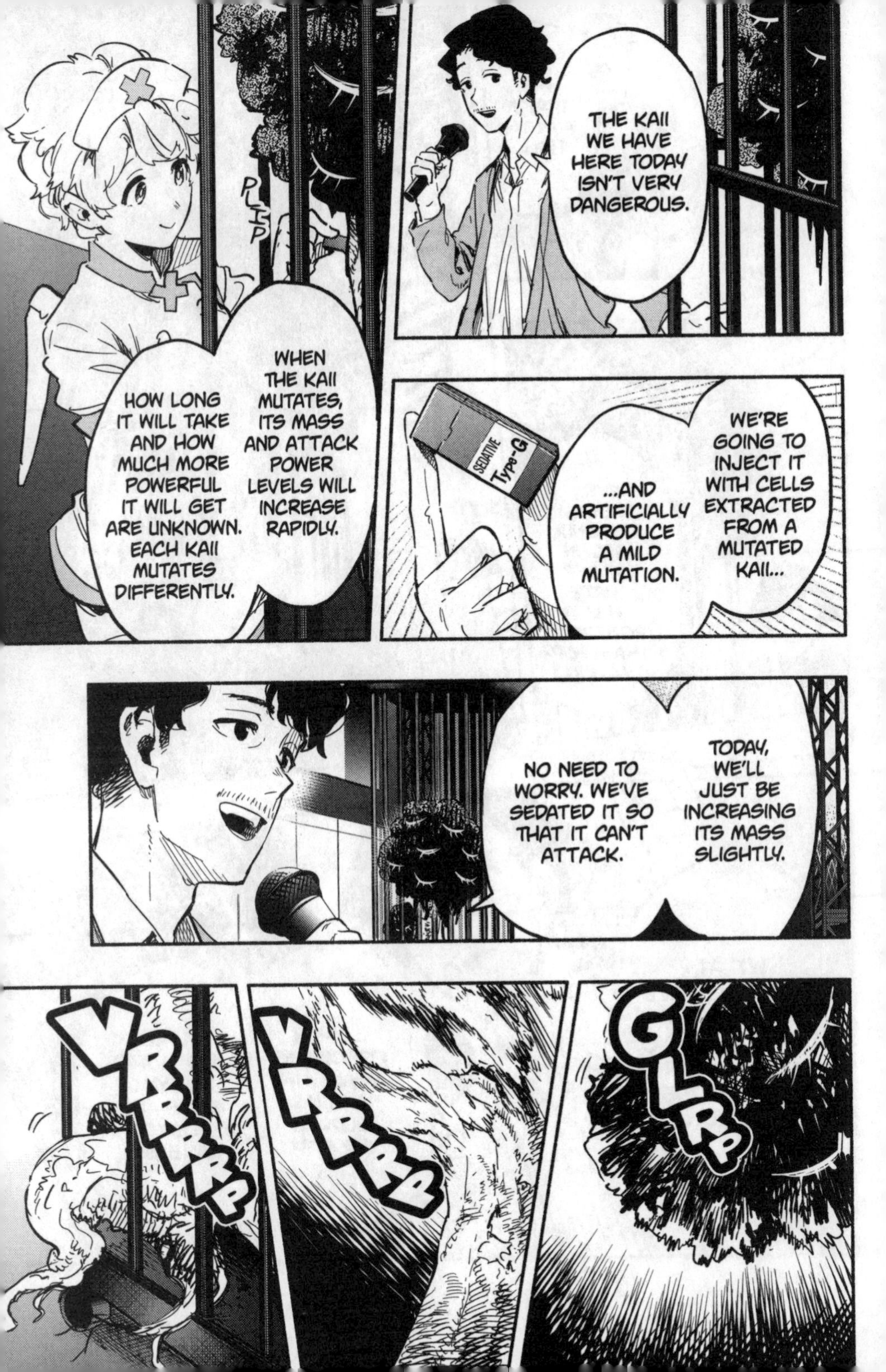
THE KAII WE HAVE HERE TODAY ISN'T VERY DANGEROUS.
SEDATIVE
Type-G
WE'RE GOING TO INJECT IT WITH CELLS EXTRACTED FROM A MUTATED KAII...
...AND ARTIFICIALLY PRODUCE A MILD MUTATION.
PLIP
WHEN THE KAII MUTATES, ITS MASS AND ATTACK POWER LEVELS WILL INCREASE RAPIDLY.
HOW LONG IT WILL TAKE AND HOW MUCH MORE POWERFUL IT WILL GET ARE UNKNOWN. EACH KAII MUTATES DIFFERENTLY.
TODAY, WE'LL JUST BE INCREASING ITS MASS SLIGHTLY.
NO NEED TO WORRY. WE'VE SEDATED IT SO THAT IT CAN'T ATTACK.
GLRP
VRRRRP
VRRRRP

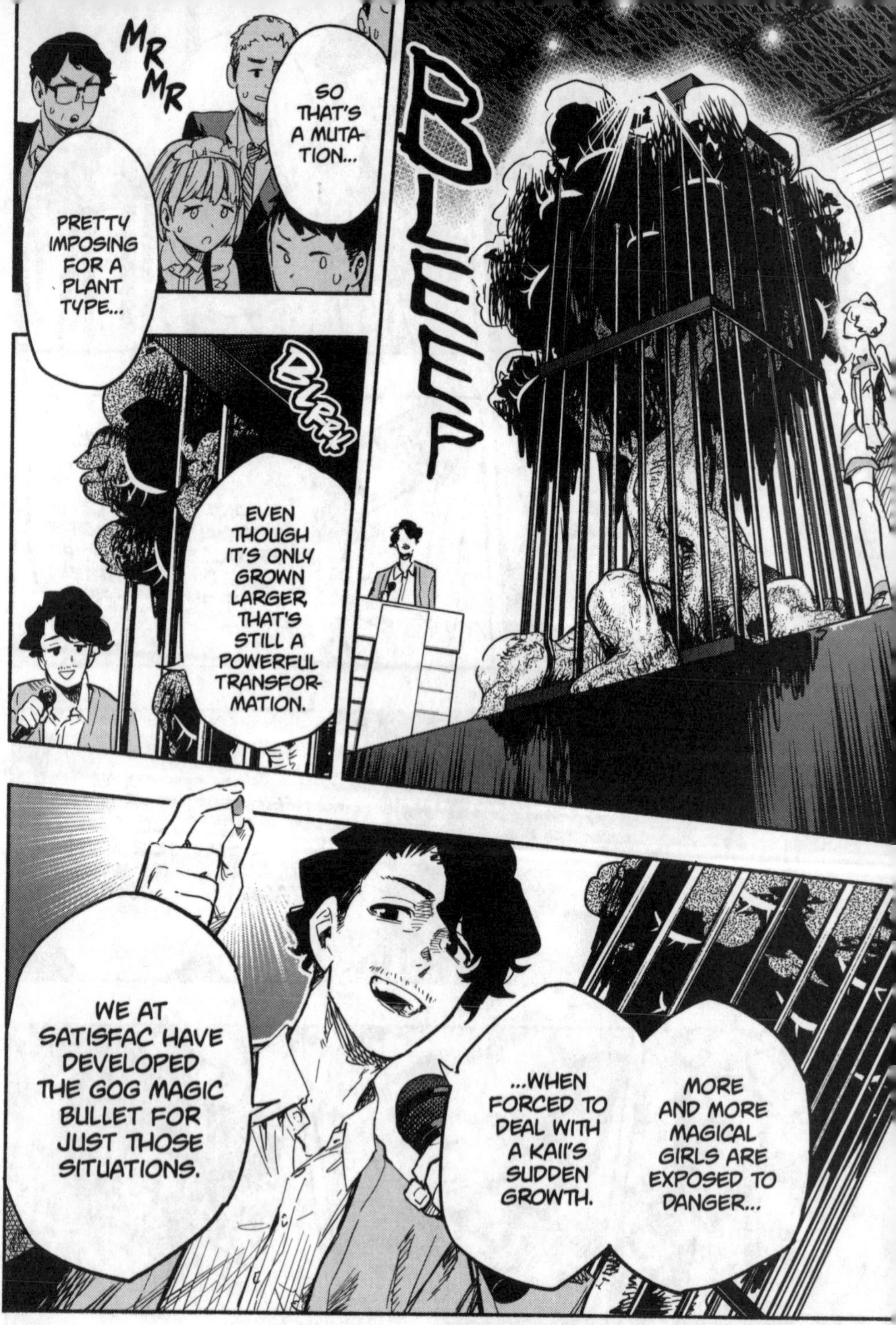
BLEEP
SO THAT'S A MUTATION...
MRMR
PRETTY IMPOSING FOR A PLANT TYPE...
BLRRK
EVEN THOUGH IT'S ONLY GROWN LARGER, THAT'S STILL A POWERFUL TRANSFORMATION.
MORE AND MORE MAGICAL GIRLS ARE EXPOSED TO DANGER...
...WHEN FORCED TO DEAL WITH A KAII'S SUDDEN GROWTH.
WE AT SATISFAC HAVE DEVELOPED THE GOG MAGIC BULLET FOR JUST THOSE SITUATIONS.

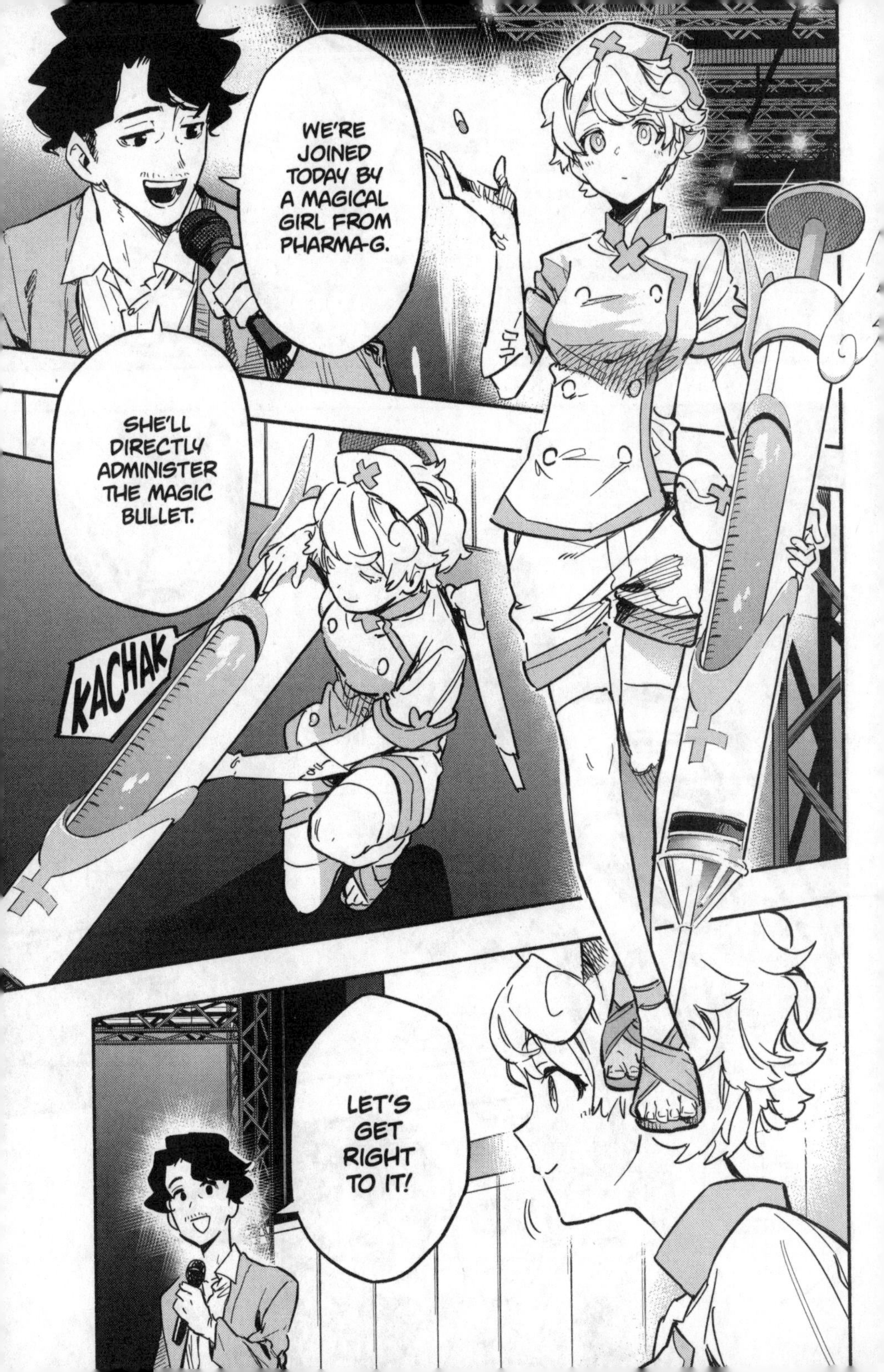
WE'RE JOINED TODAY BY A MAGICAL GIRL FROM PHARMA-G.
SHE'LL DIRECTLY ADMINISTER THE MAGIC BULLET.
KACHAK
LET'S GET RIGHT TO IT!

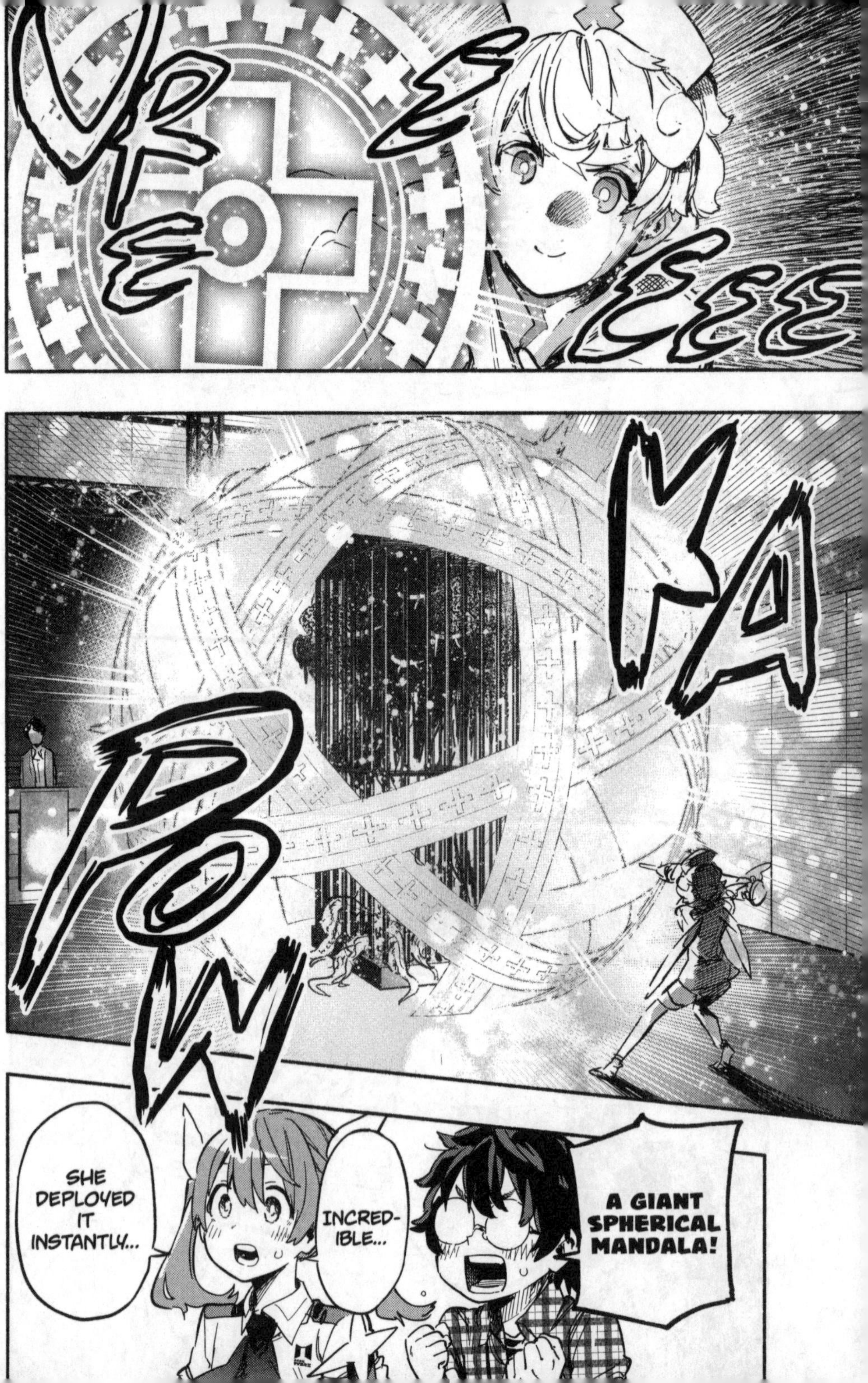
A GIANT SPHERICAL MANDALA!
INCRED-IBLE...
SHE DEPLOYED IT INSTANTLY...

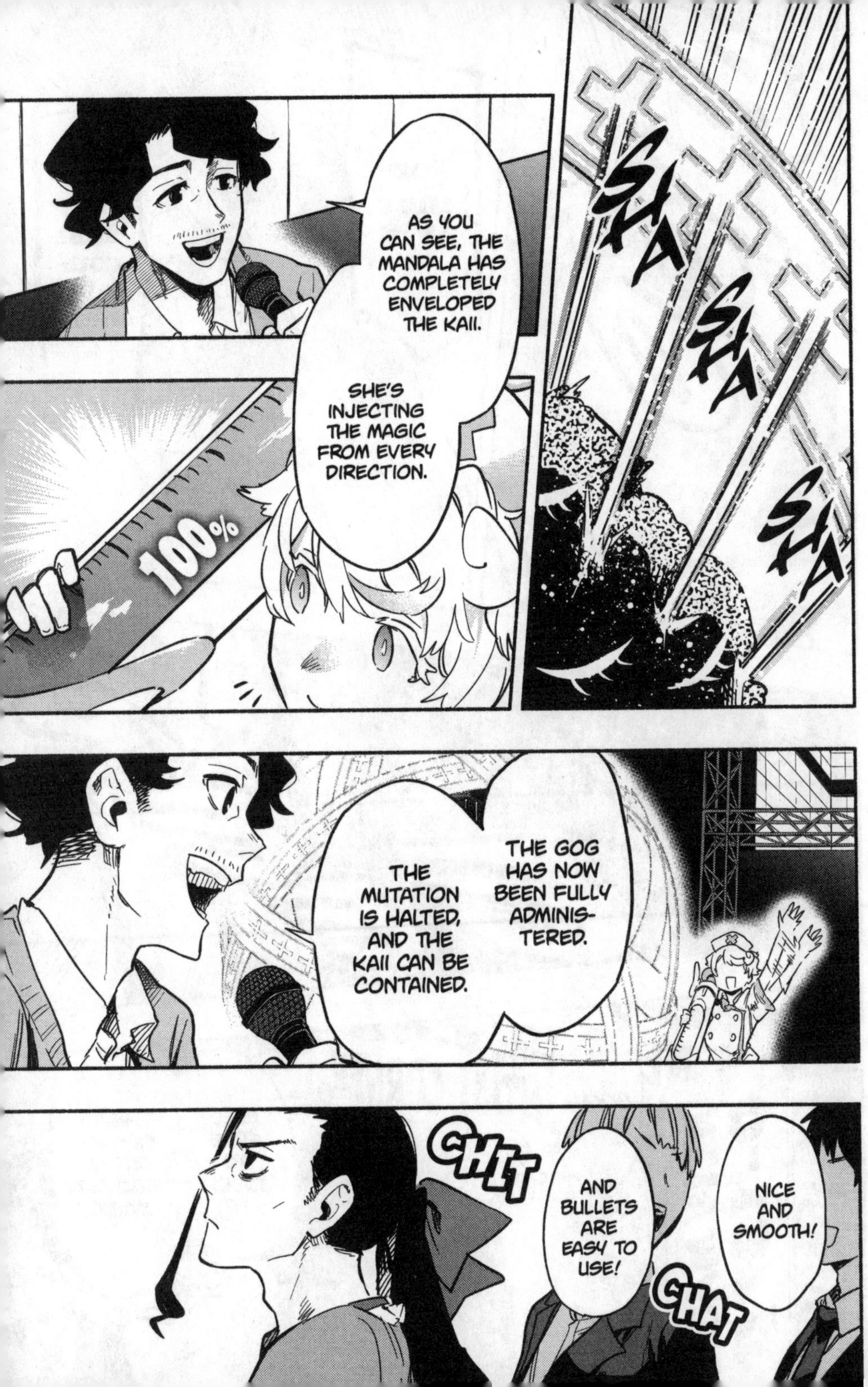
SHA
SHA
SHA
AS YOU CAN SEE, THE MANDALA HAS COMPLETELY ENVELOPED THE KAII.
SHE'S INJECTING THE MAGIC FROM EVERY DIRECTION.
100%
THE GOG HAS NOW BEEN FULLY ADMINIS-TERED.
THE MUTATION IS HALTED, AND THE KAII CAN BE CONTAINED.
NICE AND SMOOTH!
AND BULLETS ARE EASY TO USE!
CHIT
CHAT

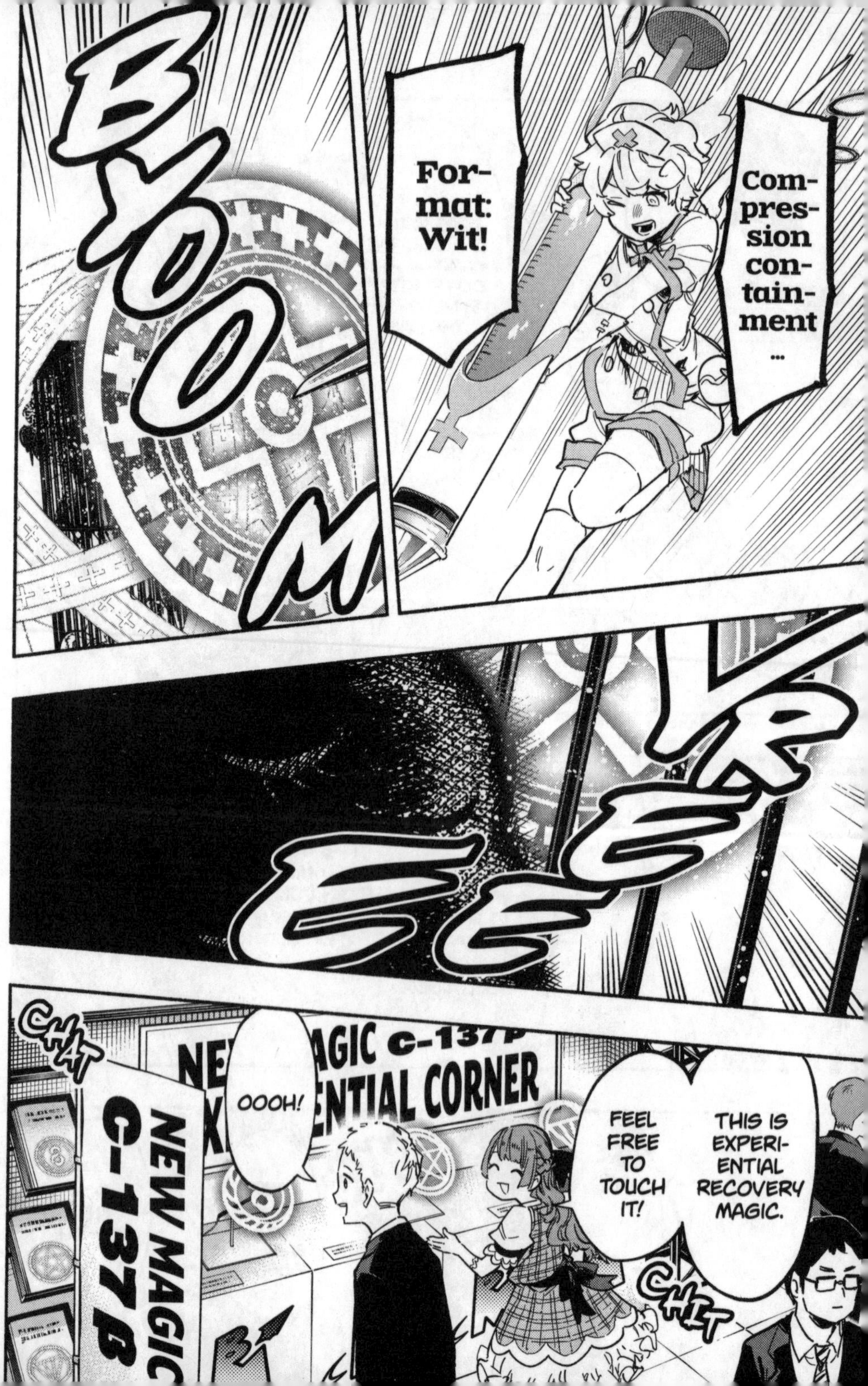
Compression containment...
Format: Wit!
BOOOM
CHAT
NEW MAGIC C-137B
AGIC C-137P
ENTIAL CORNER
THIS IS EXPERIENTIAL RECOVERY MAGIC.
FEEL FREE TO TOUCH IT!
OOOH!
CHIT

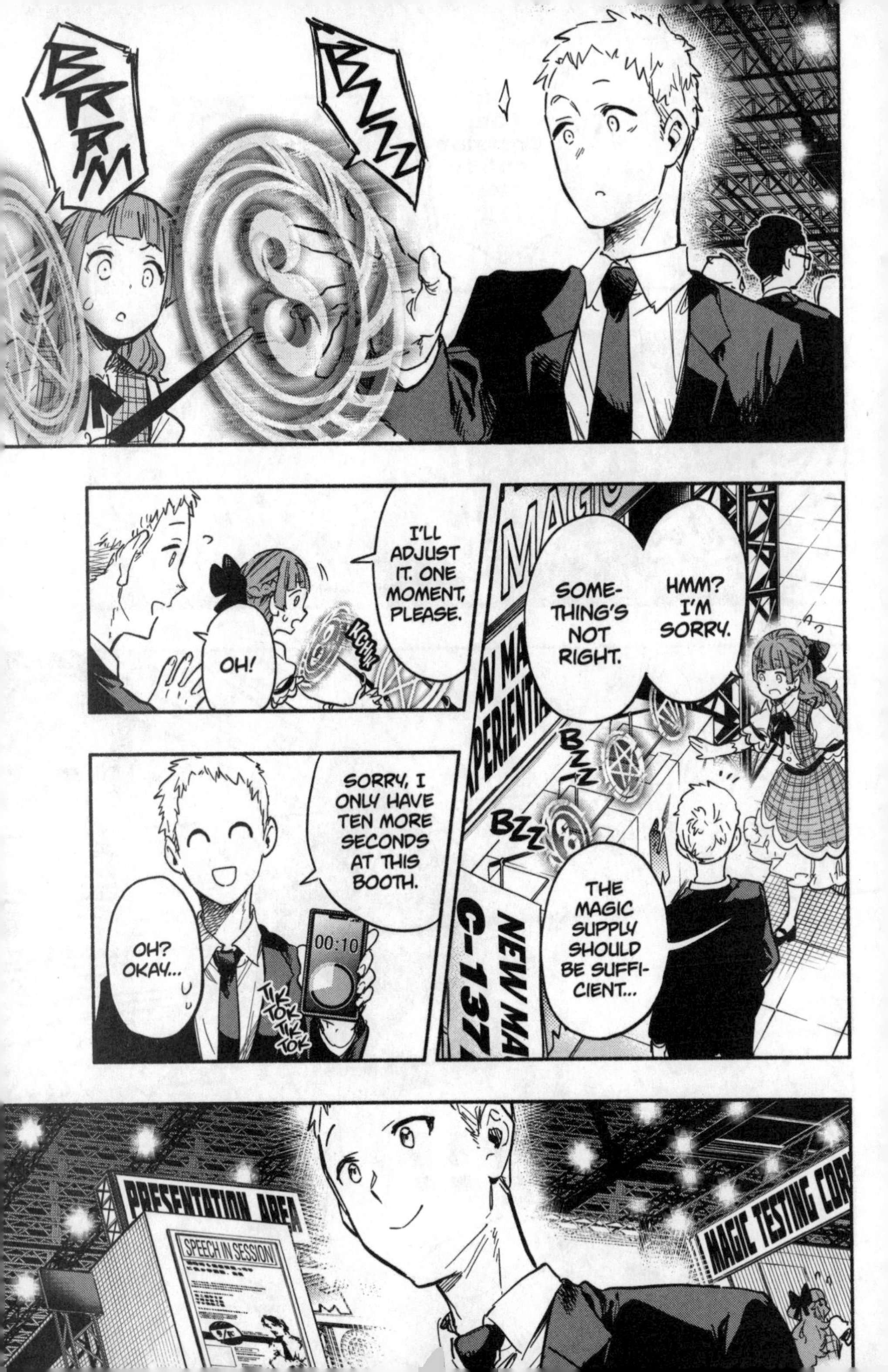
BZZZ
BRRM
HMM? I'M SORRY.
SOME-THING'S NOT RIGHT.
BZZ
BZZ
THE MAGIC SUPPLY SHOULD BE SUFFI-CIENT...
I'LL ADJUST IT. ONE MOMENT, PLEASE.
OH!
KCHK
SORRY, I ONLY HAVE TEN MORE SECONDS AT THIS BOOTH.
00:10
OH? OKAY...
TIK TOK TIK TOK
PRESENTATION AREA
SPEECH IN SESSION

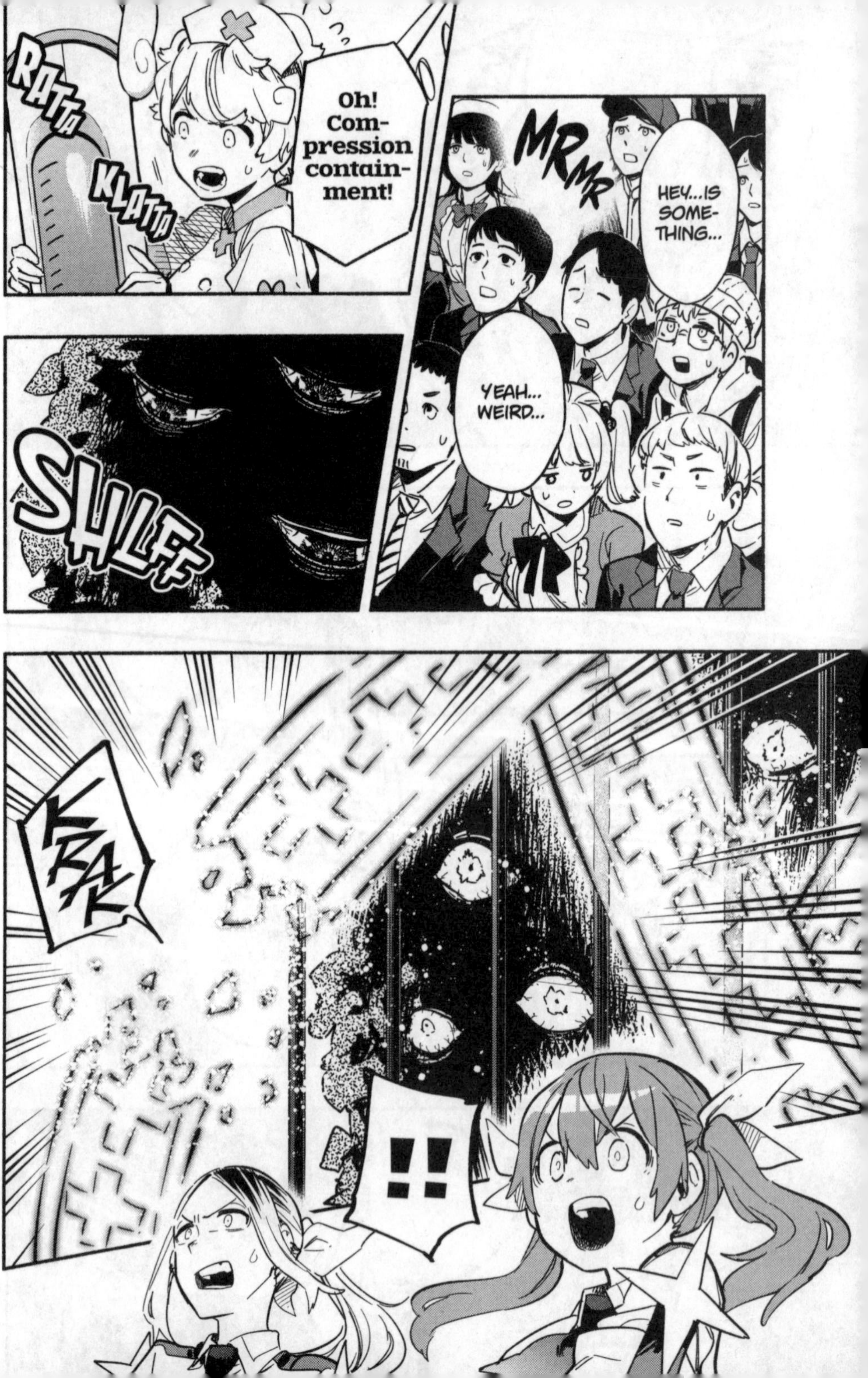
MRMR
HEY...IS SOME-THING...
YEAH... WEIRD...
RATTA
KLATTA
Oh! Com-pression contain-ment!
SHLFF
KRAK
!!

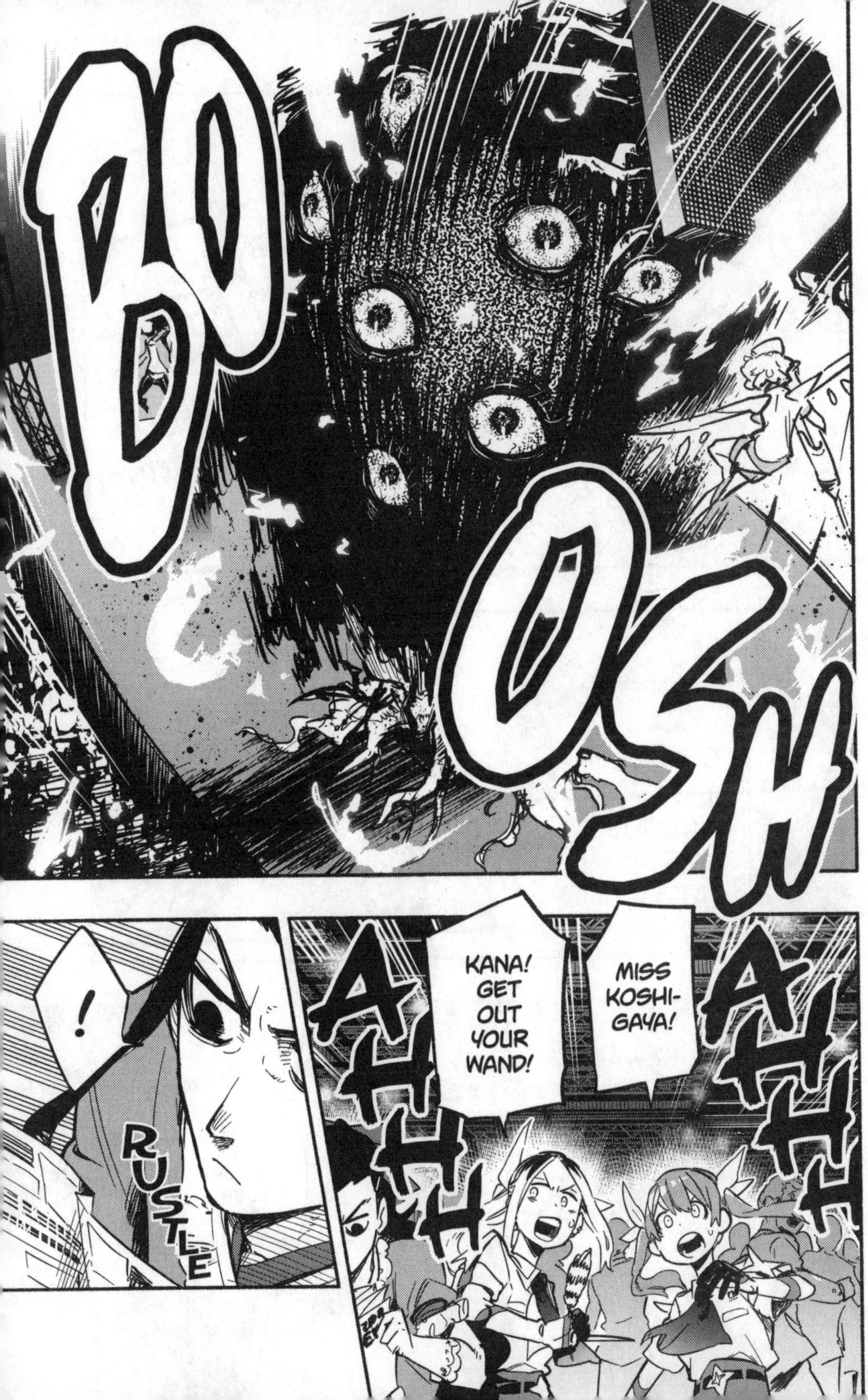
BOOSH
AHHH
AHHH
MISS KOSHI-GAYA!
KANA! GET OUT YOUR WAND!
!
RUSTLE

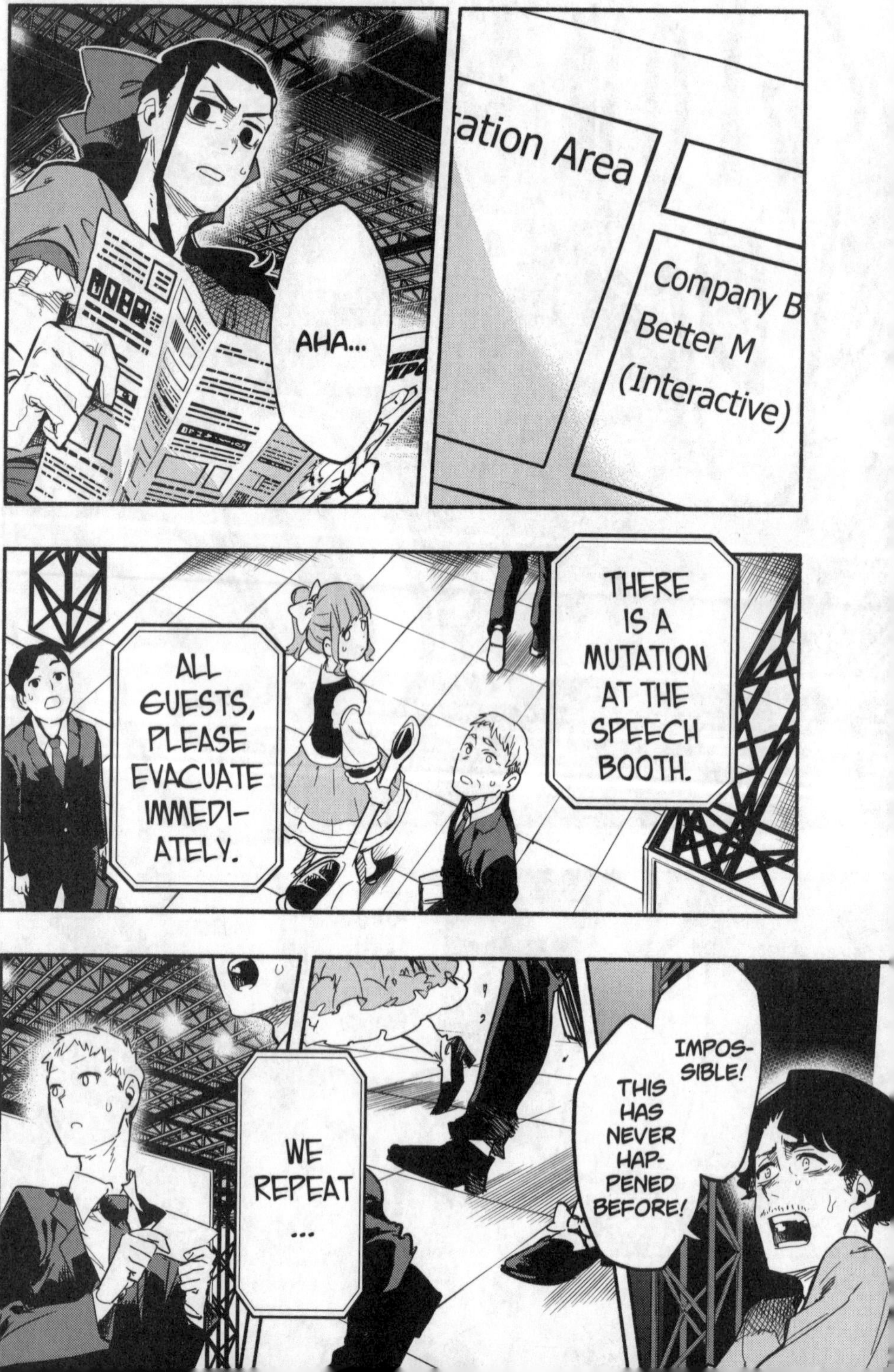
tation Area
Company B
Better M
(Interactive)
AHA...
THERE IS A MUTATION AT THE SPEECH BOOTH.
ALL GUESTS, PLEASE EVACUATE IMMEDI-ATELY.
IMPOS-SIBLE!
THIS HAS NEVER HAP-PENED BEFORE!
WE REPEAT ...

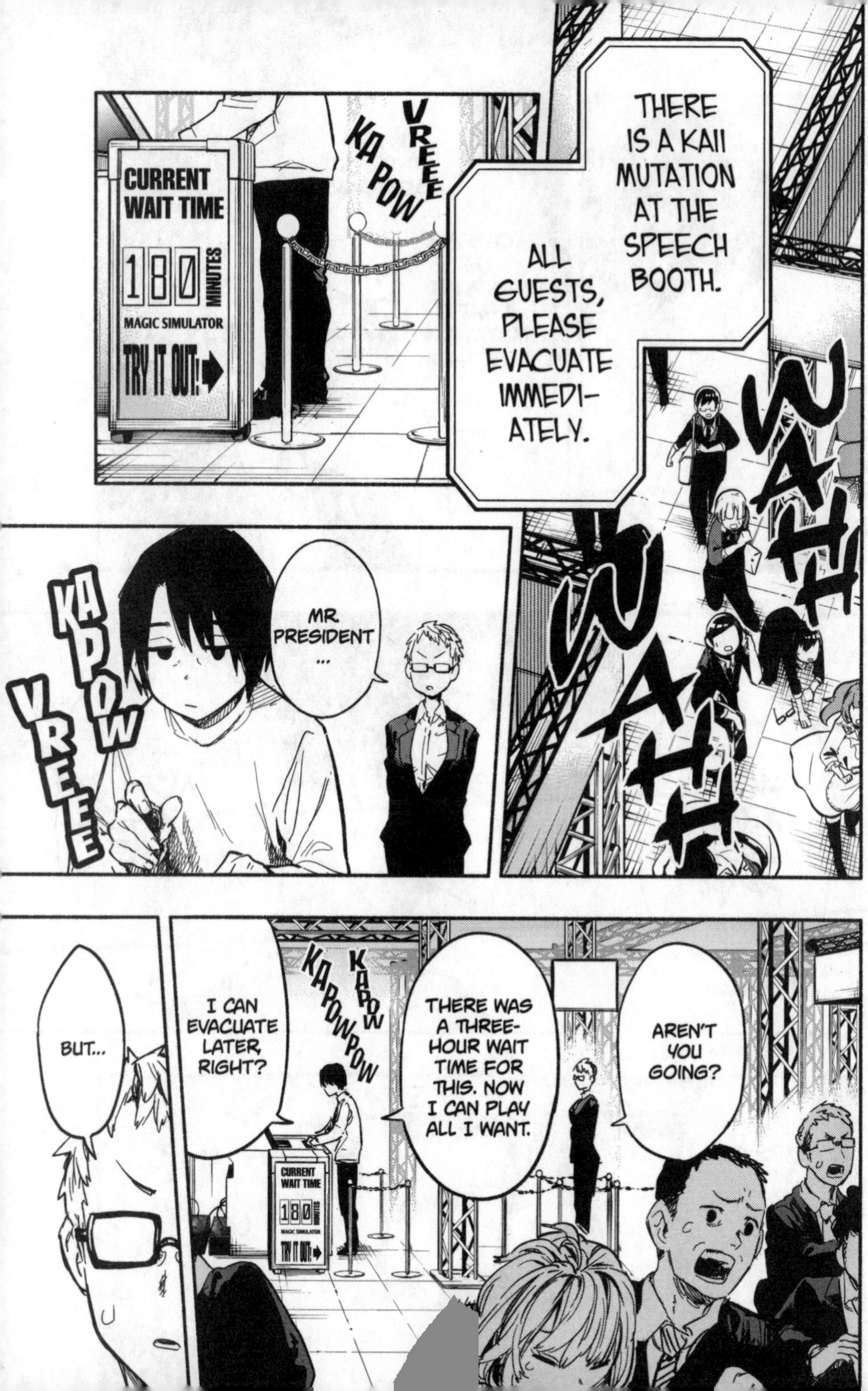
THERE IS A KAII MUTATION AT THE SPEECH BOOTH.
ALL GUESTS, PLEASE EVACUATE IMMEDIATELY.
WAH WAH
CURRENT WAIT TIME
180 MINUTES
MAGIC SIMULATOR
TRY IT OUT!
VREEE
KA POW
KAPOW
VREEE
MR. PRESIDENT...
AREN'T YOU GOING?
THERE WAS A THREE-HOUR WAIT TIME FOR THIS. NOW I CAN PLAY ALL I WANT.
KAPOW
KAPOWPOW
I CAN EVACUATE LATER, RIGHT?
BUT...

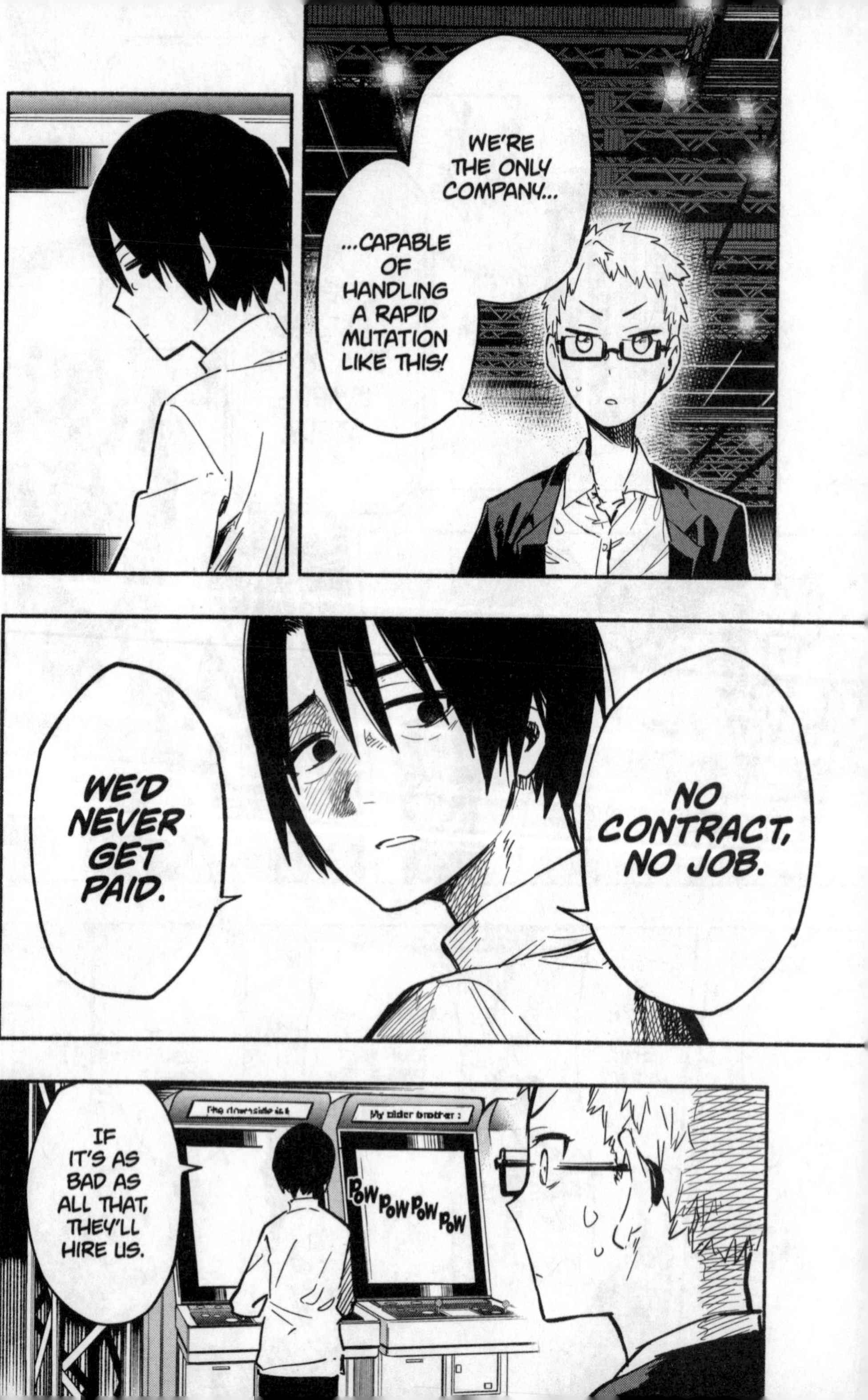
WE'RE THE ONLY COMPANY...
...CAPABLE OF HANDLING A RAPID MUTATION LIKE THIS!
NO CONTRACT, NO JOB.
WE'D NEVER GET PAID.
The downside is :
My elder brother :
POW POW POW POW
IF IT'S AS BAD AS ALL THAT, THEY'LL HIRE US.

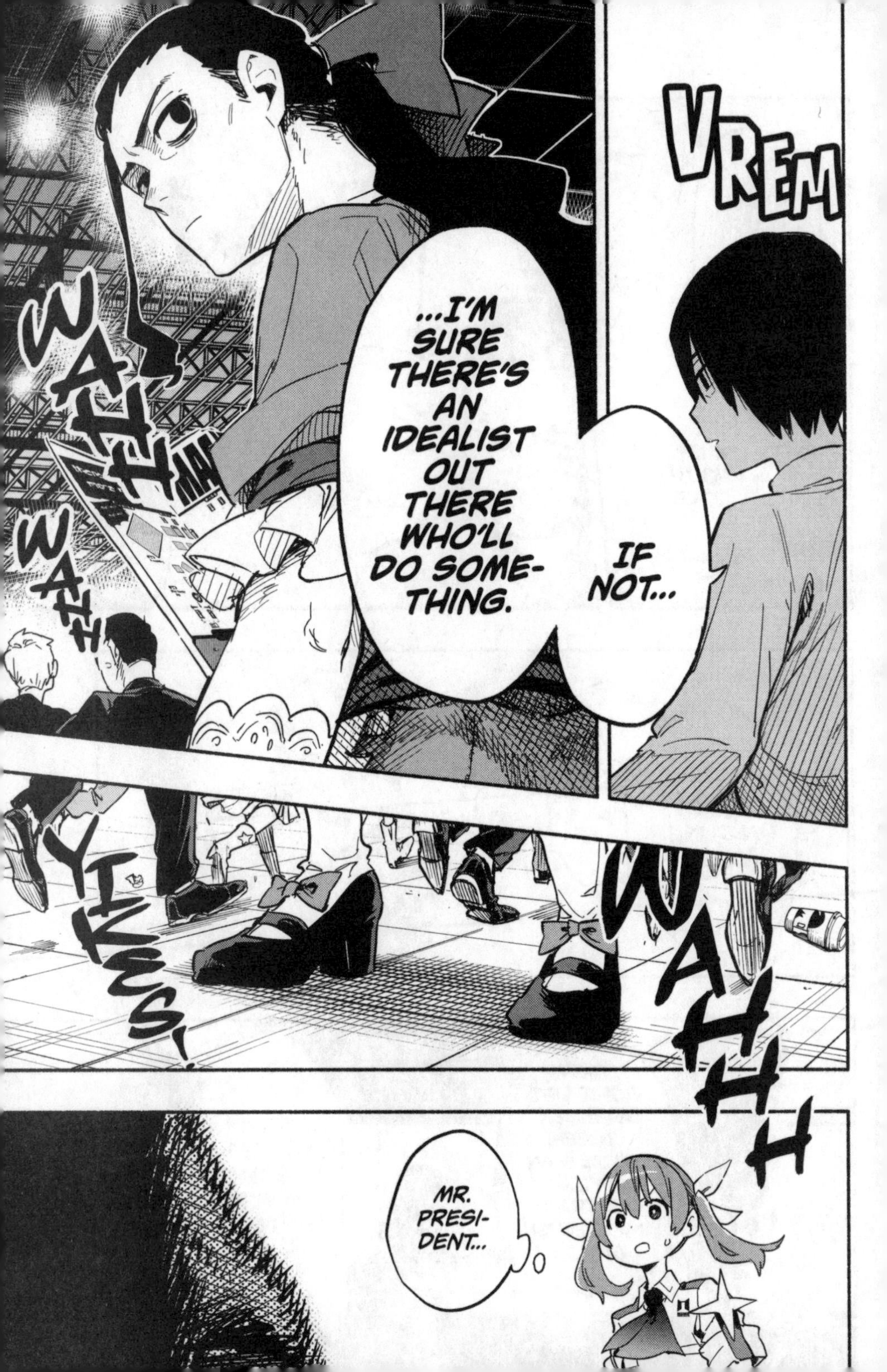
VREM
IF NOT...
...I'M SURE THERE'S AN IDEALIST OUT THERE WHO'LL DO SOME-THING.
WAAH
WAHH
WAHHHH
YIKES!
MR. PRESI-DENT...

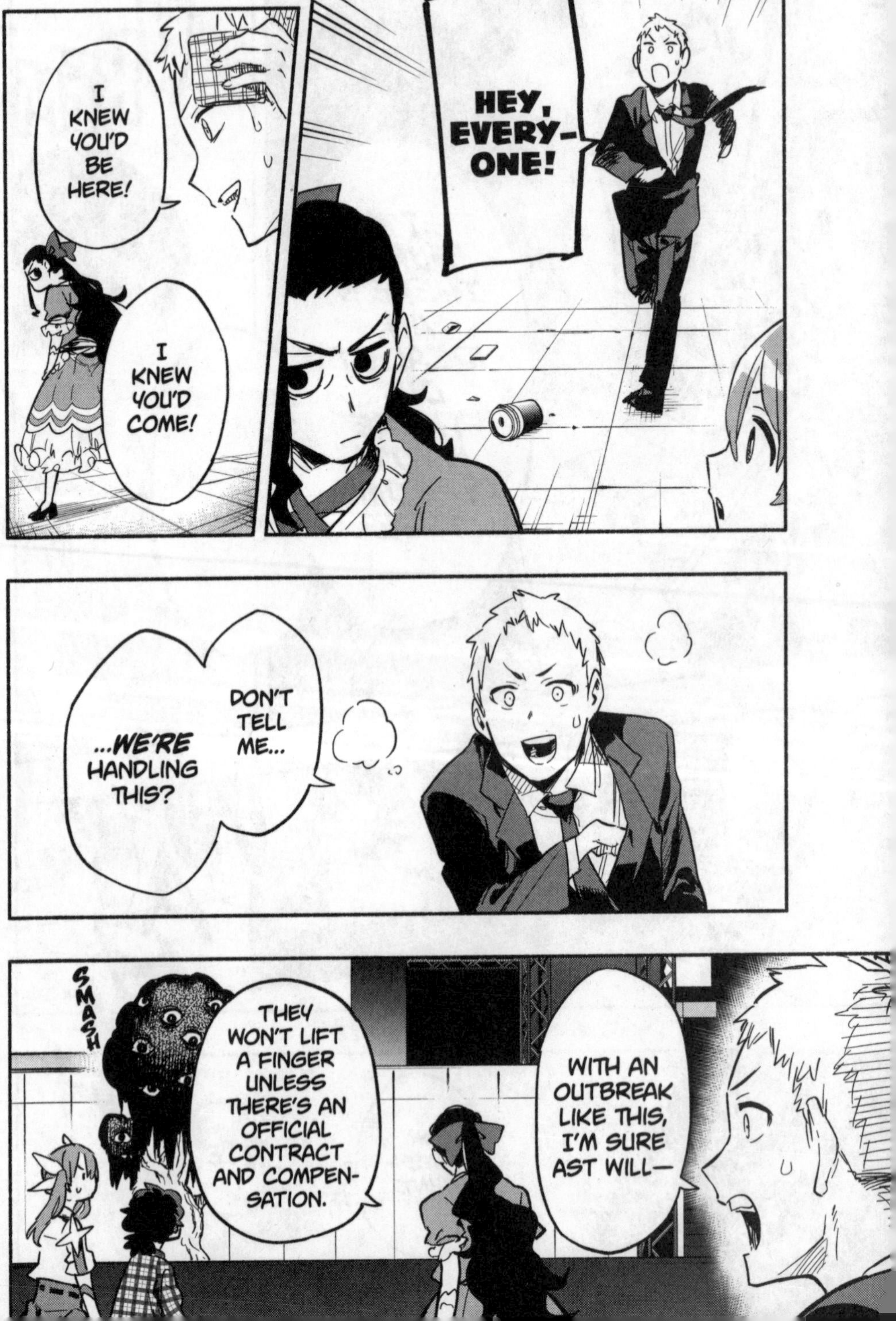
HEY, EVERYONE!
I KNEW YOU'D BE HERE!
I KNEW YOU'D COME!
DON'T TELL ME...
...WE'RE HANDLING THIS?
WITH AN OUTBREAK LIKE THIS, I'M SURE AST WILL—
THEY WON'T LIFT A FINGER UNLESS THERE'S AN OFFICIAL CONTRACT AND COMPENSATION.
SMASH

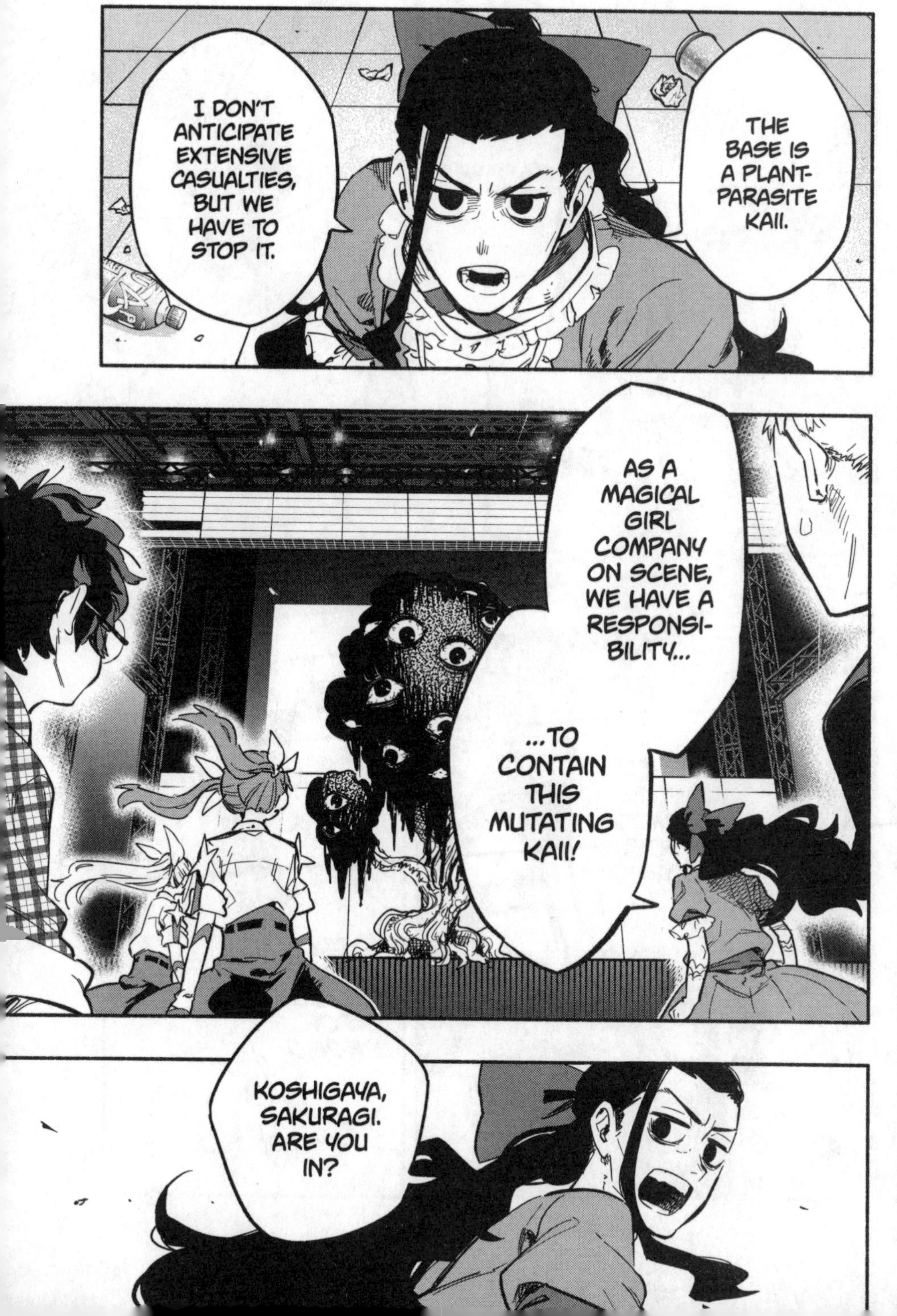
THE BASE IS A PLANT-PARASITE KAII.
I DON'T ANTICIPATE EXTENSIVE CASUALTIES, BUT WE HAVE TO STOP IT.
AS A MAGICAL GIRL COMPANY ON SCENE, WE HAVE A RESPONSI-BILITY...
...TO CONTAIN THIS MUTATING KAII!
KOSHIGAYA, SAKURAGI. ARE YOU IN?

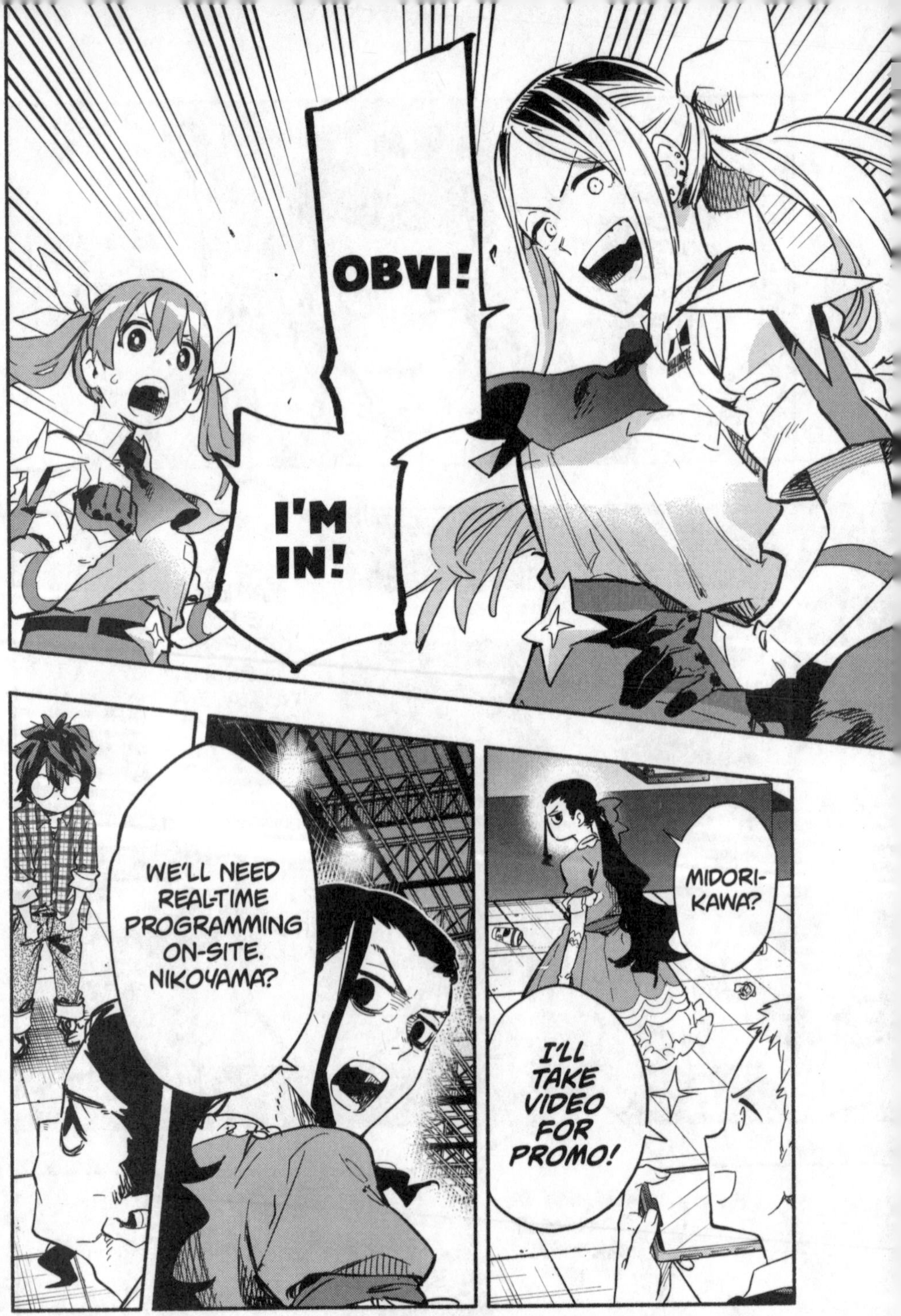
OBVI!
I'M IN!
MIDORI-KAWA?
I'LL TAKE VIDEO FOR PROMO!
WE'LL NEED REAL-TIME PROGRAMMING ON-SITE. NIKOYAMA?

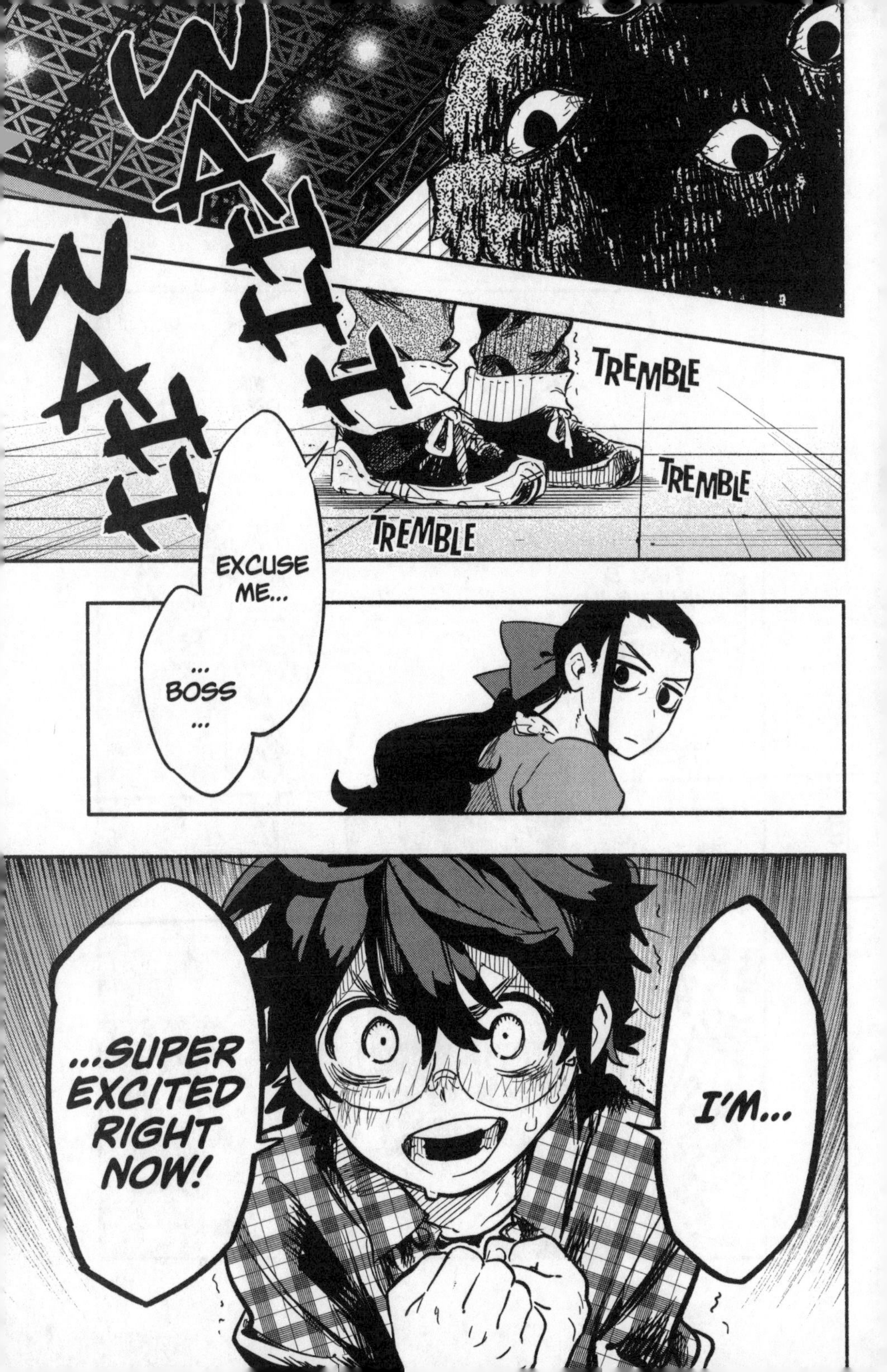
WAAAH
WAAAH
TREMBLE
TREMBLE
TREMBLE
EXCUSE ME...
... BOSS ...
I'M...
...SUPER EXCITED RIGHT NOW!

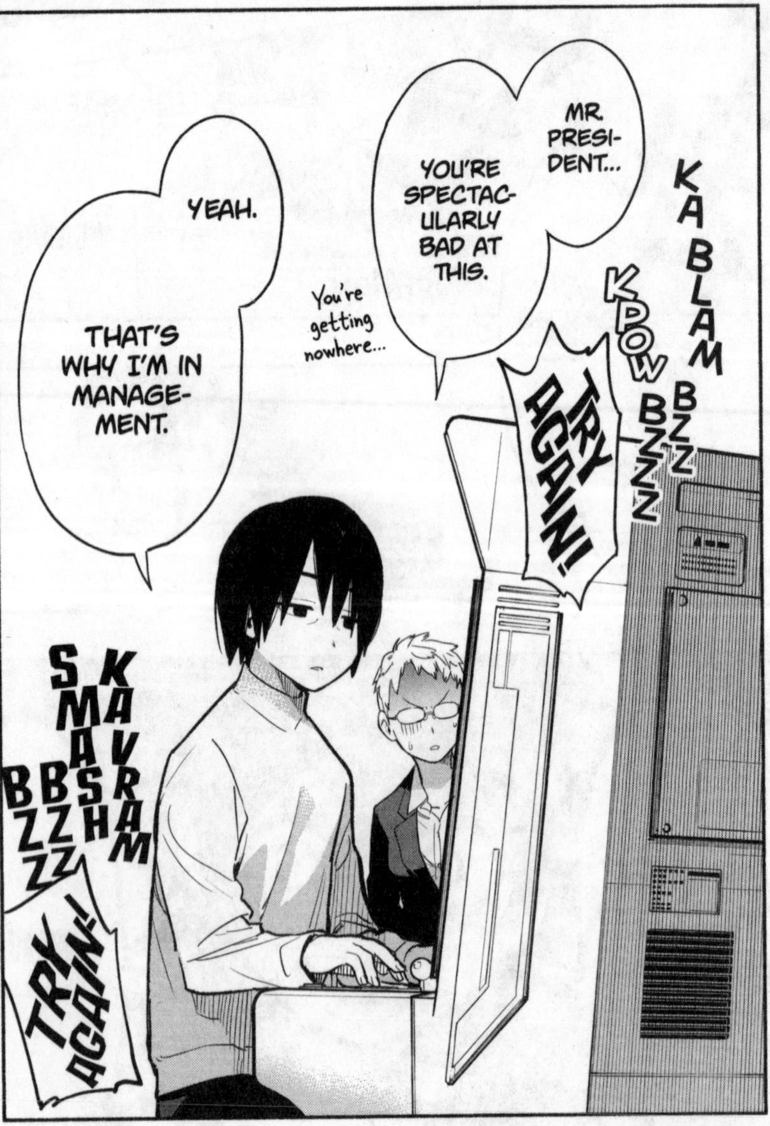
MR. PRESIDENT...
YOU'RE SPECTACULARLY BAD AT THIS.
You're getting nowhere...
KABLAM
KPOW
BZZ
BZZZ
TRY AGAIN!
YEAH.
THAT'S WHY I'M IN MANAGEMENT.
KAVRAM
SMASH
BZZZ
BZZ
TRY AGAIN!

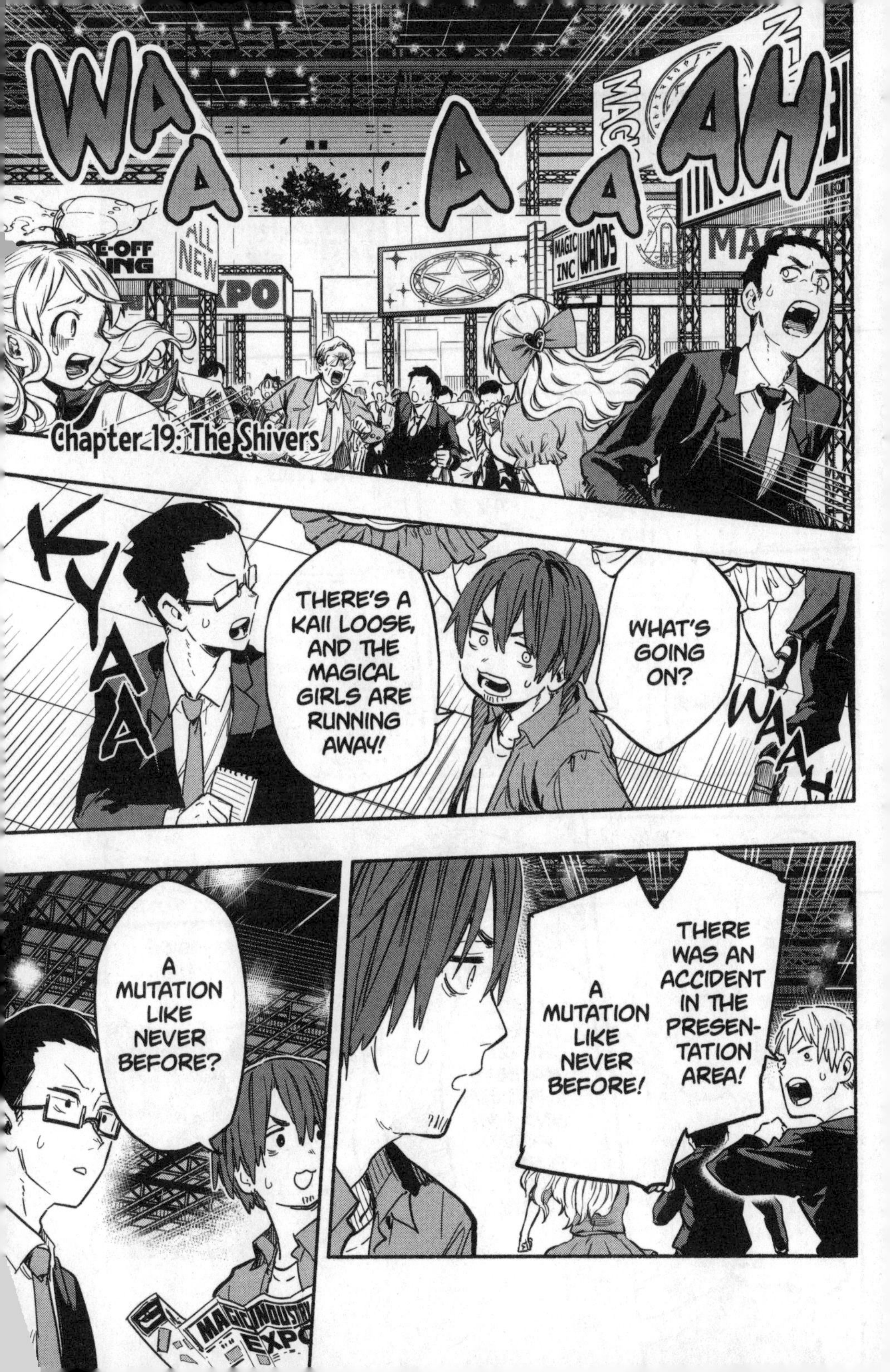
WAAAAAH
MAGIC INC
WANDS
ALL NEW
EXPO
Chapter 19: The Shivers
WAAAH
WHAT'S GOING ON?
THERE'S A KAII LOOSE, AND THE MAGICAL GIRLS ARE RUNNING AWAY!
KYAAA
THERE WAS AN ACCIDENT IN THE PRESENTATION AREA!
A MUTATION LIKE NEVER BEFORE!
A MUTATION LIKE NEVER BEFORE?

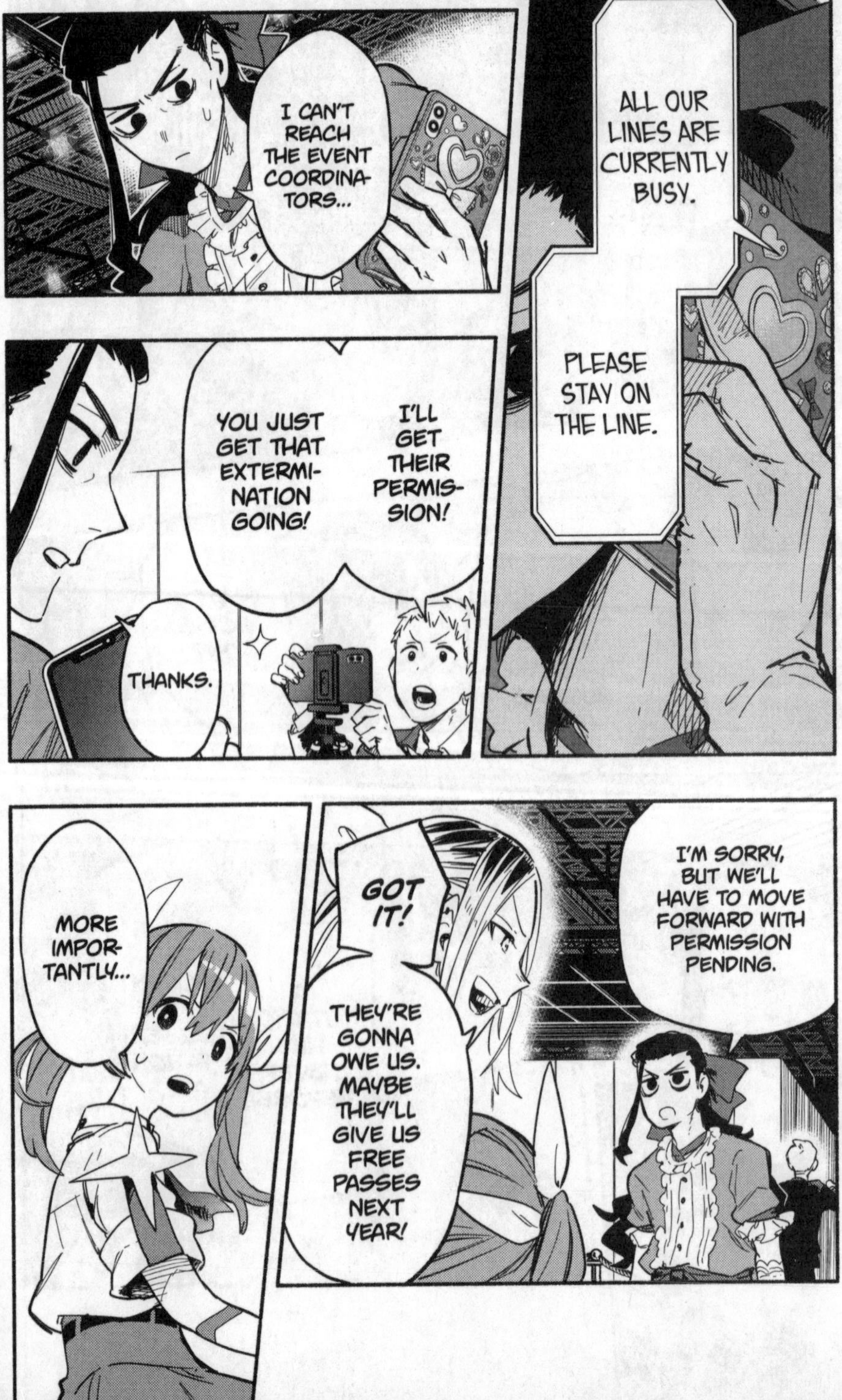
ALL OUR LINES ARE CURRENTLY BUSY.
PLEASE STAY ON THE LINE.
I CAN'T REACH THE EVENT COORDINATORS...
I'LL GET THEIR PERMISSION!
YOU JUST GET THAT EXTERMINATION GOING!
THANKS.
I'M SORRY, BUT WE'LL HAVE TO MOVE FORWARD WITH PERMISSION PENDING.
GOT IT!
THEY'RE GONNA OWE US. MAYBE THEY'LL GIVE US FREE PASSES NEXT YEAR!
MORE IMPORTANTLY...

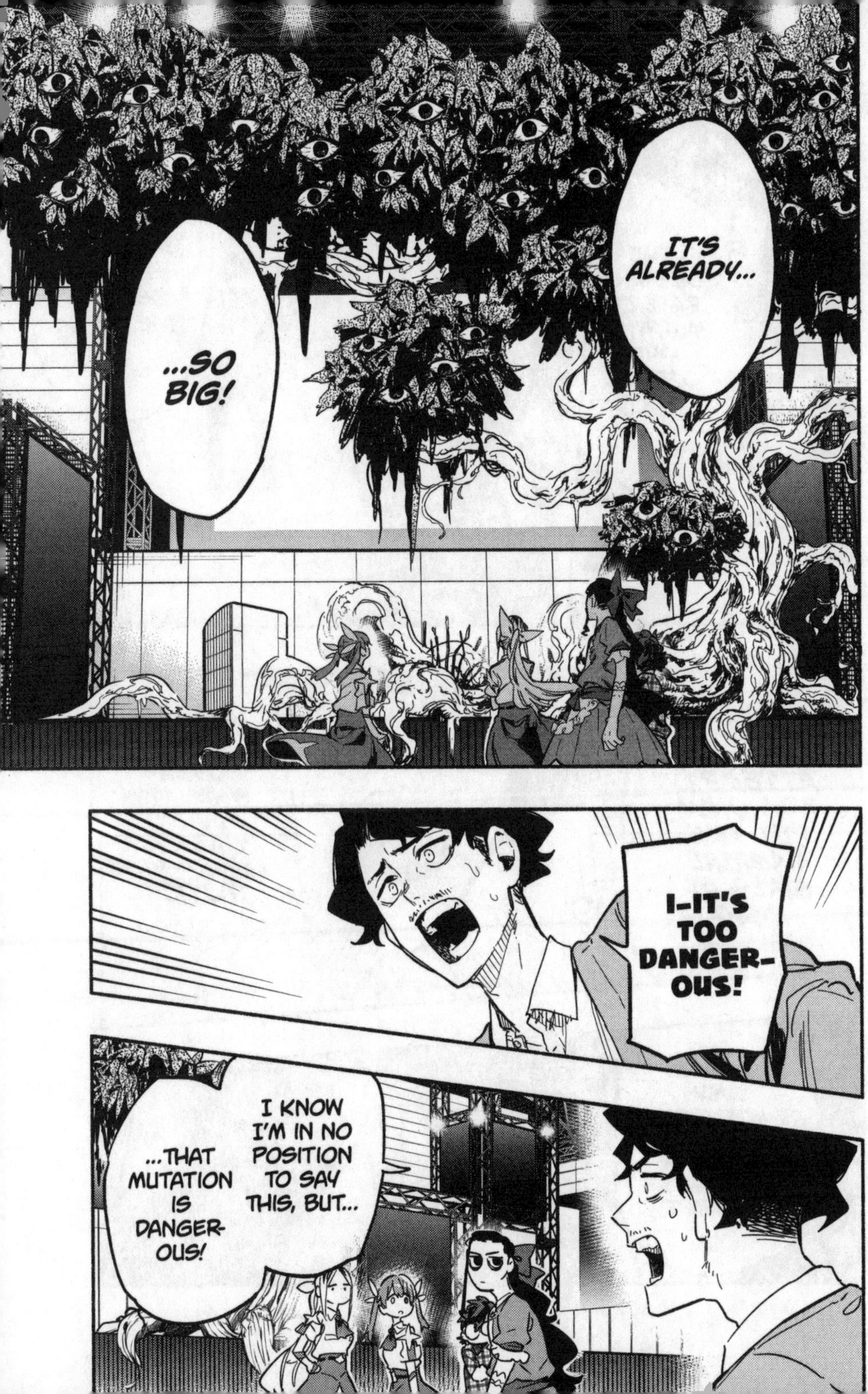
IT'S ALREADY...
...SO BIG!
I-IT'S TOO DANGER-OUS!
I KNOW I'M IN NO POSITION TO SAY THIS, BUT...
...THAT MUTATION IS DANGER-OUS!

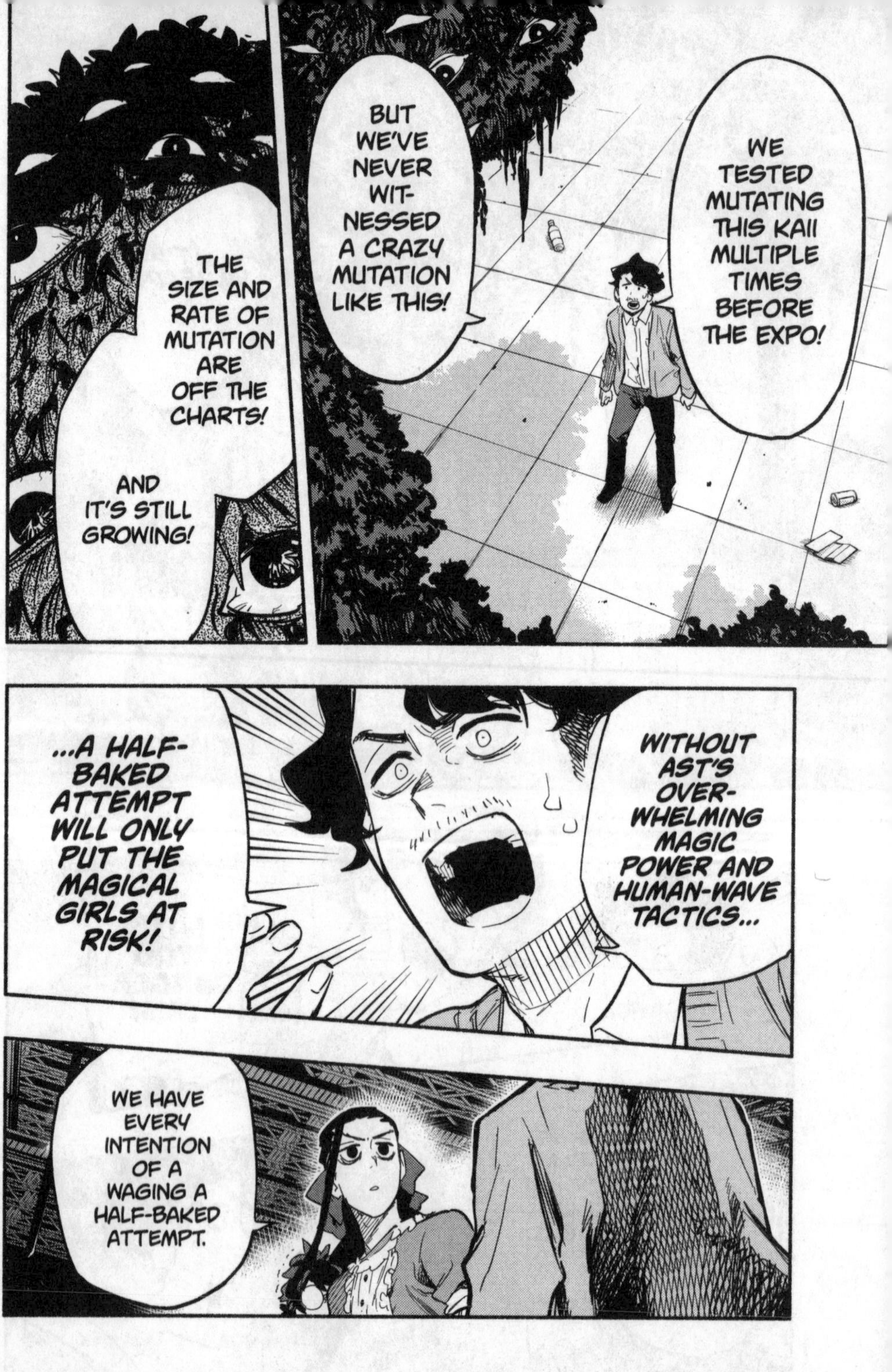
WE TESTED MUTATING THIS KAII MULTIPLE TIMES BEFORE THE EXPO!
BUT WE'VE NEVER WIT-NESSED A CRAZY MUTATION LIKE THIS!
THE SIZE AND RATE OF MUTATION ARE OFF THE CHARTS!
AND IT'S STILL GROWING!
WITHOUT AST'S OVER-WHELMING MAGIC POWER AND HUMAN-WAVE TACTICS...
...A HALF-BAKED ATTEMPT WILL ONLY PUT THE MAGICAL GIRLS AT RISK!
WE HAVE EVERY INTENTION OF A WAGING A HALF-BAKED ATTEMPT.

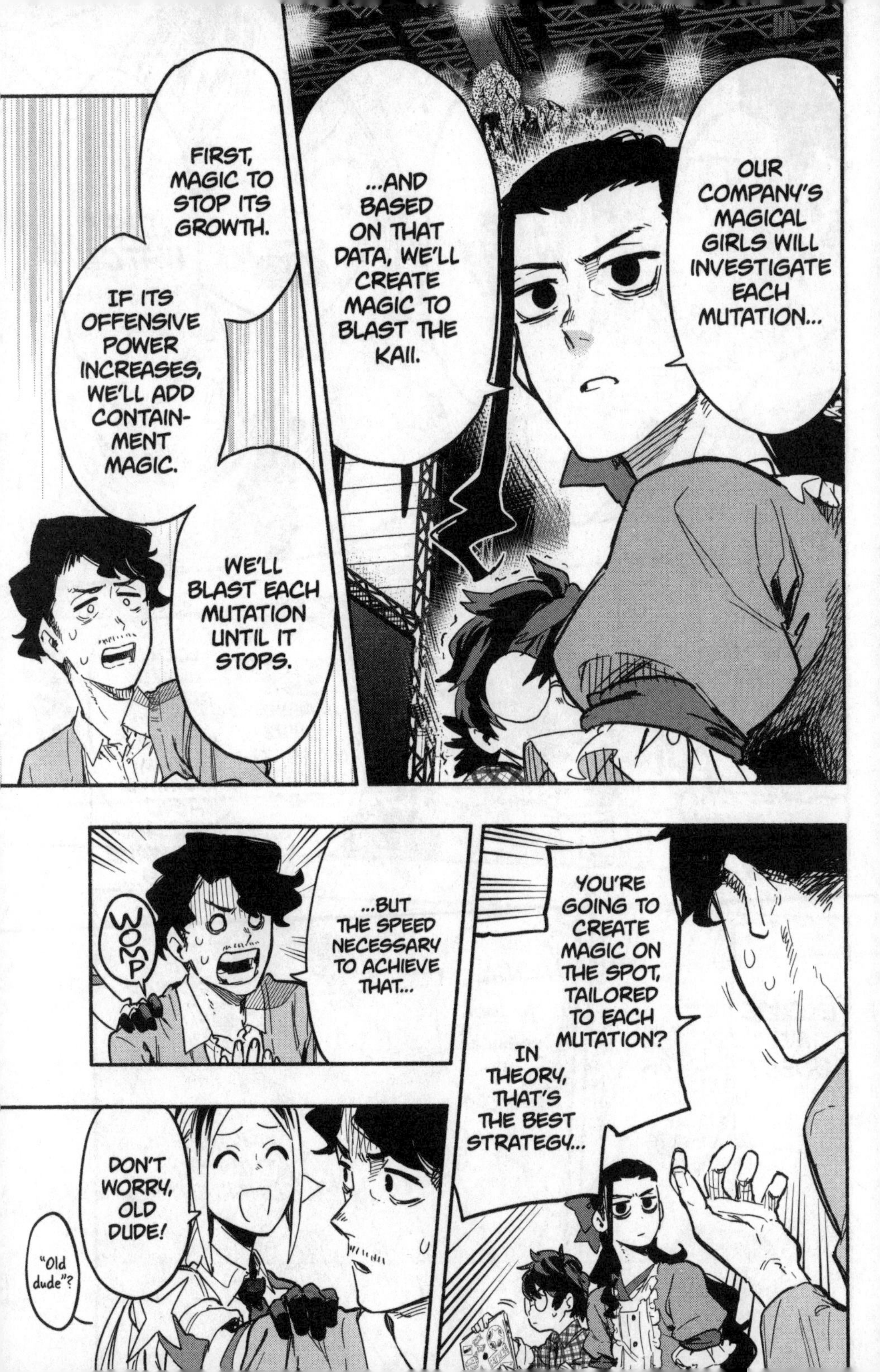
OUR COMPANY'S MAGICAL GIRLS WILL INVESTIGATE EACH MUTATION...
...AND BASED ON THAT DATA, WE'LL CREATE MAGIC TO BLAST THE KAII.
FIRST, MAGIC TO STOP ITS GROWTH.
IF ITS OFFENSIVE POWER INCREASES, WE'LL ADD CONTAIN-MENT MAGIC.
WE'LL BLAST EACH MUTATION UNTIL IT STOPS.
YOU'RE GOING TO CREATE MAGIC ON THE SPOT, TAILORED TO EACH MUTATION?
WOMP
...BUT THE SPEED NECESSARY TO ACHIEVE THAT...
IN THEORY, THAT'S THE BEST STRATEGY...
DON'T WORRY, OLD DUDE!
"Old dude"?

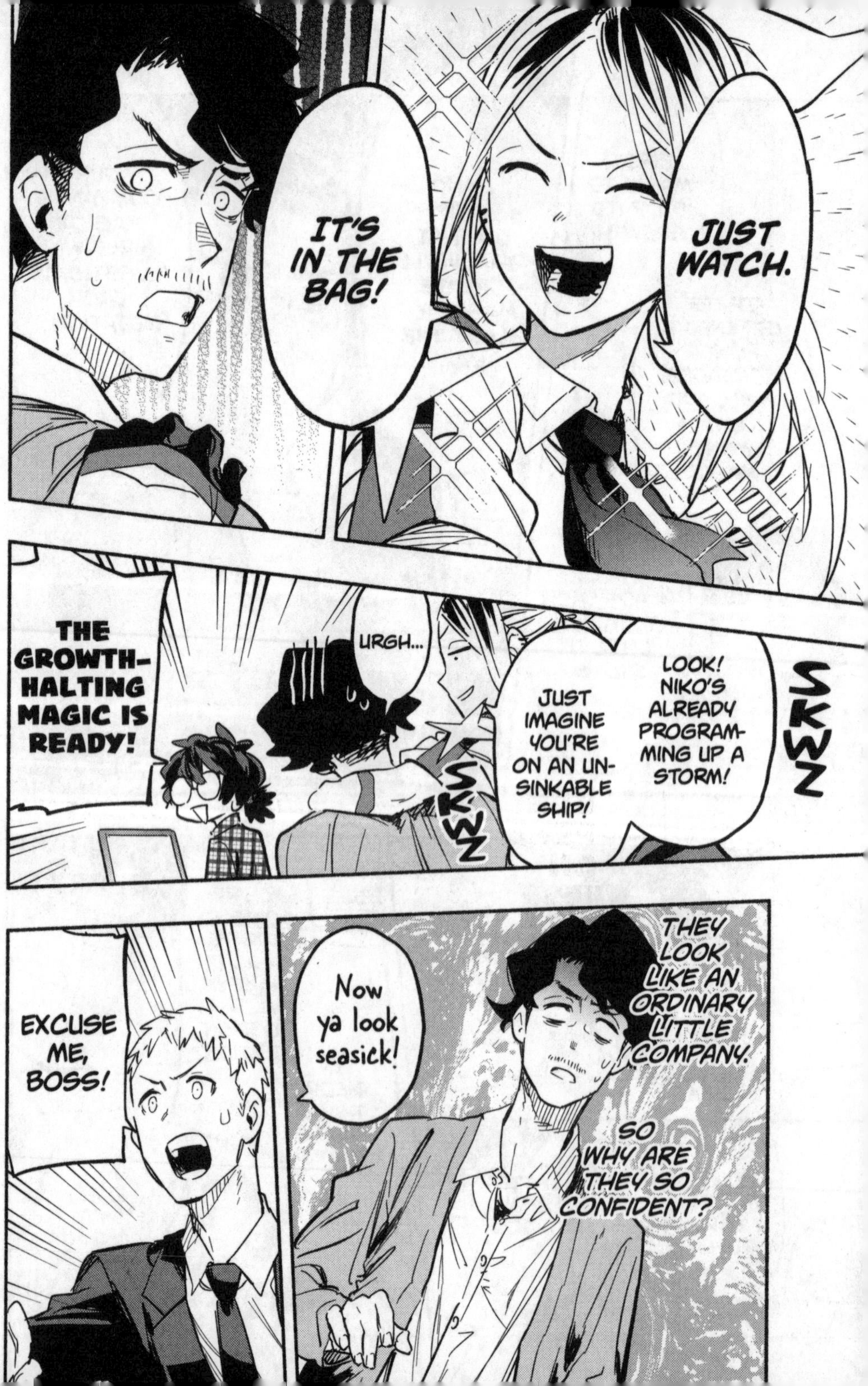
JUST WATCH.
IT'S IN THE BAG!
SKWZ
LOOK! NIKO'S ALREADY PROGRAMMING UP A STORM!
JUST IMAGINE YOU'RE ON AN UNSINKABLE SHIP!
SKWZ
URGH...
THE GROWTH-HALTING MAGIC IS READY!
THEY LOOK LIKE AN ORDINARY LITTLE COMPANY.
SO WHY ARE THEY SO CONFIDENT?
Now ya look seasick!
EXCUSE ME, BOSS!

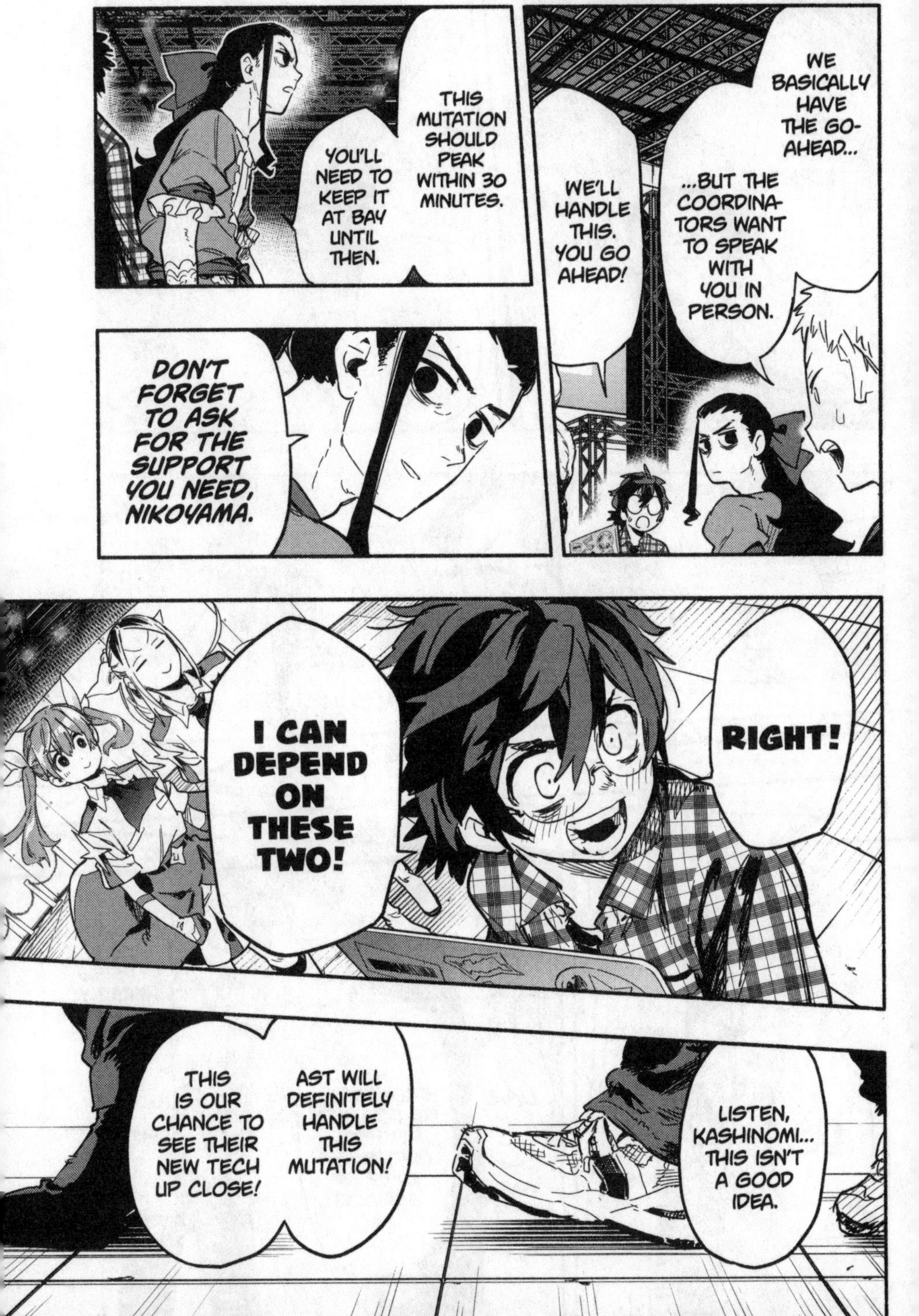
WE BASICALLY HAVE THE GO-AHEAD...
...BUT THE COORDINATORS WANT TO SPEAK WITH YOU IN PERSON.
WE'LL HANDLE THIS. YOU GO AHEAD!
THIS MUTATION SHOULD PEAK WITHIN 30 MINUTES.
YOU'LL NEED TO KEEP IT AT BAY UNTIL THEN.
DON'T FORGET TO ASK FOR THE SUPPORT YOU NEED, NIKOYAMA.
RIGHT!
I CAN DEPEND ON THESE TWO!
LISTEN, KASHINOMI... THIS ISN'T A GOOD IDEA.
AST WILL DEFINITELY HANDLE THIS MUTATION!
THIS IS OUR CHANCE TO SEE THEIR NEW TECH UP CLOSE!

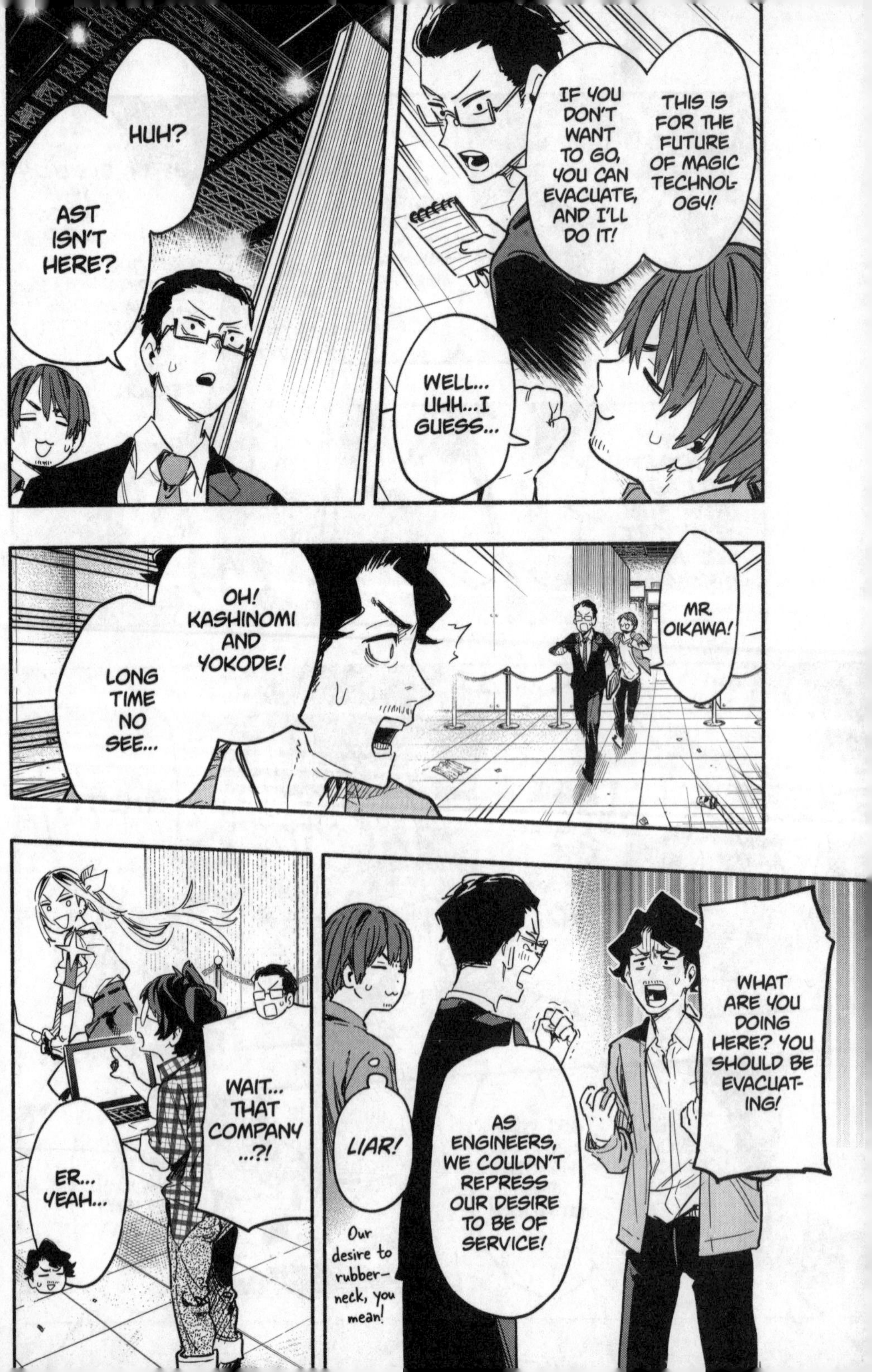
THIS IS FOR THE FUTURE OF MAGIC TECHNOLOGY!
IF YOU DON'T WANT TO GO, YOU CAN EVACUATE, AND I'LL DO IT!
WELL... UHH...I GUESS...
HUH?
AST ISN'T HERE?
MR. OIKAWA!
OH! KASHINOMI AND YOKODE!
LONG TIME NO SEE...
WHAT ARE YOU DOING HERE? YOU SHOULD BE EVACUATING!
AS ENGINEERS, WE COULDN'T REPRESS OUR DESIRE TO BE OF SERVICE!
LIAR!
Our desire to rubberneck, you mean!
WAIT... THAT COMPANY ...?!
ER... YEAH...

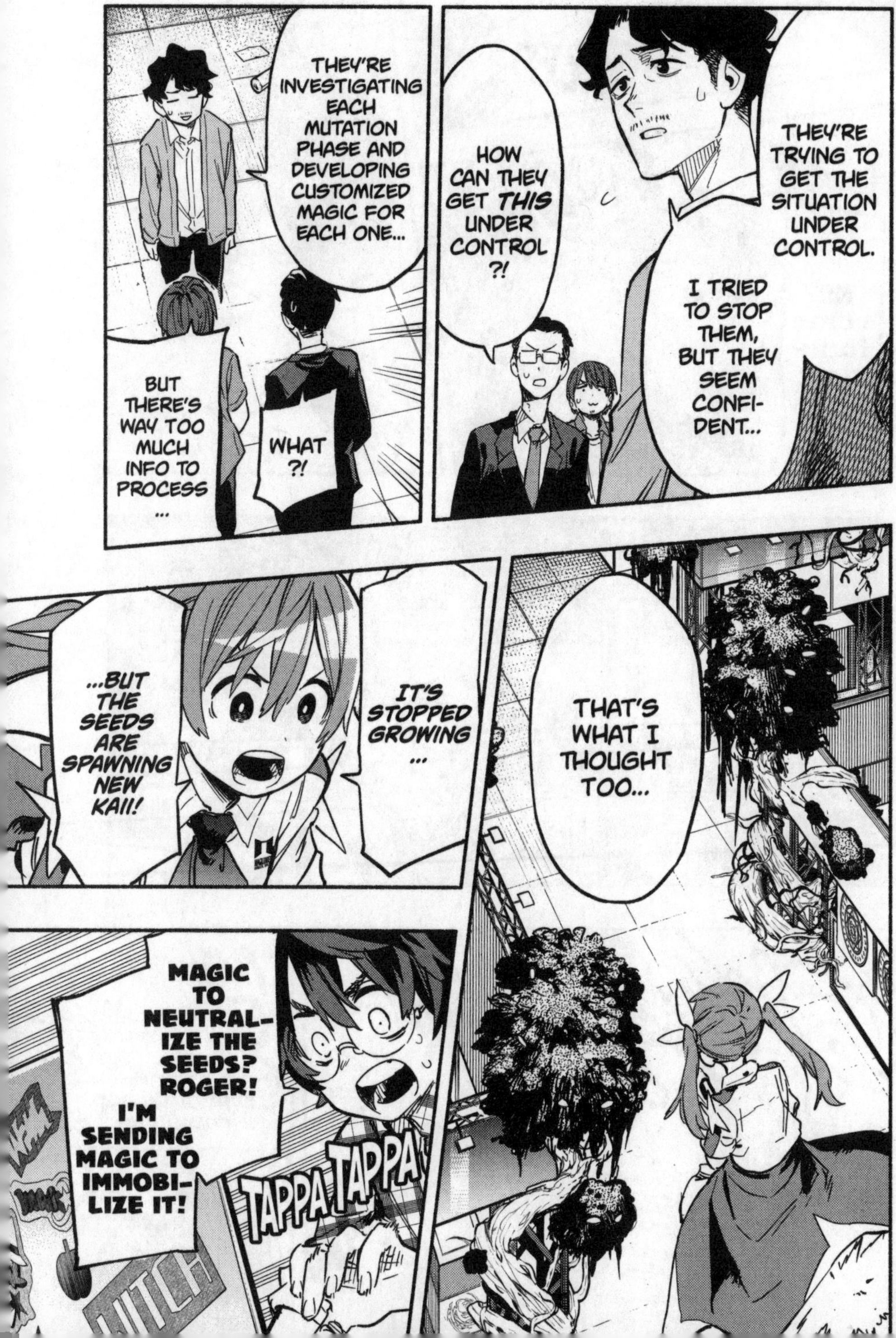
THEY'RE TRYING TO GET THE SITUATION UNDER CONTROL.
I TRIED TO STOP THEM, BUT THEY SEEM CONFIDENT...
HOW CAN THEY GET THIS UNDER CONTROL?!
THEY'RE INVESTIGATING EACH MUTATION PHASE AND DEVELOPING CUSTOMIZED MAGIC FOR EACH ONE...
WHAT?!
BUT THERE'S WAY TOO MUCH INFO TO PROCESS...
THAT'S WHAT I THOUGHT TOO...
IT'S STOPPED GROWING...
...BUT THE SEEDS ARE SPAWNING NEW KAII!
MAGIC TO NEUTRALIZE THE SEEDS? ROGER!
I'M SENDING MAGIC TO IMMOBILIZE IT!
TAPPA TAPPA

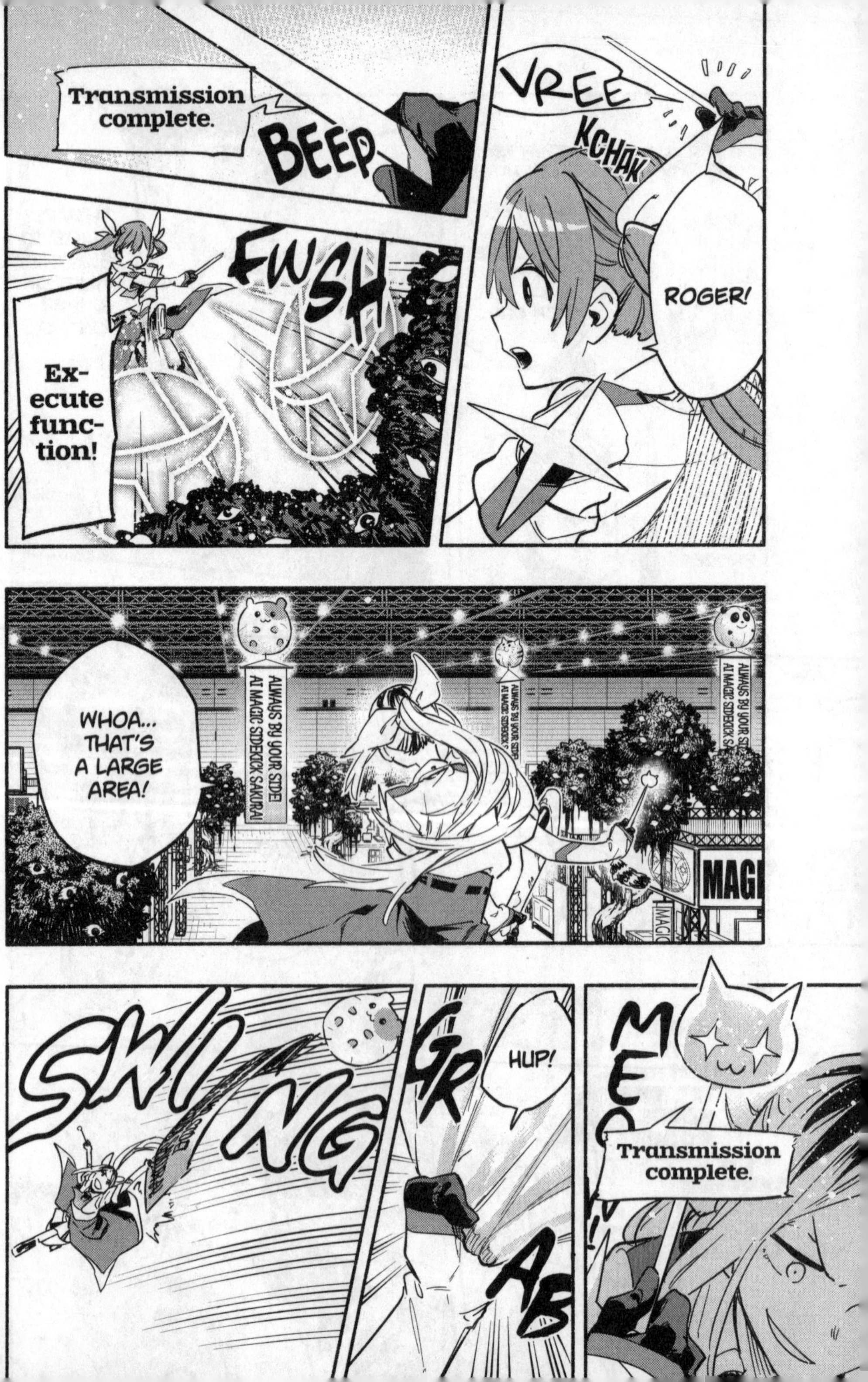
VREE
KCHAK
ROGER!
Transmission complete.
BEEP
FWSH
Ex-ecute func-tion!
WHOA... THAT'S A LARGE AREA!
ALWAYS BY YOUR SIDE! AI MAGIC SIDEKICK SAKURA!
ALWAYS BY YOUR SIDE! AI MAGIC SIDEKICK SAKURA!
ALWAYS BY YOUR SIDE! AI MAGIC SIDEKICK
MAGI
Transmission complete.
HUP!
GR
AB
SWING

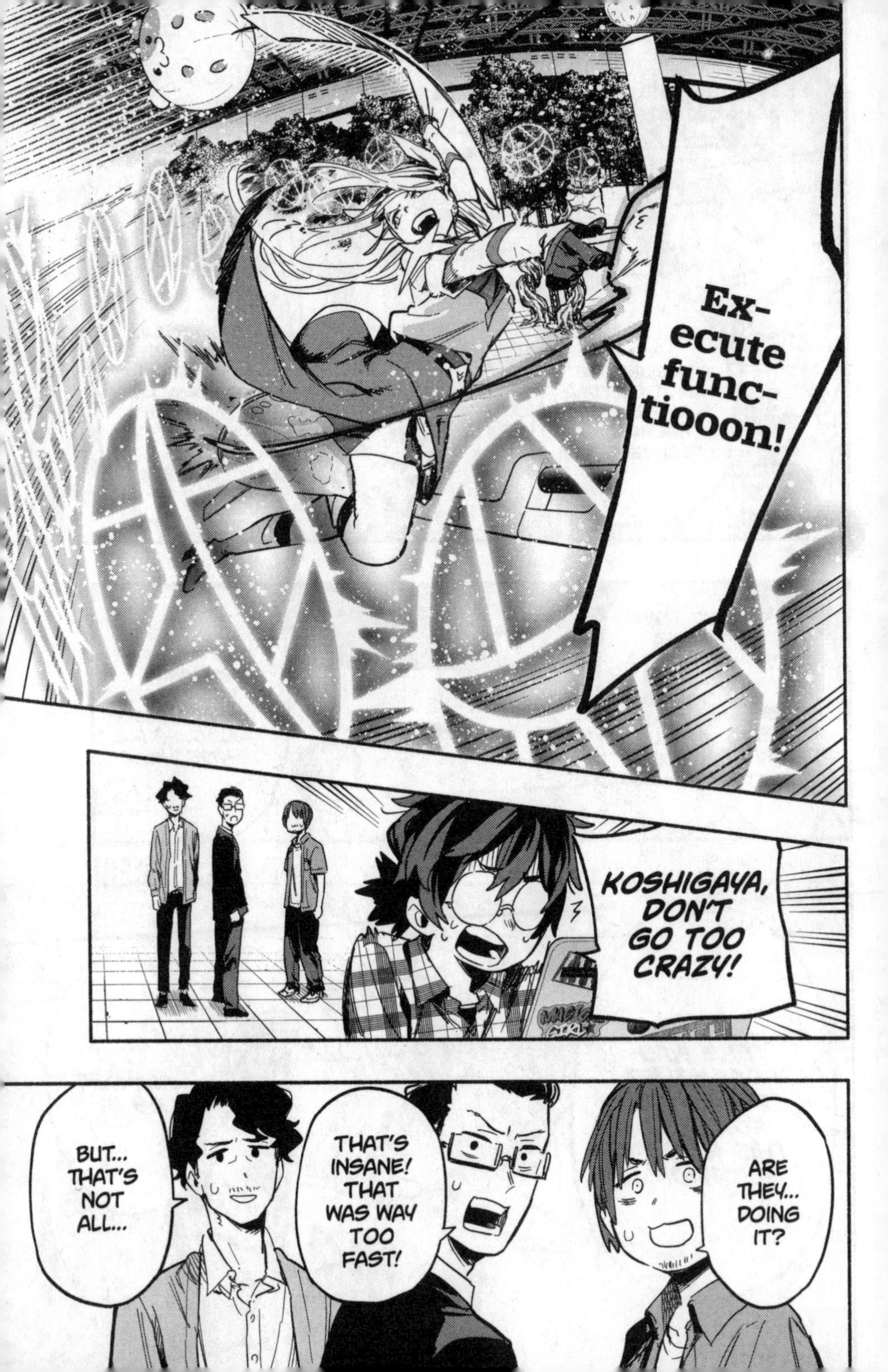
Ex-ecute func-tiooon!
KOSHIGAYA, DON'T GO TOO CRAZY!
ARE THEY... DOING IT?
THAT'S INSANE! THAT WAS WAY TOO FAST!
BUT... THAT'S NOT ALL...

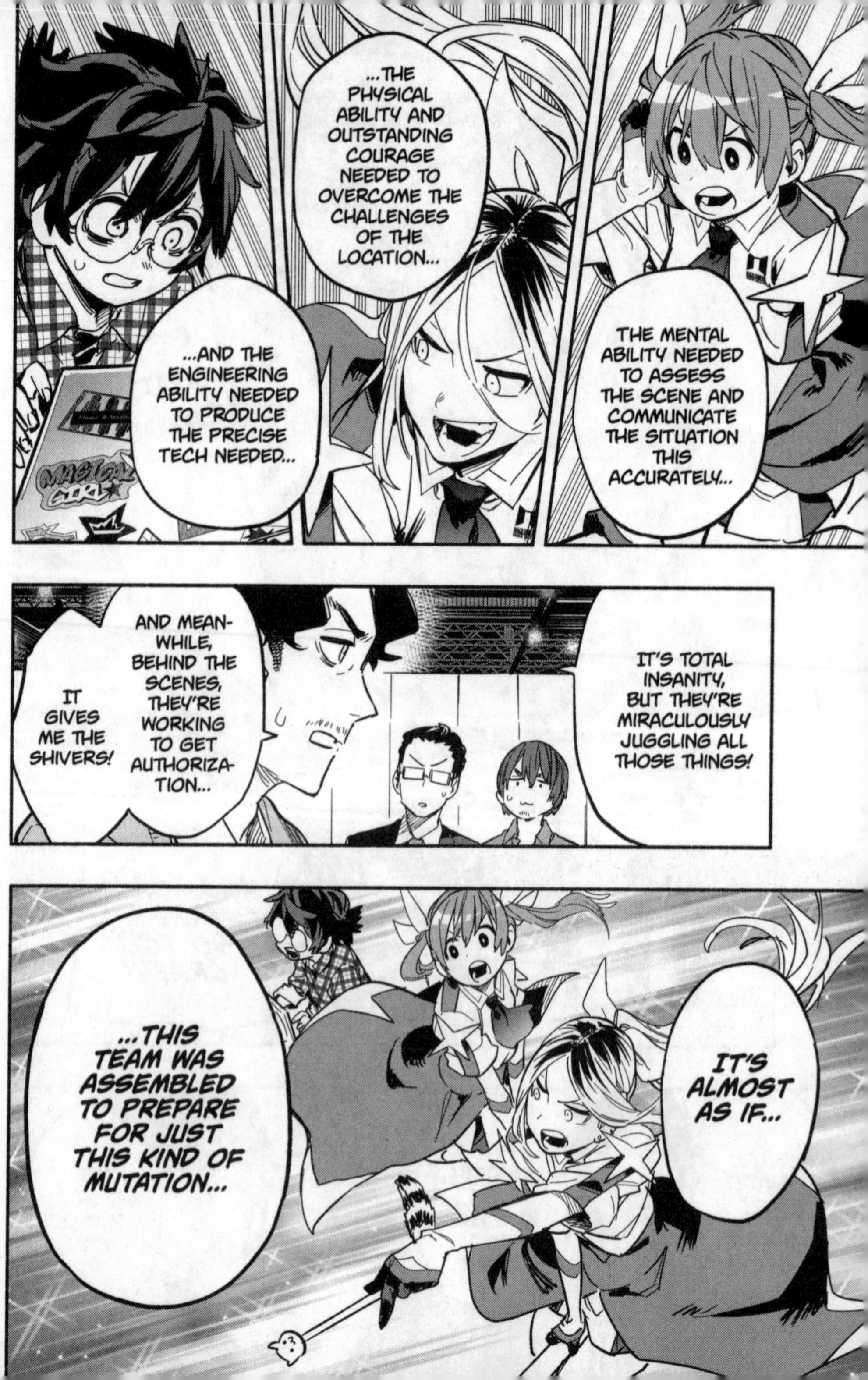
THE MENTAL ABILITY NEEDED TO ASSESS THE SCENE AND COMMUNICATE THE SITUATION THIS ACCURATELY...
...THE PHYSICAL ABILITY AND OUTSTANDING COURAGE NEEDED TO OVERCOME THE CHALLENGES OF THE LOCATION...
...AND THE ENGINEERING ABILITY NEEDED TO PRODUCE THE PRECISE TECH NEEDED...
IT'S TOTAL INSANITY, BUT THEY'RE MIRACULOUSLY JUGGLING ALL THOSE THINGS!
AND MEAN-WHILE, BEHIND THE SCENES, THEY'RE WORKING TO GET AUTHORIZA-TION...
IT GIVES ME THE SHIVERS!
IT'S ALMOST AS IF...
...THIS TEAM WAS ASSEMBLED TO PREPARE FOR JUST THIS KIND OF MUTATION...

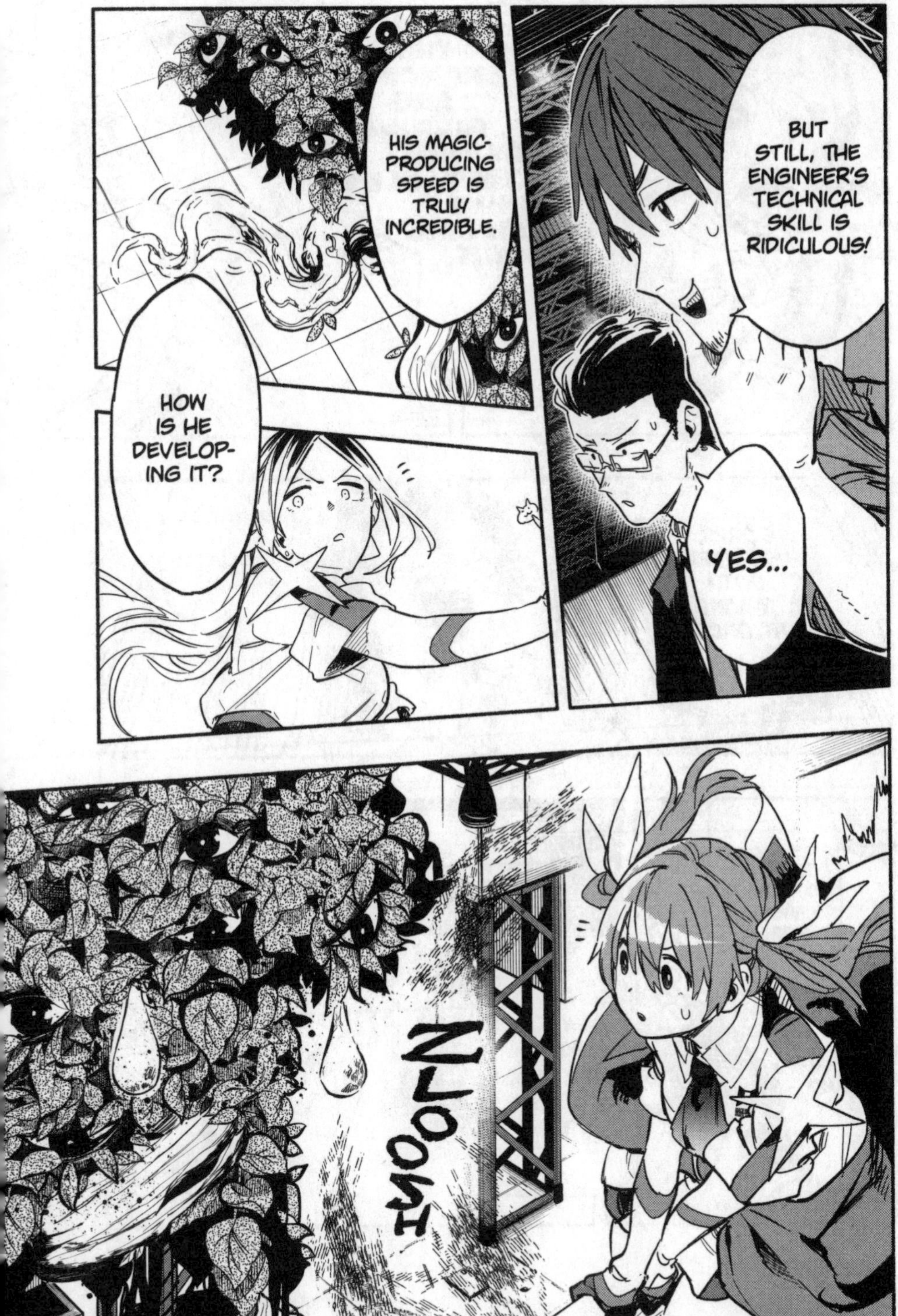
BUT STILL, THE ENGINEER'S TECHNICAL SKILL IS RIDICULOUS!
YES...
HIS MAGIC-PRODUCING SPEED IS TRULY INCREDIBLE.
HOW IS HE DEVELOPING IT?
ZLOOSH

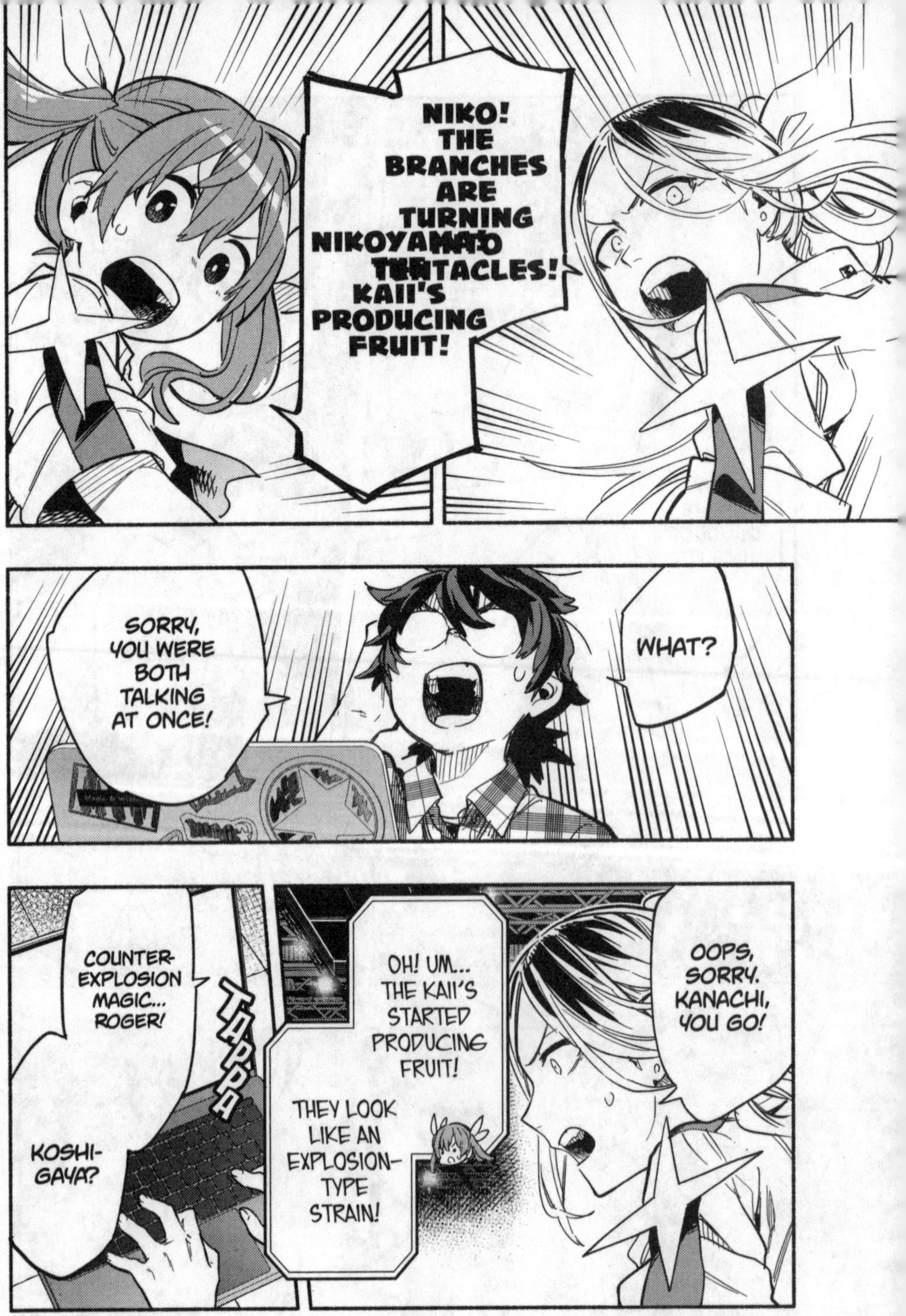
NIKO! THE BRANCHES ARE TURNING INTO TENTACLES!
NIKOYAMA! KAII'S PRODUCING FRUIT!
WHAT?
SORRY, YOU WERE BOTH TALKING AT ONCE!
OOPS, SORRY. KANACHI, YOU GO!
OH! UM... THE KAII'S STARTED PRODUCING FRUIT!
THEY LOOK LIKE AN EXPLOSION-TYPE STRAIN!
COUNTER-EXPLOSION MAGIC... ROGER!
TAPPA
KOSHI-GAYA?

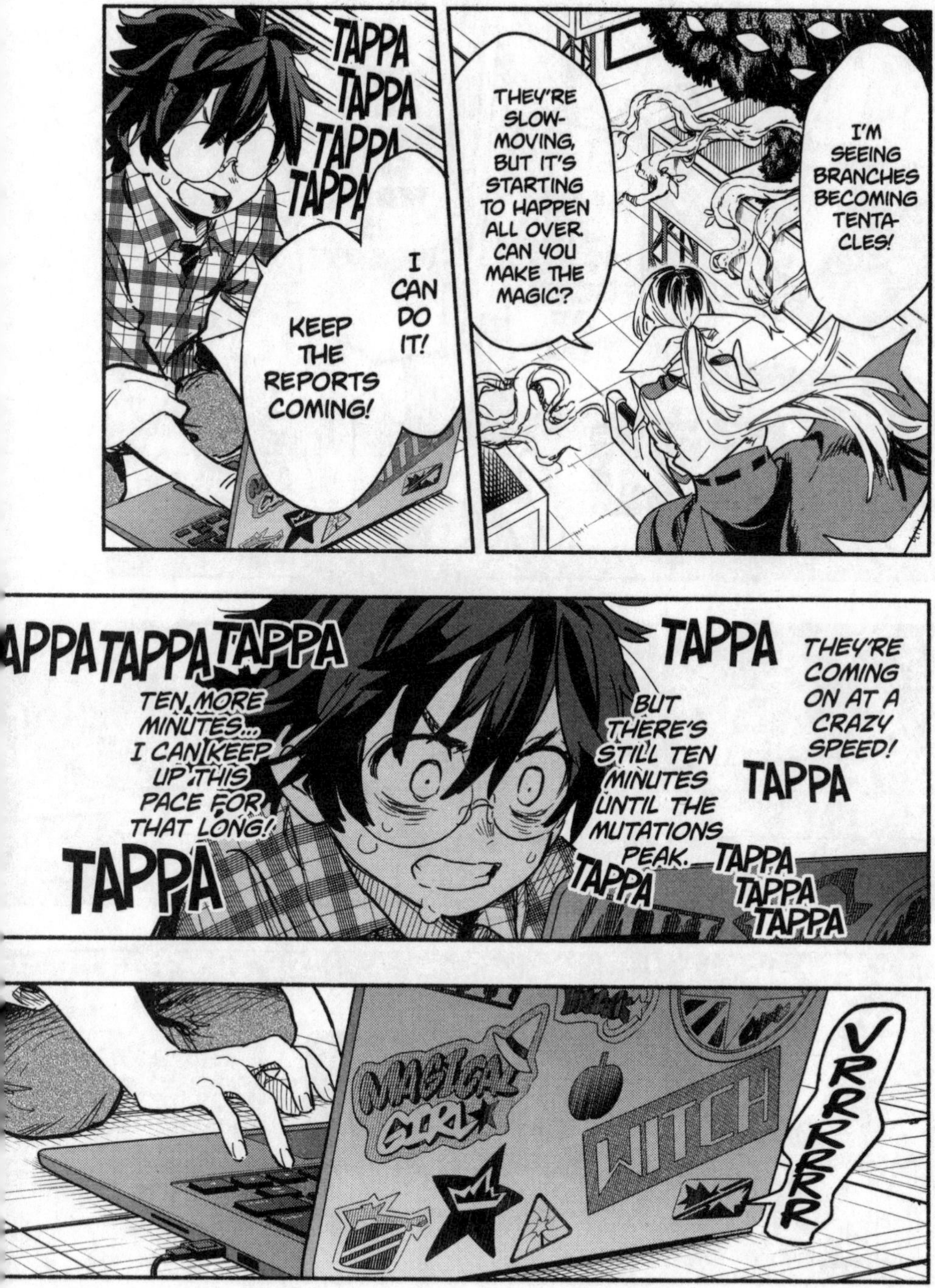
I'M SEEING BRANCHES BECOMING TENTACLES!
THEY'RE SLOW-MOVING, BUT IT'S STARTING TO HAPPEN ALL OVER. CAN YOU MAKE THE MAGIC?
TAPPA TAPPA TAPPA TAPPA
I CAN DO IT!
KEEP THE REPORTS COMING!
THEY'RE COMING ON AT A CRAZY SPEED!
TAPPA
TAPPA
BUT THERE'S STILL TEN MINUTES UNTIL THE MUTATIONS PEAK.
TAPPA TAPPA TAPPA
TAPPA
TAPPA TAPPA TAPPA
TEN MORE MINUTES... I CAN KEEP UP THIS PACE FOR THAT LONG!
TAPPA
VRRRRRR
WITCH
MAGICAL GIRL

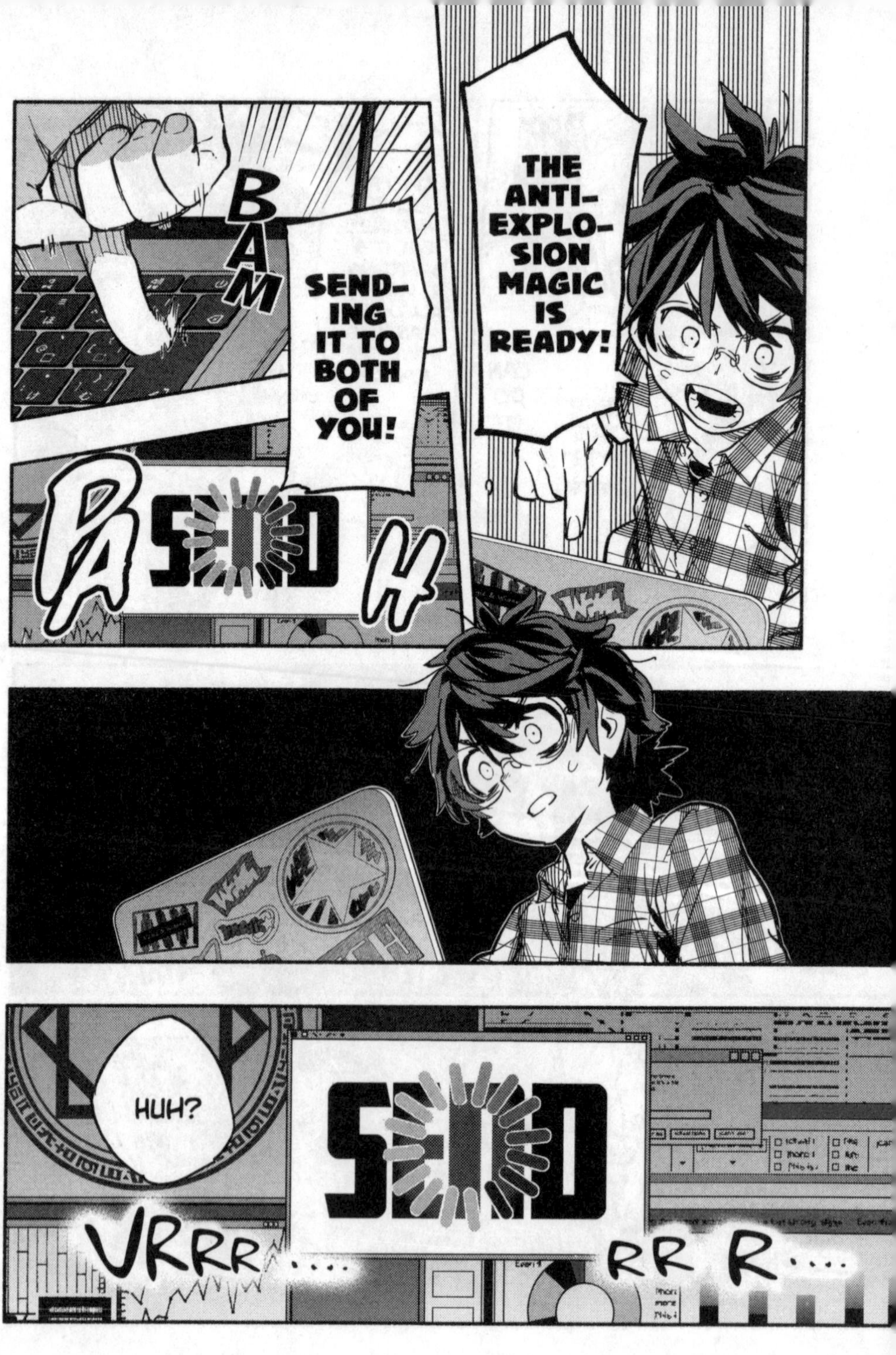
THE ANTI-EXPLOSION MAGIC IS READY!
BAM
SENDING IT TO BOTH OF YOU!
PASH
SEND
HUH?
SEND
VRRR.... RR R....

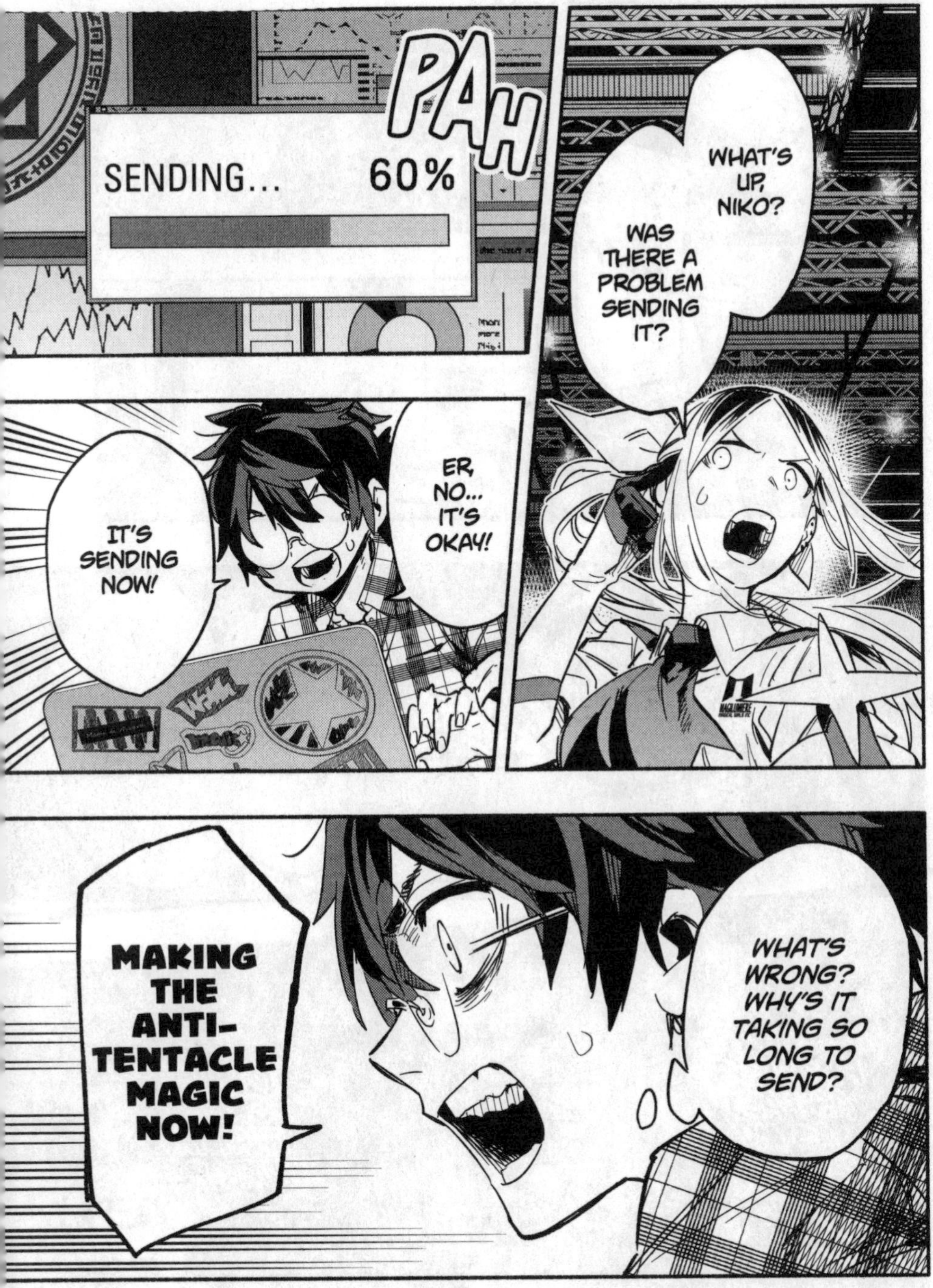
WHAT'S UP, NIKO?
WAS THERE A PROBLEM SENDING IT?
SENDING... 60%
PAH
ER, NO... IT'S OKAY!
IT'S SENDING NOW!
WHAT'S WRONG? WHY'S IT TAKING SO LONG TO SEND?
MAKING THE ANTI-TENTACLE MAGIC NOW!

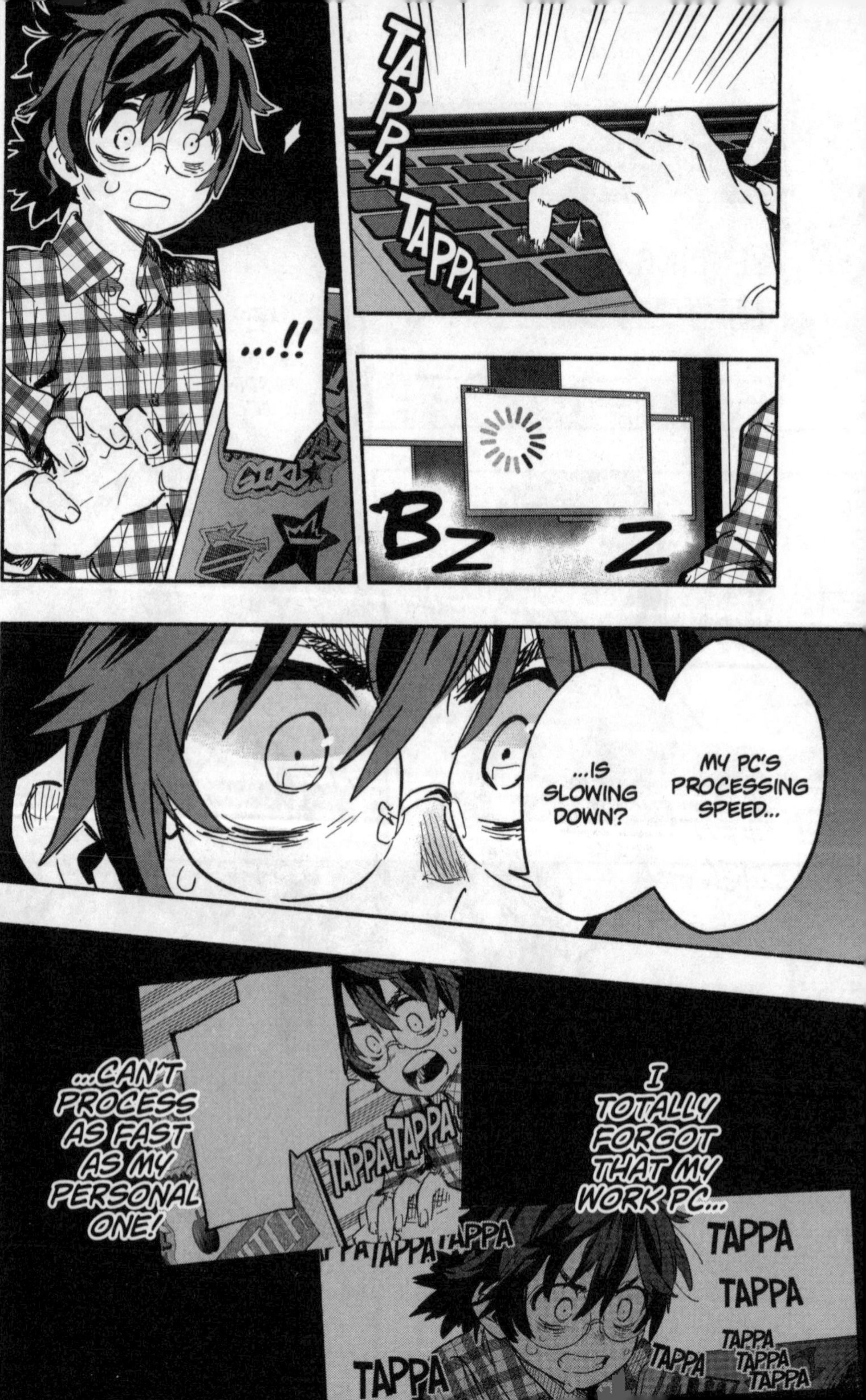
TAPPA
TAPPA
TAPPA
BZZ
...!!
MY PC'S PROCESSING SPEED...
...IS SLOWING DOWN?
I TOTALLY FORGOT THAT MY WORK PC...
TAPPA
TAPPA
TAPPA TAPPA TAPPA
TAPPA
TAPPA
...CAN'T PROCESS AS FAST AS MY PERSONAL ONE!
TAPPA TAPPA
TAPPA TAPPA TAPPA

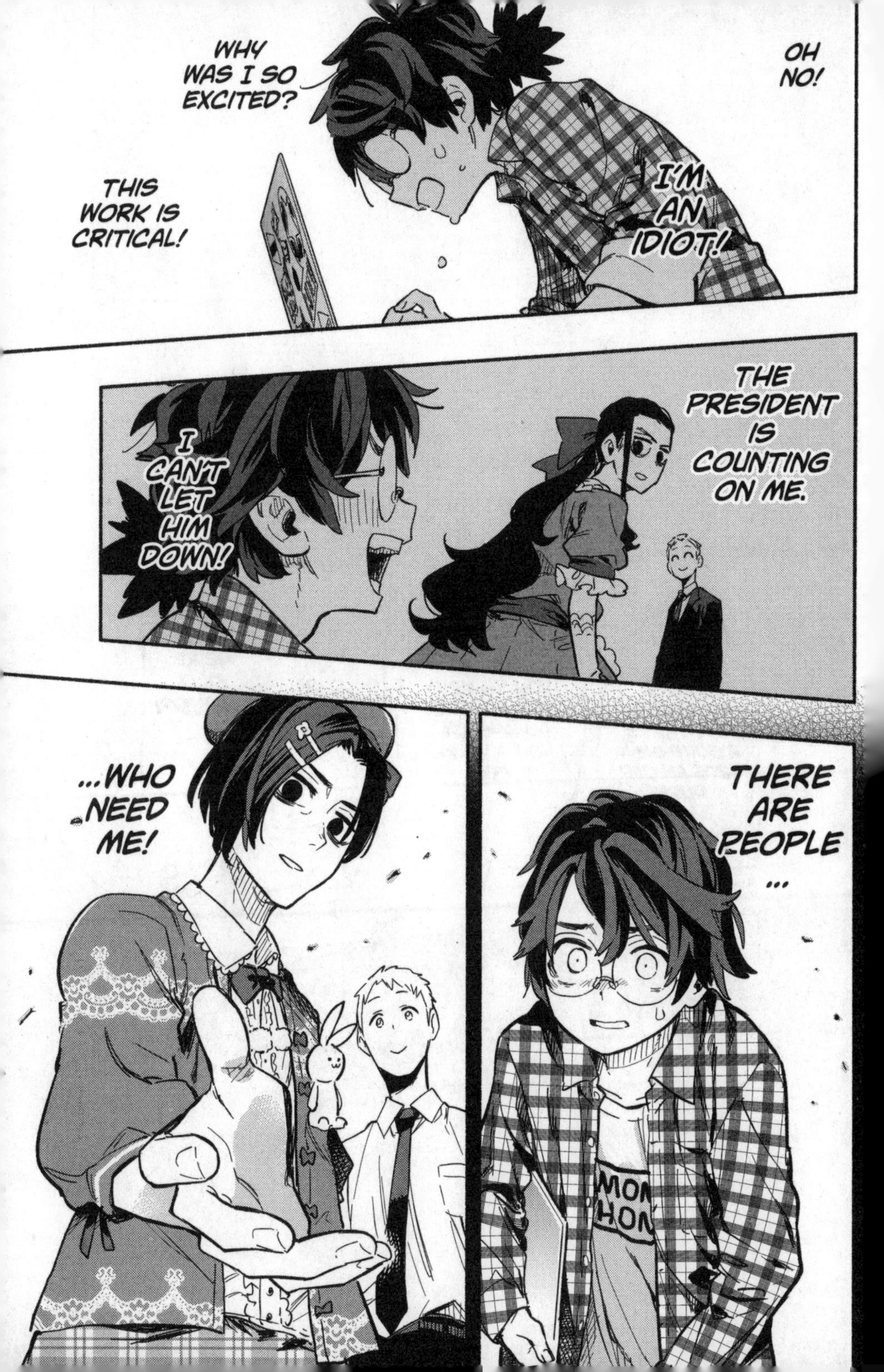
OH NO!
I'M AN IDIOT!
WHY WAS I SO EXCITED?
THIS WORK IS CRITICAL!
THE PRESIDENT IS COUNTING ON ME.
I CAN'T LET HIM DOWN!
THERE ARE PEOPLE ...
...WHO NEED ME!

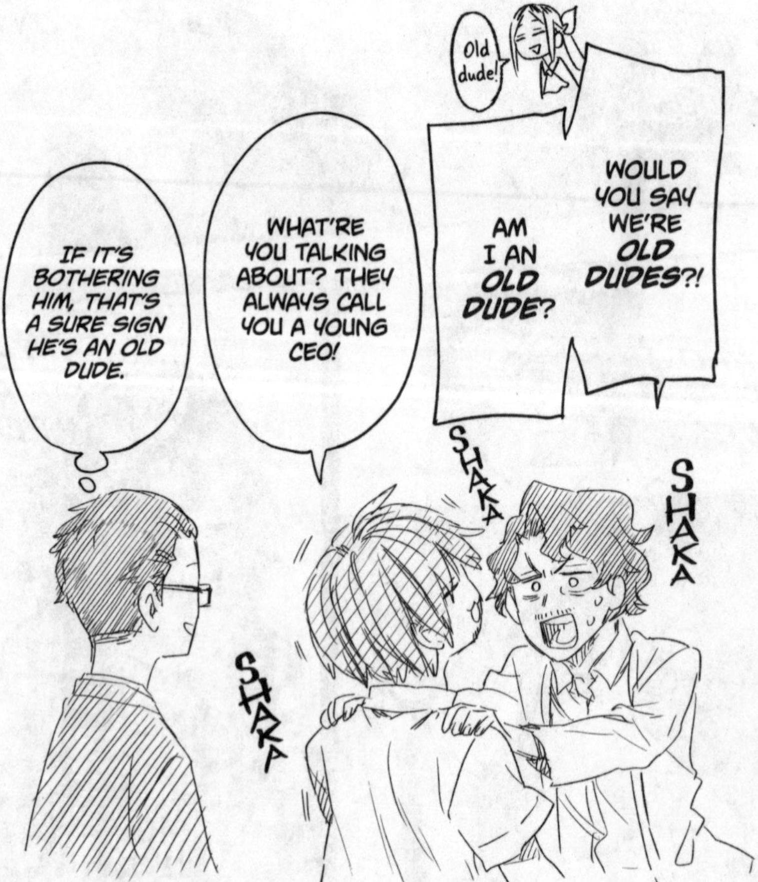

WOULD YOU SAY WE'RE OLD DUDES?!
AM I AN OLD DUDE?
Old dude!
SHAKA
SHAKA
WHAT'RE YOU TALKING ABOUT? THEY ALWAYS CALL YOU A YOUNG CEO!
SHAKA
IF IT'S BOTHERING HIM, THAT'S A SURE SIGN HE'S AN OLD DUDE.

Chapter 20: Friends

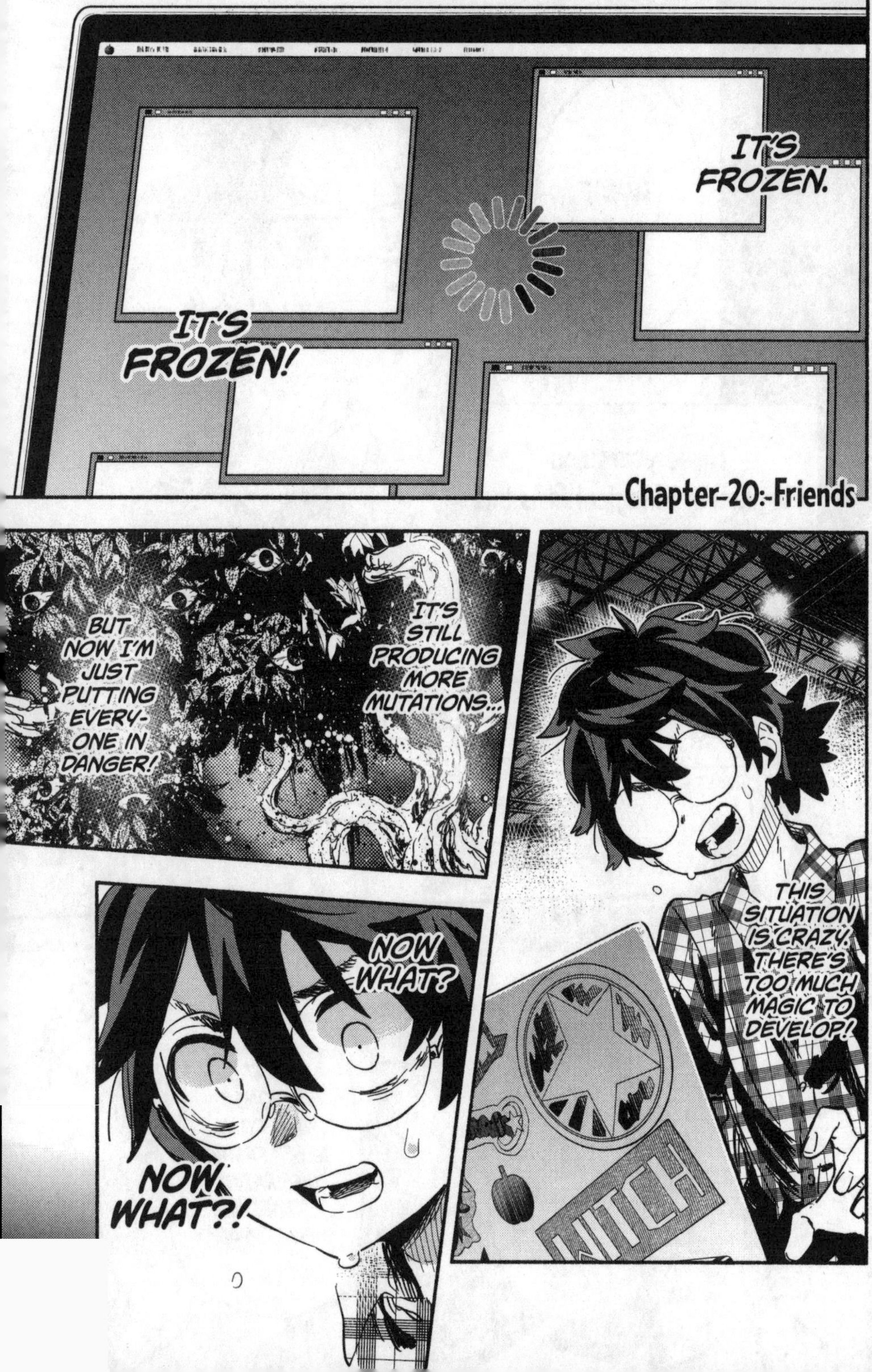
IT'S FROZEN.
IT'S FROZEN!
THIS SITUATION IS CRAZY. THERE'S TOO MUCH MAGIC TO DEVELOP!
IT'S STILL PRODUCING MORE MUTATIONS...
BUT NOW I'M JUST PUTTING EVERY-ONE IN DANGER!
NOW WHAT?
NOW WHAT?!
WITCH

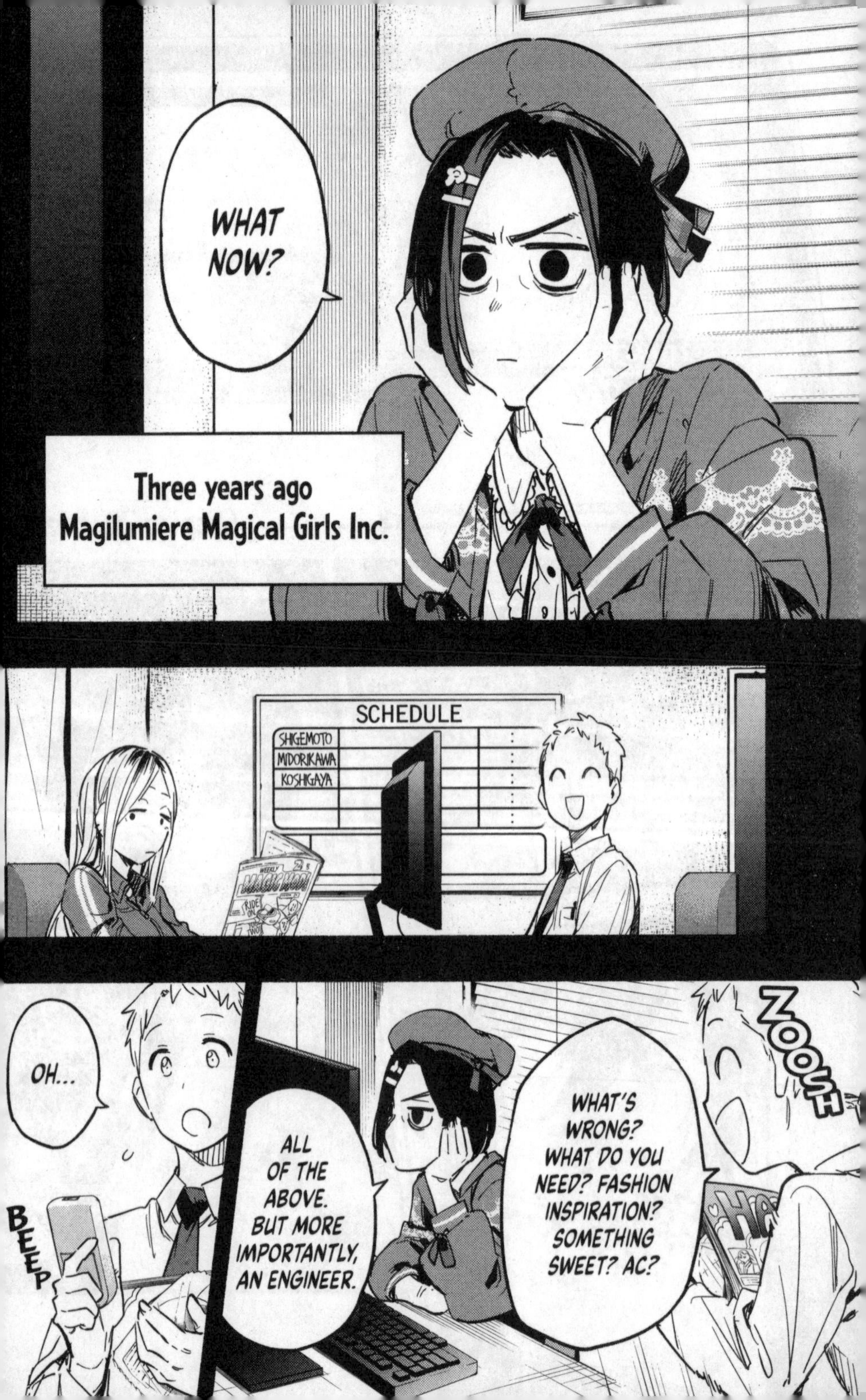
WHAT NOW?
Three years ago Magilumiere Magical Girls Inc.
SCHEDULE
SHIGEMOTO
MIDORIKAWA
KOSHIGAYA
ZOOOSH
WHAT'S WRONG? WHAT DO YOU NEED? FASHION INSPIRATION? SOMETHING SWEET? AC?
ALL OF THE ABOVE. BUT MORE IMPORTANTLY, AN ENGINEER.
OH...
BEEP

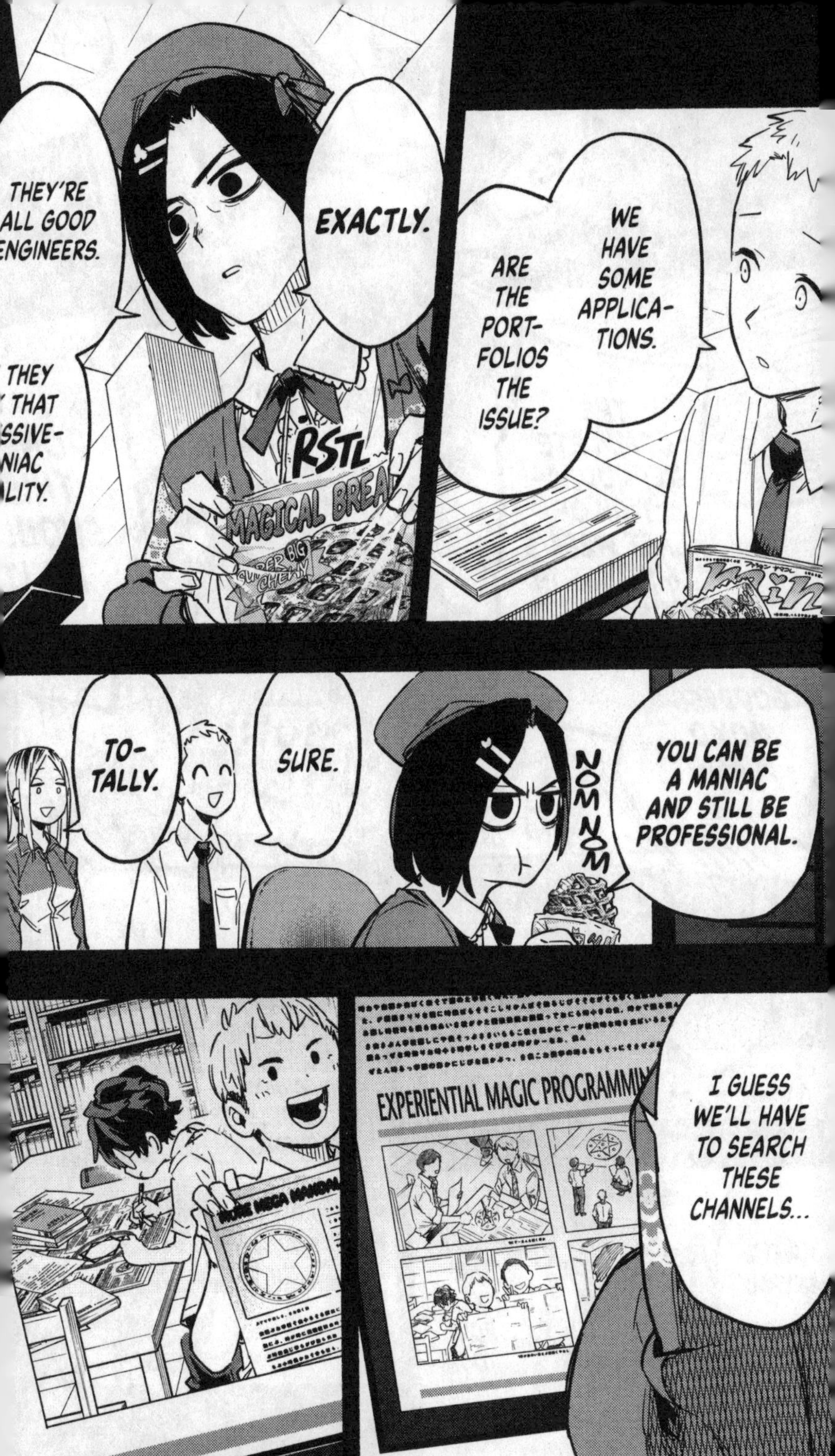
ARE THE PORT-FOLIOS THE ISSUE?
WE HAVE SOME APPLICA-TIONS.
EXACTLY.
THEY'RE ALL GOOD ENGINEERS.
THEY THAT SSIVE- NIAC LITY.
RSTL
MAGICAL BREA
YOU CAN BE A MANIAC AND STILL BE PROFESSIONAL.
NOM NOM
SURE.
TO-TALLY.
I GUESS WE'LL HAVE TO SEARCH THESE CHANNELS...
EXPERIENTIAL MAGIC PROGRAMMIN

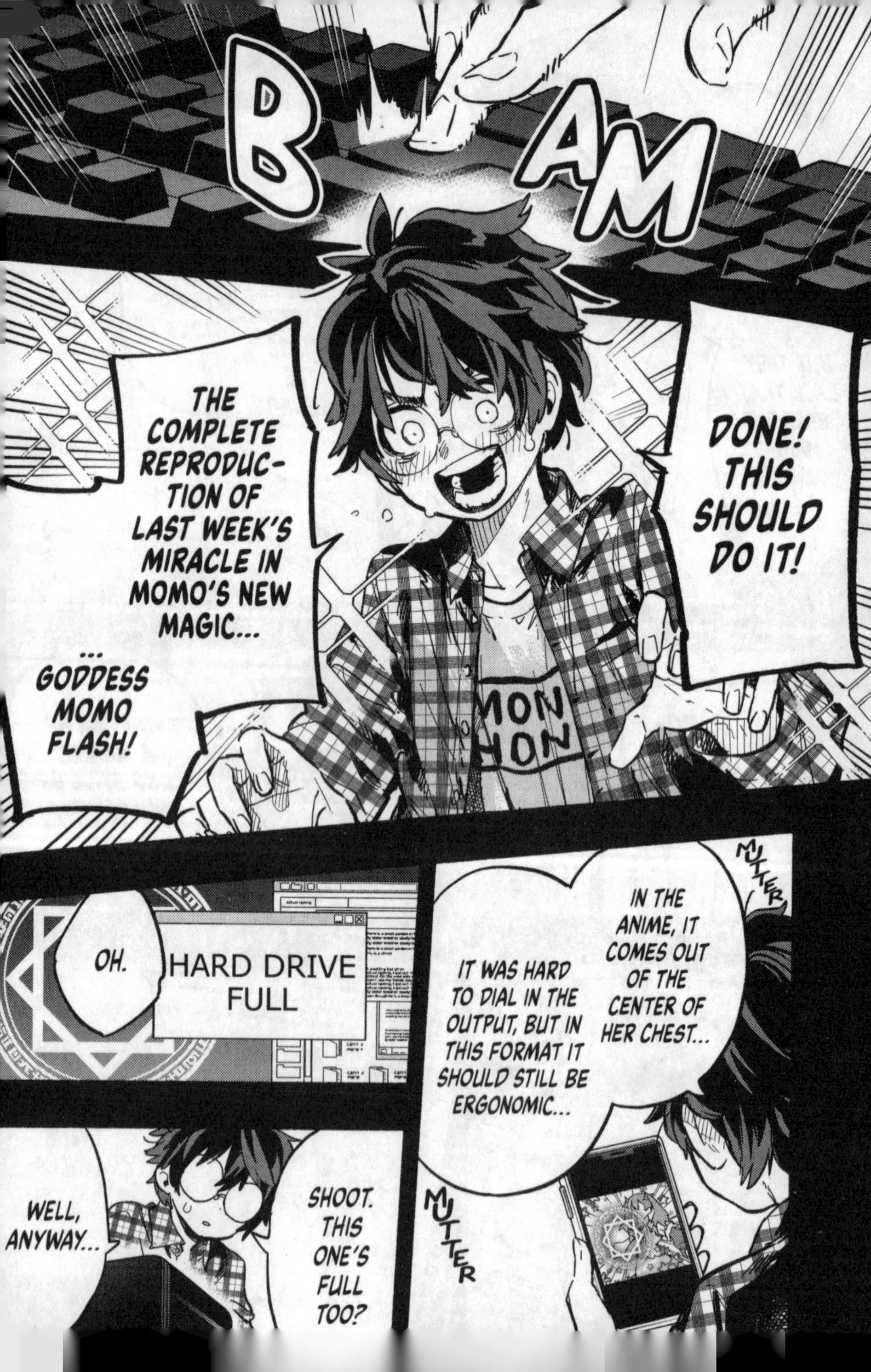
BAM
DONE! THIS SHOULD DO IT!
THE COMPLETE REPRODUCTION OF LAST WEEK'S MIRACLE IN MOMO'S NEW MAGIC...
...GODDESS MOMO FLASH!
MUTTER
IN THE ANIME, IT COMES OUT OF THE CENTER OF HER CHEST...
IT WAS HARD TO DIAL IN THE OUTPUT, BUT IN THIS FORMAT IT SHOULD STILL BE ERGONOMIC...
MUTTER
OH.
HARD DRIVE FULL
SHOOT. THIS ONE'S FULL TOO?
WELL, ANYWAY...

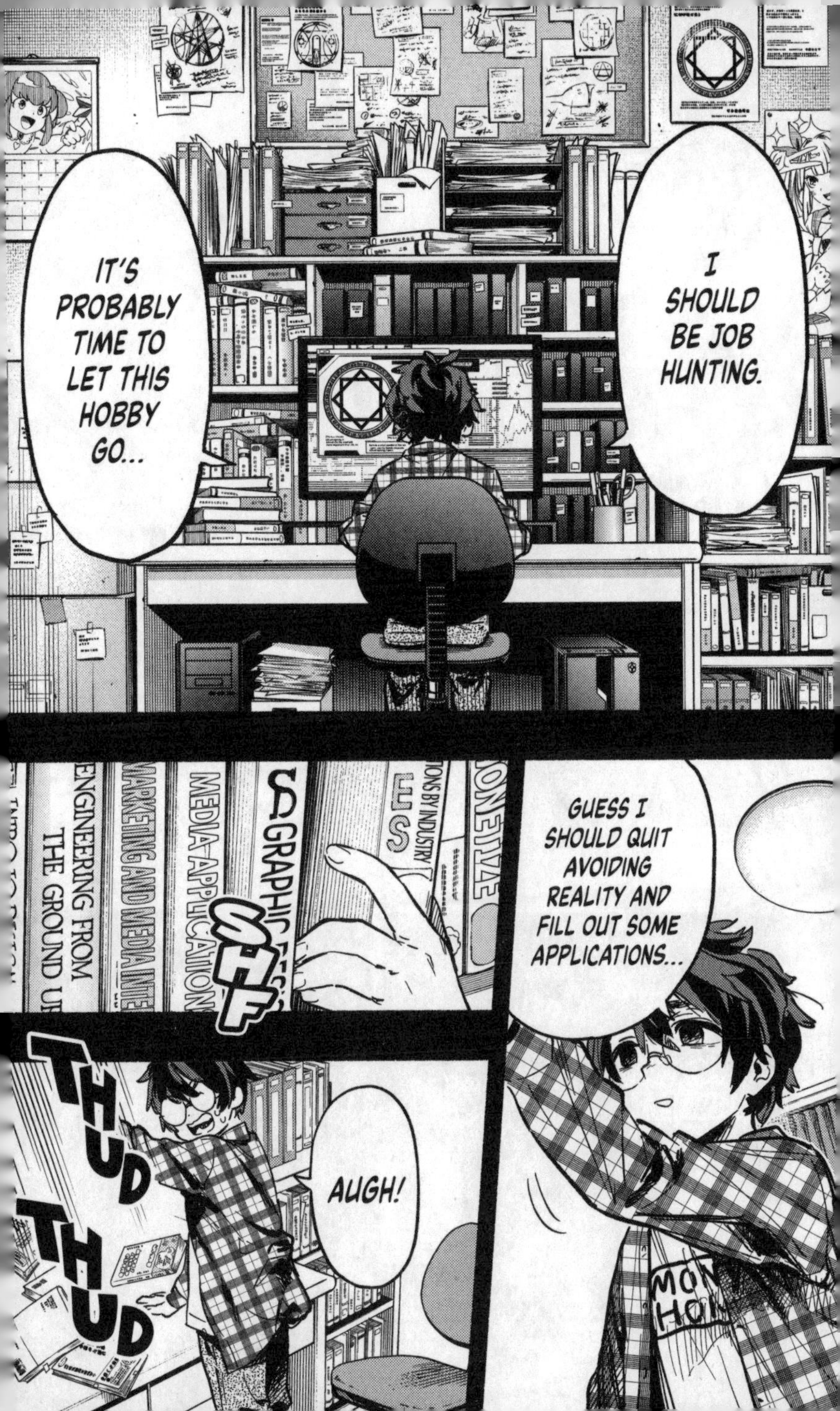
I SHOULD BE JOB HUNTING.
IT'S PROBABLY TIME TO LET THIS HOBBY GO...
GUESS I SHOULD QUIT AVOIDING REALITY AND FILL OUT SOME APPLICATIONS...
SHF
THUD
THUD
THUD
AUGH!

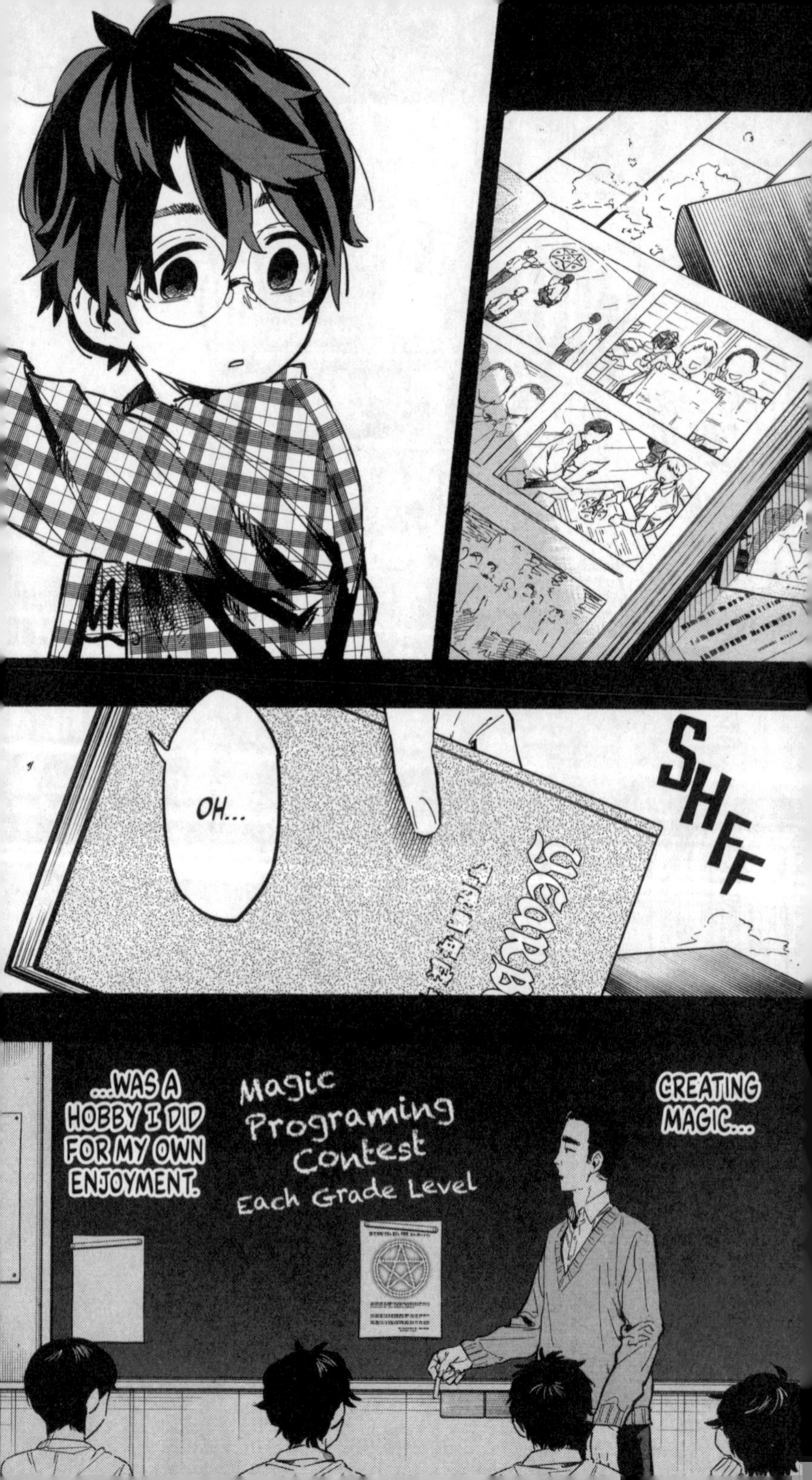
SHFF
OH...
CREATING MAGIC...
Magic Programing Contest
Each Grade Level
...WAS A HOBBY I DID FOR MY OWN ENJOYMENT.

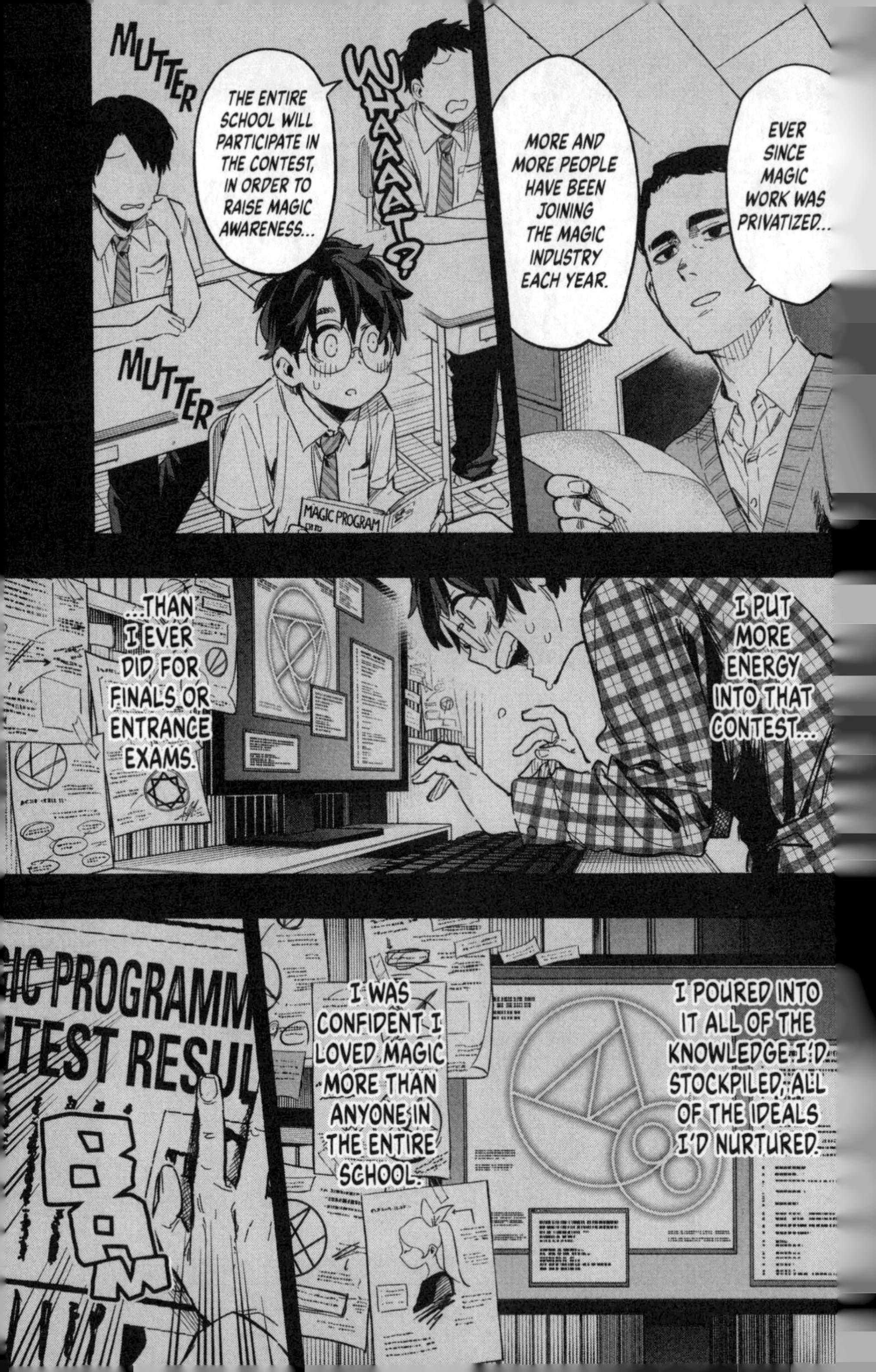
EVER SINCE MAGIC WORK WAS PRIVATIZED...
MORE AND MORE PEOPLE HAVE BEEN JOINING THE MAGIC INDUSTRY EACH YEAR.
THE ENTIRE SCHOOL WILL PARTICIPATE IN THE CONTEST, IN ORDER TO RAISE MAGIC AWARENESS...
WHAAAAT!?
MUTTER
MUTTER
MAGIC PROGRAM
I PUT MORE ENERGY INTO THAT CONTEST...
...THAN I EVER DID FOR FINALS OR ENTRANCE EXAMS.
I POURED INTO IT ALL OF THE KNOWLEDGE I'D STOCKPILED, ALL OF THE IDEALS I'D NURTURED.
I WAS CONFIDENT I LOVED MAGIC MORE THAN ANYONE IN THE ENTIRE SCHOOL.
IC PROGRAMM
TEST RESU
8

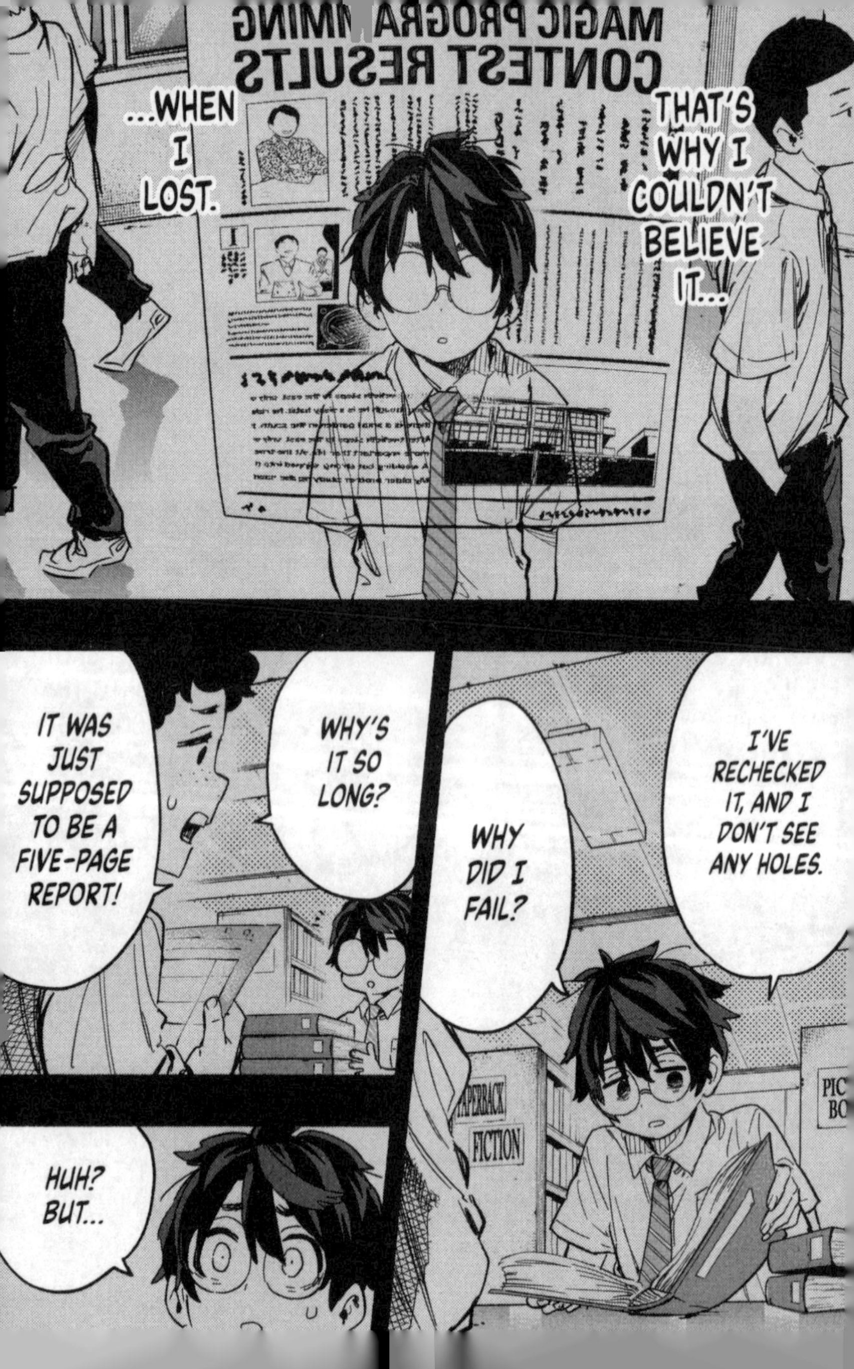
MAGIC PROGRAMMING CONTEST RESULTS
THAT'S WHY I COULDN'T BELIEVE IT...
...WHEN I LOST.
I'VE RECHECKED IT, AND I DON'T SEE ANY HOLES.
WHY DID I FAIL?
FICTION
WHY'S IT SO LONG?
IT WAS JUST SUPPOSED TO BE A FIVE-PAGE REPORT!
HUH? BUT...

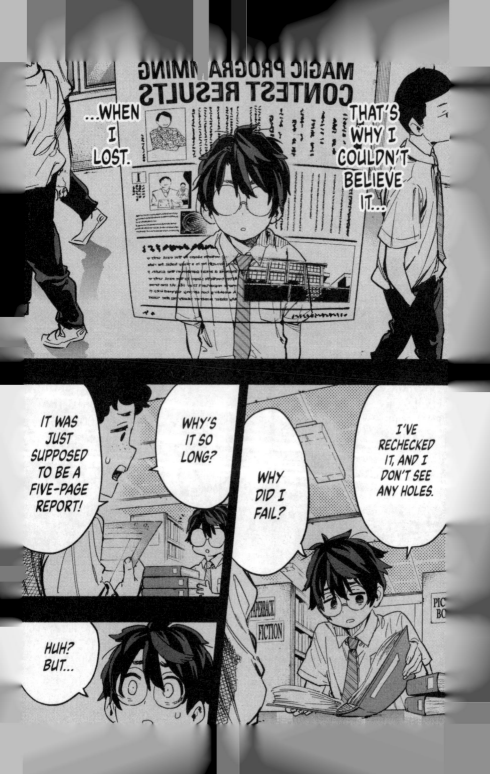

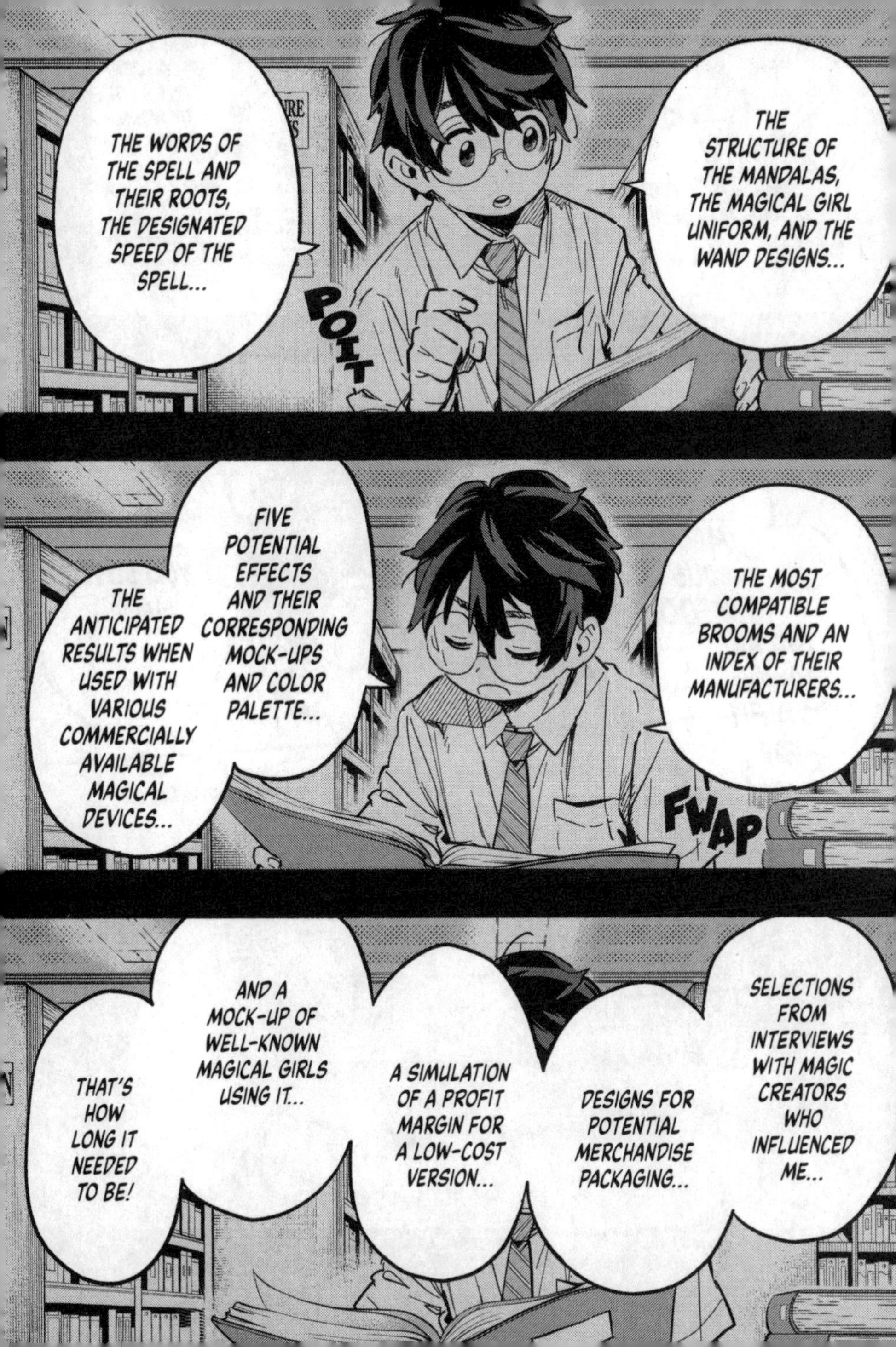
THE STRUCTURE OF THE MANDALAS, THE MAGICAL GIRL UNIFORM, AND THE WAND DESIGNS...
THE WORDS OF THE SPELL AND THEIR ROOTS, THE DESIGNATED SPEED OF THE SPELL...
POIT
THE MOST COMPATIBLE BROOMS AND AN INDEX OF THEIR MANUFACTURERS...
FWAP
FIVE POTENTIAL EFFECTS AND THEIR CORRESPONDING MOCK-UPS AND COLOR PALETTE...
THE ANTICIPATED RESULTS WHEN USED WITH VARIOUS COMMERCIALLY AVAILABLE MAGICAL DEVICES...
SELECTIONS FROM INTERVIEWS WITH MAGIC CREATORS WHO INFLUENCED ME...
DESIGNS FOR POTENTIAL MERCHANDISE PACKAGING...
A SIMULATION OF A PROFIT MARGIN FOR A LOW-COST VERSION...
AND A MOCK-UP OF WELL-KNOWN MAGICAL GIRLS USING IT...
THAT'S HOW LONG IT NEEDED TO BE!

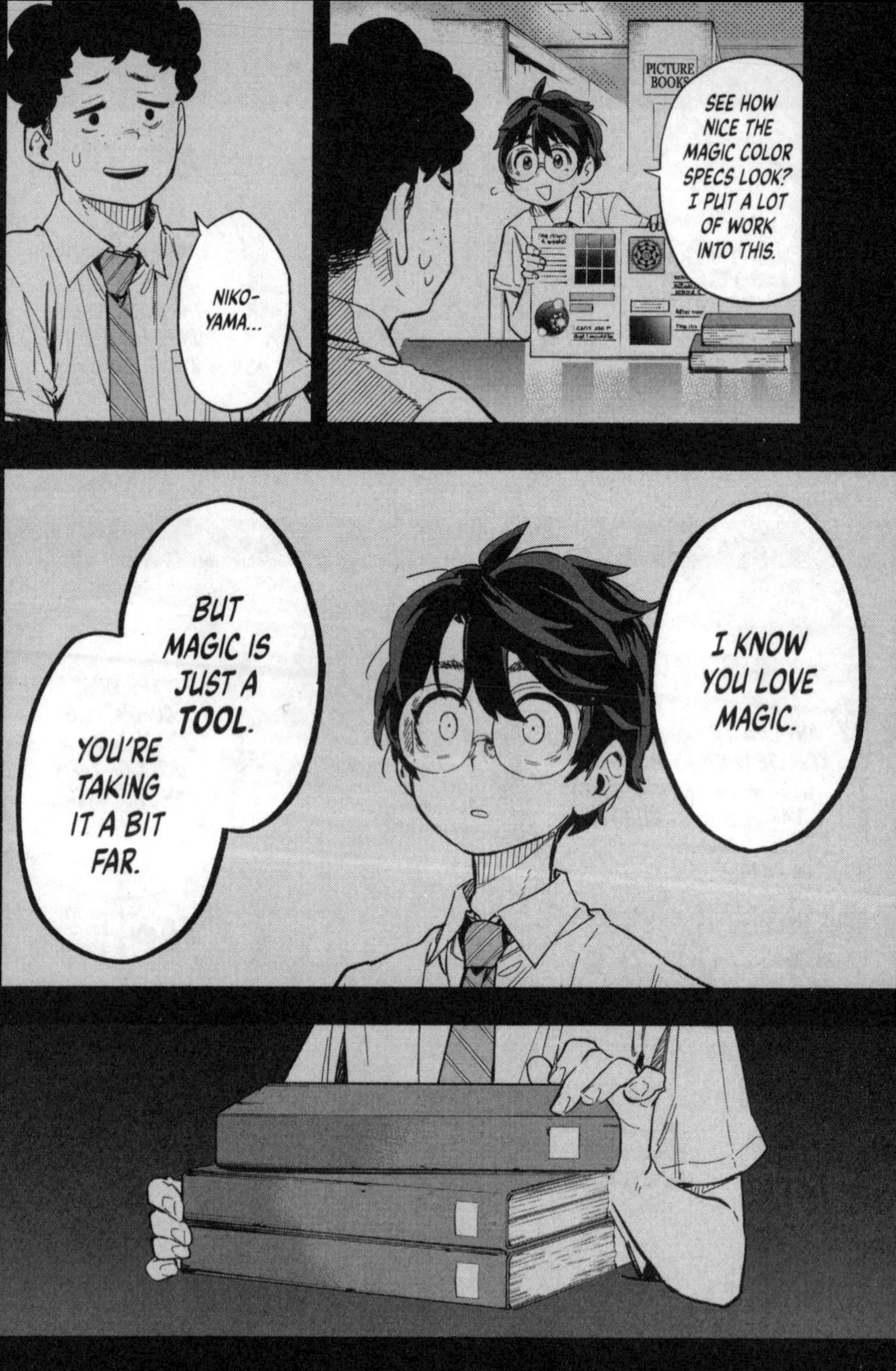
PICTURE BOOKS
SEE HOW NICE THE MAGIC COLOR SPECS LOOK? I PUT A LOT OF WORK INTO THIS.
NIKO-YAMA...
I KNOW YOU LOVE MAGIC.
BUT MAGIC IS JUST A TOOL.
YOU'RE TAKING IT A BIT FAR.

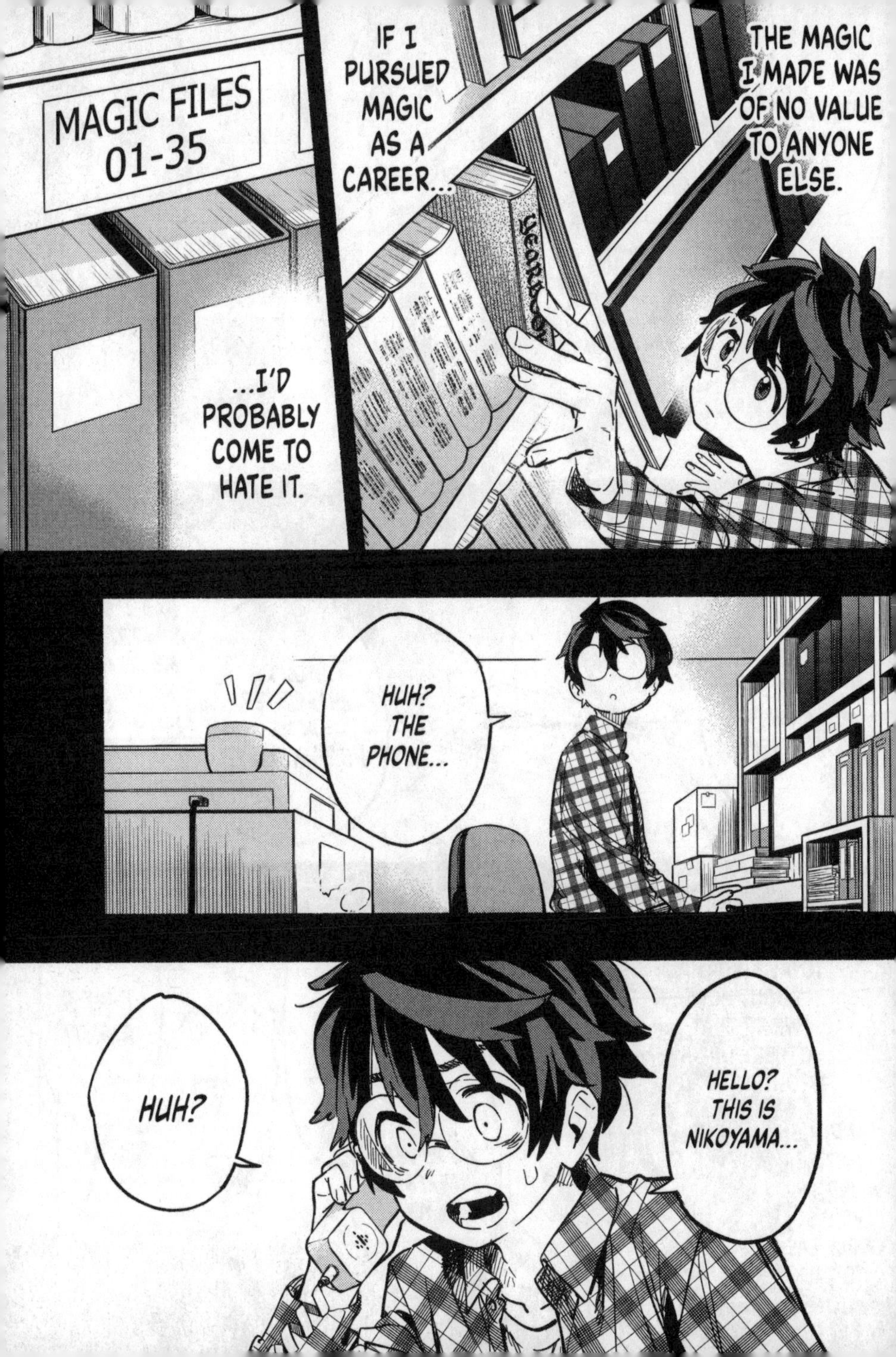
THE MAGIC I MADE WAS OF NO VALUE TO ANYONE ELSE.
IF I PURSUED MAGIC AS A CAREER...
YEARBOOK
MAGIC FILES 01-35
...I'D PROBABLY COME TO HATE IT.
HUH? THE PHONE...
HELLO? THIS IS NIKOYAMA...
HUH?

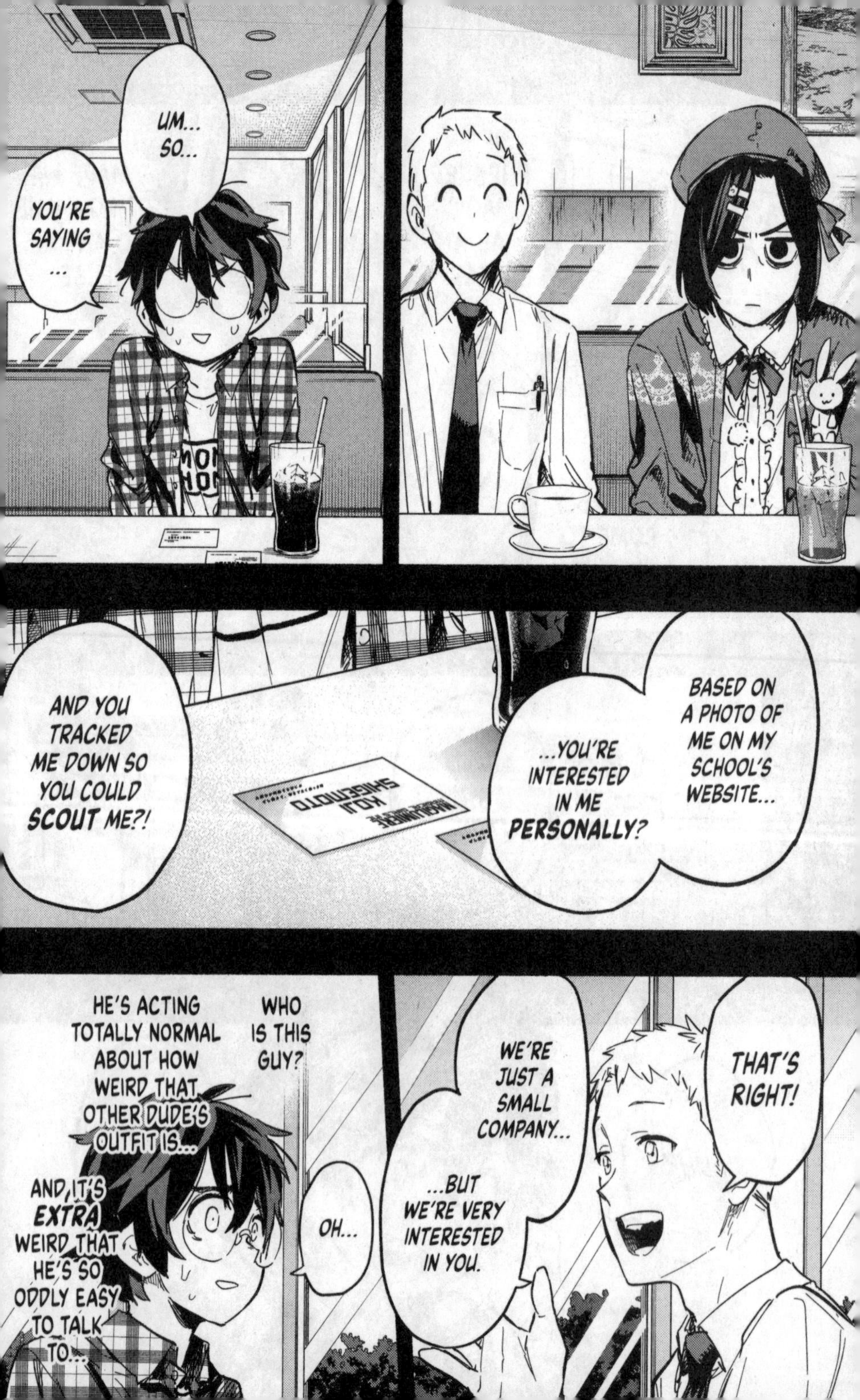
UM... SO...
YOU'RE SAYING ...
BASED ON A PHOTO OF ME ON MY SCHOOL'S WEBSITE...
...YOU'RE INTERESTED IN ME PERSONALLY?
AND YOU TRACKED ME DOWN SO YOU COULD SCOUT ME?!
THAT'S RIGHT!
WE'RE JUST A SMALL COMPANY...
...BUT WE'RE VERY INTERESTED IN YOU.
WHO IS THIS GUY?
HE'S ACTING TOTALLY NORMAL ABOUT HOW WEIRD THAT OTHER DUDE'S OUTFIT IS...
OH...
AND IT'S EXTRA WEIRD THAT HE'S SO ODDLY EASY TO TALK TO...

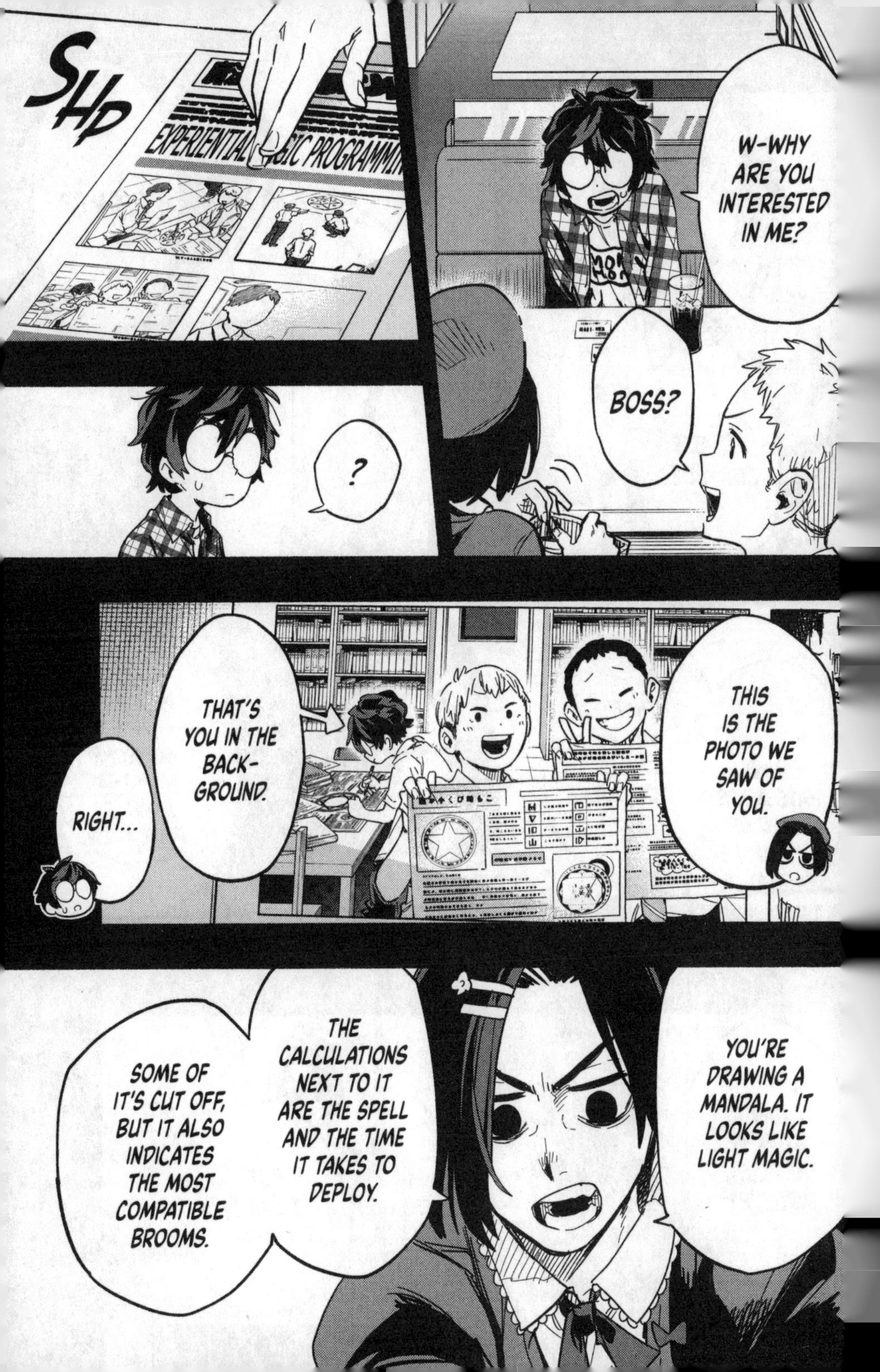
W-WHY ARE YOU INTERESTED IN ME?
SHP
BOSS?
?
THIS IS THE PHOTO WE SAW OF YOU.
THAT'S YOU IN THE BACK-GROUND.
RIGHT...
YOU'RE DRAWING A MANDALA. IT LOOKS LIKE LIGHT MAGIC.
THE CALCULATIONS NEXT TO IT ARE THE SPELL AND THE TIME IT TAKES TO DEPLOY.
SOME OF IT'S CUT OFF, BUT IT ALSO INDICATES THE MOST COMPATIBLE BROOMS.

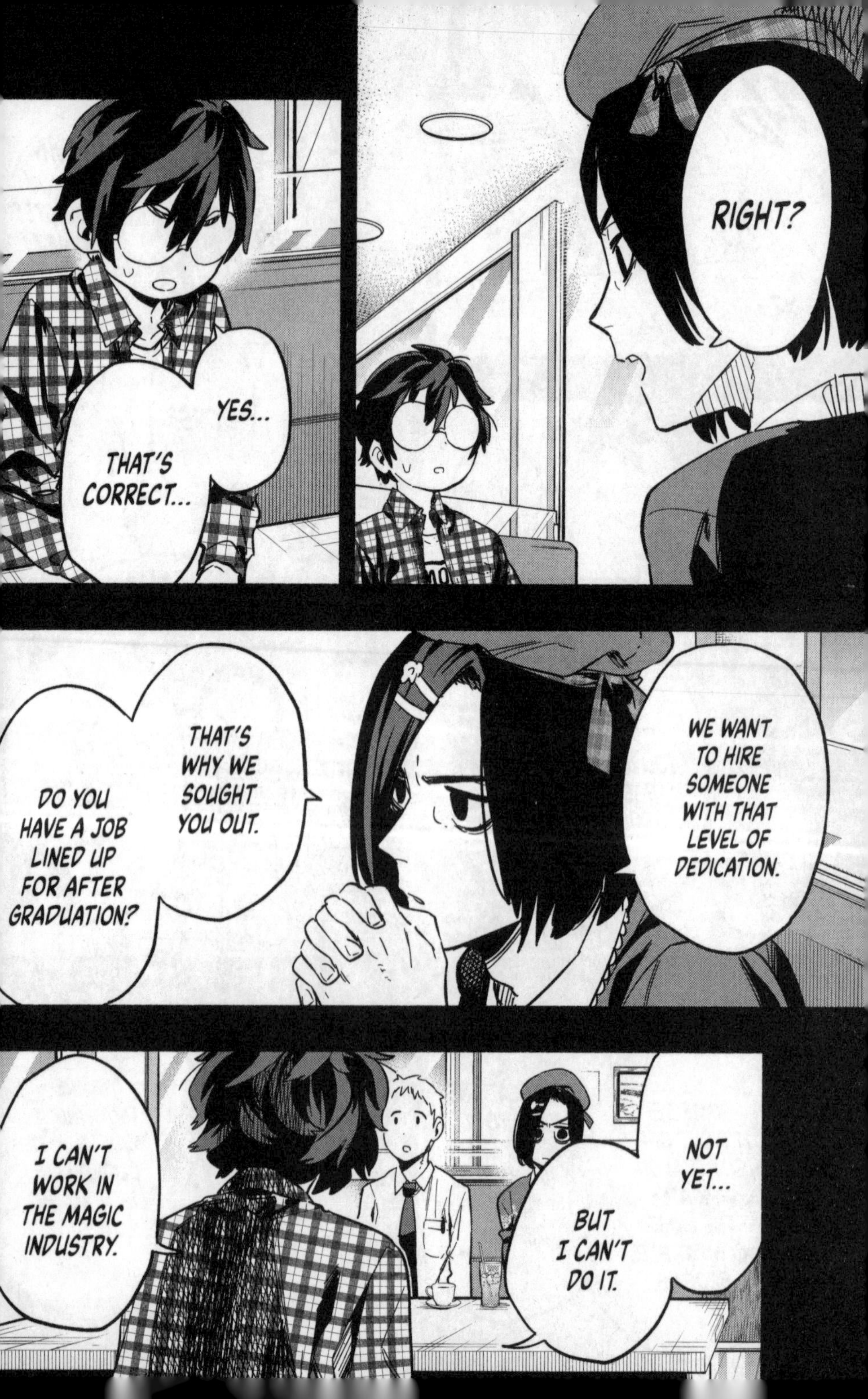
RIGHT?
YES... THAT'S CORRECT...
WE WANT TO HIRE SOMEONE WITH THAT LEVEL OF DEDICATION.
THAT'S WHY WE SOUGHT YOU OUT. DO YOU HAVE A JOB LINED UP FOR AFTER GRADUATION?
NOT YET... BUT I CAN'T DO IT.
I CAN'T WORK IN THE MAGIC INDUSTRY.

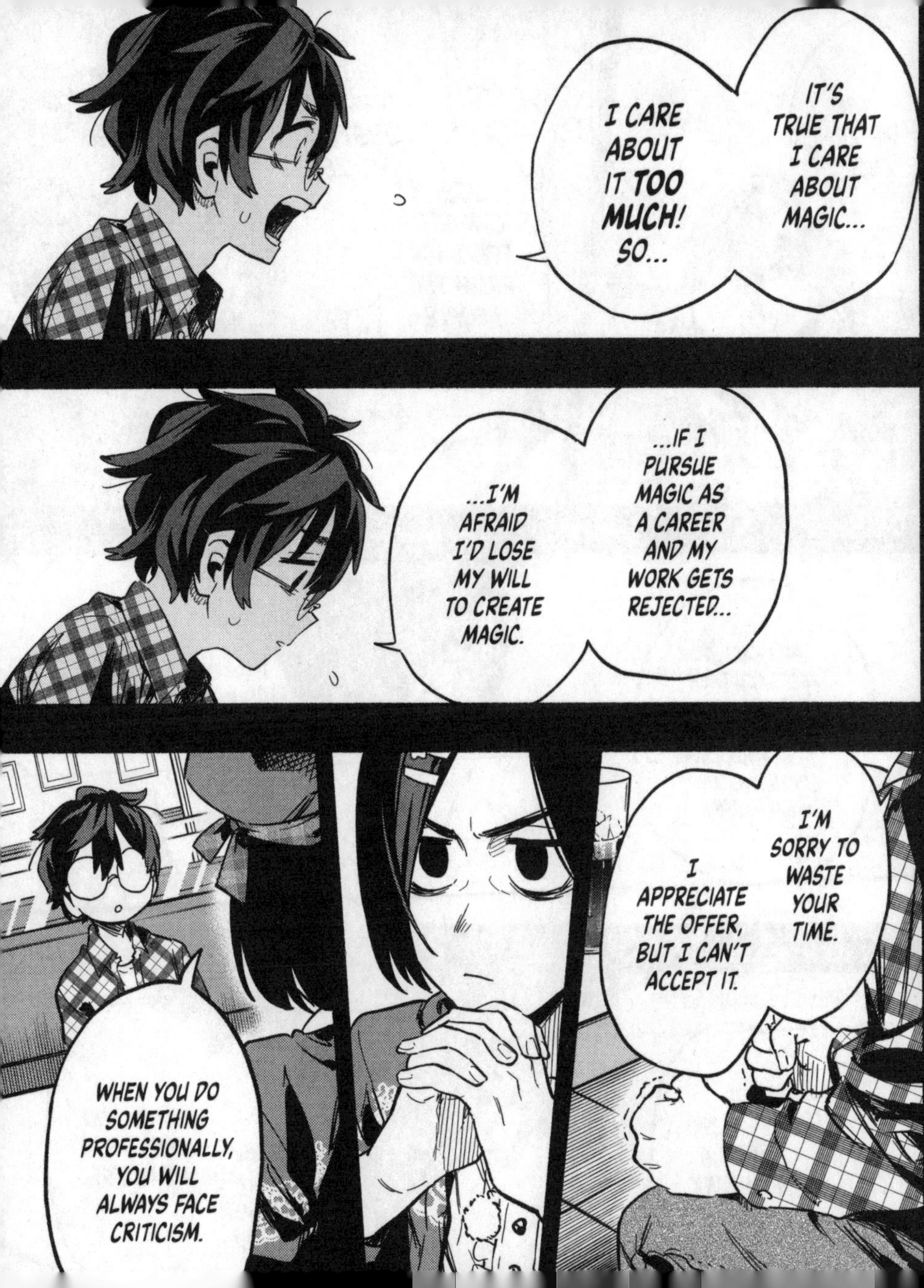
IT'S TRUE THAT I CARE ABOUT MAGIC...
I CARE ABOUT IT **TOO MUCH**! SO...
...IF I PURSUE MAGIC AS A CAREER AND MY WORK GETS REJECTED...
...I'M AFRAID I'D LOSE MY WILL TO CREATE MAGIC.
I'M SORRY TO WASTE YOUR TIME.
I APPRECIATE THE OFFER, BUT I CAN'T ACCEPT IT.
WHEN YOU DO SOMETHING PROFESSIONALLY, YOU WILL ALWAYS FACE CRITICISM.

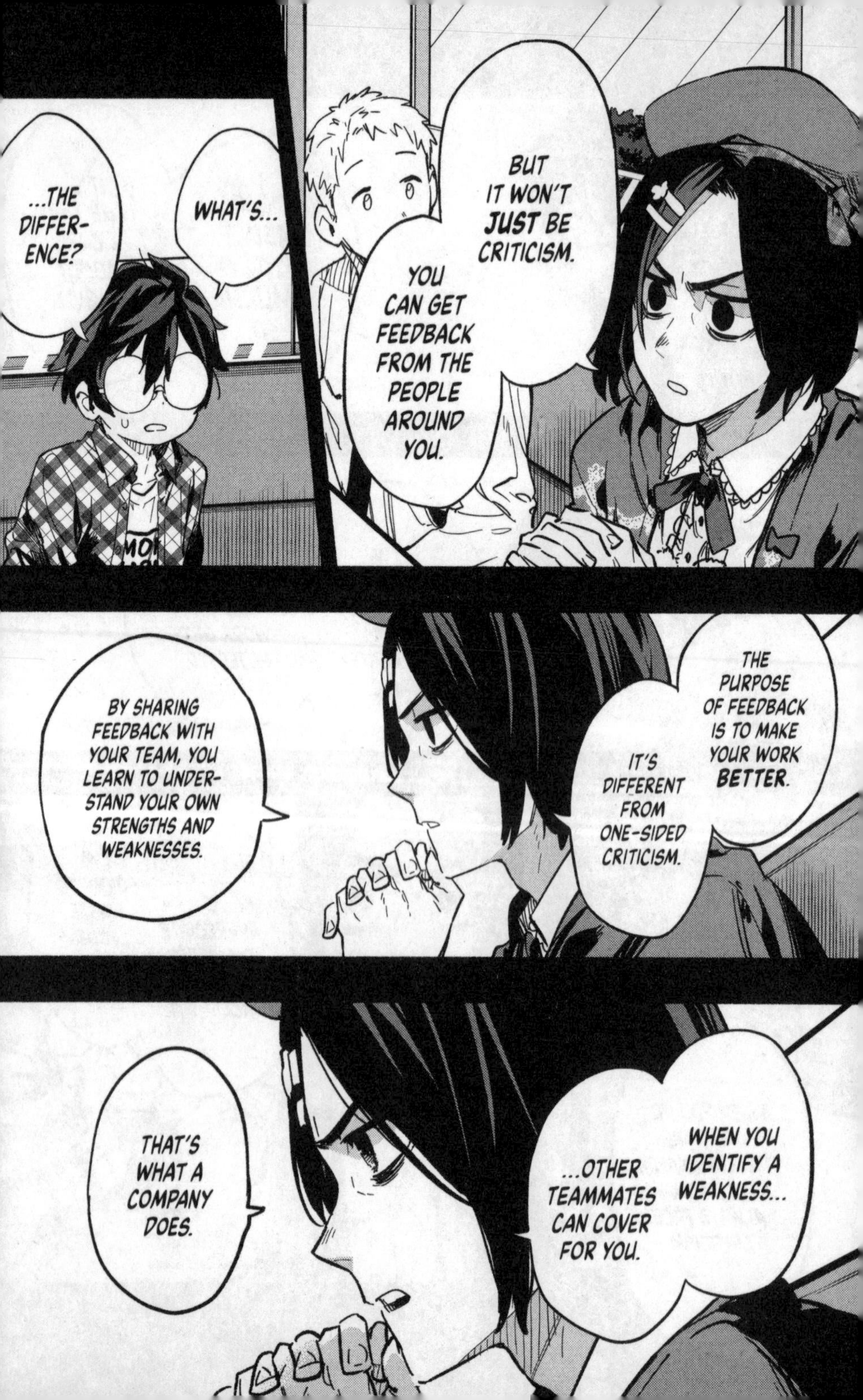
BUT IT WON'T JUST BE CRITICISM.
YOU CAN GET FEEDBACK FROM THE PEOPLE AROUND YOU.
WHAT'S...
...THE DIFFER-ENCE?
THE PURPOSE OF FEEDBACK IS TO MAKE YOUR WORK BETTER.
IT'S DIFFERENT FROM ONE-SIDED CRITICISM.
BY SHARING FEEDBACK WITH YOUR TEAM, YOU LEARN TO UNDER-STAND YOUR OWN STRENGTHS AND WEAKNESSES.
WHEN YOU IDENTIFY A WEAKNESS...
...OTHER TEAMMATES CAN COVER FOR YOU.
THAT'S WHAT A COMPANY DOES.

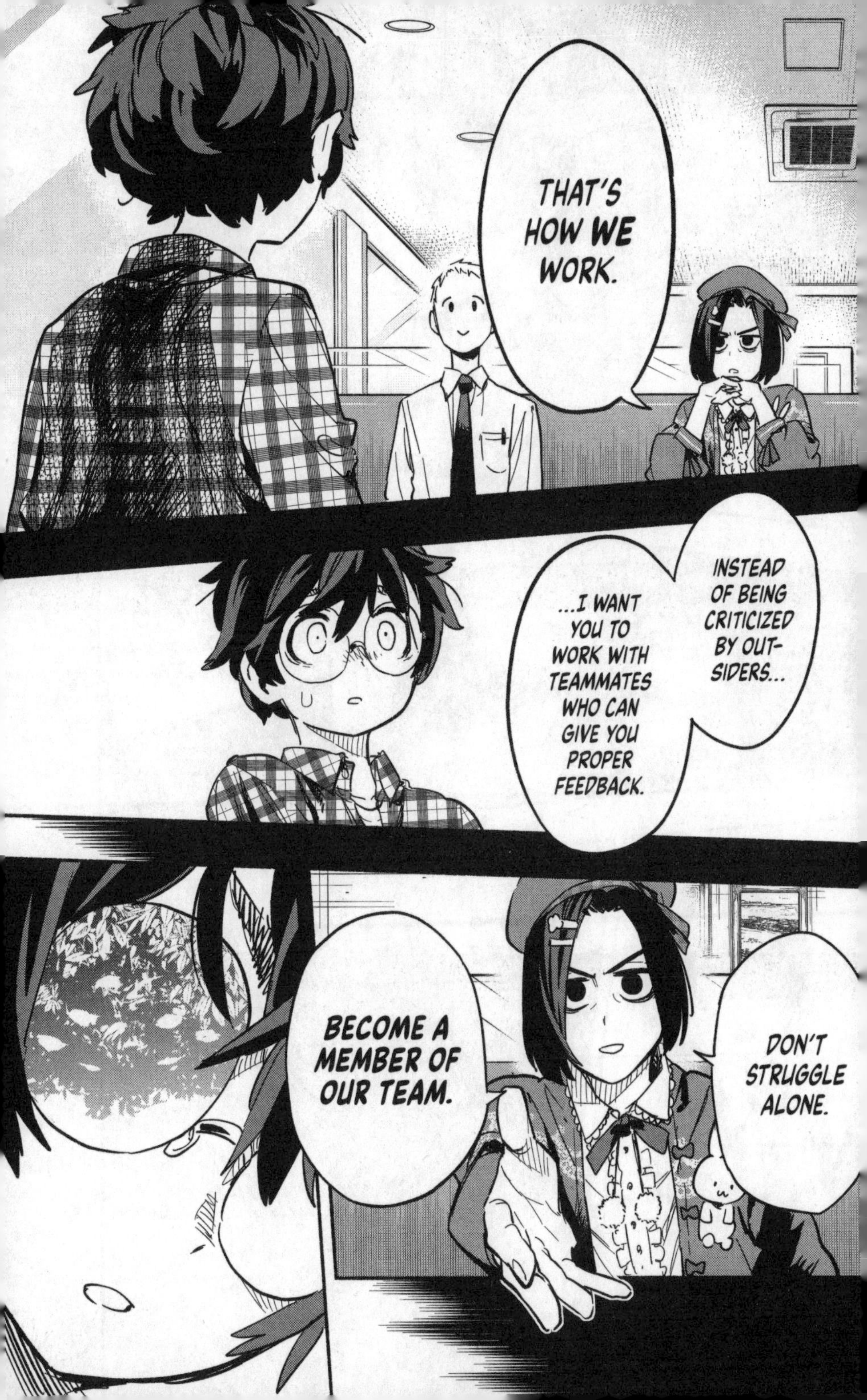
THAT'S HOW WE WORK.
INSTEAD OF BEING CRITICIZED BY OUT-SIDERS...
...I WANT YOU TO WORK WITH TEAMMATES WHO CAN GIVE YOU PROPER FEEDBACK.
DON'T STRUGGLE ALONE.
BECOME A MEMBER OF OUR TEAM.

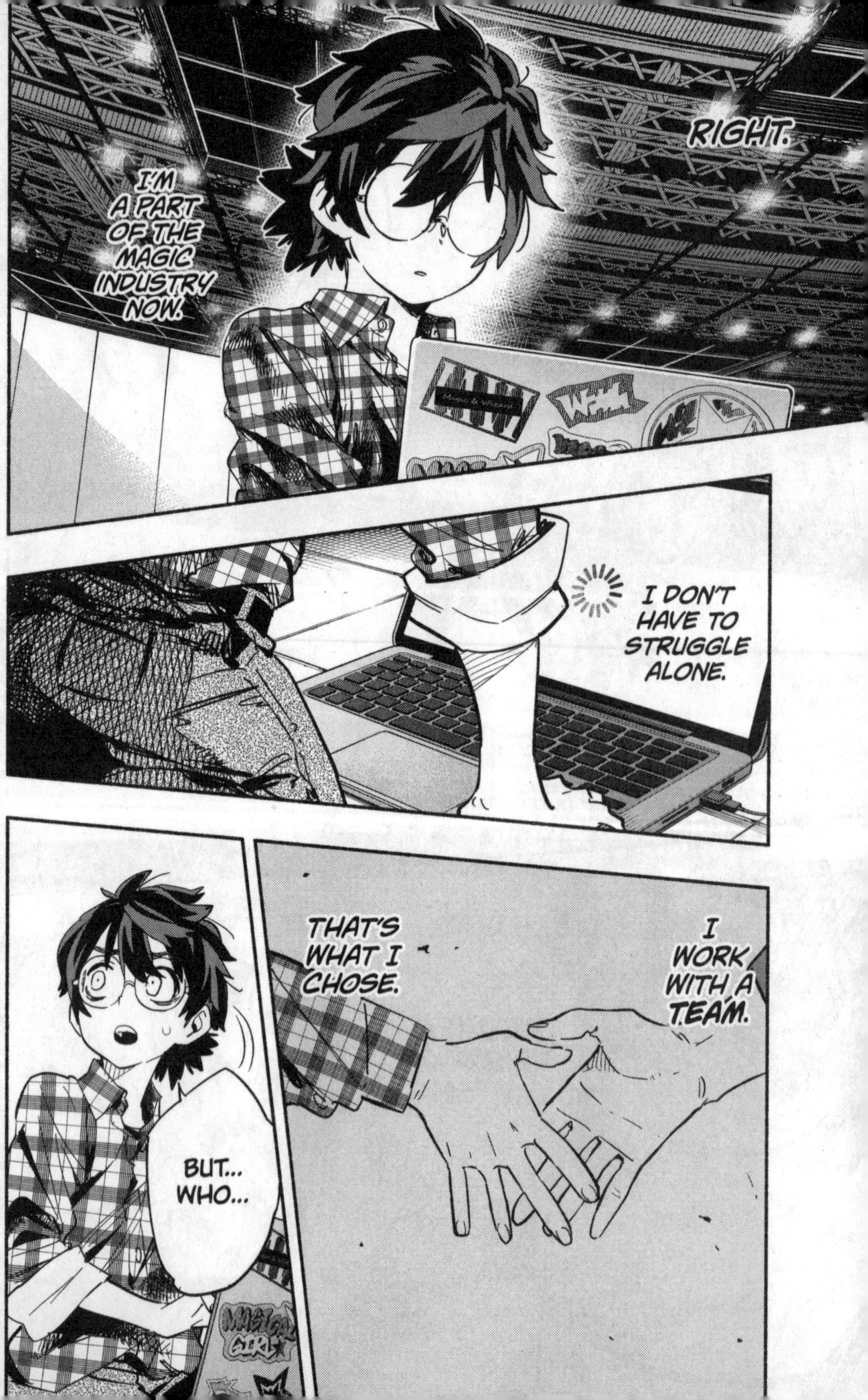
RIGHT.
I'M A PART OF THE MAGIC INDUSTRY NOW.
I DON'T HAVE TO STRUGGLE ALONE.
I WORK WITH A TEAM.
THAT'S WHAT I CHOSE.
BUT... WHO...

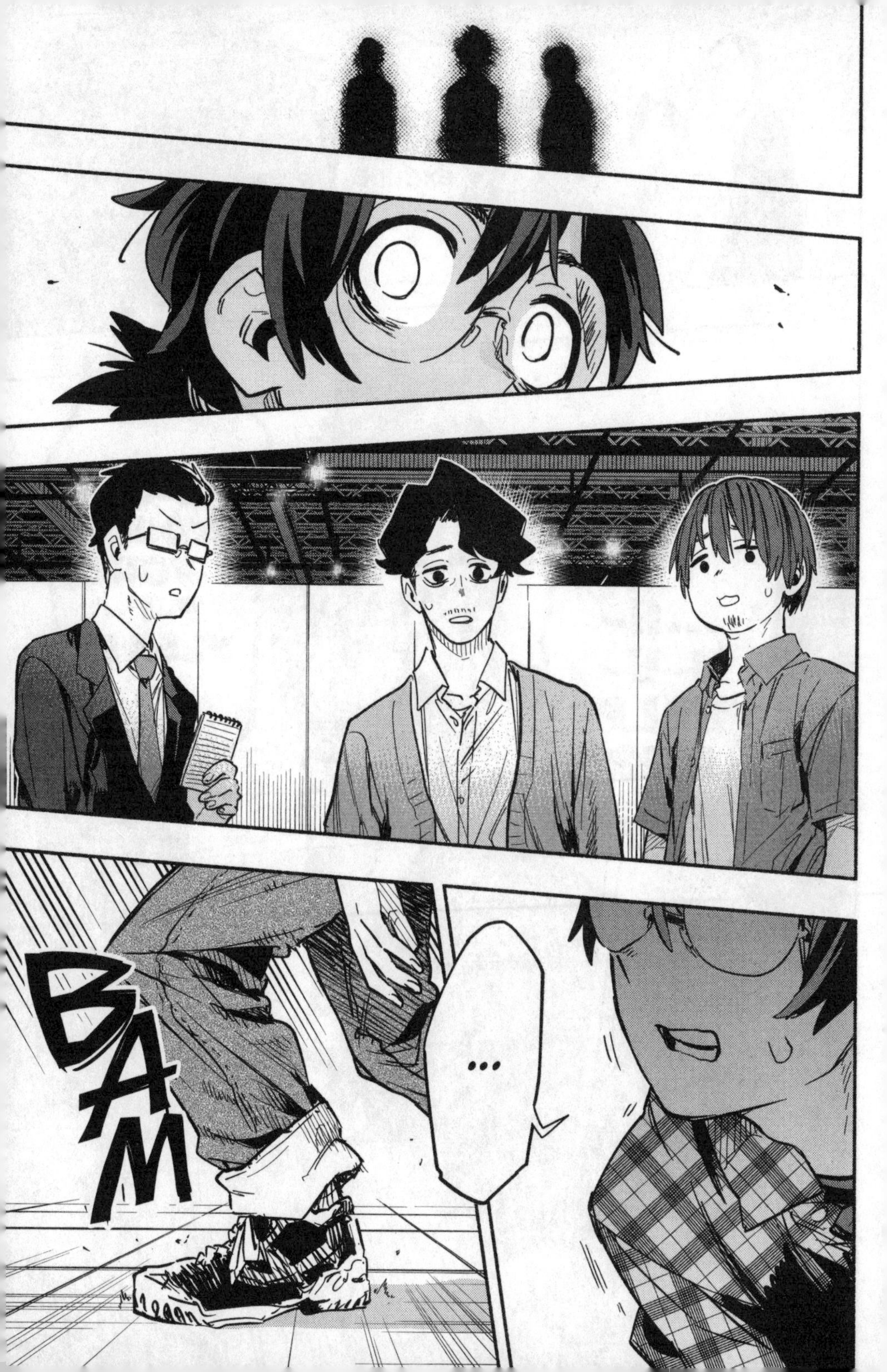

...
BAM

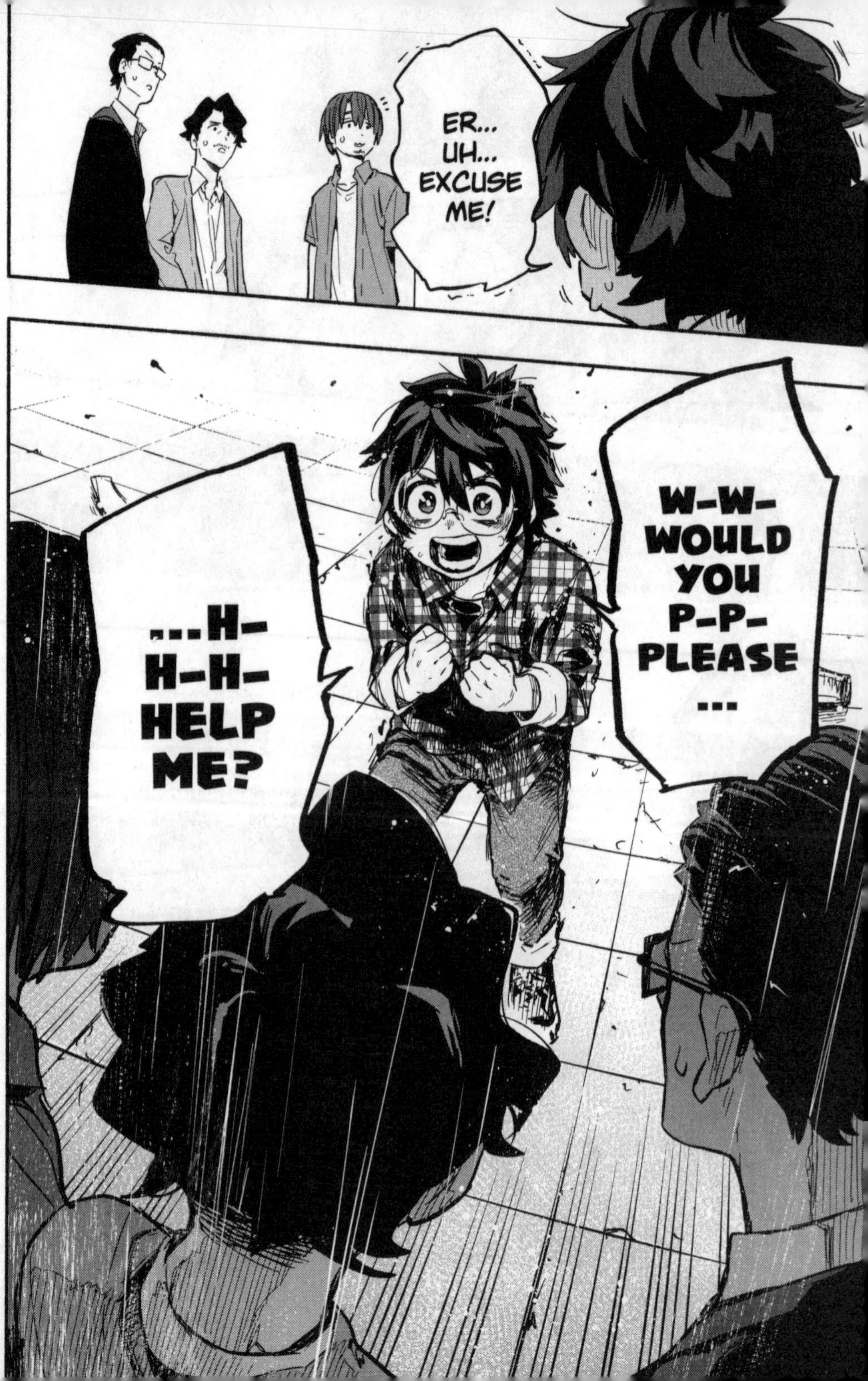
ER... UH... EXCUSE ME!
W-W-WOULD YOU P-P-PLEASE ...
...H-H-H-HELP ME?

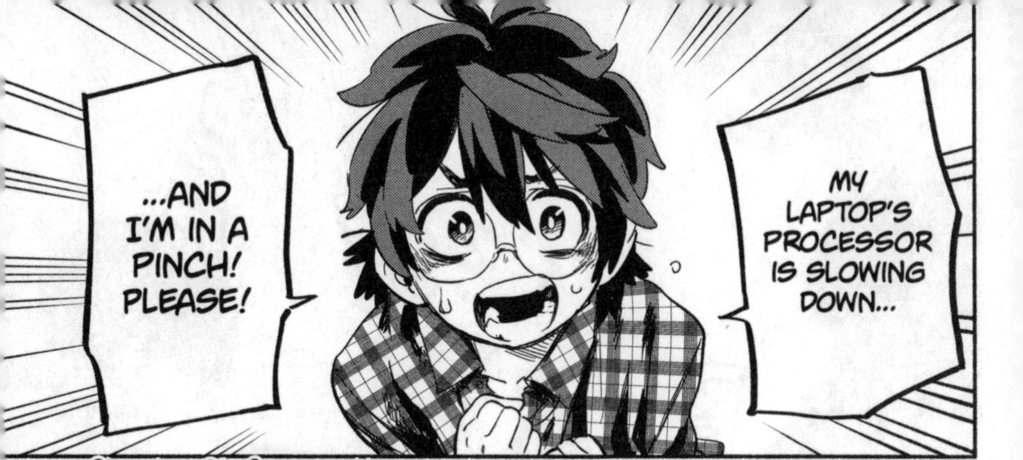
MY LAPTOP'S PROCESSOR IS SLOWING DOWN...
...AND I'M IN A PINCH! PLEASE!

Chapter 21: Cooperation

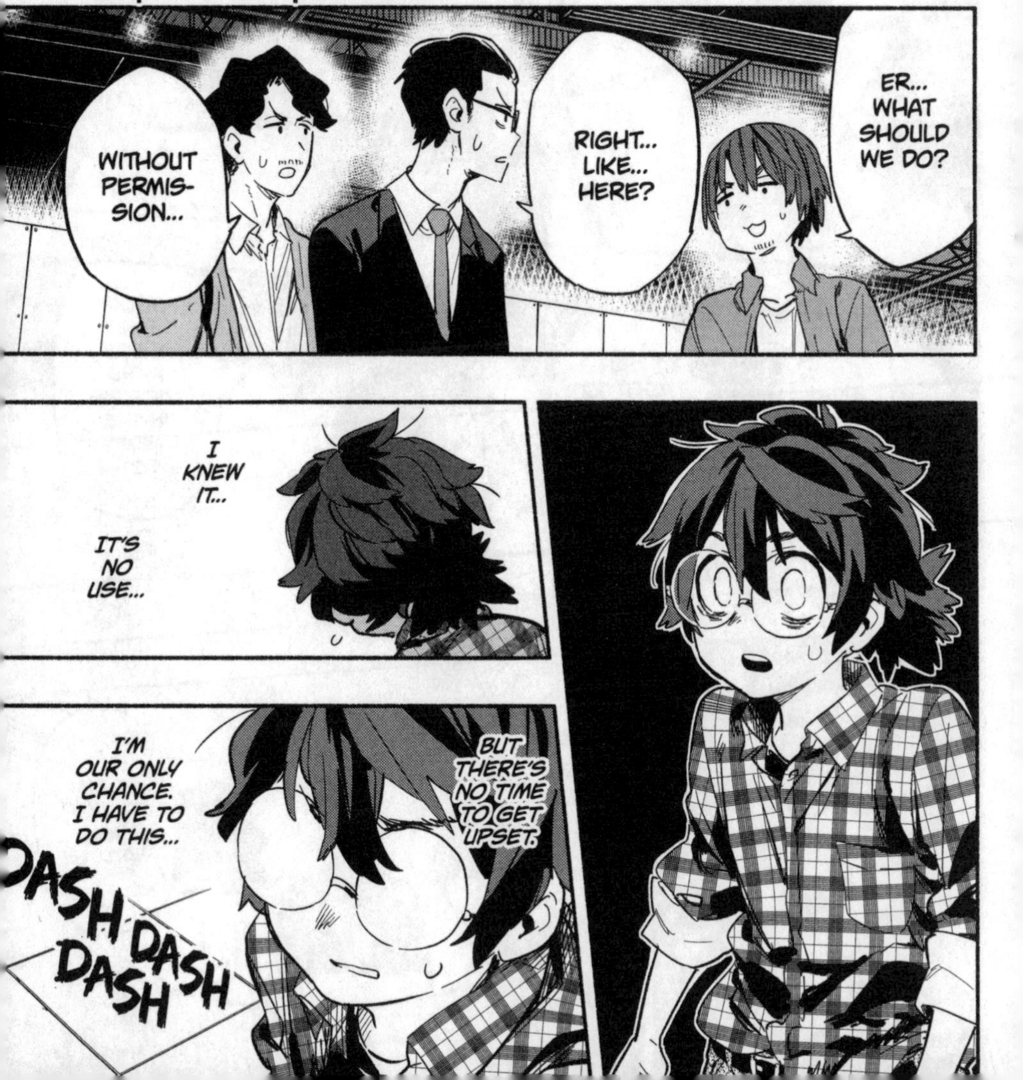
ER... WHAT SHOULD WE DO?
RIGHT... LIKE... HERE?
WITHOUT PERMISSION...
I KNEW IT...
IT'S NO USE...
BUT THERE'S NO TIME TO GET UPSET.
I'M OUR ONLY CHANCE. I HAVE TO DO THIS...
DASH DASH
DASH DASH

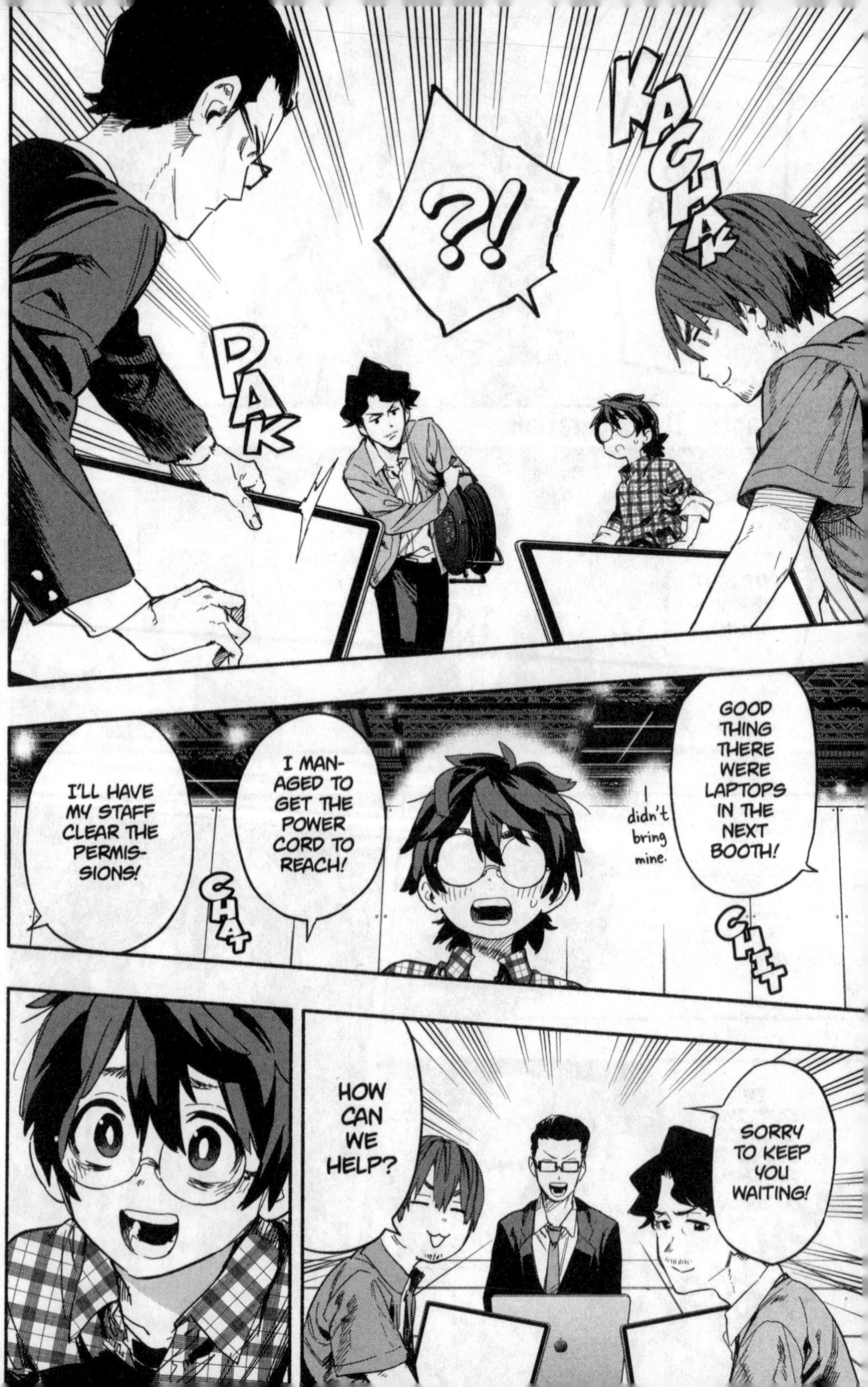
KACHAK
?!
DAK
GOOD THING THERE WERE LAPTOPS IN THE NEXT BOOTH!
CHIT
I didn't bring mine.
I MAN-AGED TO GET THE POWER CORD TO REACH!
CHAT
I'LL HAVE MY STAFF CLEAR THE PERMIS-SIONS!
SORRY TO KEEP YOU WAITING!
HOW CAN WE HELP?

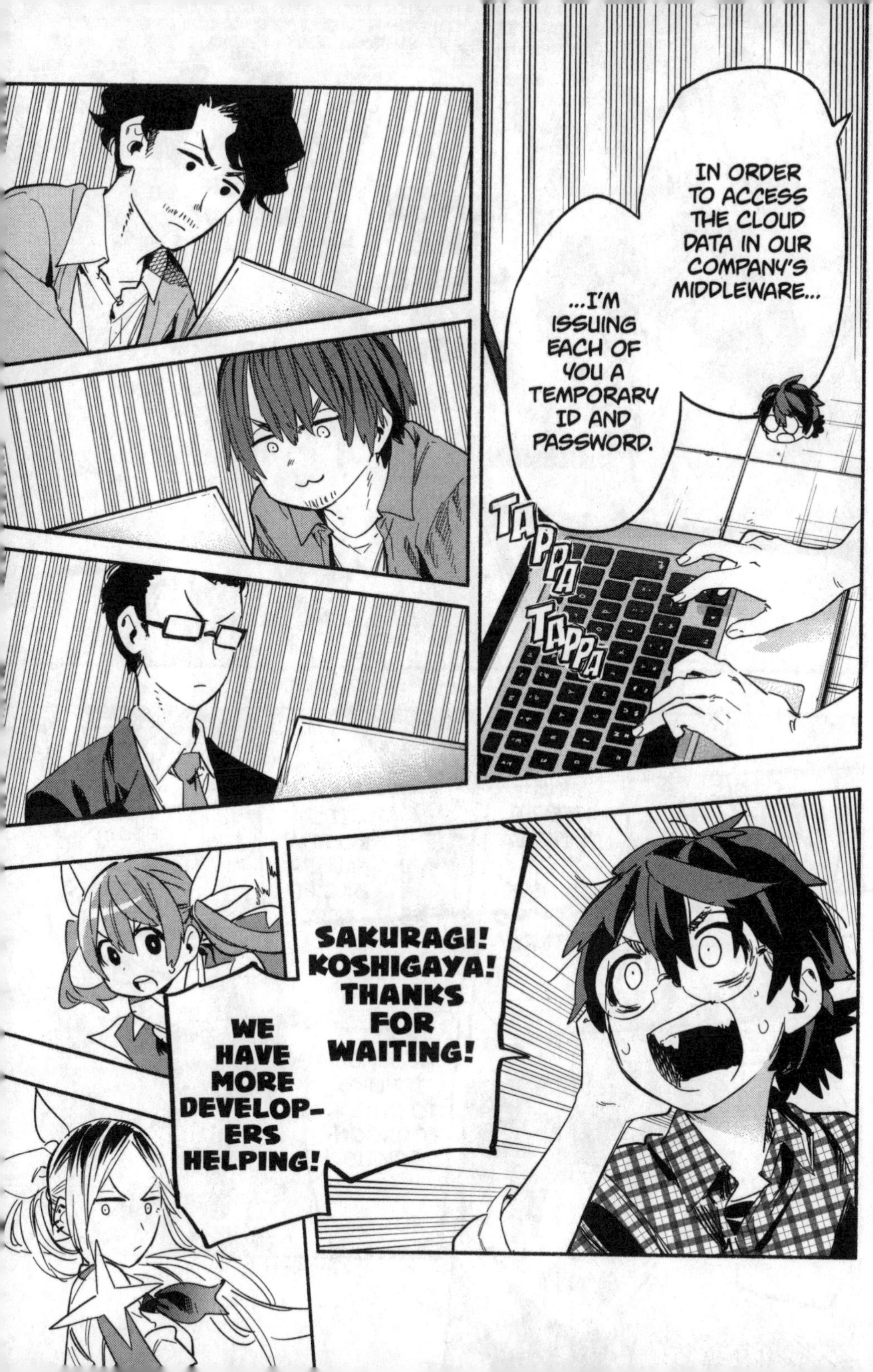
IN ORDER TO ACCESS THE CLOUD DATA IN OUR COMPANY'S MIDDLEWARE...
...I'M ISSUING EACH OF YOU A TEMPORARY ID AND PASSWORD.
TAPPA
TAPPA
SAKURAGI! KOSHIGAYA! THANKS FOR WAITING!
WE HAVE MORE DEVELOP-ERS HELPING!

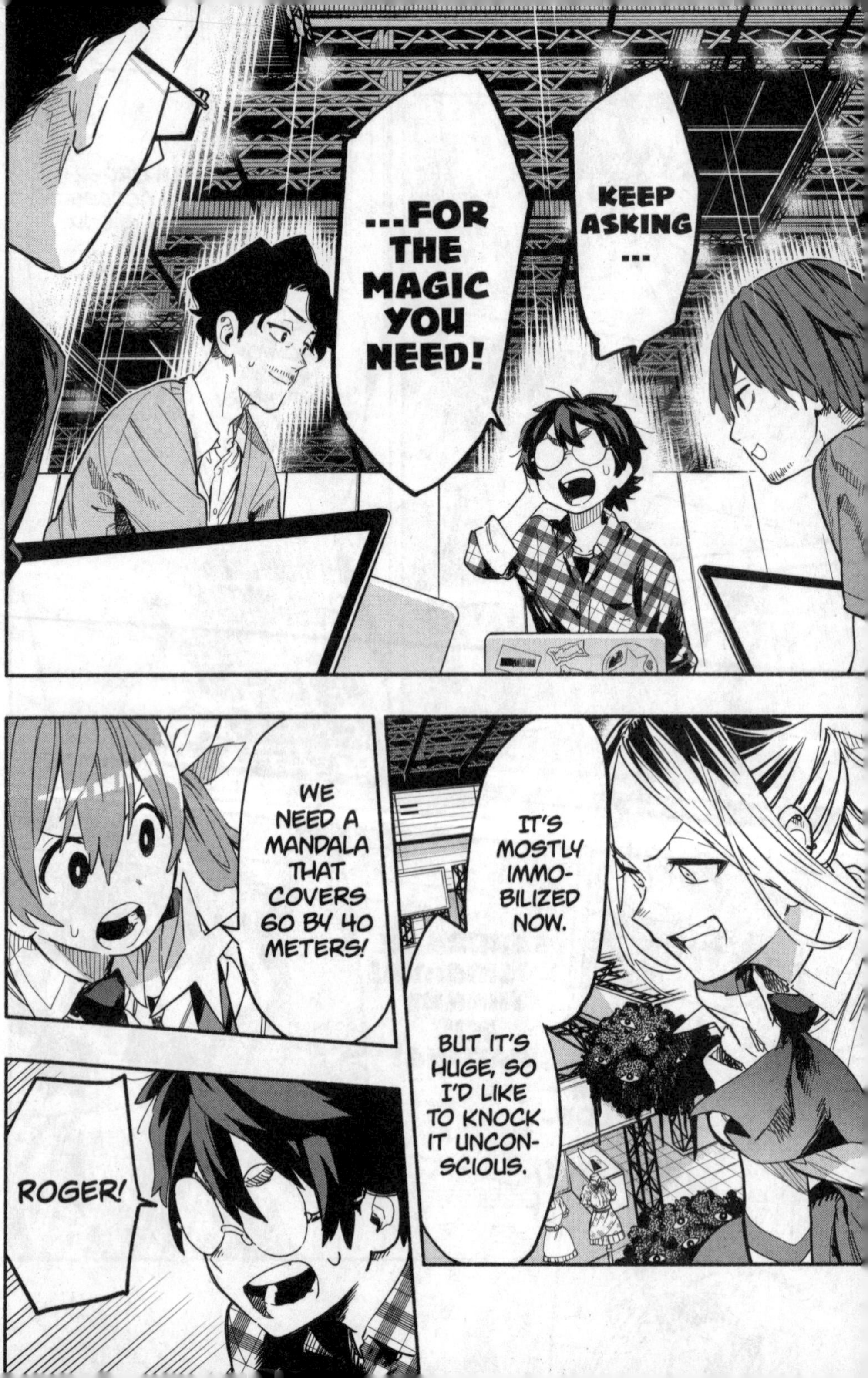
KEEP ASKING ...
...FOR THE MAGIC YOU NEED!
IT'S MOSTLY IMMO-BILIZED NOW.
BUT IT'S HUGE, SO I'D LIKE TO KNOCK IT UNCON-SCIOUS.
WE NEED A MANDALA THAT COVERS 60 BY 40 METERS!
ROGER!

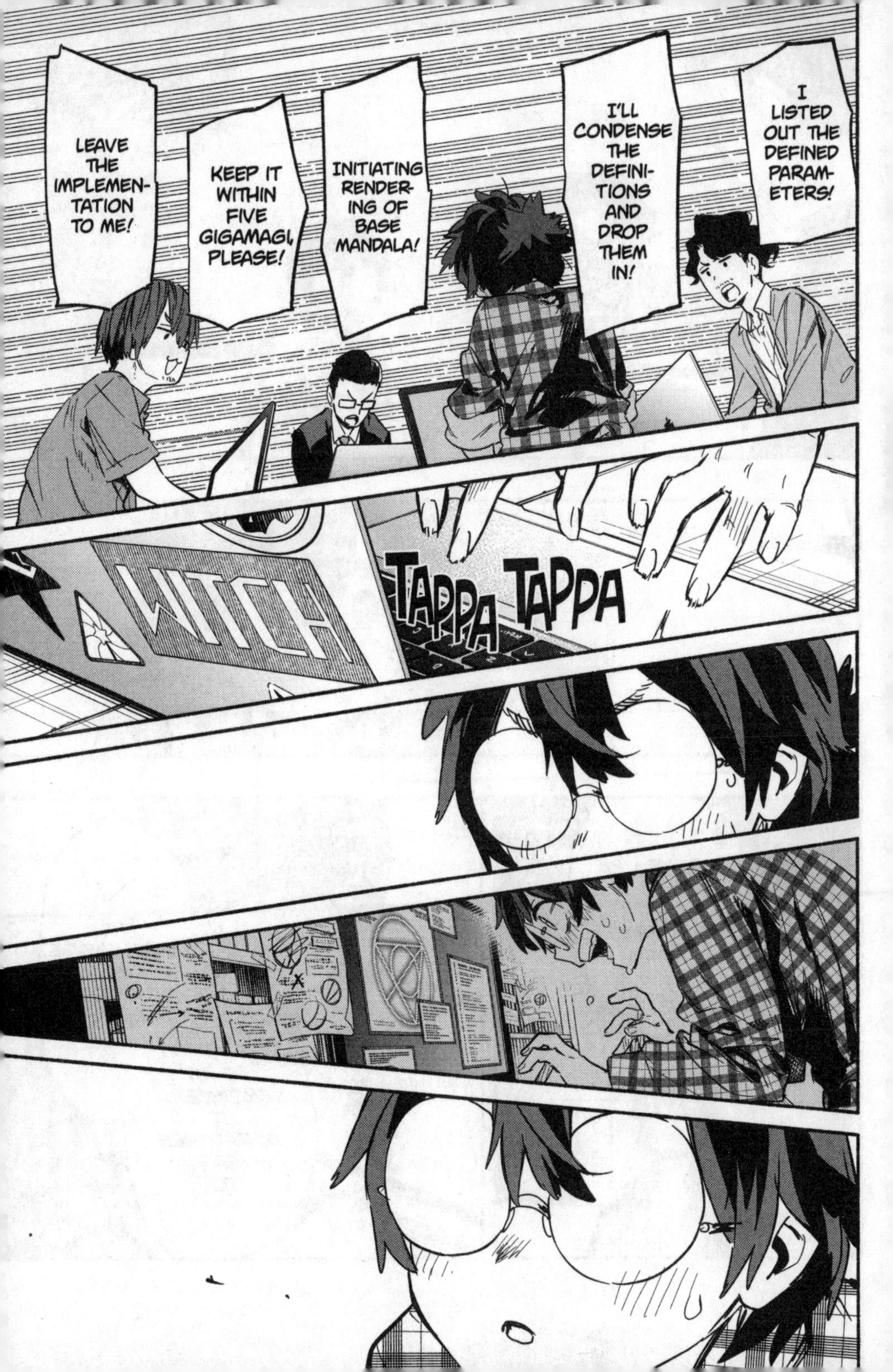
I LISTED OUT THE DEFINED PARAMETERS!
I'LL CONDENSE THE DEFINITIONS AND DROP THEM IN!
INITIATING RENDERING OF BASE MANDALA!
KEEP IT WITHIN FIVE GIGAMAGI, PLEASE!
LEAVE THE IMPLEMENTATION TO ME!
WITCH
TAPPA TAPPA

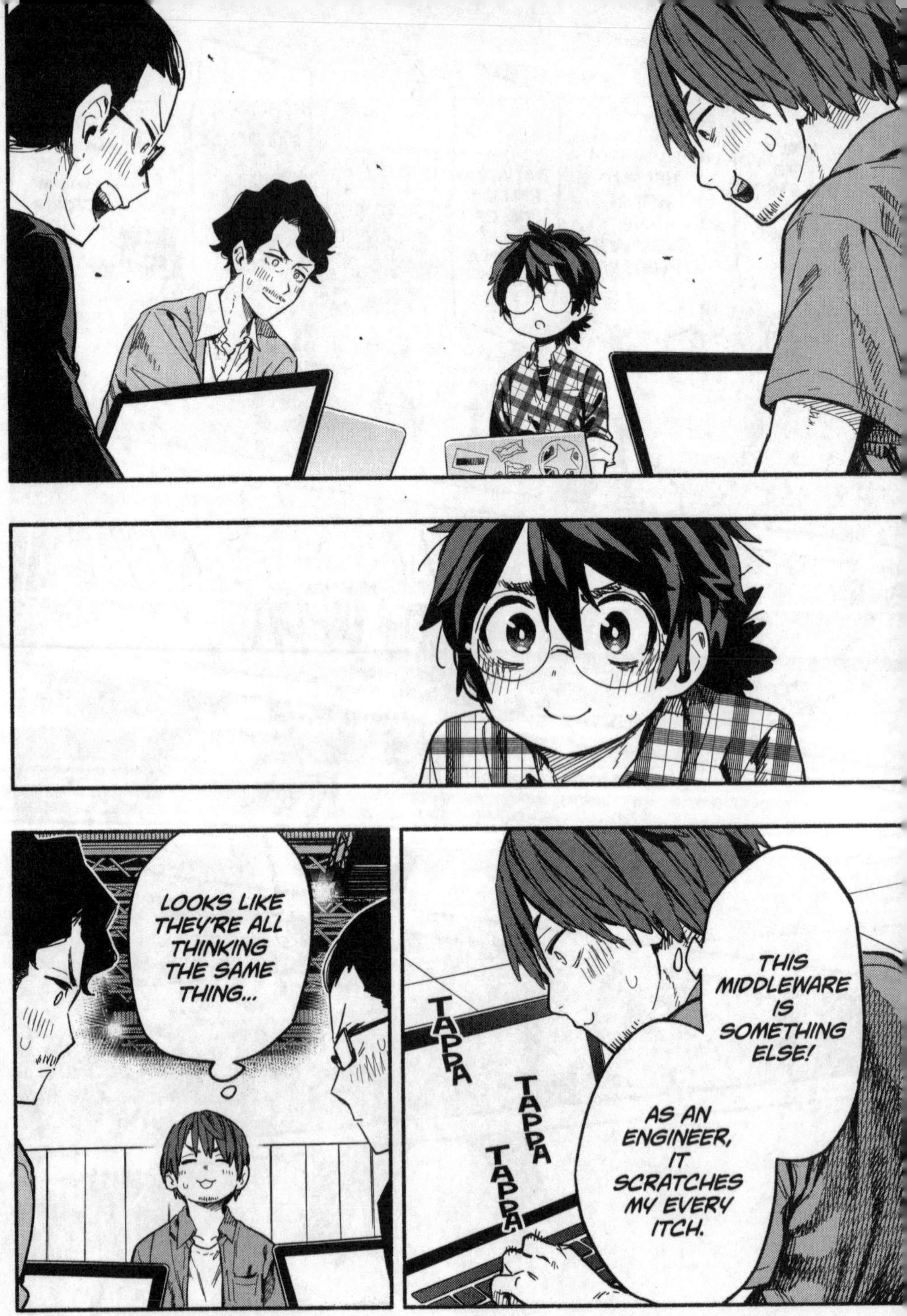
THIS MIDDLEWARE IS SOMETHING ELSE!
AS AN ENGINEER, IT SCRATCHES MY EVERY ITCH.
TAPPA
TAPPA
TAPPA
TAPPA
LOOKS LIKE THEY'RE ALL THINKING THE SAME THING...

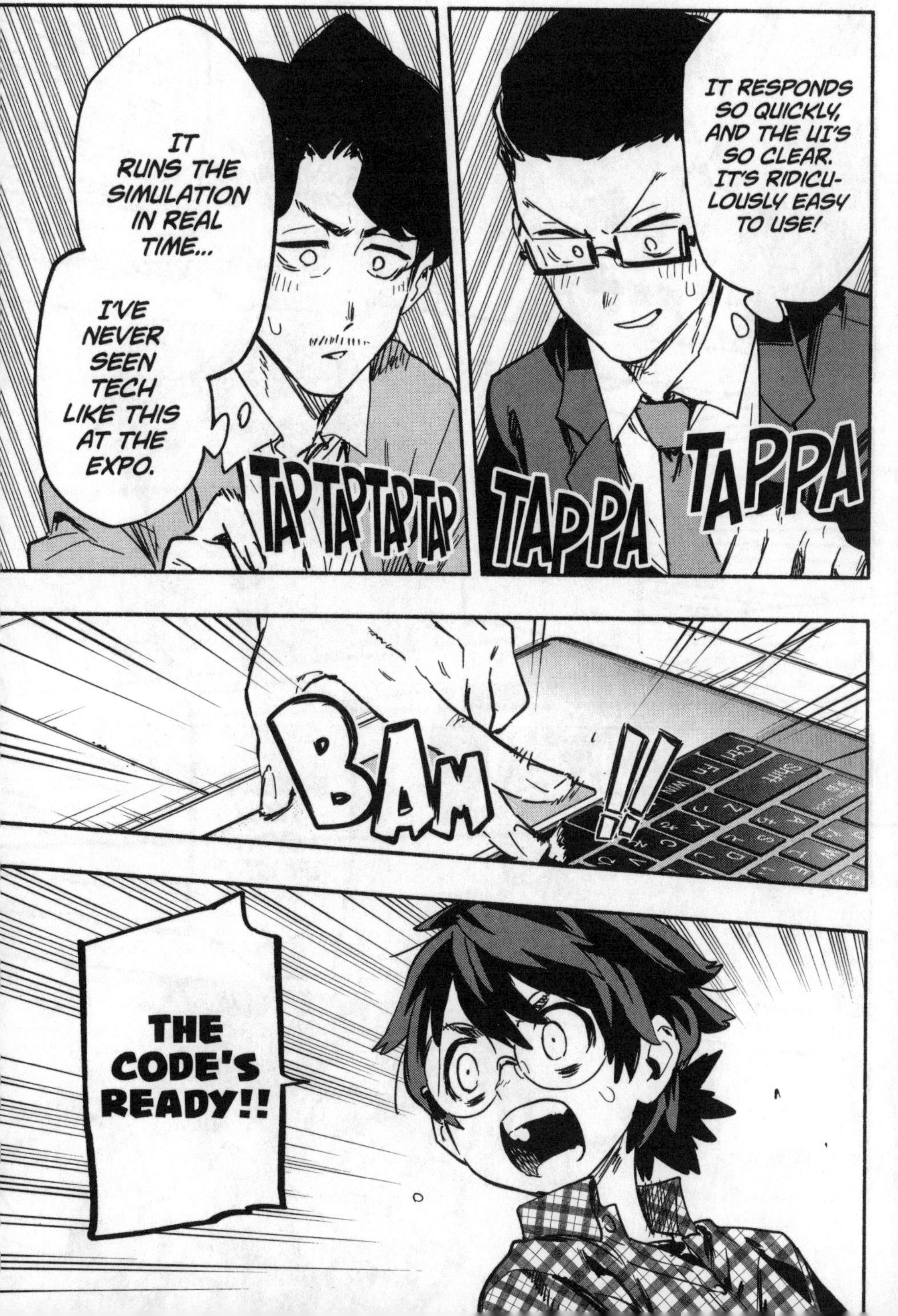
IT RESPONDS SO QUICKLY, AND THE UI'S SO CLEAR. IT'S RIDICU-LOUSLY EASY TO USE!
TAPPA TAPPA
IT RUNS THE SIMULATION IN REAL TIME...
I'VE NEVER SEEN TECH LIKE THIS AT THE EXPO.
TAP TAP TAP TAP
BAM!!
THE CODE'S READY!!

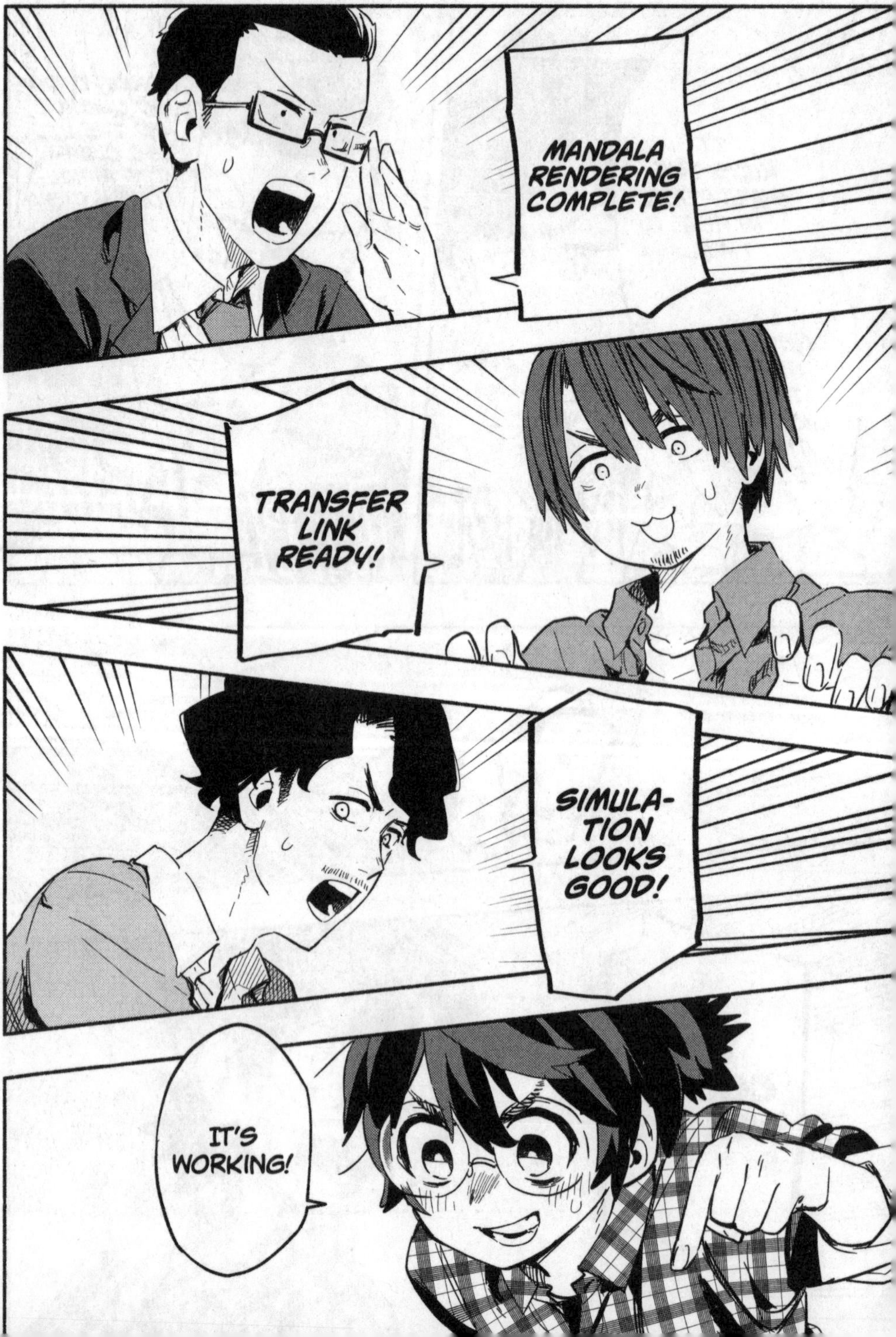
MANDALA RENDERING COMPLETE!
TRANSFER LINK READY!
SIMULA-TION LOOKS GOOD!
IT'S WORKING!

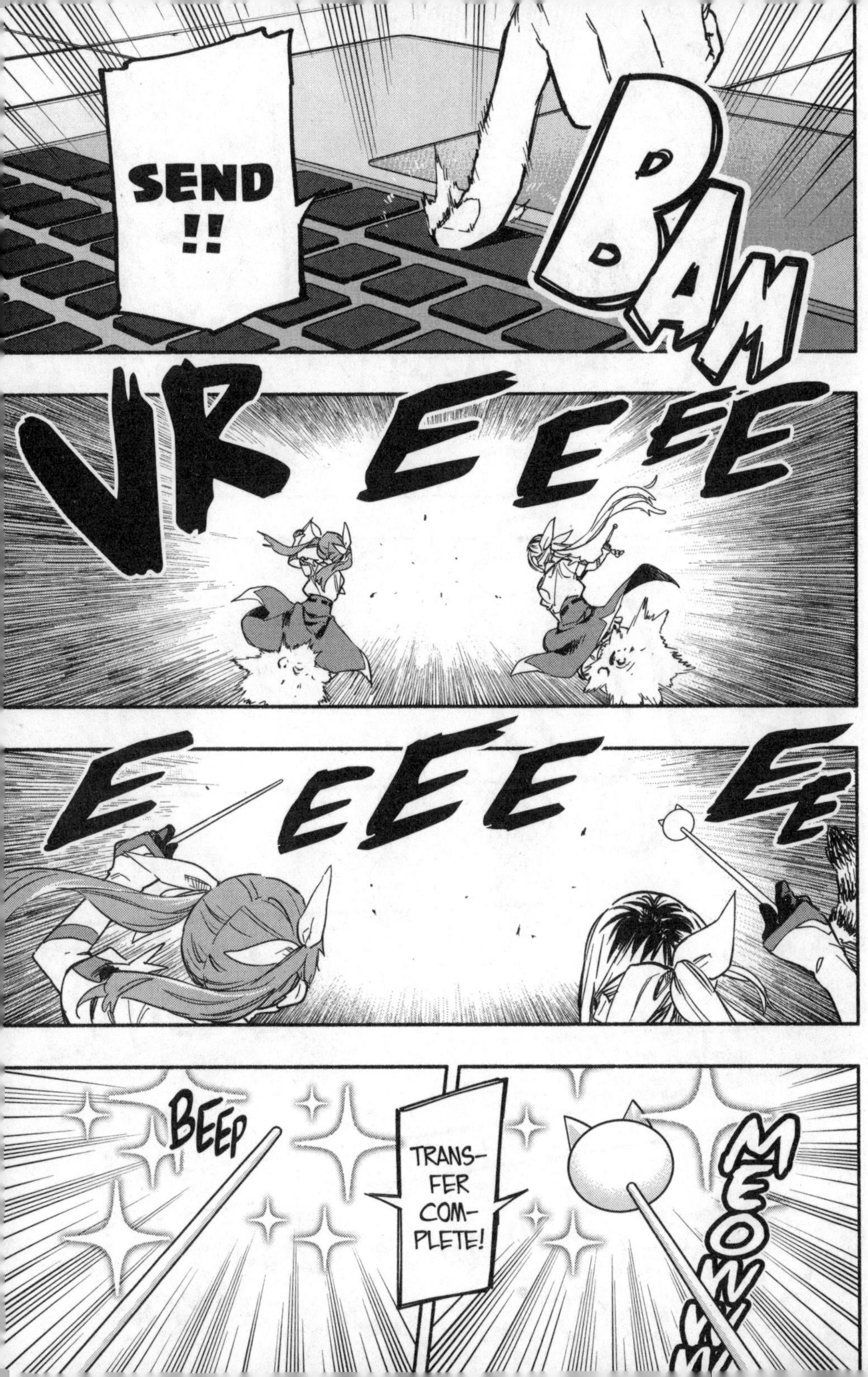
BAM
SEND !!
VREEEEEEEEEE
BEEP
TRANS-FER COM-PLETE!
MEOW

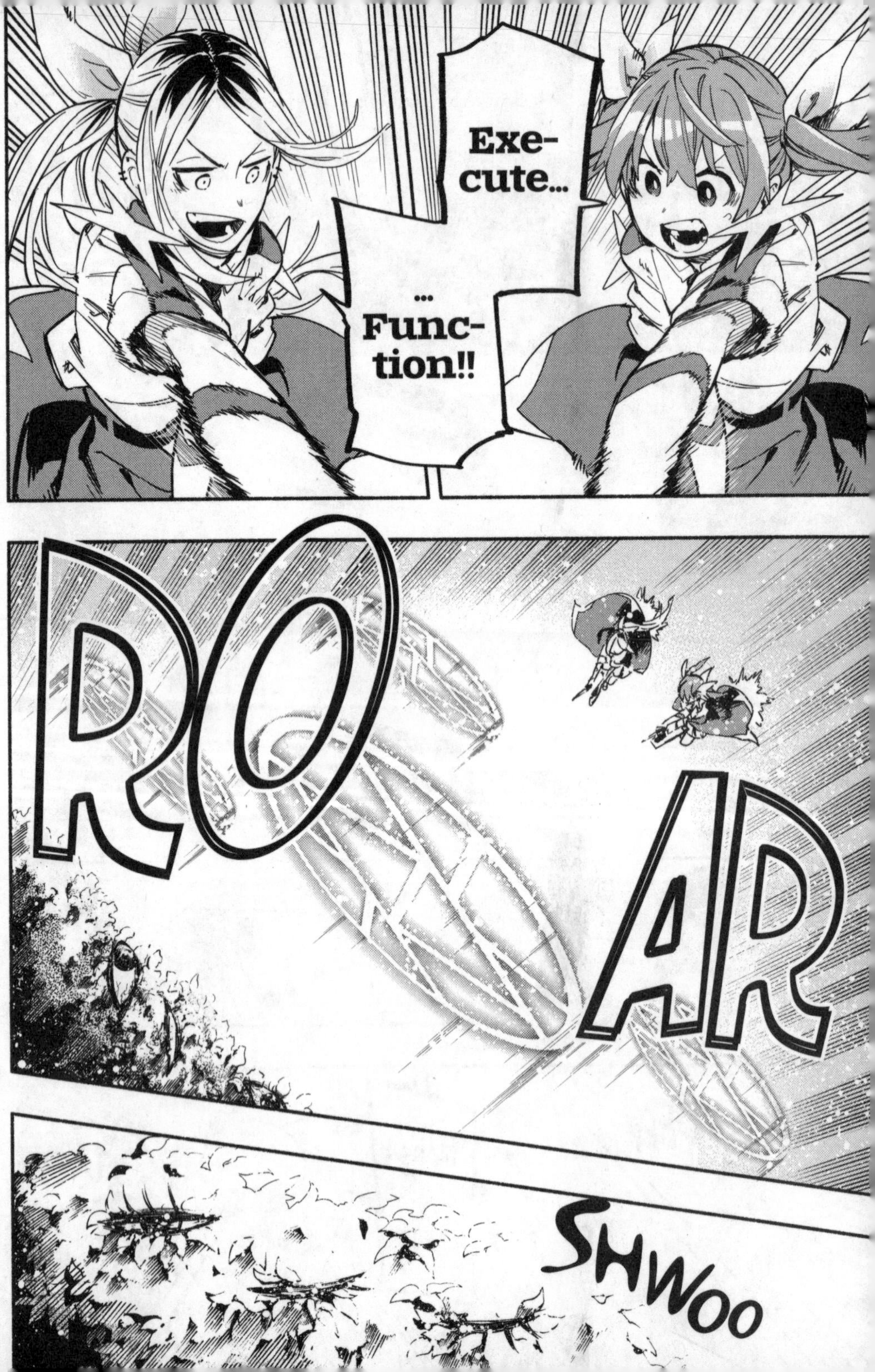
Exe-
cute...
...
Func-
tion!!
ROAR
SHWOO

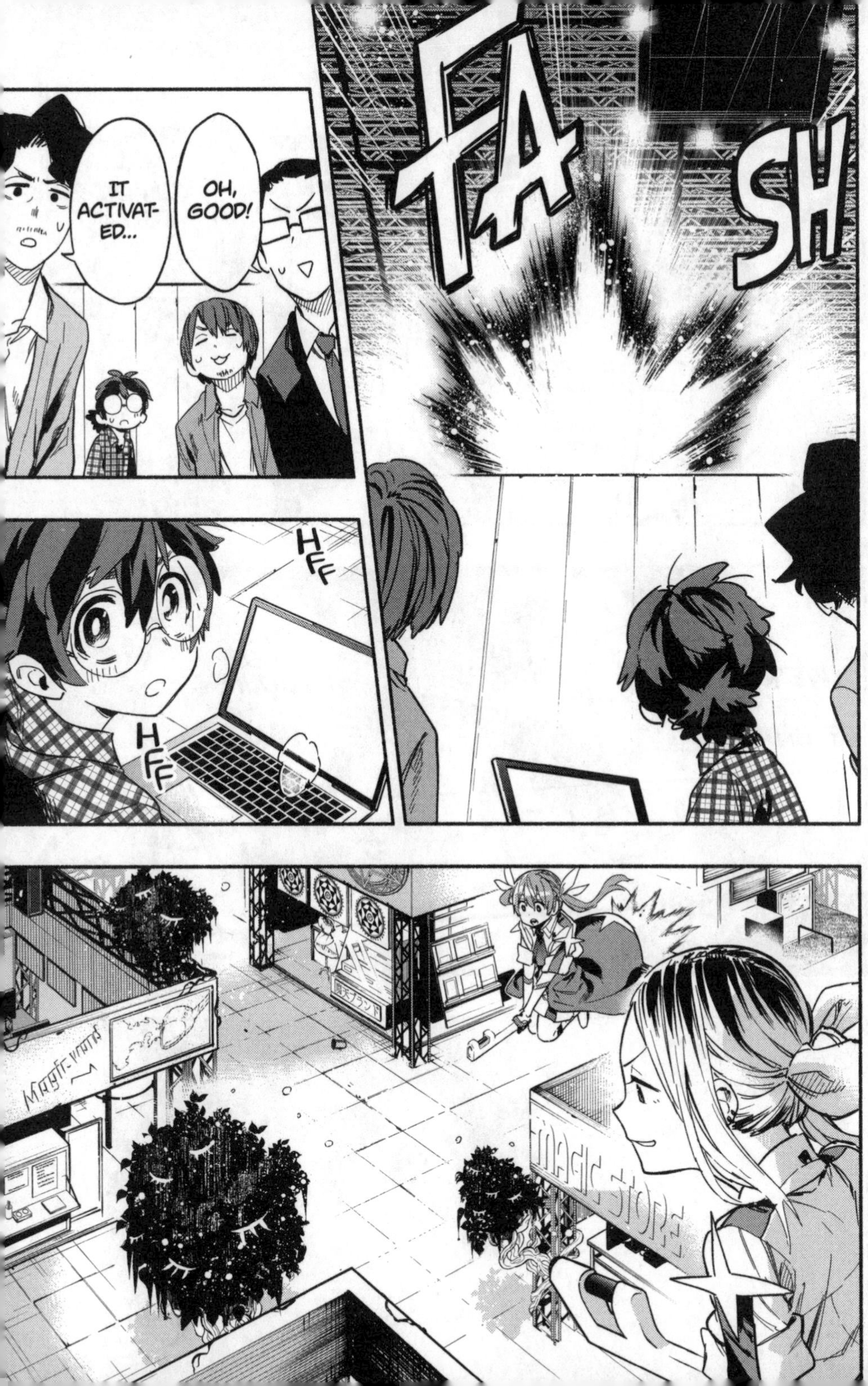
TASH
OH, GOOD!
IT ACTIVATED...
HFF
HFF
MAGIC STORE

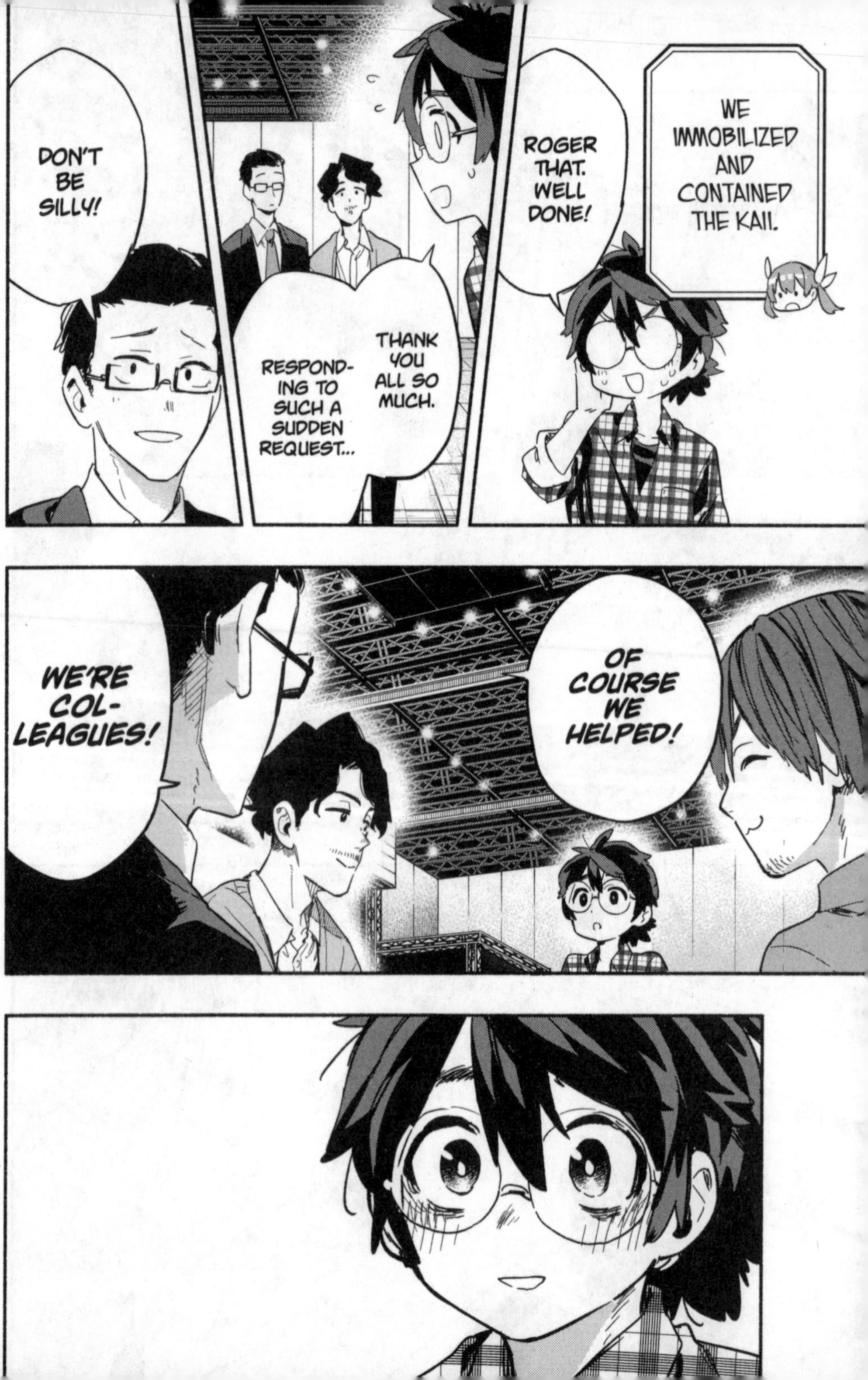
WE IMMOBILIZED AND CONTAINED THE KAIL.
ROGER THAT. WELL DONE!
THANK YOU ALL SO MUCH.
RESPOND-ING TO SUCH A SUDDEN REQUEST...
DON'T BE SILLY!
OF COURSE WE HELPED!
WE'RE COL-LEAGUES!

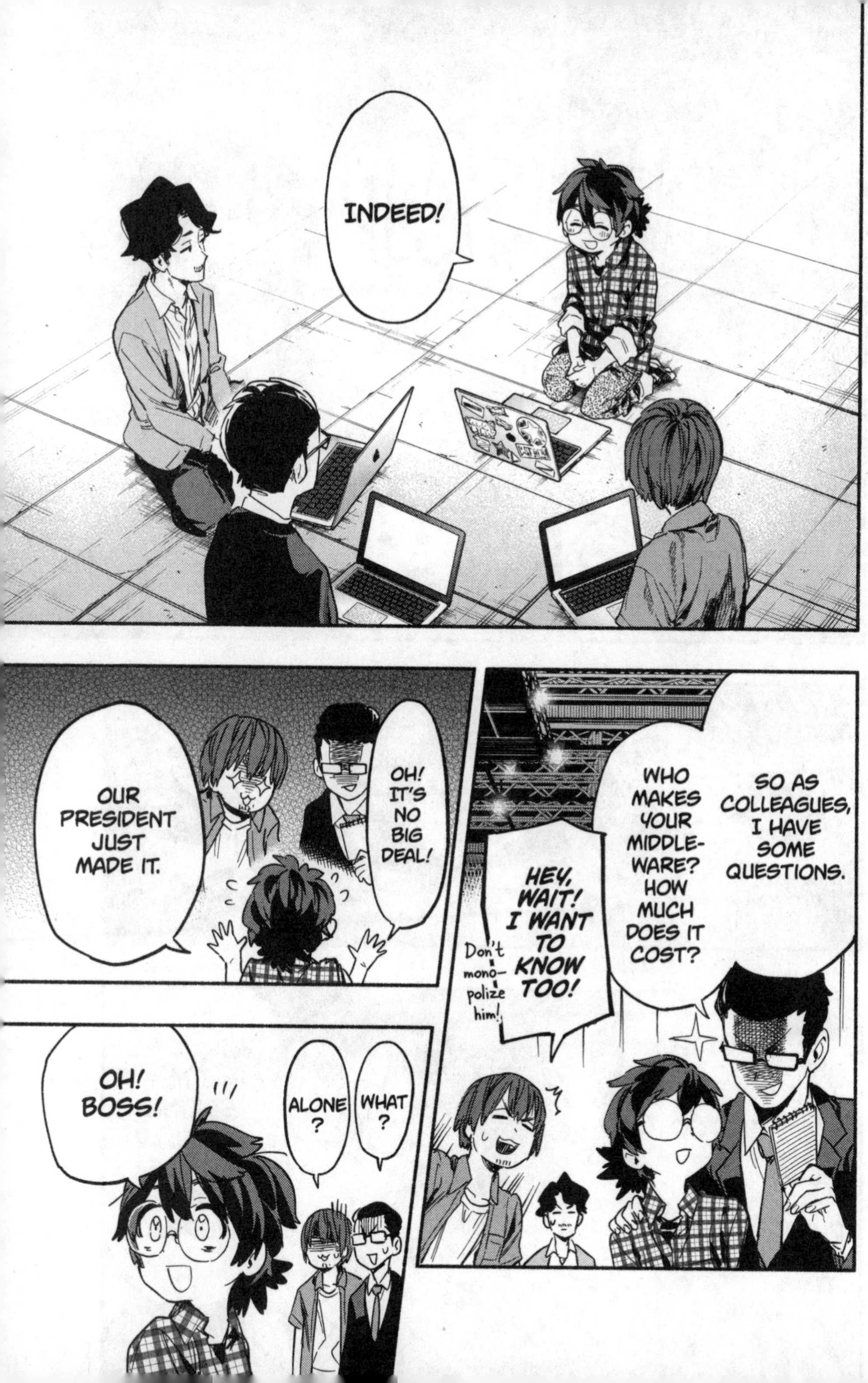
INDEED!
SO AS COLLEAGUES, I HAVE SOME QUESTIONS.
WHO MAKES YOUR MIDDLE-WARE? HOW MUCH DOES IT COST?
HEY, WAIT! I WANT TO KNOW TOO!
Don't monopolize him!
OH! IT'S NO BIG DEAL!
OUR PRESIDENT JUST MADE IT.
WHAT?
ALONE?
OH! BOSS!

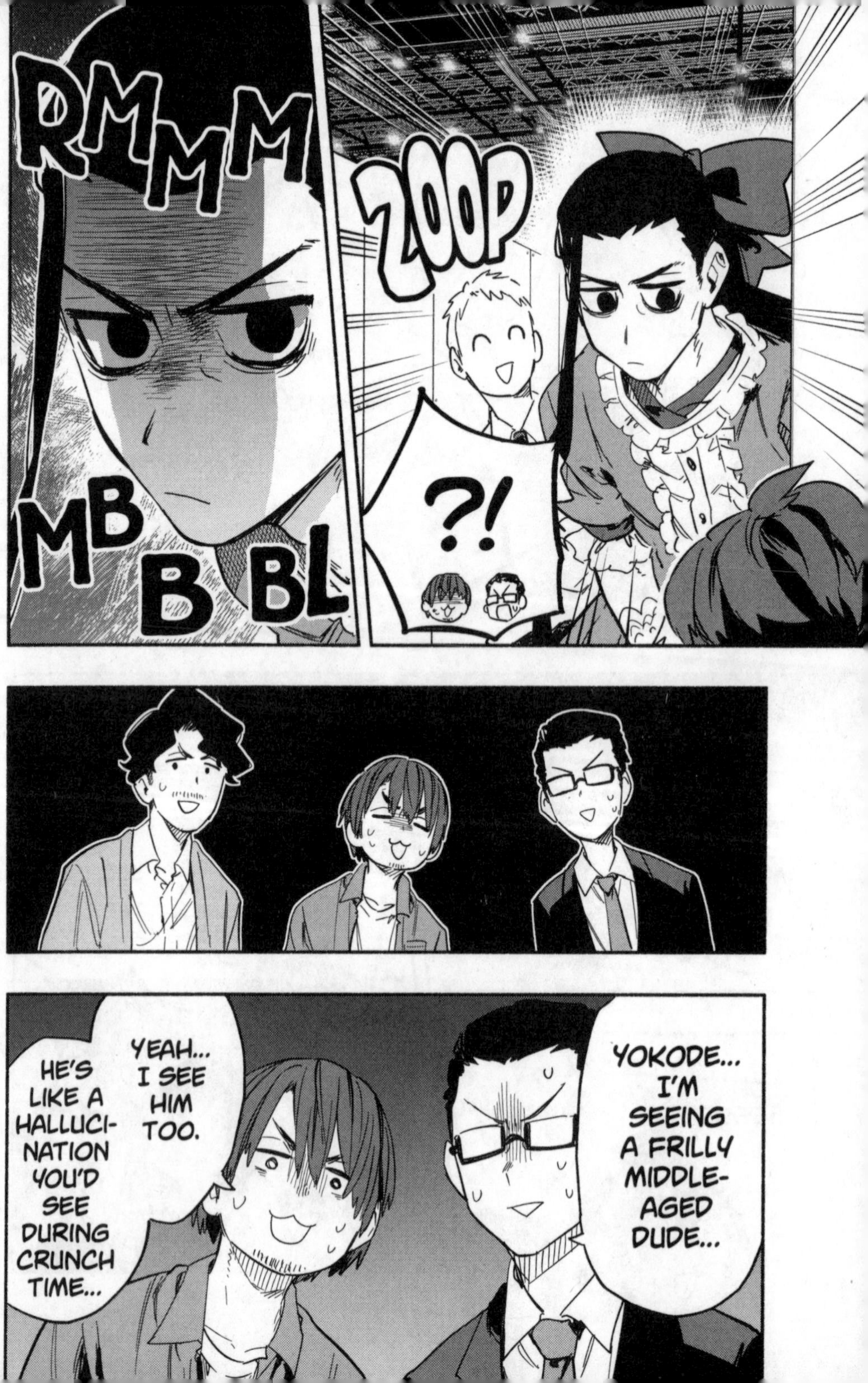
ZOOP
?!
RMMMM
MB B BL
YOKODE... I'M SEEING A FRILLY MIDDLE-AGED DUDE...
YEAH... I SEE HIM TOO.
HE'S LIKE A HALLUCINATION YOU'D SEE DURING CRUNCH TIME...

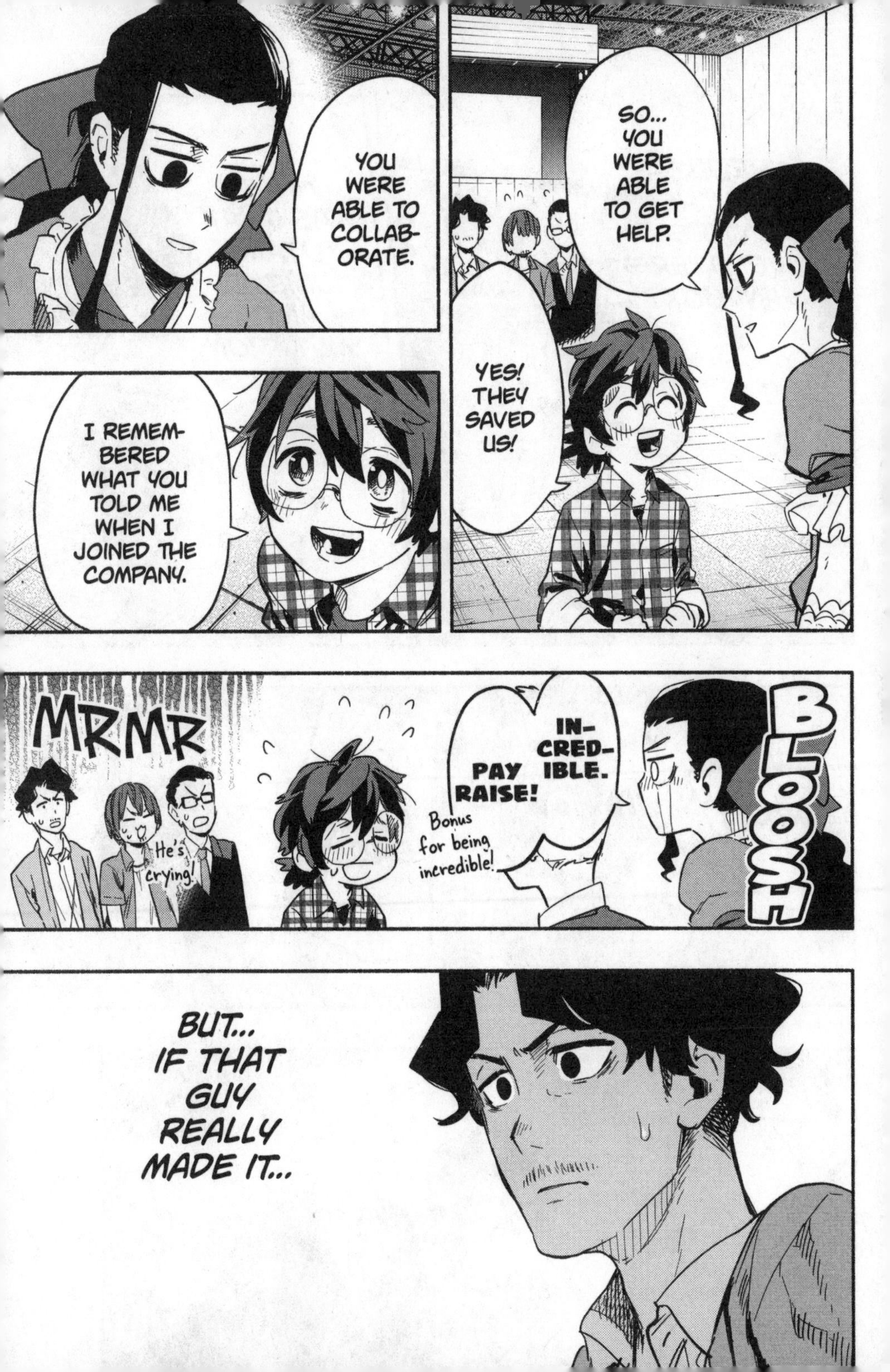

SO... YOU WERE ABLE TO GET HELP.
YES! THEY SAVED US!
YOU WERE ABLE TO COLLABORATE.
I REMEMBERED WHAT YOU TOLD ME WHEN I JOINED THE COMPANY.
BLOOSH
INCREDIBLE. PAY RAISE!
Bonus for being incredible!
He's crying!
MRMR
BUT... IF THAT GUY REALLY MADE IT...

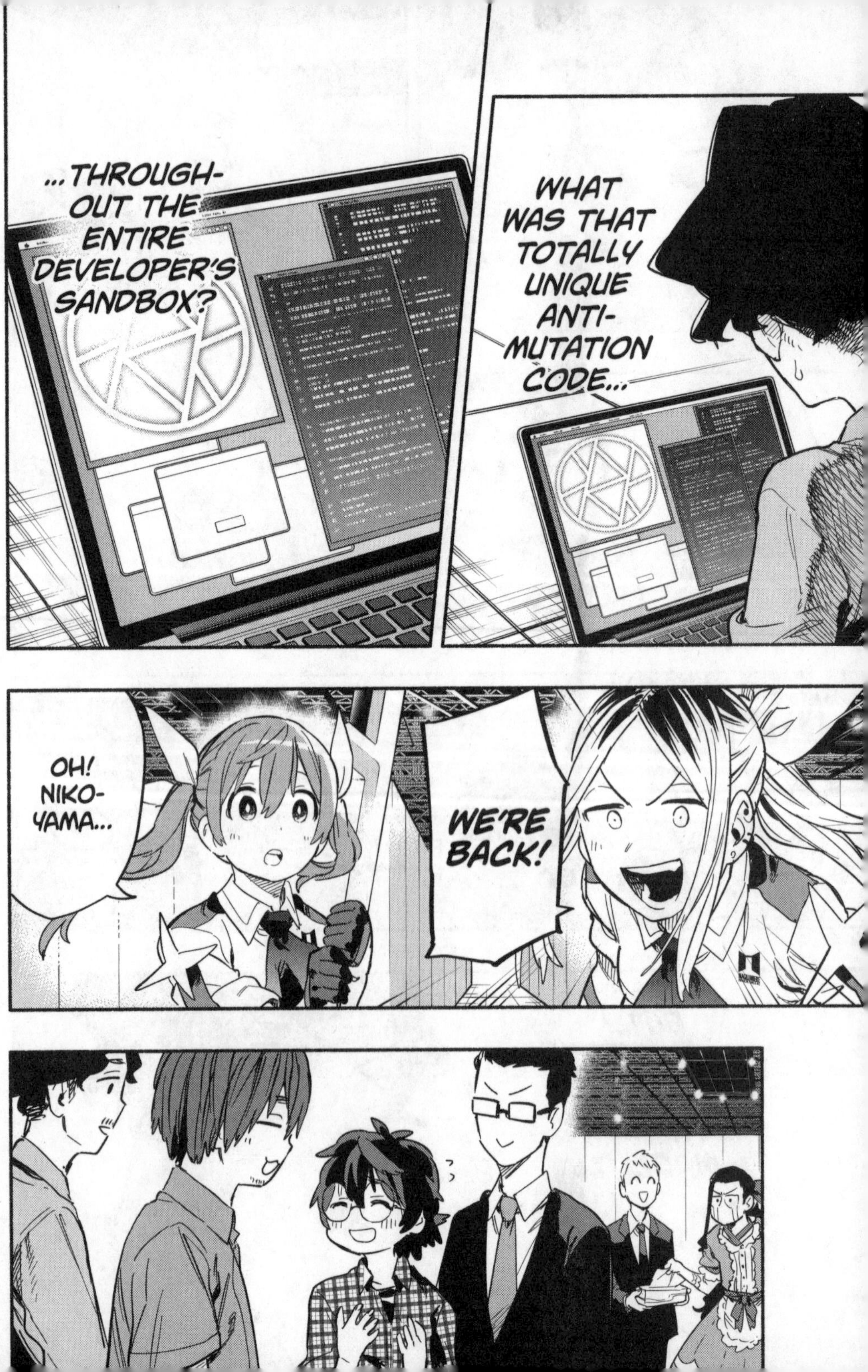
WHAT WAS THAT TOTALLY UNIQUE ANTI-MUTATION CODE...
...THROUGH-OUT THE ENTIRE DEVELOPER'S SANDBOX?
WE'RE BACK!
OH! NIKO-YAMA...

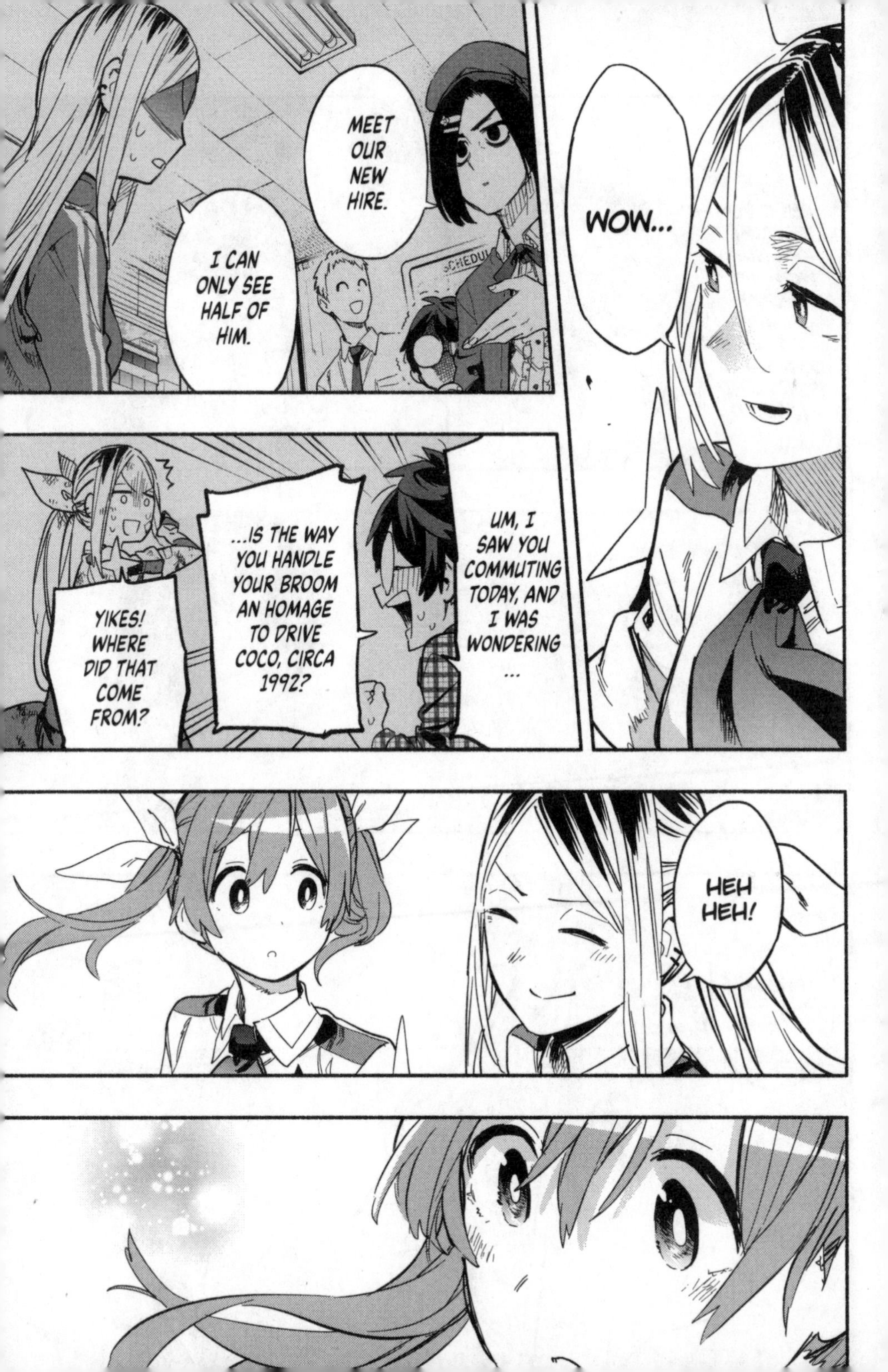
WOW...
MEET OUR NEW HIRE.
I CAN ONLY SEE HALF OF HIM.
UM, I SAW YOU COMMUTING TODAY, AND I WAS WONDERING...
...IS THE WAY YOU HANDLE YOUR BROOM AN HOMAGE TO DRIVE COCO, CIRCA 1992?
YIKES! WHERE DID THAT COME FROM?
HEH HEH!

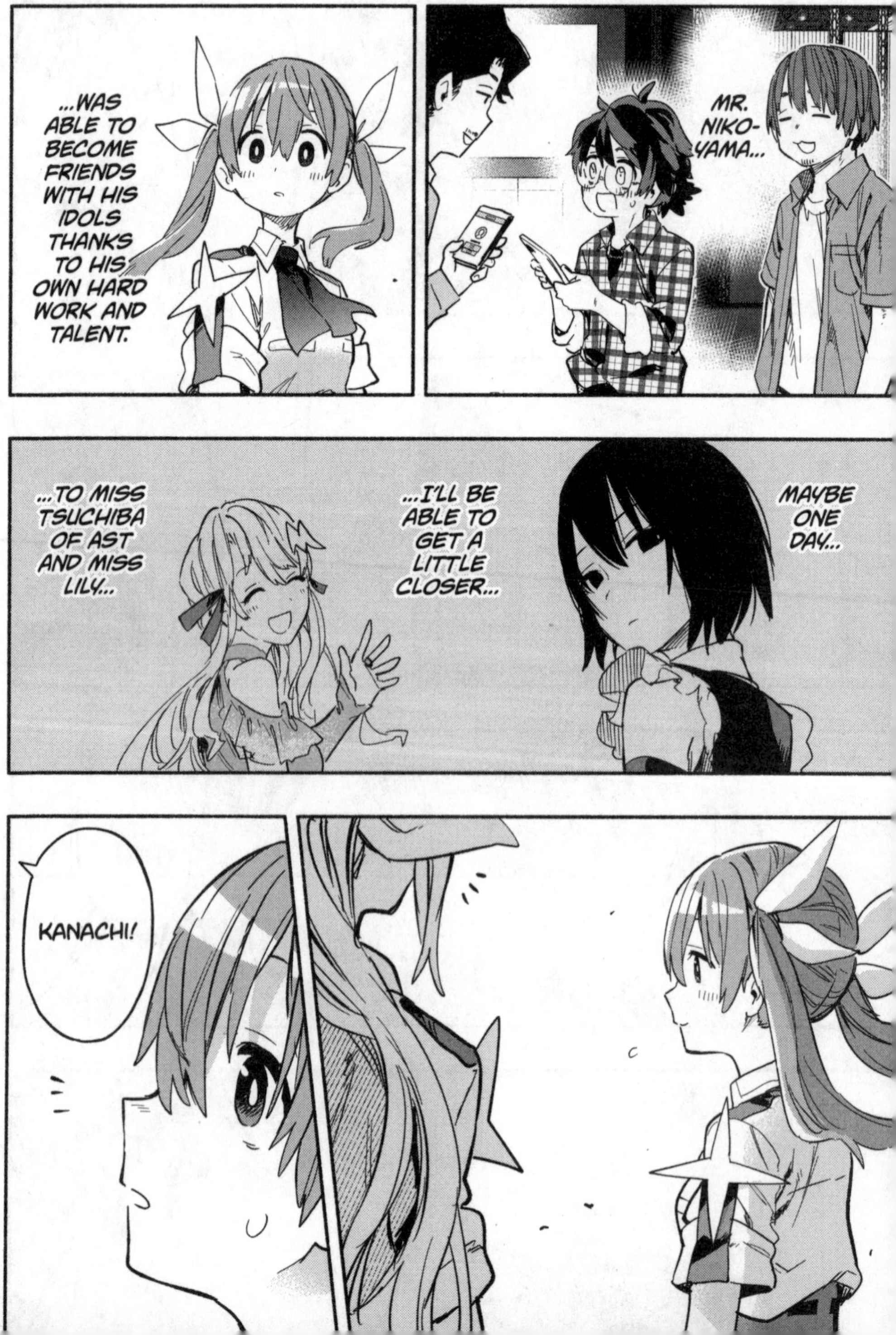
MR. NIKO-YAMA...
...WAS ABLE TO BECOME FRIENDS WITH HIS IDOLS THANKS TO HIS OWN HARD WORK AND TALENT.
MAYBE ONE DAY...
...I'LL BE ABLE TO GET A LITTLE CLOSER...
...TO MISS TSUCHIBA OF AST AND MISS LILY...
KANACHI!

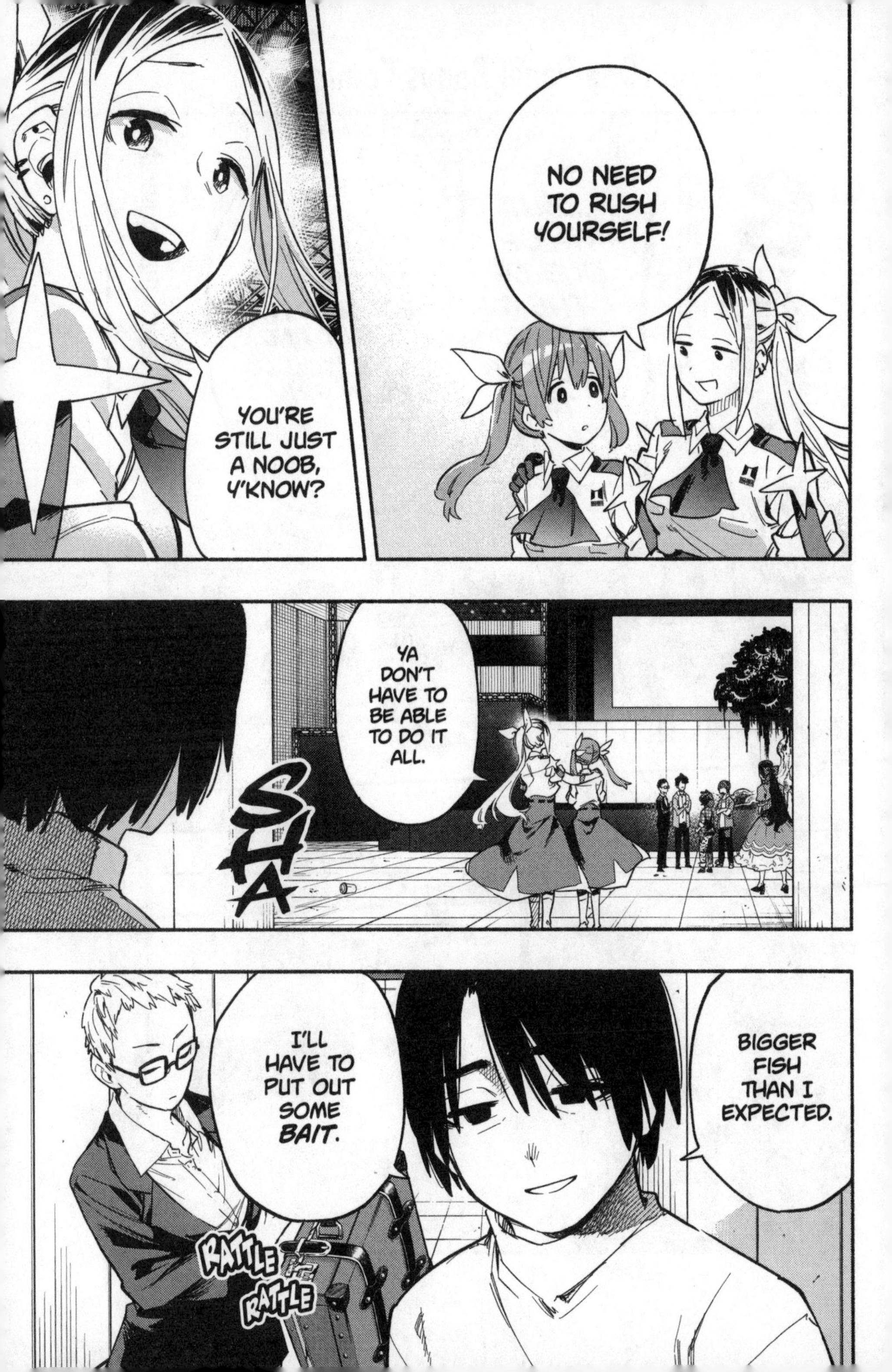
NO NEED TO RUSH YOURSELF!
YOU'RE STILL JUST A NOOB, Y'KNOW?
YA DON'T HAVE TO BE ABLE TO DO IT ALL.
SHA
BIGGER FISH THAN I EXPECTED.
I'LL HAVE TO PUT OUT SOME BAIT.
RATTLE RATTLE

One-Panel Bonus Comic

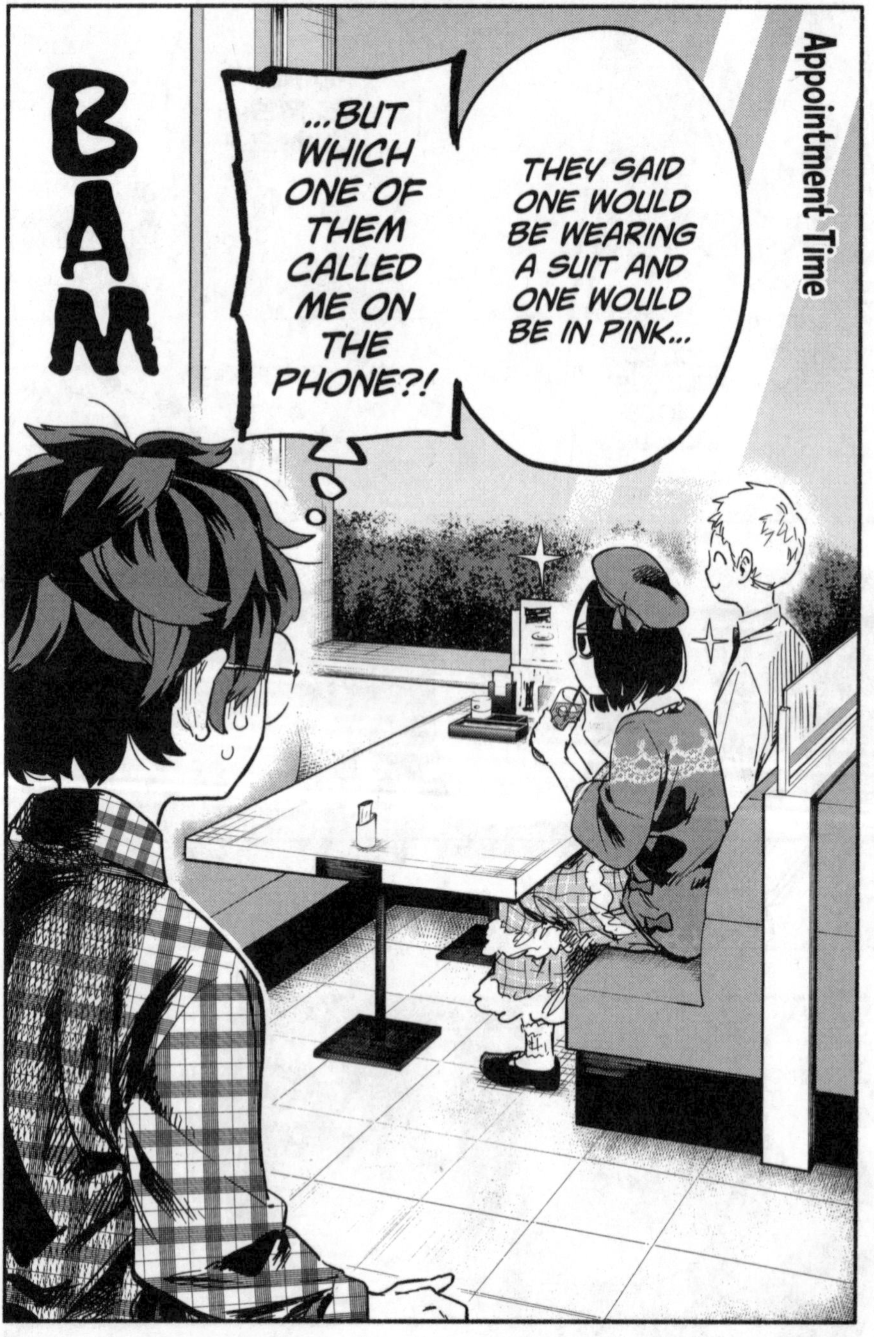
Appointment Time
THEY SAID ONE WOULD BE WEARING A SUIT AND ONE WOULD BE IN PINK...
...BUT WHICH ONE OF THEM CALLED ME ON THE PHONE?!
BAM

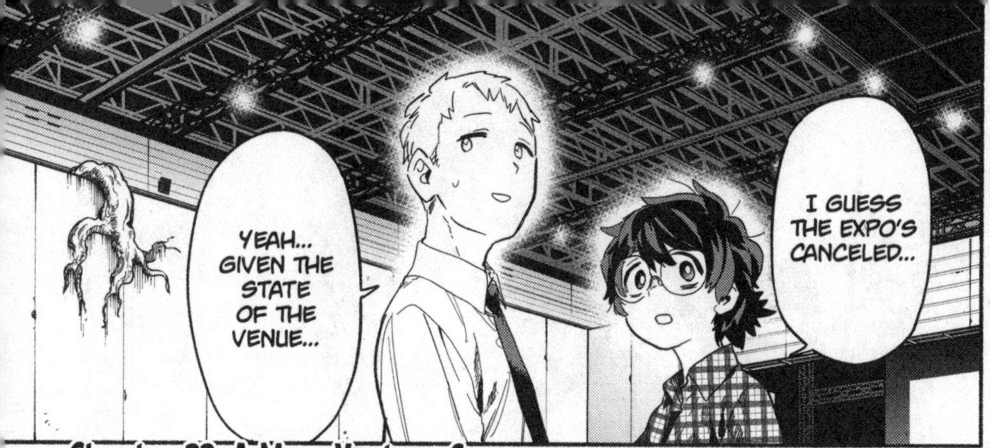
I GUESS THE EXPO'S CANCELED...
YEAH... GIVEN THE STATE OF THE VENUE...

Chapter 22: A Mere Venture Company

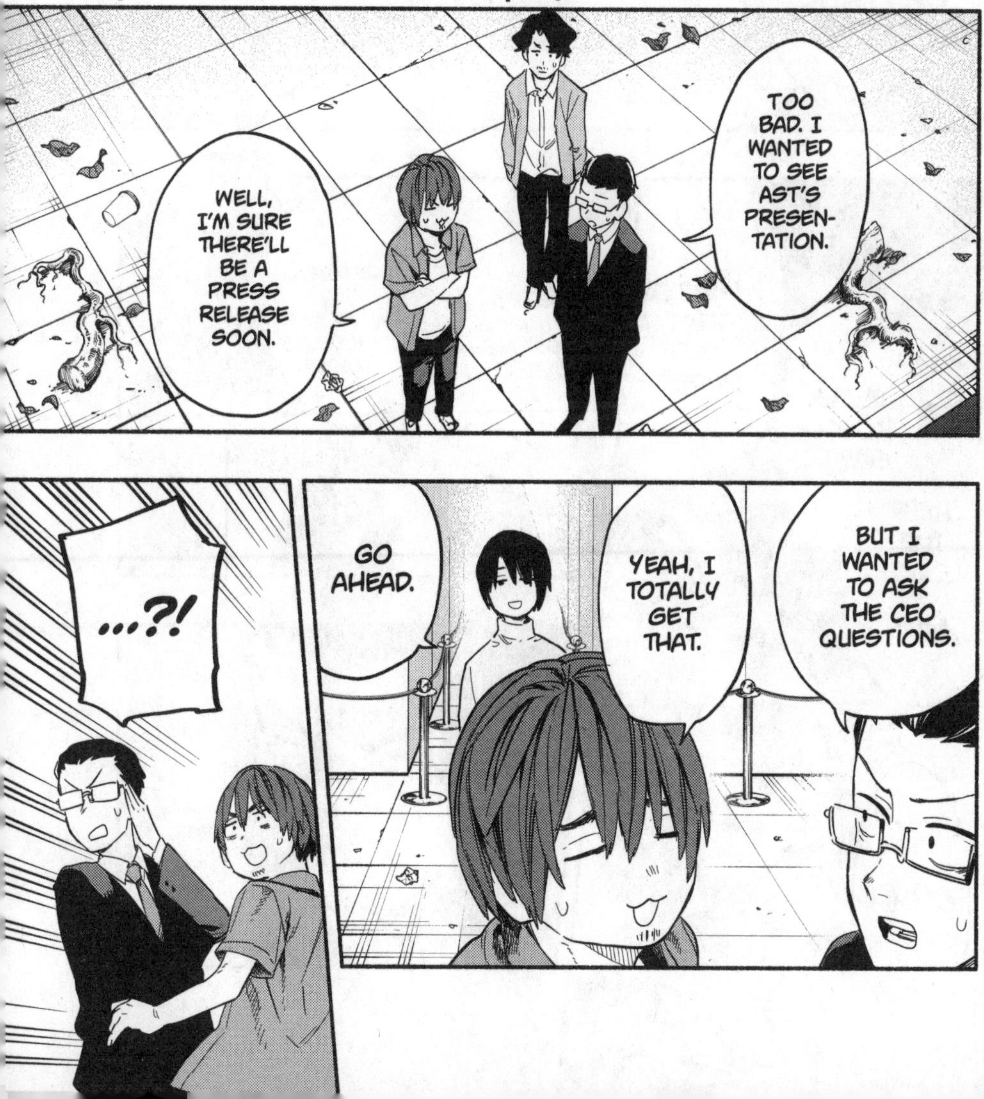
TOO BAD. I WANTED TO SEE AST'S PRESEN-TATION.
WELL, I'M SURE THERE'LL BE A PRESS RELEASE SOON.
BUT I WANTED TO ASK THE CEO QUESTIONS.
YEAH, I TOTALLY GET THAT.
GO AHEAD.
...?!

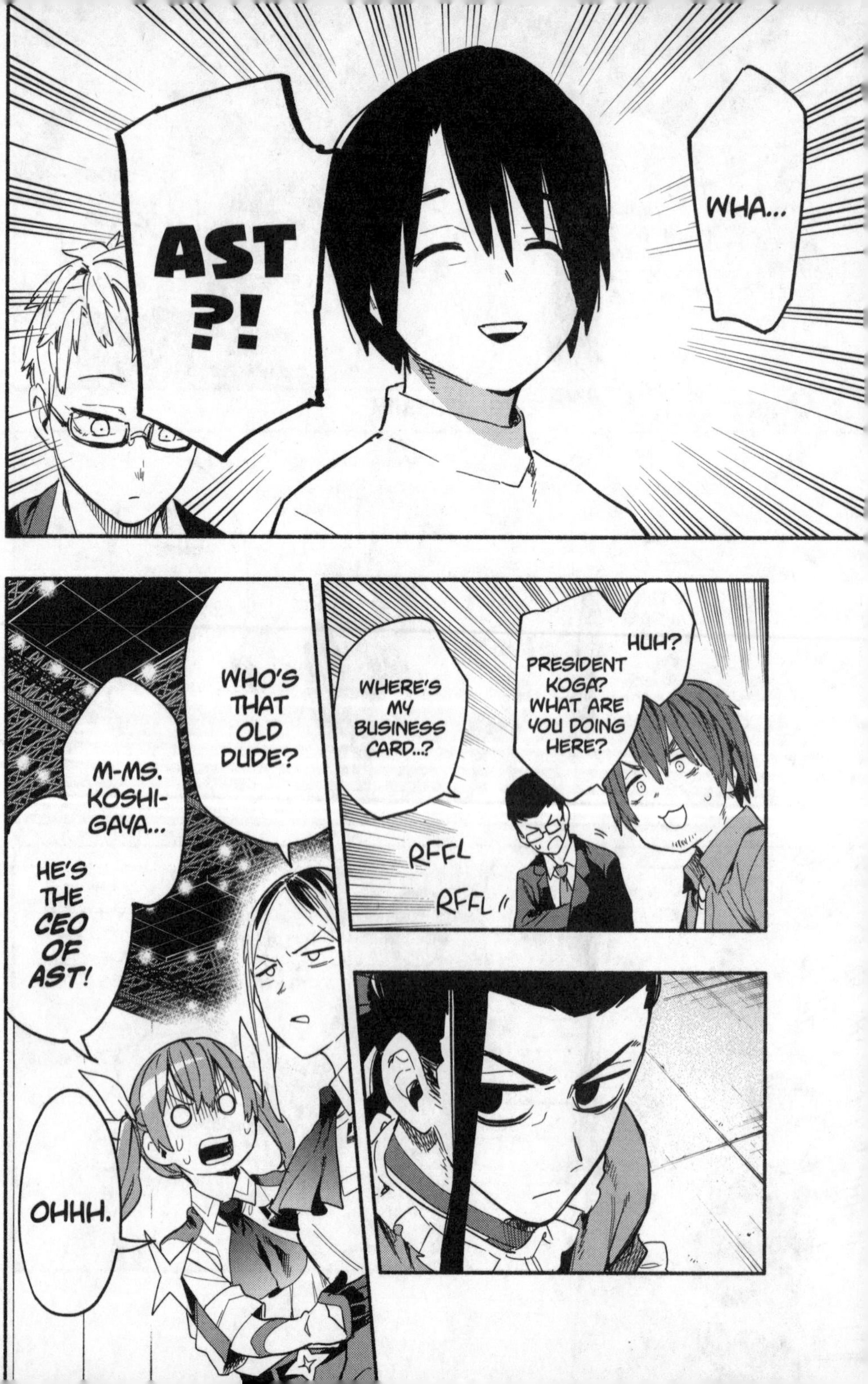
WHA...
AST ?!
HUH? PRESIDENT KOGA? WHAT ARE YOU DOING HERE?
WHERE'S MY BUSINESS CARD..?
RFFL
RFFL
WHO'S THAT OLD DUDE?
M-MS. KOSHI-GAYA...
HE'S THE CEO OF AST!
OHHH.

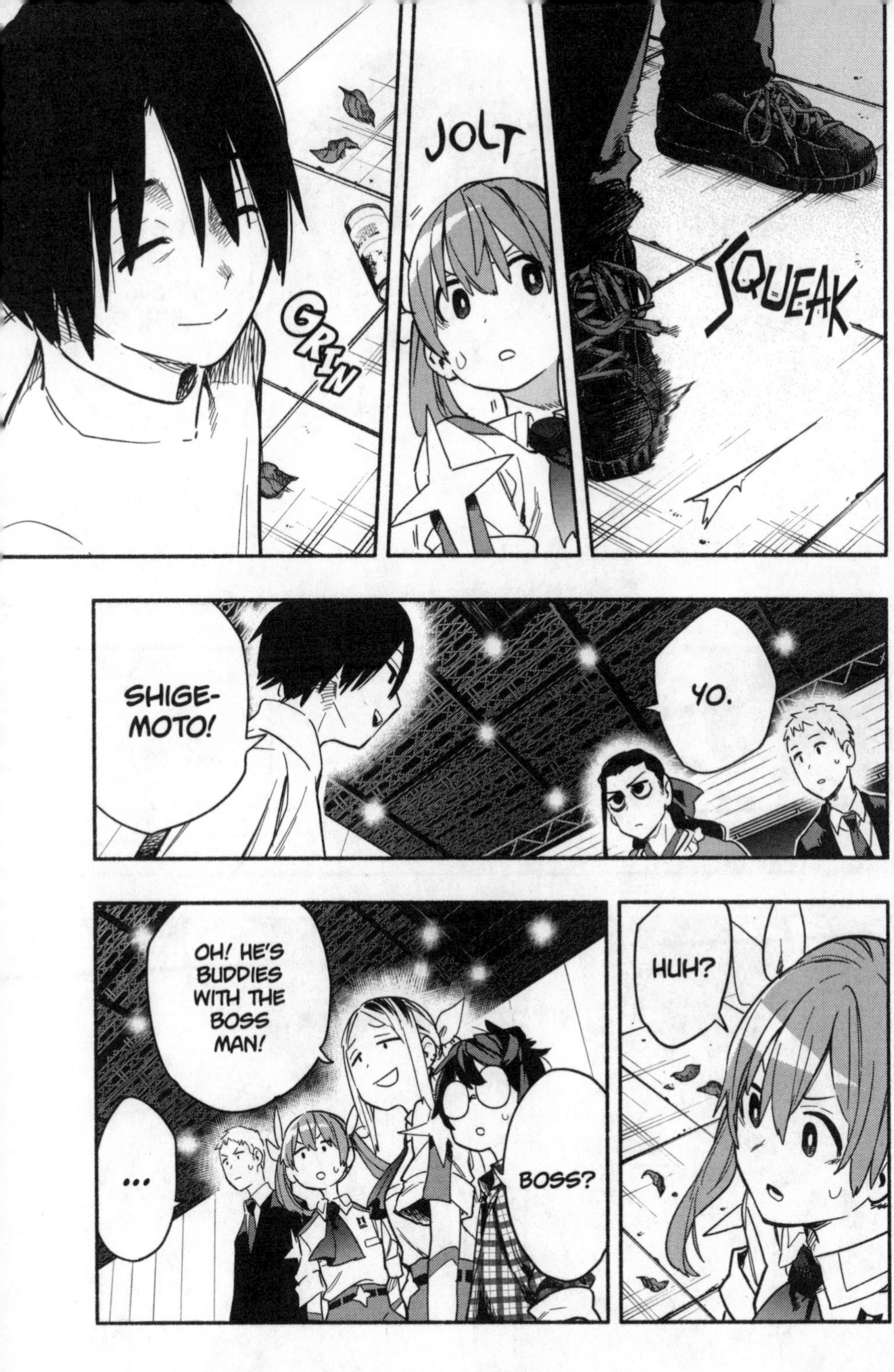
SQUEAK
JOLT
GRIN
YO.
SHIGE-MOTO!
HUH?
OH! HE'S BUDDIES WITH THE BOSS MAN!
BOSS?
...

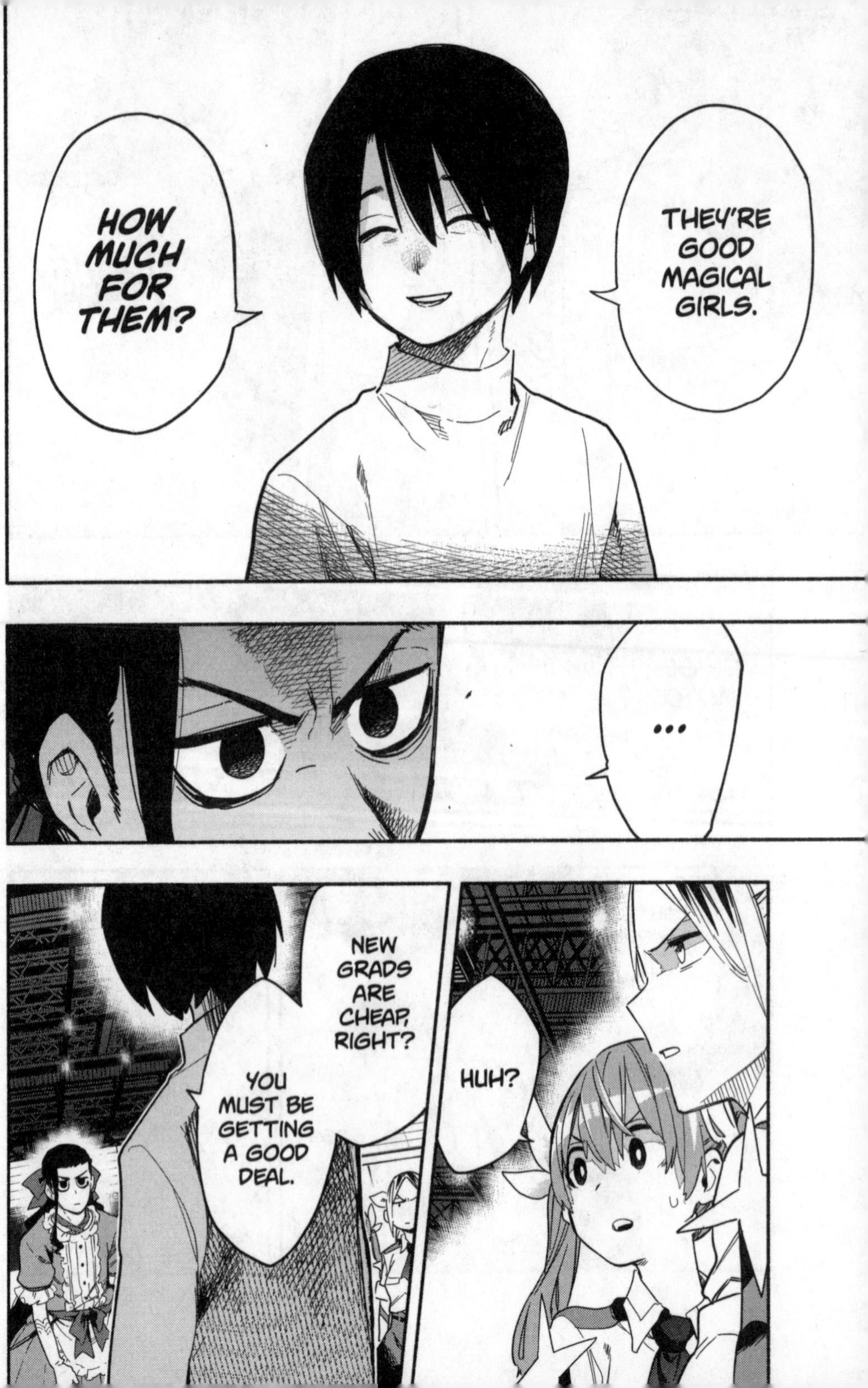
THEY'RE GOOD MAGICAL GIRLS.
HOW MUCH FOR THEM?
...
NEW GRADS ARE CHEAP, RIGHT?
YOU MUST BE GETTING A GOOD DEAL.
HUH?

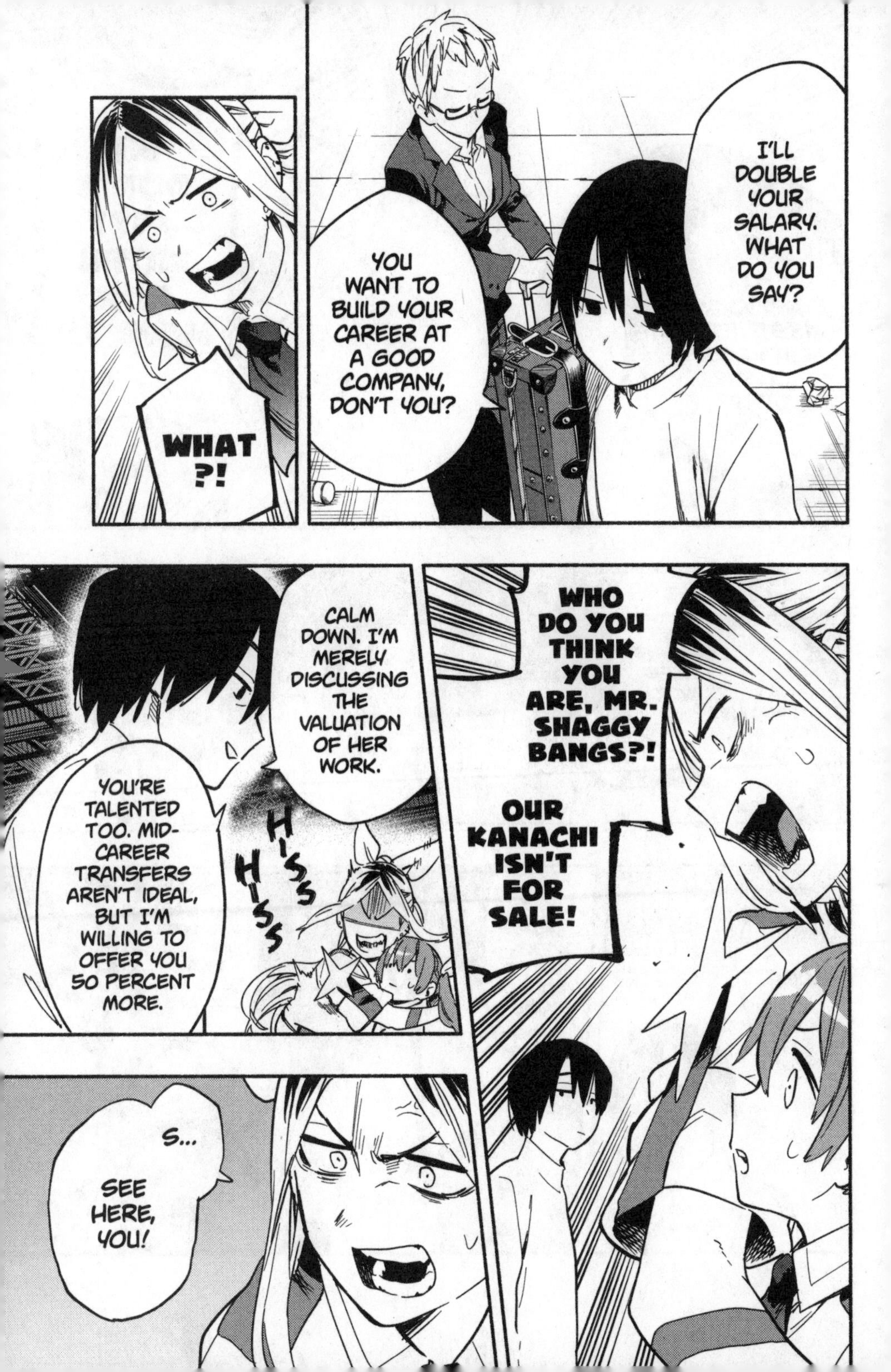
I'LL DOUBLE YOUR SALARY. WHAT DO YOU SAY?
YOU WANT TO BUILD YOUR CAREER AT A GOOD COMPANY, DON'T YOU?
WHAT?!
WHO DO YOU THINK YOU ARE, MR. SHAGGY BANGS?!
OUR KANACHI ISN'T FOR SALE!
CALM DOWN. I'M MERELY DISCUSSING THE VALUATION OF HER WORK.
YOU'RE TALENTED TOO. MID-CAREER TRANSFERS AREN'T IDEAL, BUT I'M WILLING TO OFFER YOU 50 PERCENT MORE.
HISS
HISS
S...
SEE HERE, YOU!

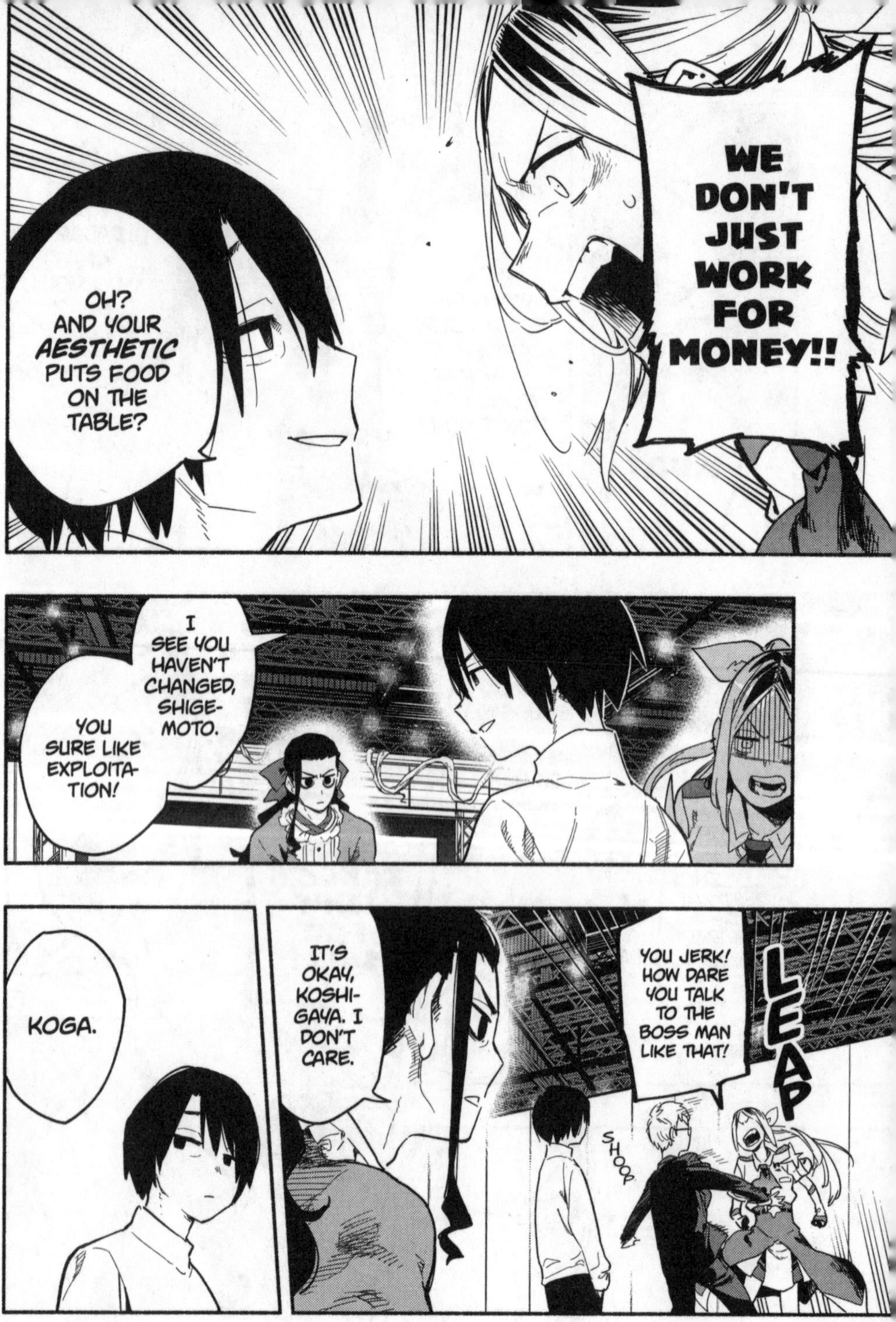
WE DON'T JUST WORK FOR MONEY!!
OH? AND YOUR AESTHETIC PUTS FOOD ON THE TABLE?
I SEE YOU HAVEN'T CHANGED, SHIGE-MOTO.
YOU SURE LIKE EXPLOITA-TION!
YOU JERK! HOW DARE YOU TALK TO THE BOSS MAN LIKE THAT!
LEAP
SHOOP
IT'S OKAY, KOSHI-GAYA. I DON'T CARE.
KOGA.

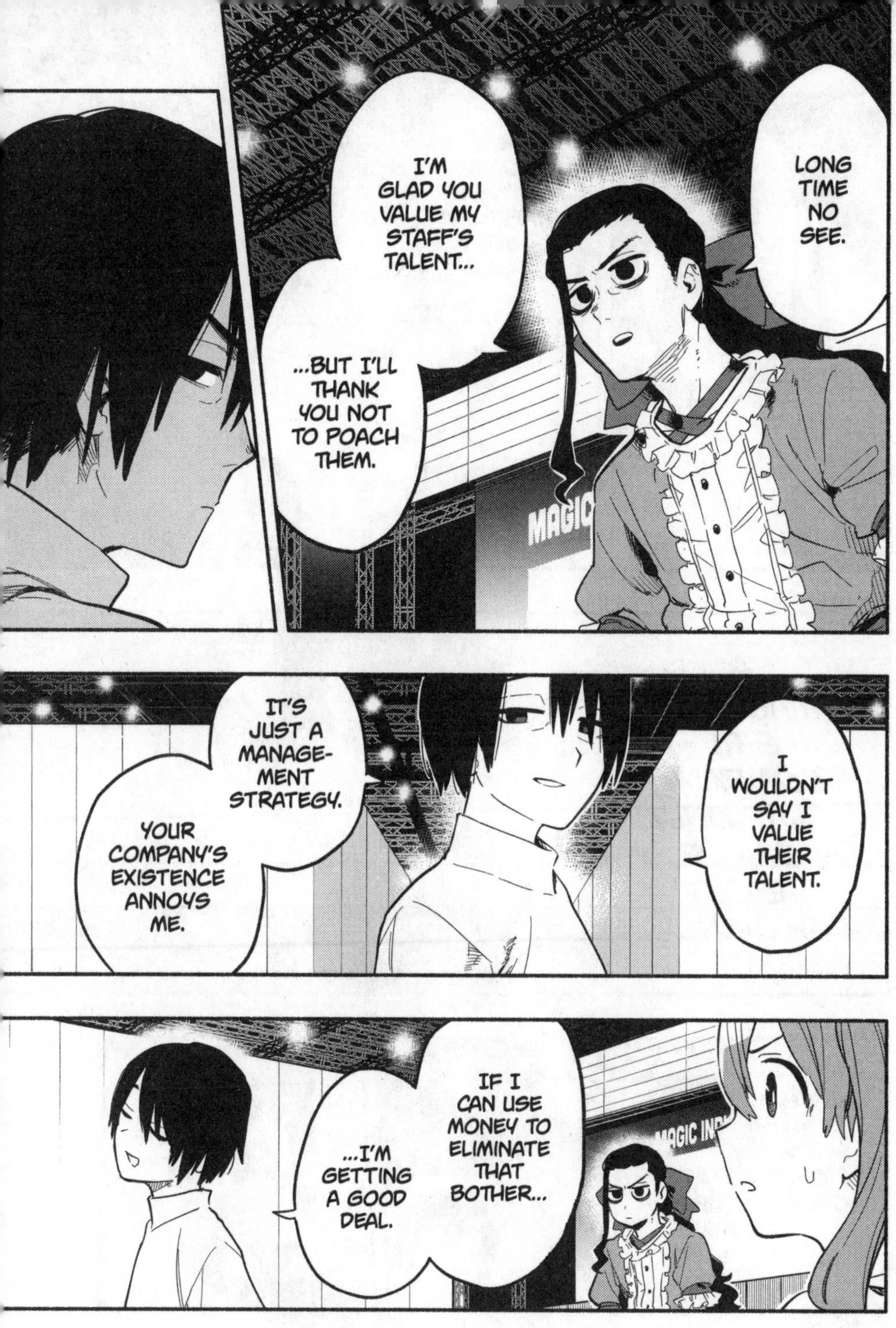
LONG TIME NO SEE.
I'M GLAD YOU VALUE MY STAFF'S TALENT...
...BUT I'LL THANK YOU NOT TO POACH THEM.
MAGIC
I WOULDN'T SAY I VALUE THEIR TALENT.
IT'S JUST A MANAGE-MENT STRATEGY.
YOUR COMPANY'S EXISTENCE ANNOYS ME.
IF I CAN USE MONEY TO ELIMINATE THAT BOTHER...
...I'M GETTING A GOOD DEAL.

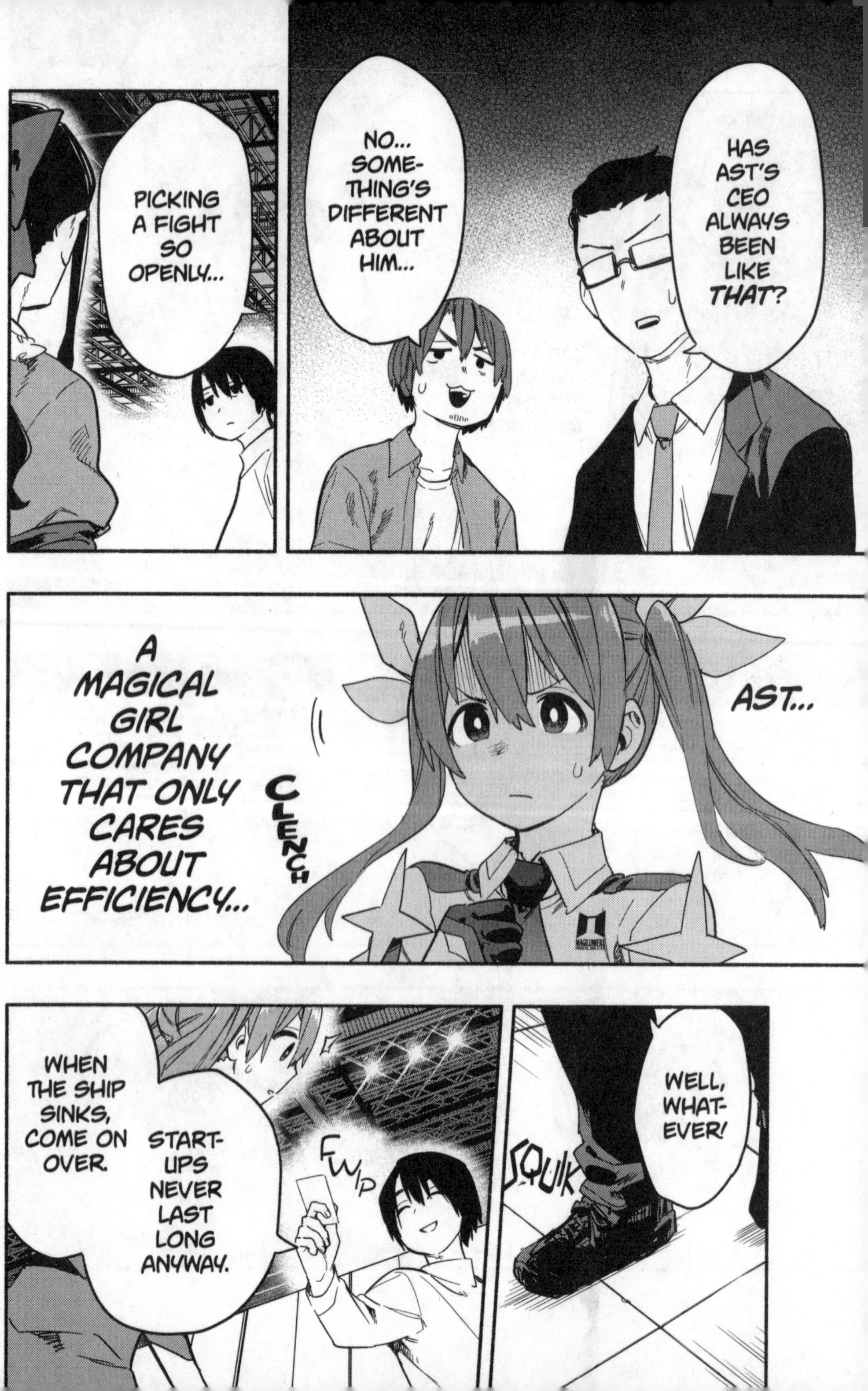
HAS AST'S CEO ALWAYS BEEN LIKE THAT?
NO... SOME-THING'S DIFFERENT ABOUT HIM...
PICKING A FIGHT SO OPENLY...
AST...
CLENCH
A MAGICAL GIRL COMPANY THAT ONLY CARES ABOUT EFFICIENCY...
WELL, WHAT-EVER!
SQUIK
START-UPS NEVER LAST LONG ANYWAY.
WHEN THE SHIP SINKS, COME ON OVER.
FWIP

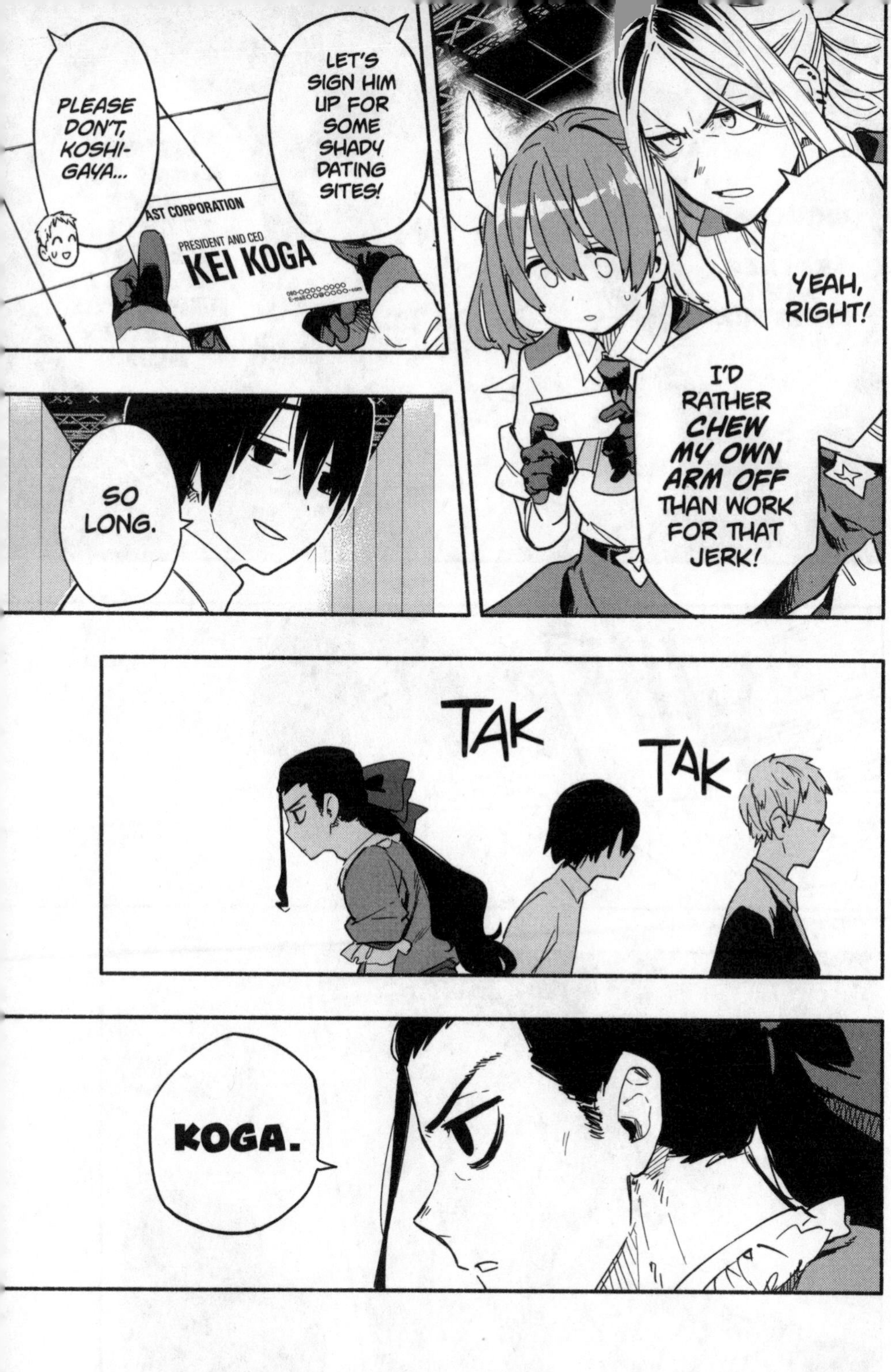
YEAH, RIGHT!
I'D RATHER CHEW MY OWN ARM OFF THAN WORK FOR THAT JERK!
LET'S SIGN HIM UP FOR SOME SHADY DATING SITES!
PLEASE DON'T, KOSHI-GAYA...
AST CORPORATION
PRESIDENT AND CEO
KEI KOGA
SO LONG.
TAK
TAK
KOGA.

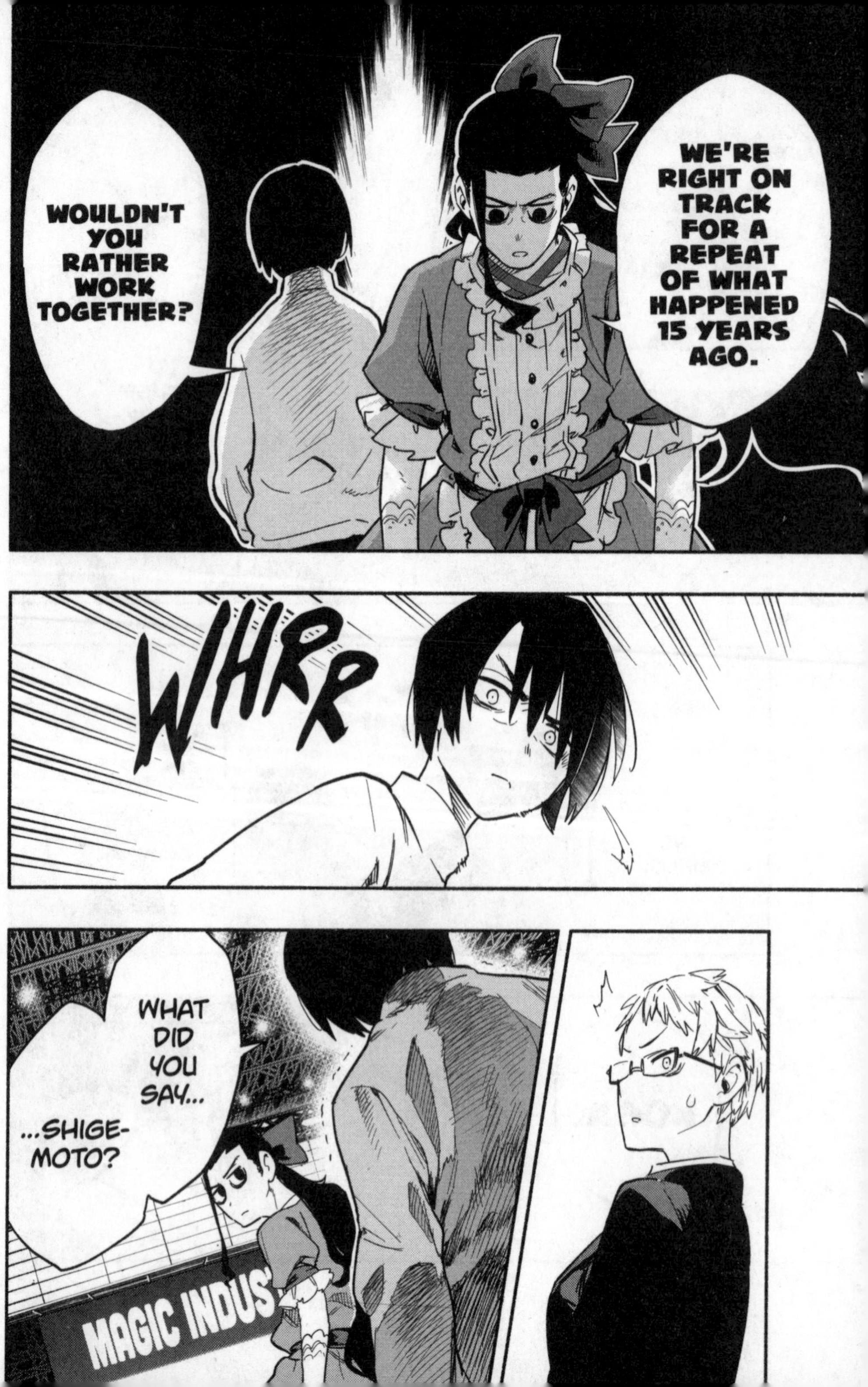
WE'RE RIGHT ON TRACK FOR A REPEAT OF WHAT HAPPENED 15 YEARS AGO.
WOULDN'T YOU RATHER WORK TOGETHER?
WHRR
WHAT DID YOU SAY...
...SHIGE-MOTO?
MAGIC INDUS

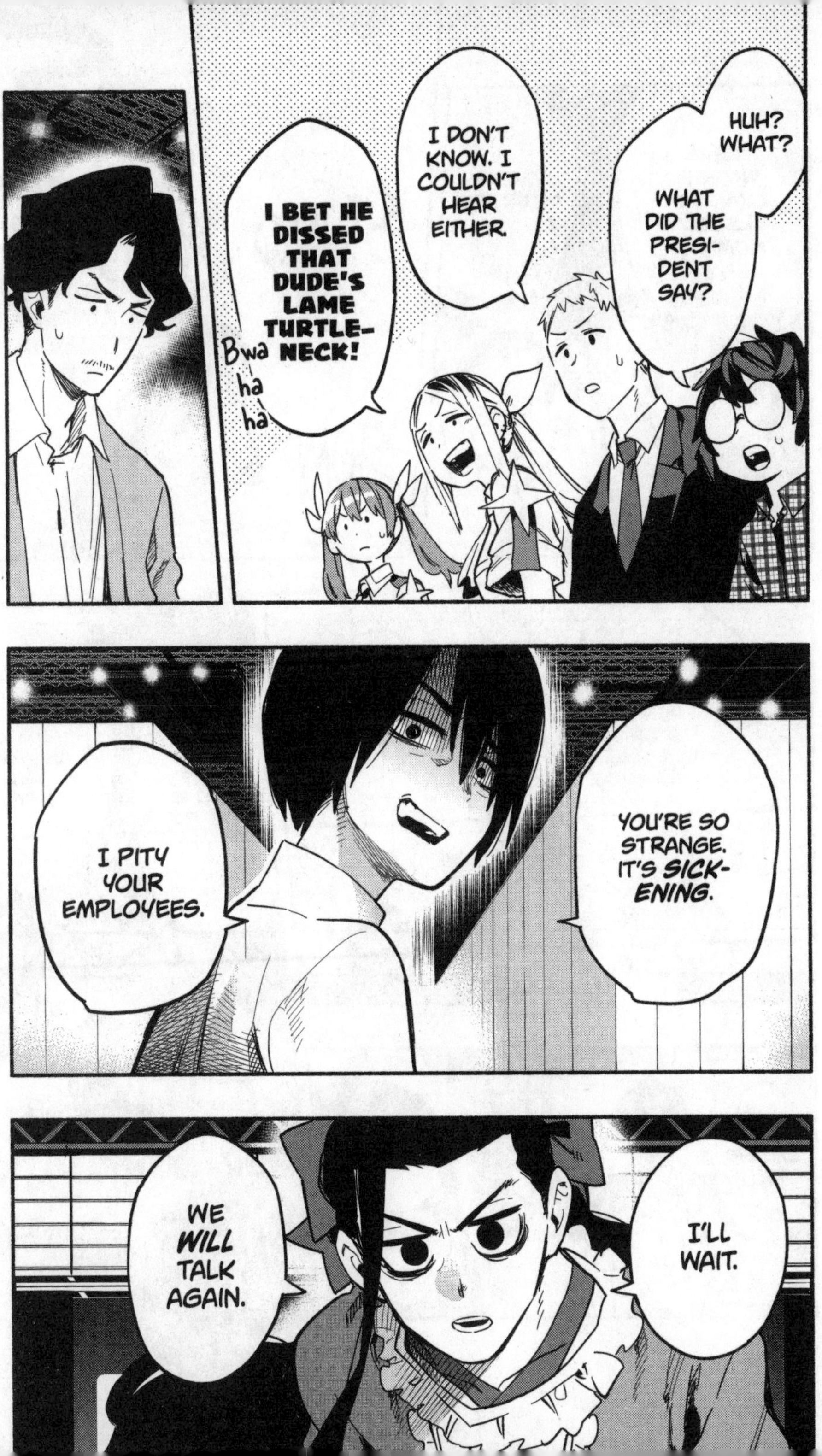
HUH? WHAT?
WHAT DID THE PRESIDENT SAY?
I DON'T KNOW. I COULDN'T HEAR EITHER.
I BET HE DISSED THAT DUDE'S LAME TURTLENECK!
Bwa ha ha
YOU'RE SO STRANGE. IT'S SICKENING.
I PITY YOUR EMPLOYEES.
I'LL WAIT.
WE WILL TALK AGAIN.

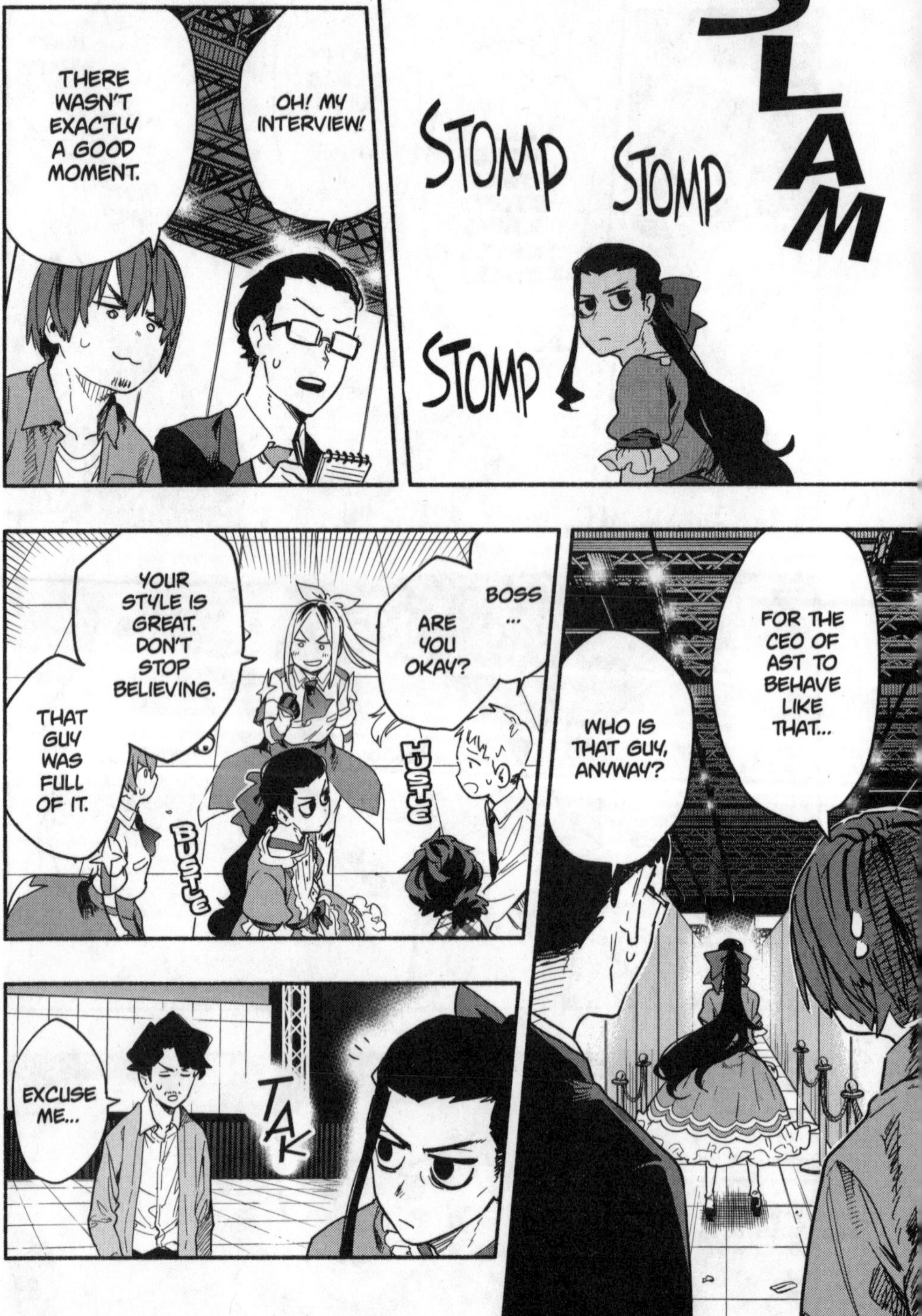
SLAM
STOMP
STOMP
STOMP
OH! MY INTERVIEW!
THERE WASN'T EXACTLY A GOOD MOMENT.
FOR THE CEO OF AST TO BEHAVE LIKE THAT...
WHO IS THAT GUY, ANYWAY?
BOSS ...
ARE YOU OKAY?
HUSTLE
YOUR STYLE IS GREAT. DON'T STOP BELIEVING.
BUSTLE
THAT GUY WAS FULL OF IT.
TAK
EXCUSE ME...

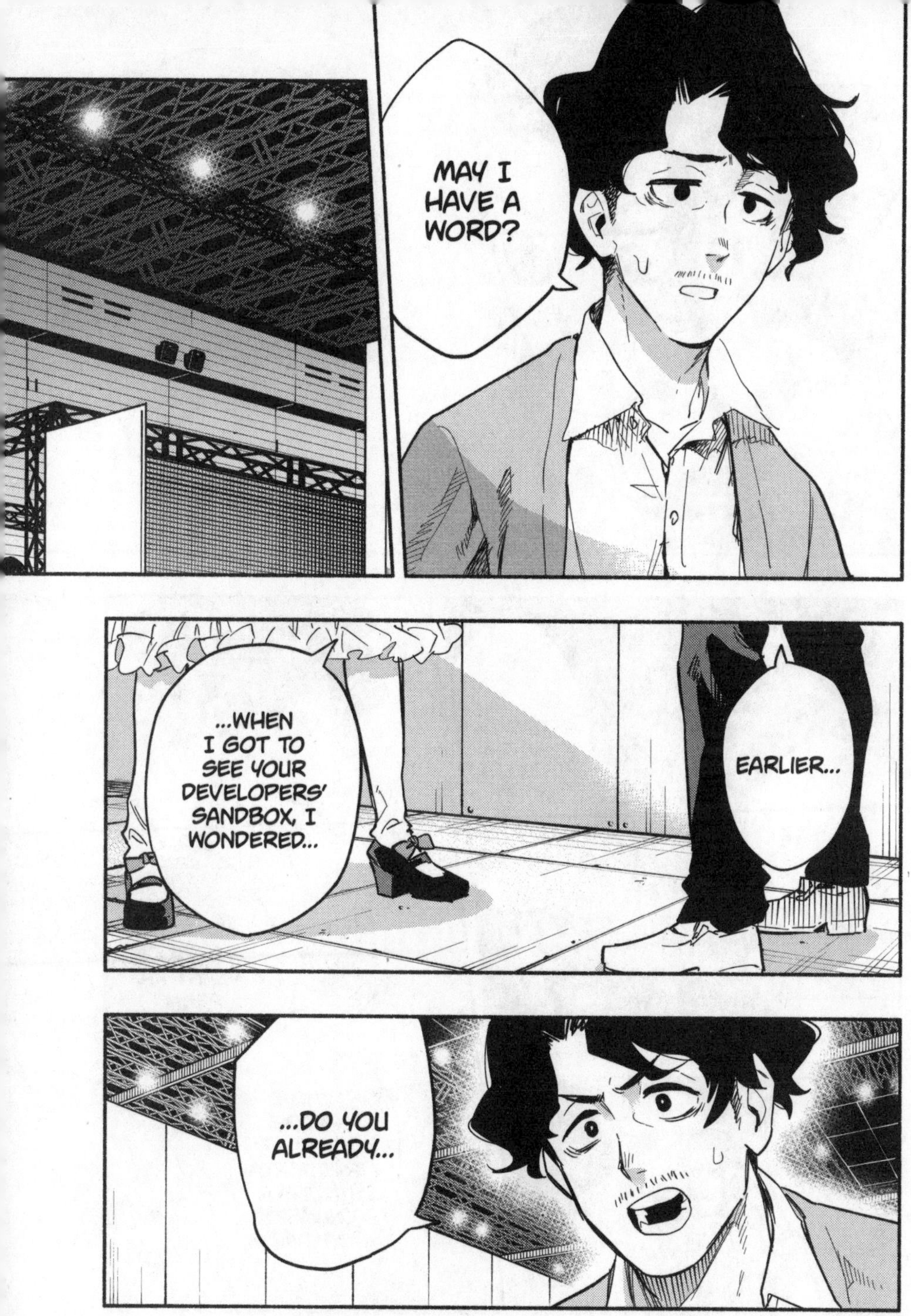
MAY I HAVE A WORD?
EARLIER...
...WHEN I GOT TO SEE YOUR DEVELOPERS' SANDBOX, I WONDERED...
...DO YOU ALREADY...

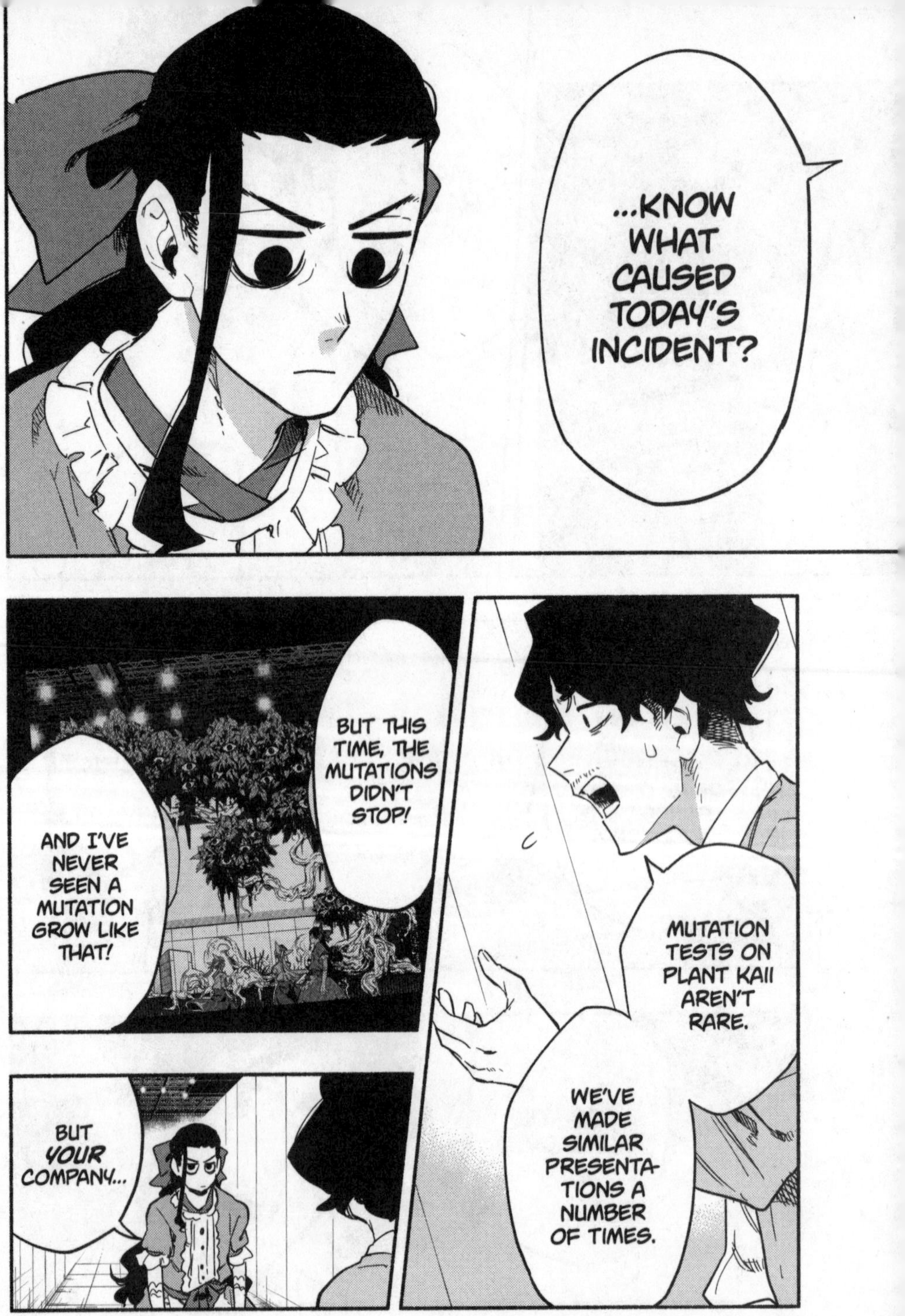
...KNOW WHAT CAUSED TODAY'S INCIDENT?
MUTATION TESTS ON PLANT KAII AREN'T RARE.
WE'VE MADE SIMILAR PRESENTATIONS A NUMBER OF TIMES.
BUT THIS TIME, THE MUTATIONS DIDN'T STOP!
AND I'VE NEVER SEEN A MUTATION GROW LIKE THAT!
BUT *YOUR* COMPANY...

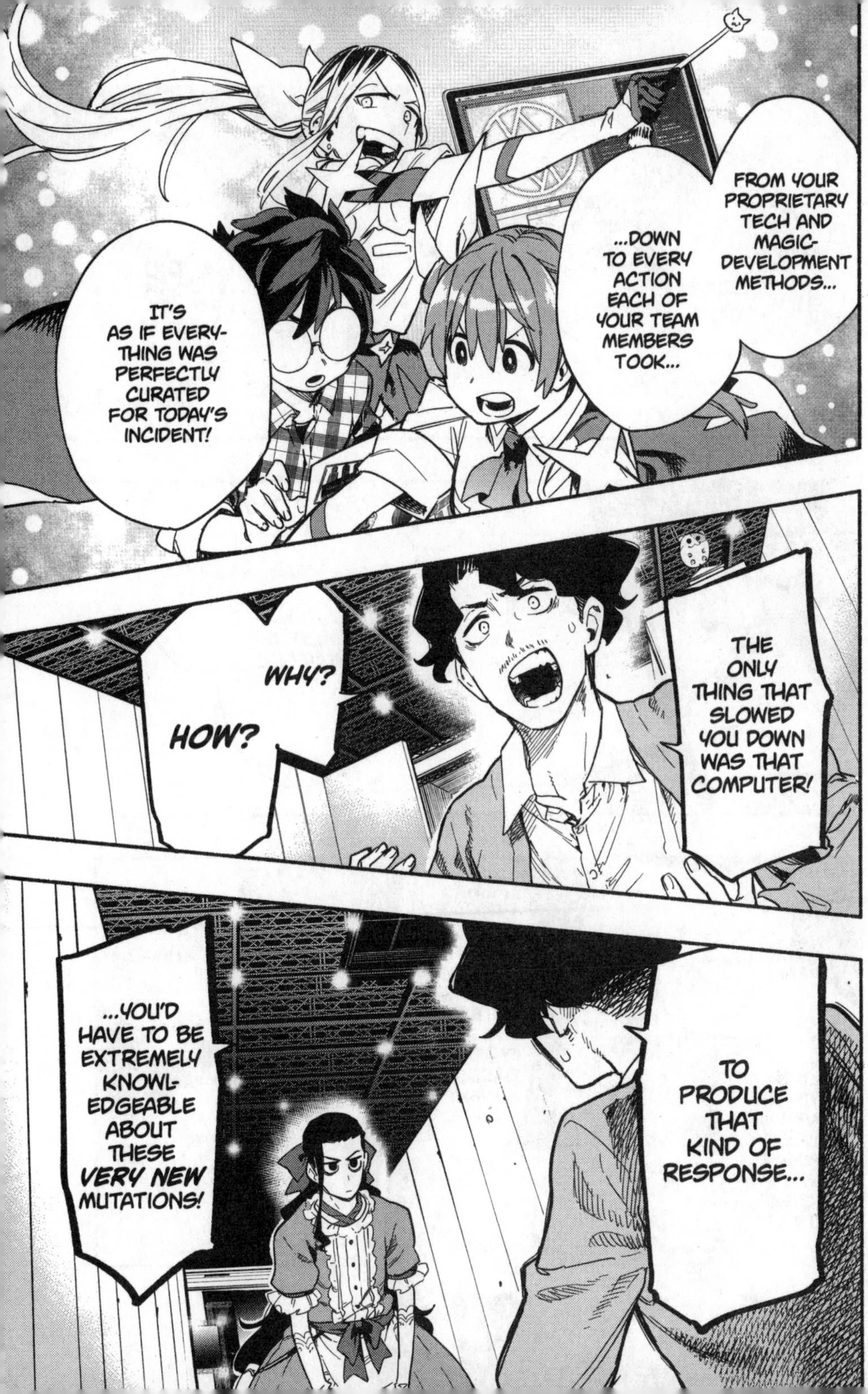
FROM YOUR PROPRIETARY TECH AND MAGIC-DEVELOPMENT METHODS...
...DOWN TO EVERY ACTION EACH OF YOUR TEAM MEMBERS TOOK...
IT'S AS IF EVERYTHING WAS PERFECTLY CURATED FOR TODAY'S INCIDENT!
THE ONLY THING THAT SLOWED YOU DOWN WAS THAT COMPUTER!
WHY?
HOW?
TO PRODUCE THAT KIND OF RESPONSE...
...YOU'D HAVE TO BE EXTREMELY KNOWLEDGEABLE ABOUT THESE VERY NEW MUTATIONS!

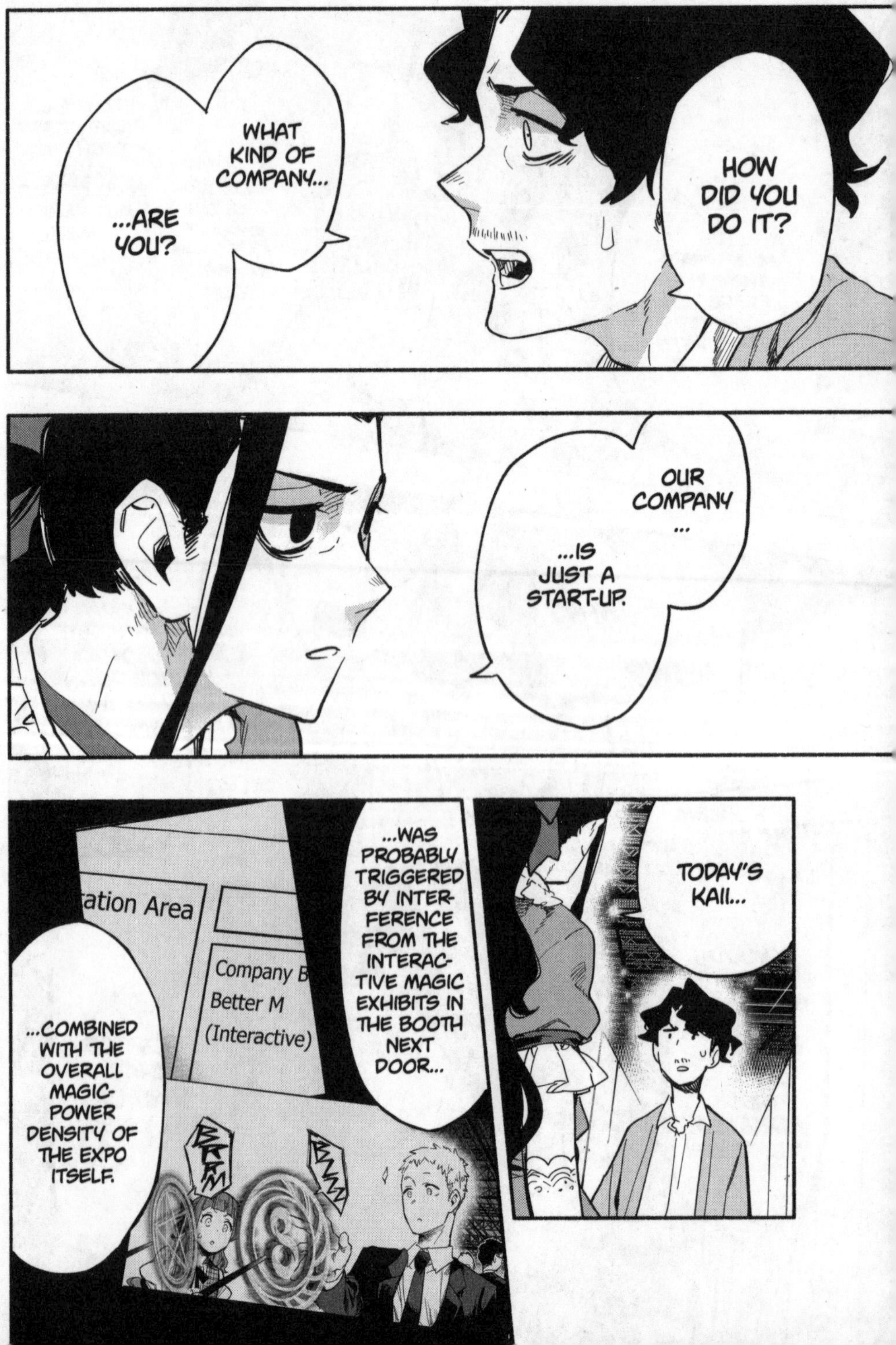
HOW DID YOU DO IT?
WHAT KIND OF COMPANY... ...ARE YOU?
OUR COMPANY... ...IS JUST A START-UP.
TODAY'S KAII...
...WAS PROBABLY TRIGGERED BY INTER-FERENCE FROM THE INTERAC-TIVE MAGIC EXHIBITS IN THE BOOTH NEXT DOOR...
ation Area
Company B
Better M
(Interactive)
...COMBINED WITH THE OVERALL MAGIC-POWER DENSITY OF THE EXPO ITSELF.
BRRM
BZZZ

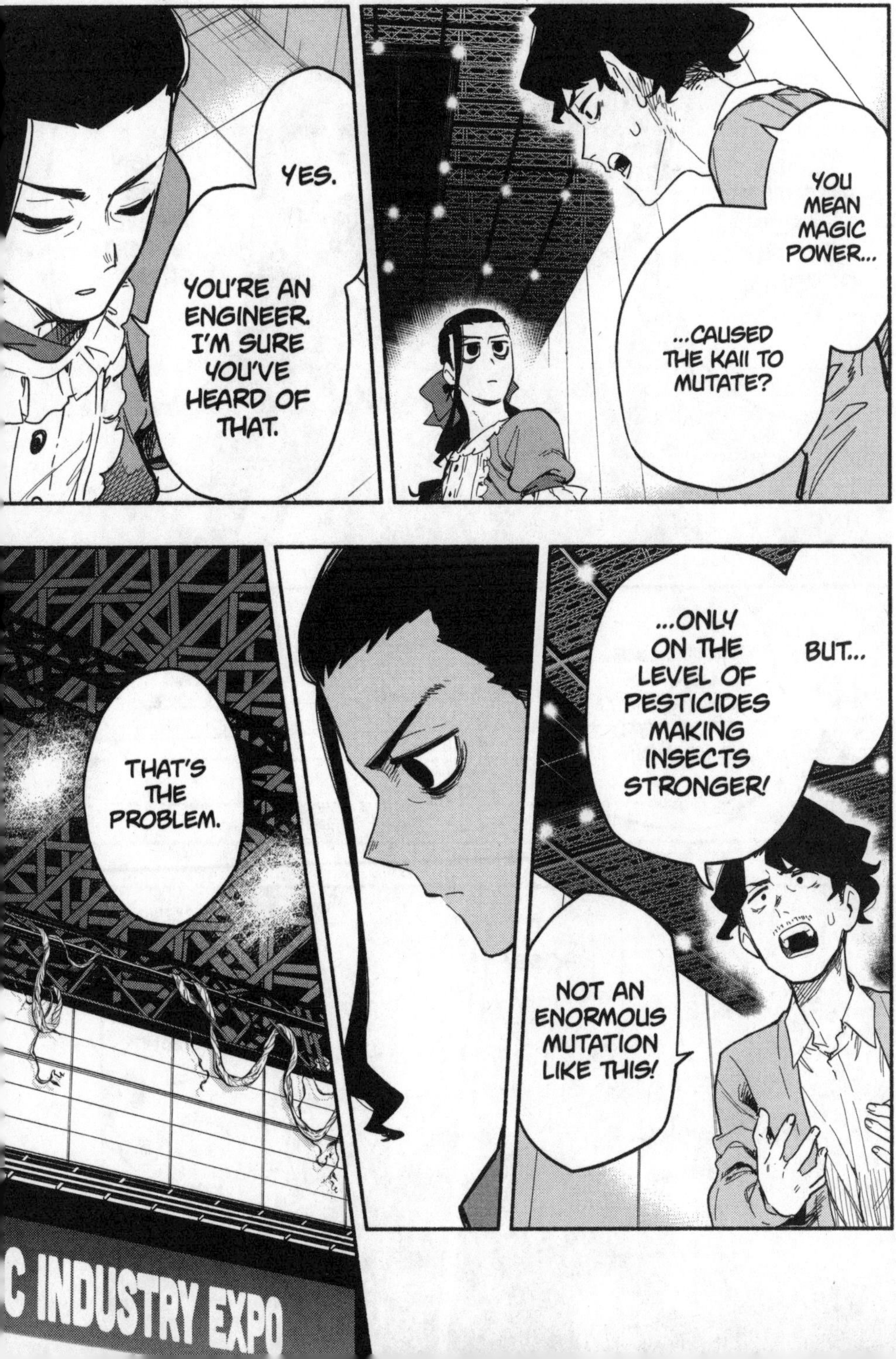
YOU MEAN MAGIC POWER...
...CAUSED THE KAII TO MUTATE?
YES.
YOU'RE AN ENGINEER. I'M SURE YOU'VE HEARD OF THAT.
BUT...
...ONLY ON THE LEVEL OF PESTICIDES MAKING INSECTS STRONGER!
NOT AN ENORMOUS MUTATION LIKE THIS!
THAT'S THE PROBLEM.
C INDUSTRY EXPO

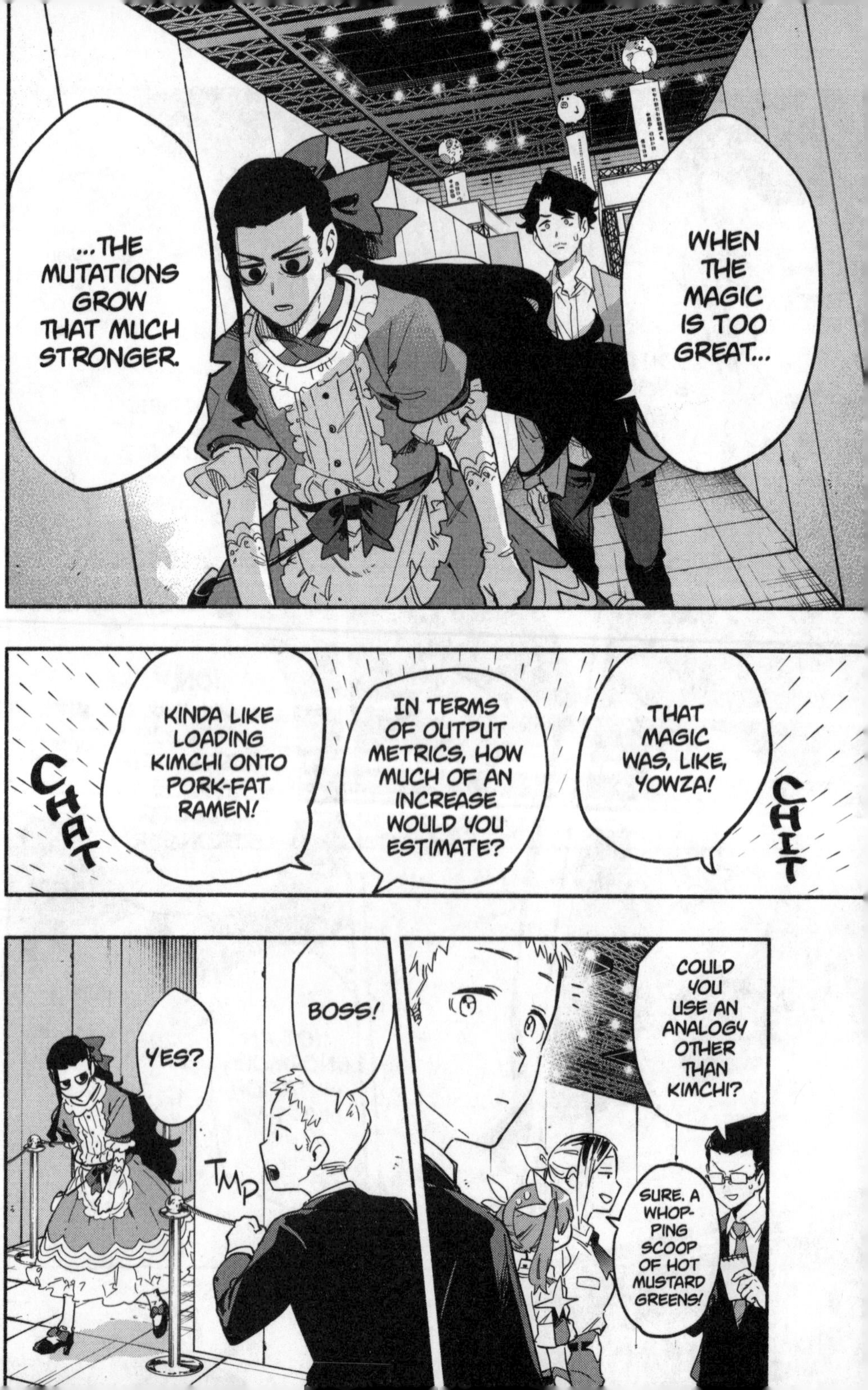
WHEN THE MAGIC IS TOO GREAT...
...THE MUTATIONS GROW THAT MUCH STRONGER.
CHIT
THAT MAGIC WAS, LIKE, YOWZA!
IN TERMS OF OUTPUT METRICS, HOW MUCH OF AN INCREASE WOULD YOU ESTIMATE?
KINDA LIKE LOADING KIMCHI ONTO PORK-FAT RAMEN!
CHAT
COULD YOU USE AN ANALOGY OTHER THAN KIMCHI?
SURE. A WHOPPING SCOOP OF HOT MUSTARD GREENS!
BOSS!
TMP
YES?

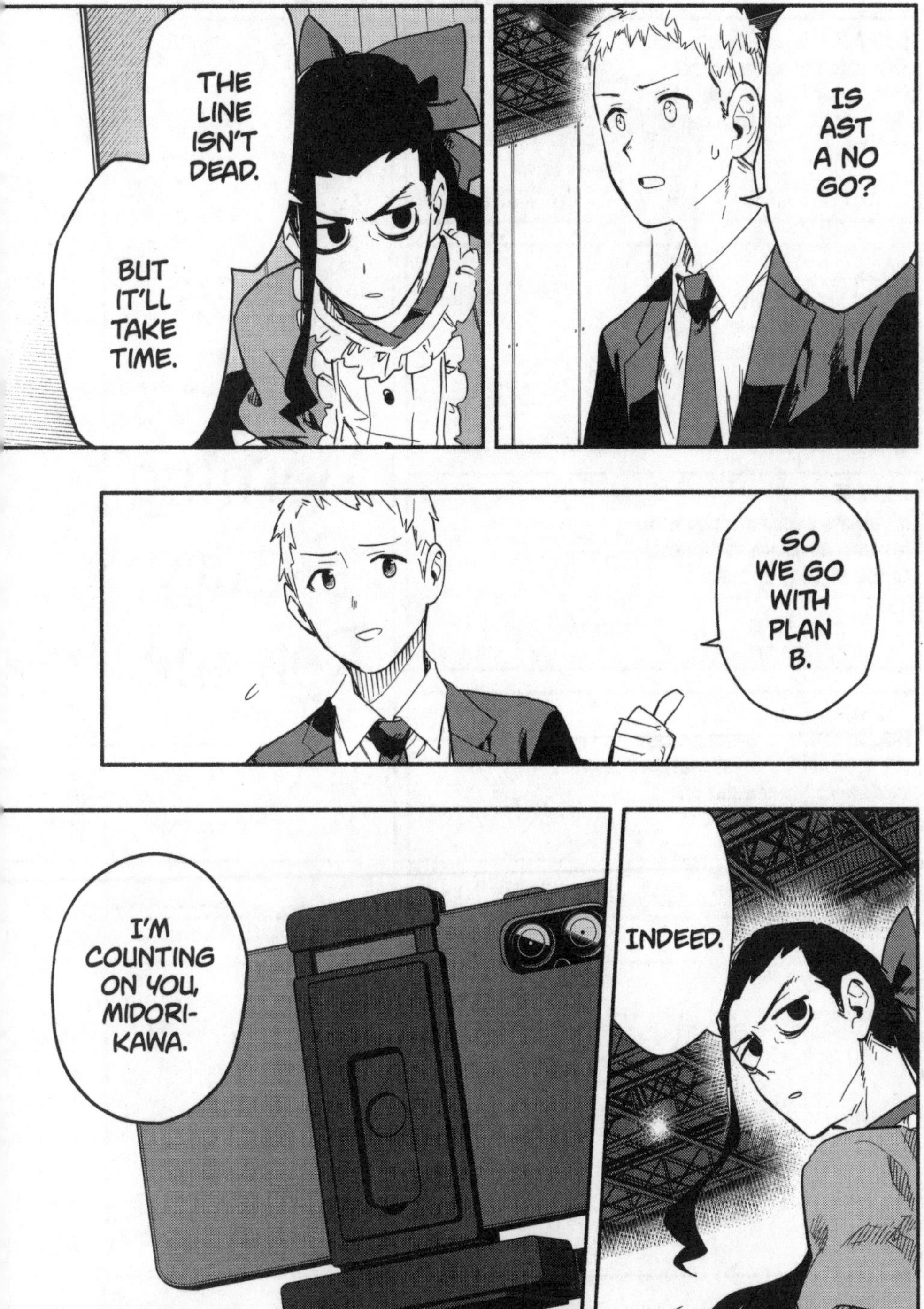
IS AST A NO GO?
THE LINE ISN'T DEAD.
BUT IT'LL TAKE TIME.
SO WE GO WITH PLAN B.
INDEED.
I'M COUNTING ON YOU, MIDORI-KAWA.

Magilumiere Magical Girls Inc. volume 3 — The End

Brand-New Bonus Comic

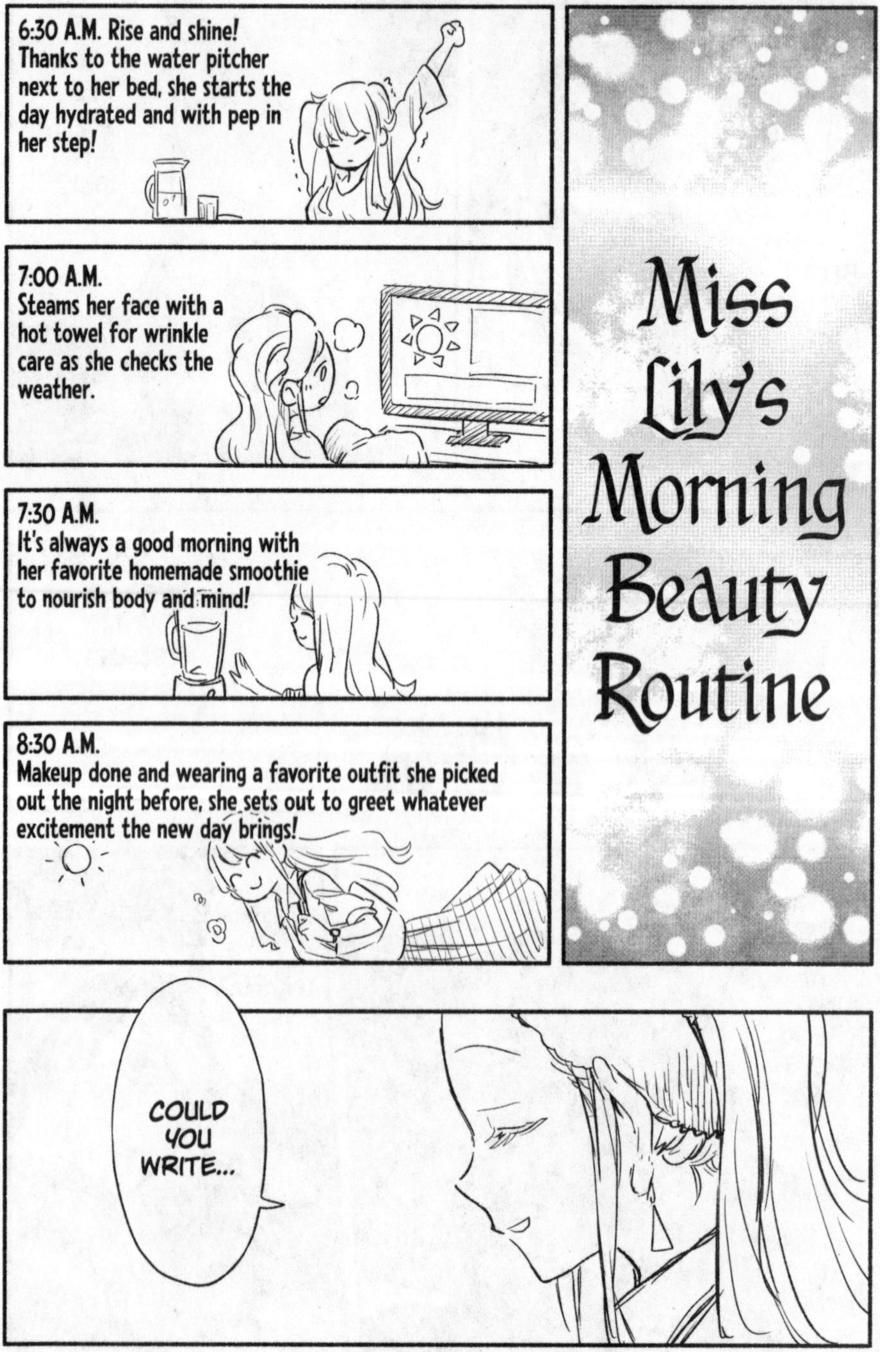
Miss Lily's Morning Beauty Routine
6:30 A.M. Rise and shine! Thanks to the water pitcher next to her bed, she starts the day hydrated and with pep in her step!
7:00 A.M. Steams her face with a hot towel for wrinkle care as she checks the weather.
7:30 A.M. It's always a good morning with her favorite homemade smoothie to nourish body and mind!
8:30 A.M. Makeup done and wearing a favorite outfit she picked out the night before, she sets out to greet whatever excitement the new day brings!
COULD YOU WRITE...

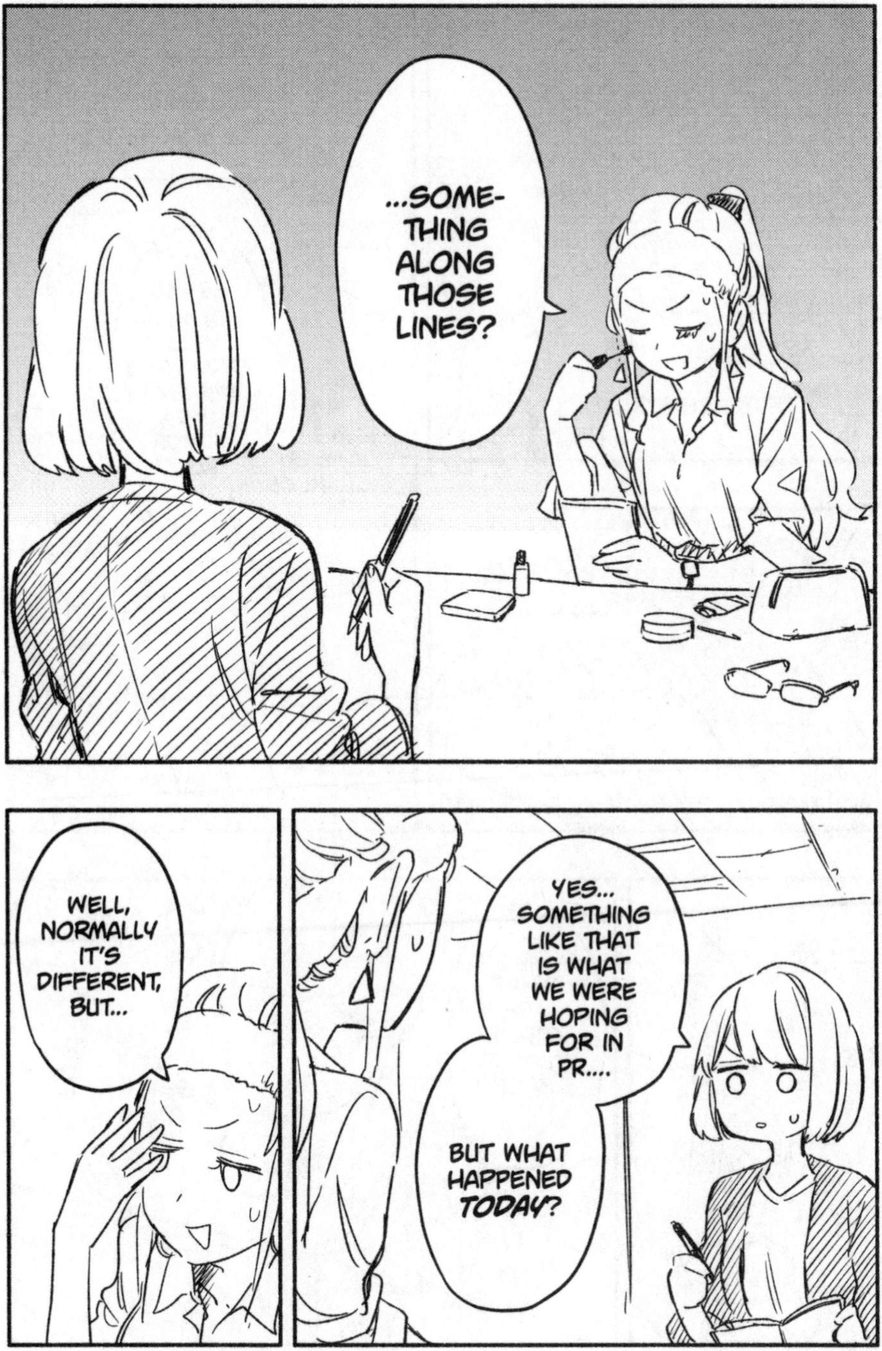
...SOME-THING ALONG THOSE LINES?
YES... SOMETHING LIKE THAT IS WHAT WE WERE HOPING FOR IN PR....
BUT WHAT HAPPENED *TODAY*?
WELL, NORMALLY IT'S DIFFERENT, BUT...

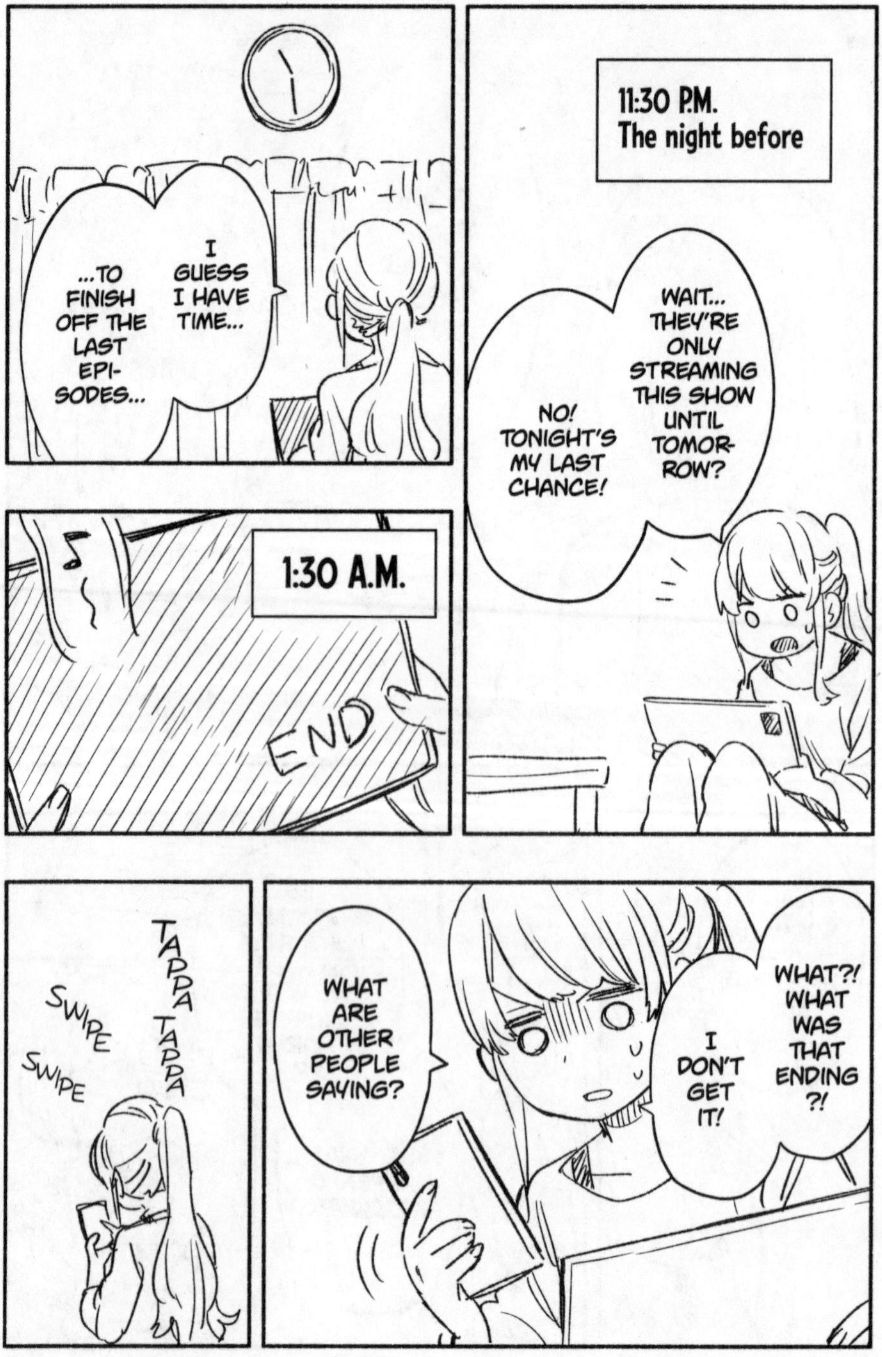
11:30 P.M. The night before
WAIT... THEY'RE ONLY STREAMING THIS SHOW UNTIL TOMOR-ROW?
NO! TONIGHT'S MY LAST CHANCE!
I GUESS I HAVE TIME...
...TO FINISH OFF THE LAST EPI-SODES...
1:30 A.M.
END
WHAT?! WHAT WAS THAT ENDING?!
I DON'T GET IT!
WHAT ARE OTHER PEOPLE SAYING?
TAPPA TAPPA
SWIPE SWIPE

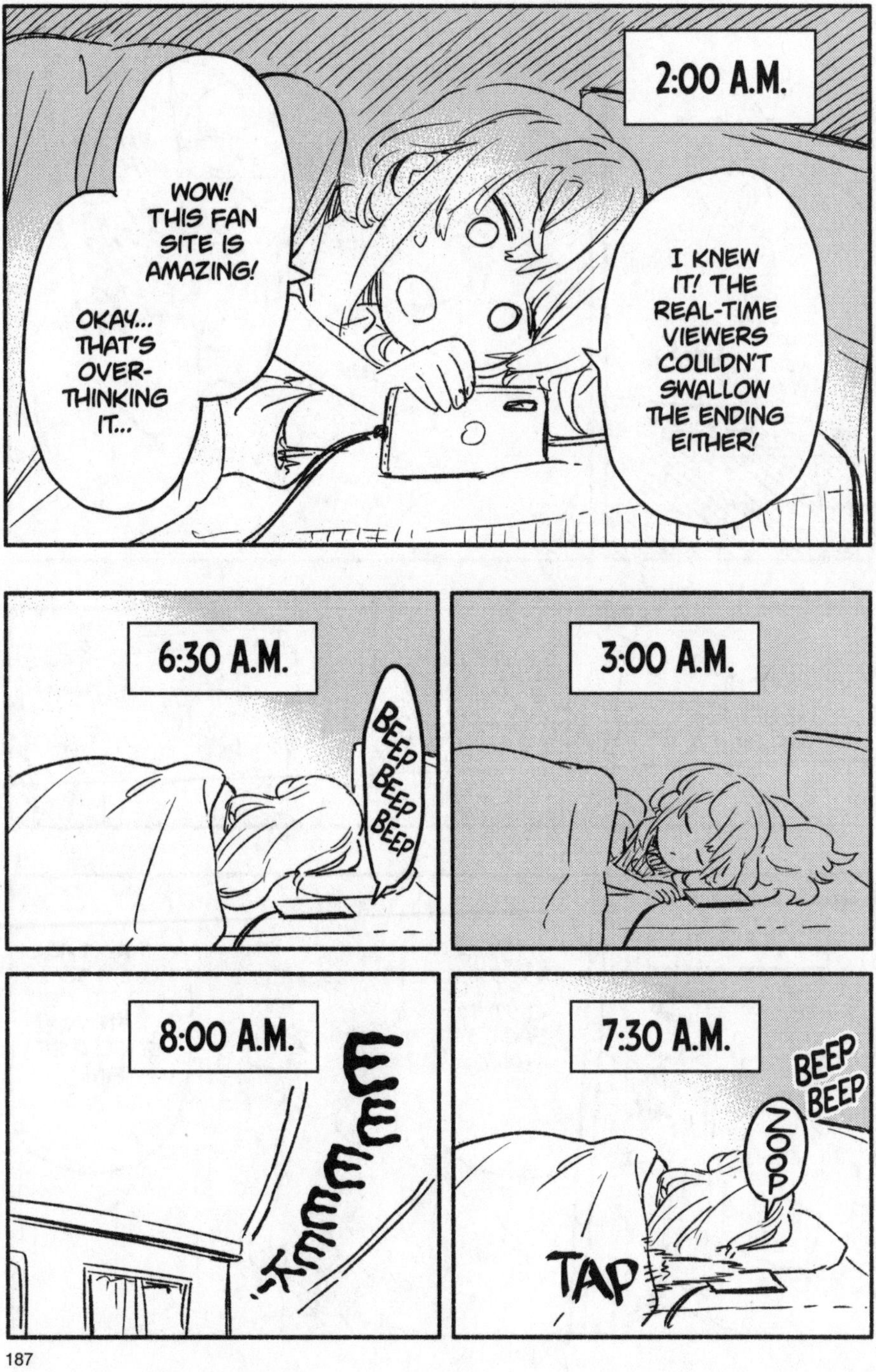
2:00 A.M.
I KNEW IT! THE REAL-TIME VIEWERS COULDN'T SWALLOW THE ENDING EITHER!
WOW! THIS FAN SITE IS AMAZING!
OKAY... THAT'S OVER-THINKING IT...
3:00 A.M.
6:30 A.M.
BEEP BEEP BEEP
7:30 A.M.
BEEP BEEP
ZOOP
TAP
8:00 A.M.
EEEEEEK!

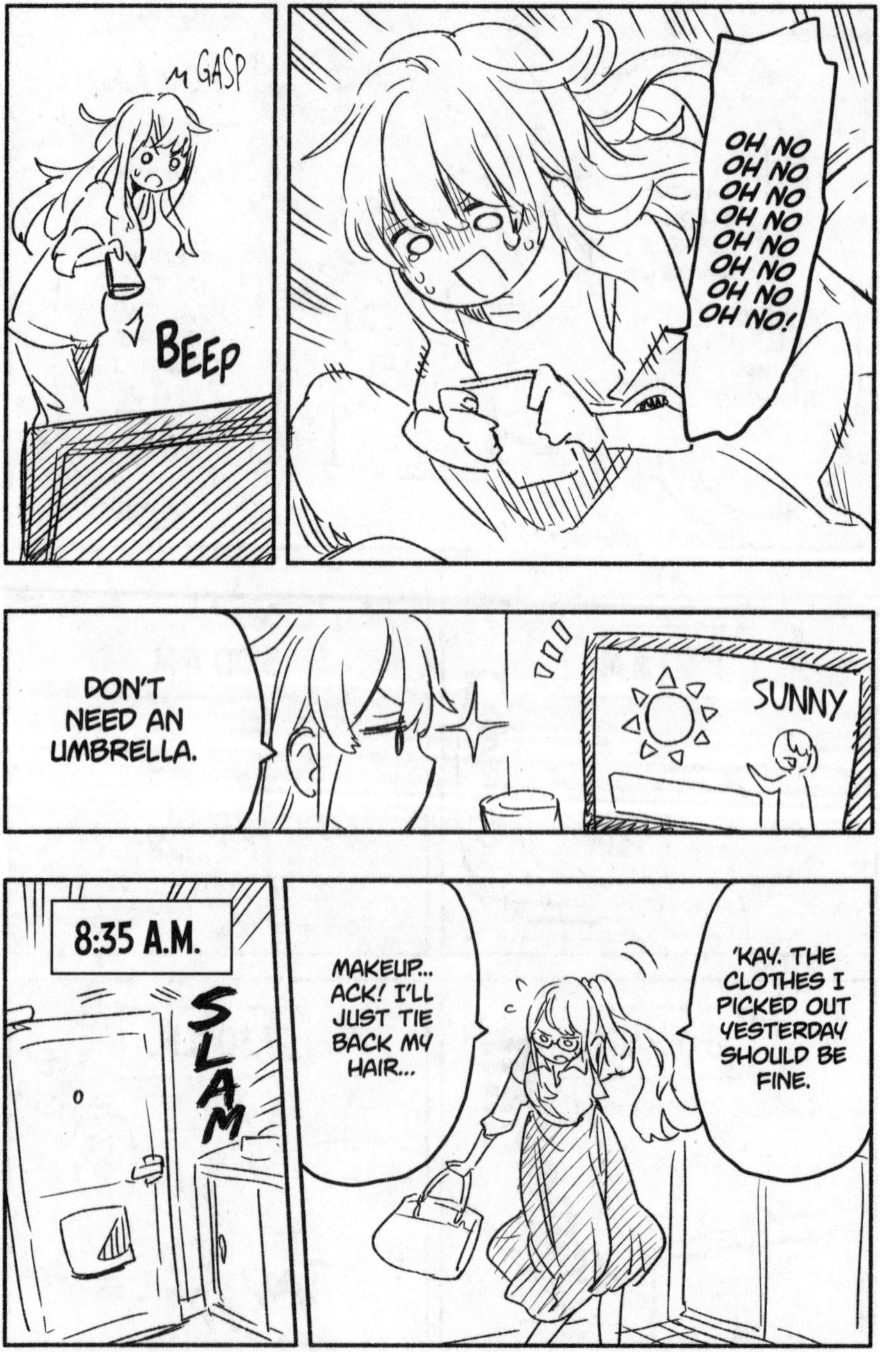
OH NO OH NO OH NO OH NO OH NO OH NO OH NO OH NO!
GASP
BEEP
SUNNY
DON'T NEED AN UMBRELLA.
'KAY. THE CLOTHES I PICKED OUT YESTERDAY SHOULD BE FINE.
MAKEUP... ACK! I'LL JUST TIE BACK MY HAIR...
8:35 A.M.
SLAM

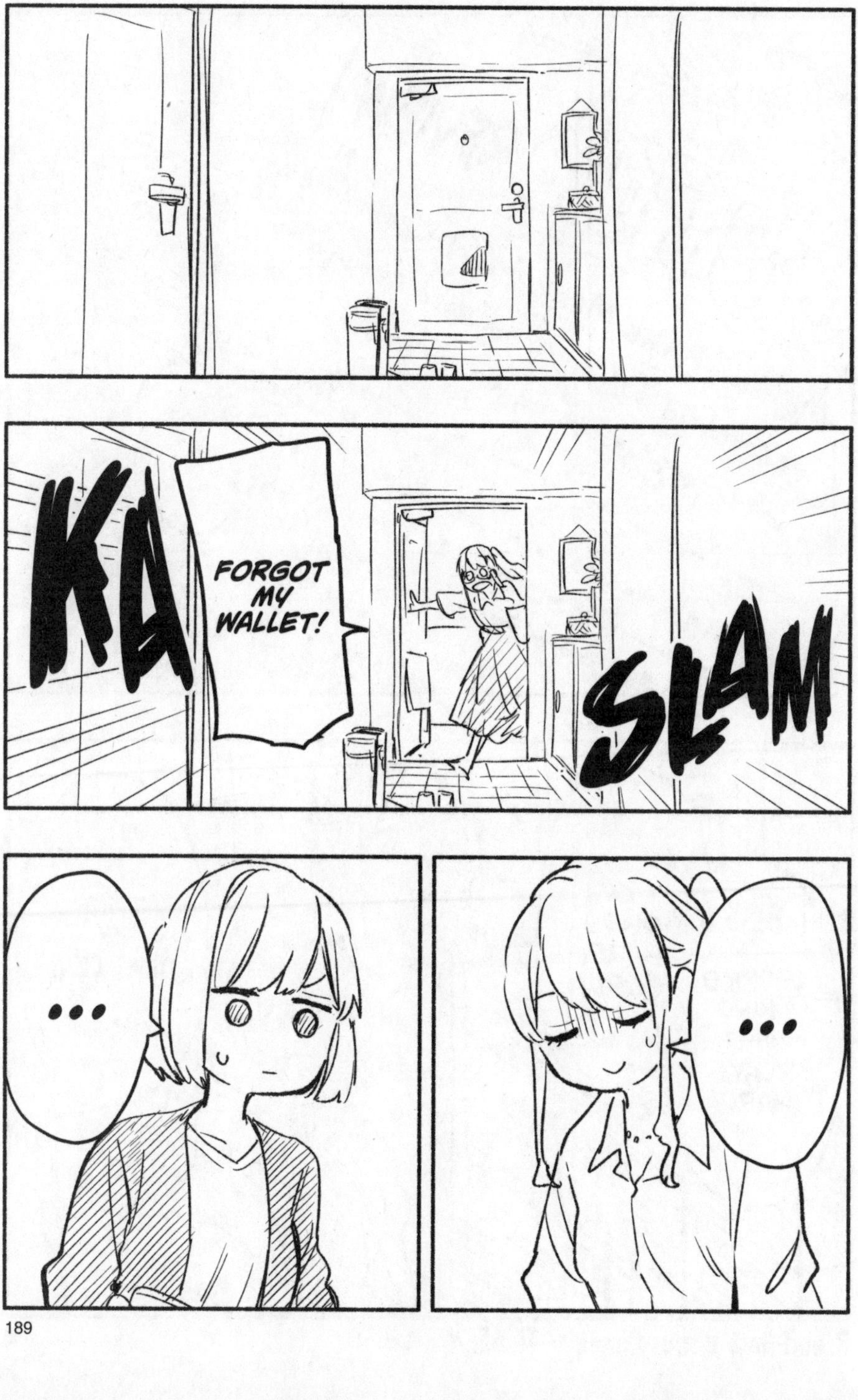
FORGOT MY WALLET!
KA
SLAM
...
...

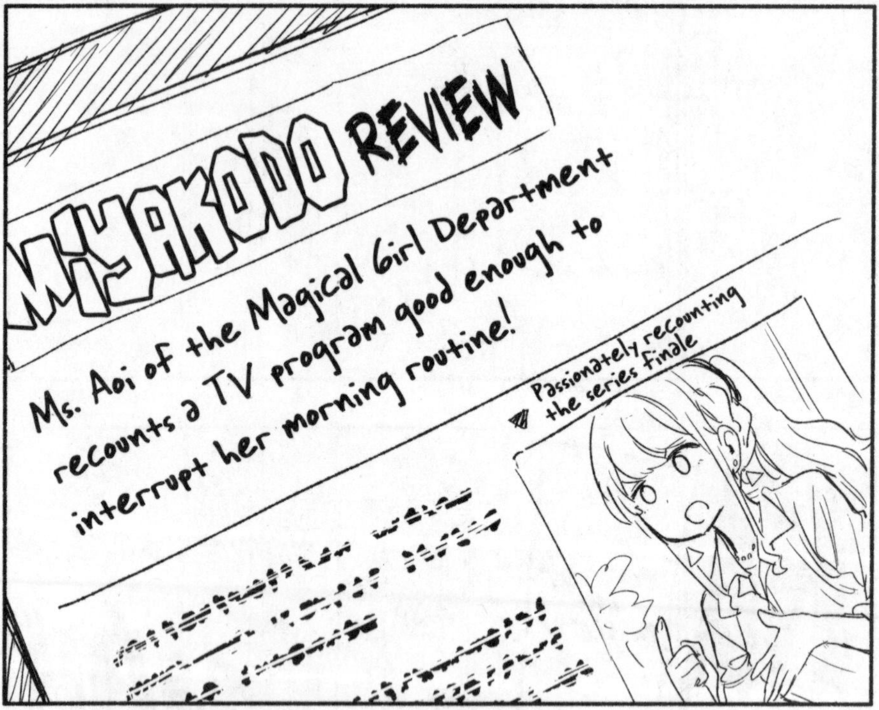
MIYAKODO REVIEW
Ms. Aoi of the Magical Girl Department recounts a TV program good enough to interrupt her morning routine!
Passionately recounting the series finale

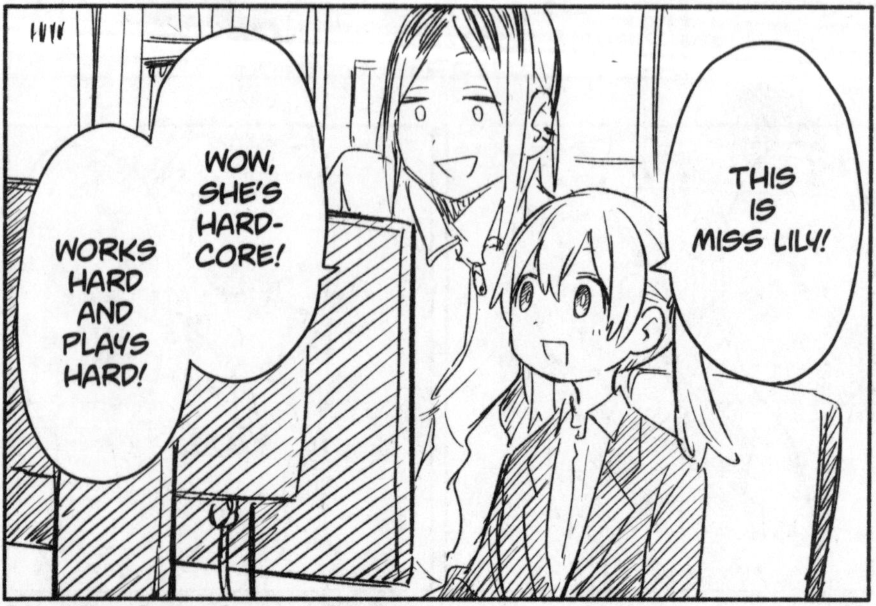
THIS IS MISS LILY!
WOW, SHE'S HARD-CORE!
WORKS HARD AND PLAYS HARD!

Brand-New Bonus Comic – The End

MAGILUMIERE MAGICAL GIRLS INC 3

STAFF LIST

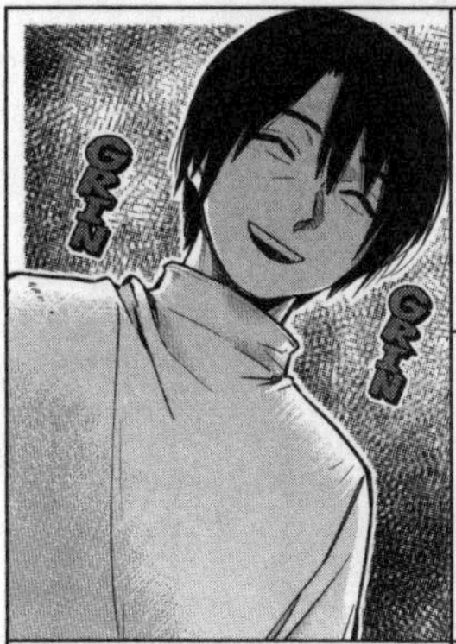
GRIN
GRIN

STAFF

CHIHIRO AIDA

Born: February 19

Enjoys while working:
Radio, rakugo storytelling

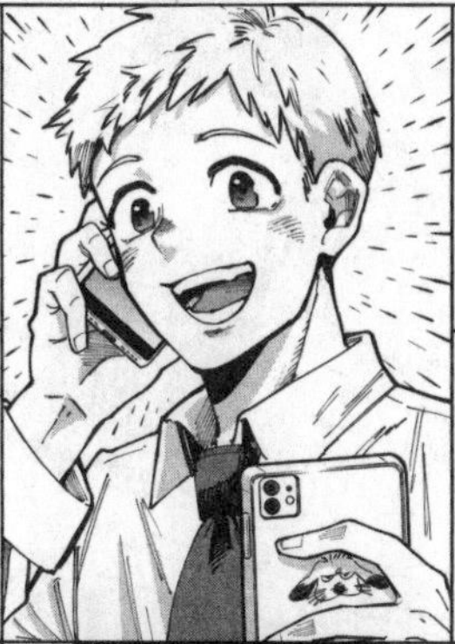

STAFF

YUTO SAEZU

Born: November 30

Enjoys while working:
Streaming real-life ghost stories

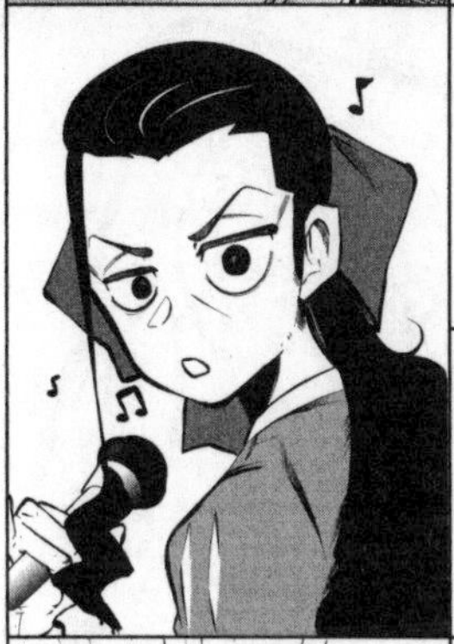

STAFF

TAKUMA TATEISHI

Born: December 23

Enjoys while working:
Monster energy drink

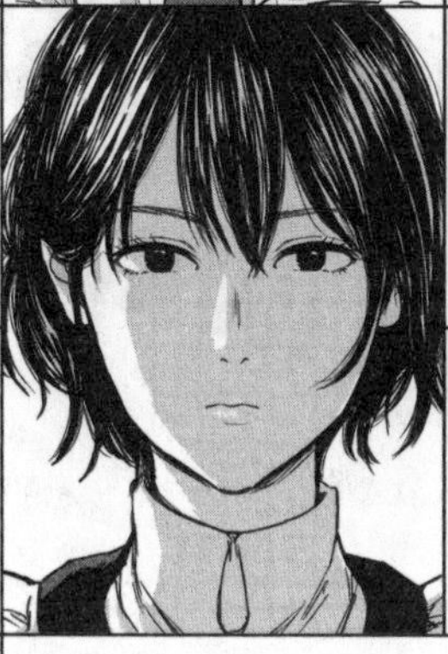

STAFF

YOH SHIORI

Born: April 27

Enjoys while working:
Music

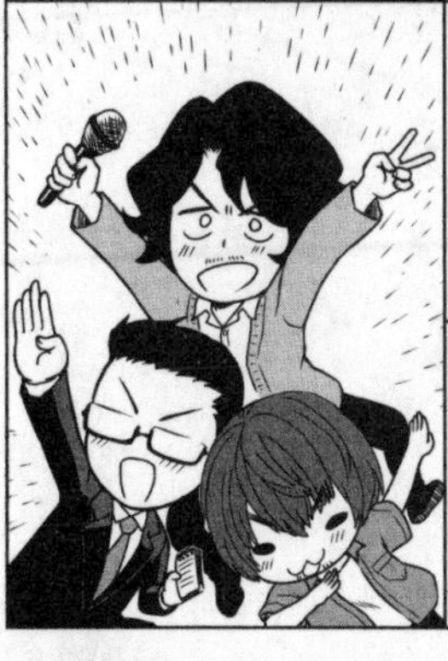

STAFF

MOMO

Born: December 20

Enjoys while working:
Sugar

MAGILUMIERE
MAGICAL GIRLS INC

Graphic Novel Designer	TADASHI HISAMOCHI SEIKO TSUCHIHASHI
Graphic Novel Editor	YUKO ABE
Editor in Chief	SHU MURAKOSHI

✦ AUTHOR ✦

SEKKA IWATA

As you may have noticed, the original storyboards for *Magilumiere* are superbly messy. It's Mr. Aoki (and the assistants) who bring that messy world into focus. Often I realize things about the story after the illustrations are done. I am always grateful.

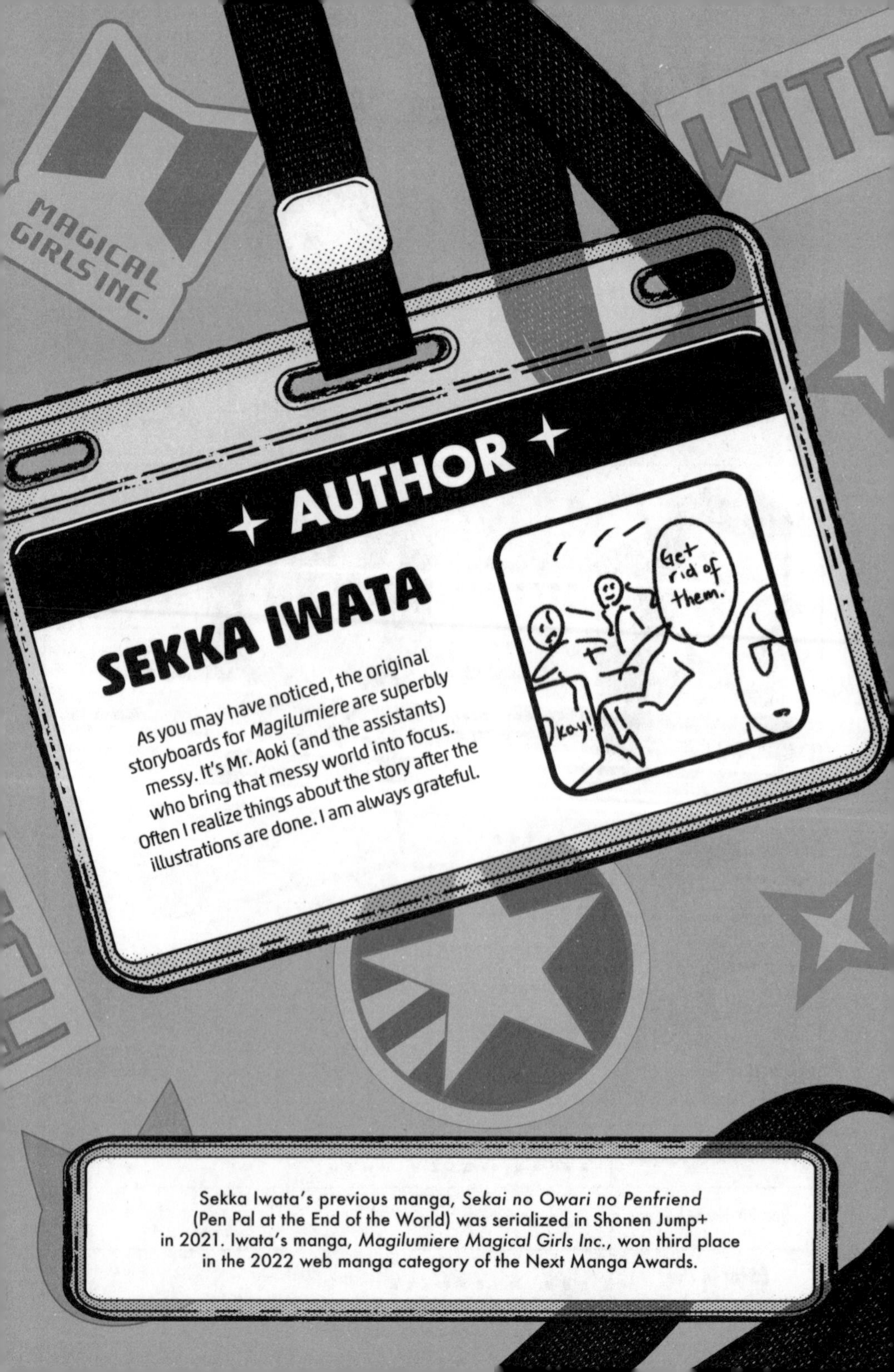
Get rid of them.
Okay!

Sekka Iwata's previous manga, *Sekai no Owari no Penfriend* (Pen Pal at the End of the World) was serialized in Shonen Jump+ in 2021. Iwata's manga, *Magilumiere Magical Girls Inc.*, won third place in the 2022 web manga category of the Next Manga Awards.

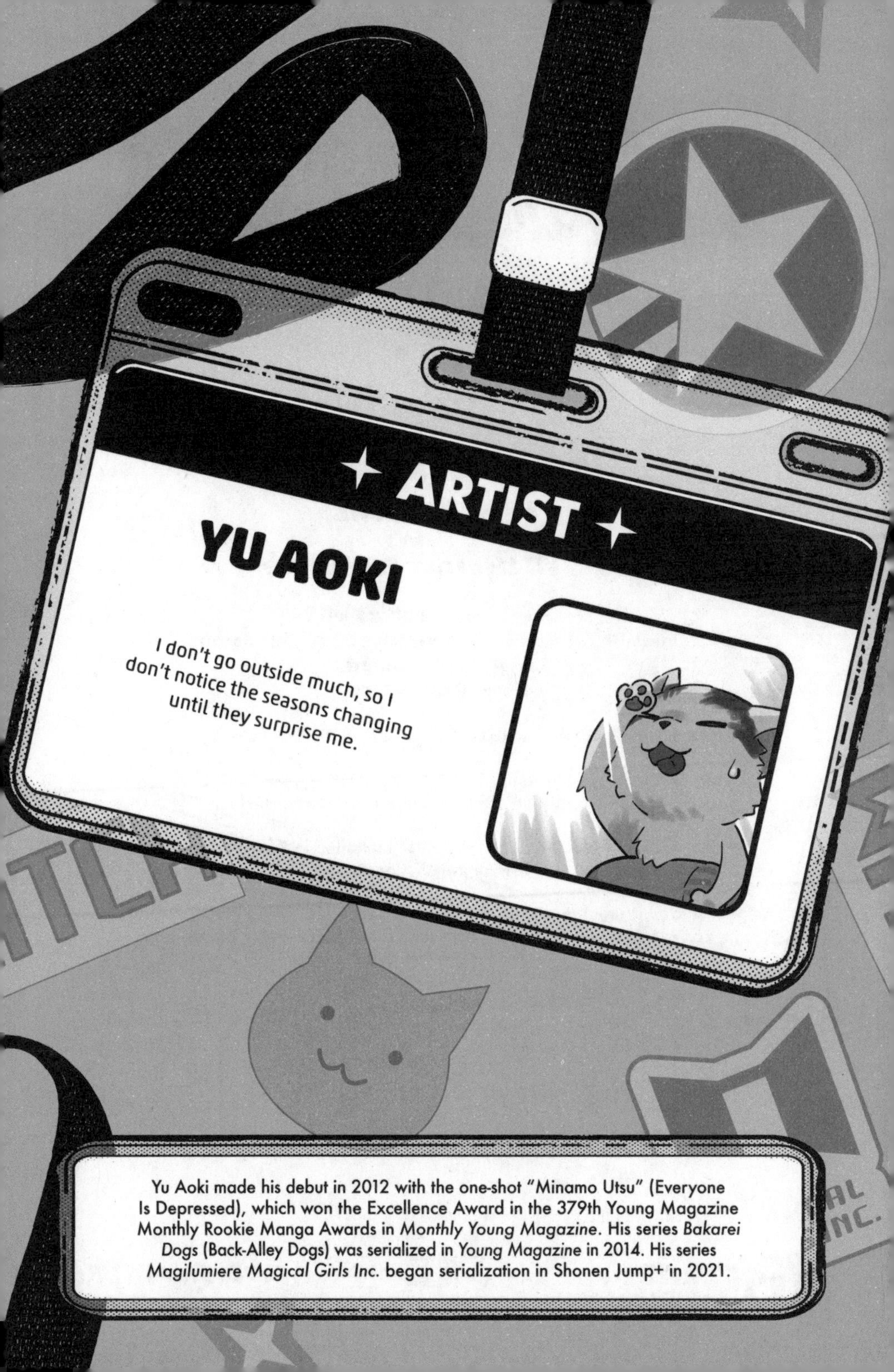
ARTIST
YU AOKI
I don't go outside much, so I don't notice the seasons changing until they surprise me.

Yu Aoki made his debut in 2012 with the one-shot "Minamo Utsu" (Everyone Is Depressed), which won the Excellence Award in the 379th Young Magazine Monthly Rookie Manga Awards in *Monthly Young Magazine*. His series *Bakarei Dogs* (Back-Alley Dogs) was serialized in *Young Magazine* in 2014. His series *Magilumiere Magical Girls Inc.* began serialization in Shonen Jump+ in 2021.

Magilumiere
MAGICAL GIRLS INC.

3

Story by **Sekka Iwata**

Art by **Yu Aoki**

✦ **VIZ Signature Edition** ✦

Translation **Camellia Nieh**
Touch-Up Art & Lettering **Annaliese "Ace" Christman**
Design **Paul Padurariu**
Editor **Pancha Diaz**

KABUSHIKIGAISHA MAGILUMIERE © 2021 by Sekka Iwata, Yu Aoki
All rights reserved.
First published in Japan in 2021 by SHUEISHA Inc., Tokyo.
English translation rights arranged by SHUEISHA Inc.

The stories, characters, and incidents mentioned in this publication
are entirely fictional.

Printed in Canada

Published by VIZ Media, LLC
P.O. Box 77010
San Francisco, CA 94107

10 9 8 7 6 5 4 3 2 1
First printing, August 2024

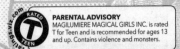

VIZ MEDIA
viz.com

VIZ SIGNATURE
vizsignature.com

BURN THE WITCH

Behind the world you think you know lies a land of magic and fairy tales—but Reverse London isn't the pretty picture that's painted in children's books. Fairy tales have teeth, and the dedicated agents of Wing Bind are the only thing standing between you and the real story.

STORY AND ART BY

TITE KUBO

A slipcased paperback edition of a modern fantasy tale set in the wider world of *Bleach*, by *Bleach* author **Tite Kubo**!

HAIKYU!!

SHOYO HINATA IS OUT TO PROVE THAT IN VOLLEYBALL YOU DON'T NEED TO BE TALL TO FLY!

Story and Art by **HARUICHI FURUDATE**

Ever since he saw the legendary player known as the "Little Giant" compete at the national volleyball finals, Shoyo Hinata has been aiming to be the best volleyball player ever! He decides to join the team at the high school the Little Giant went to—and then surpass him. Who says you need to be tall to play volleyball when you can jump higher than anyone else?

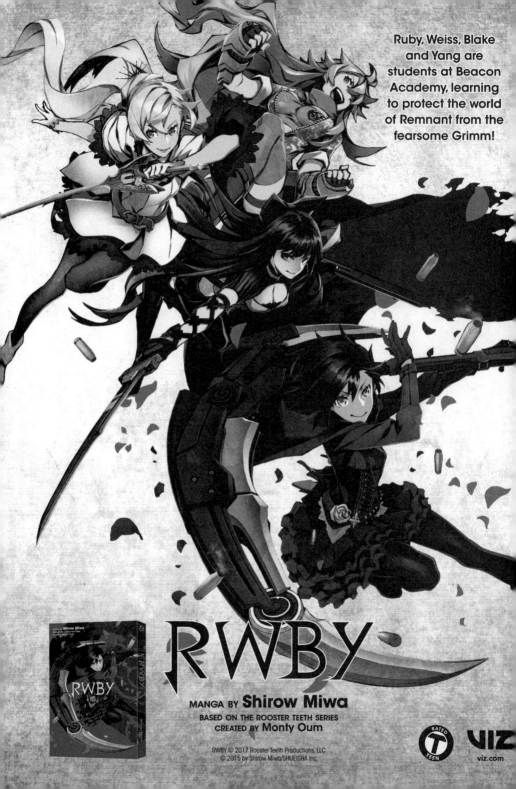

THE PROMISED NEVERLAND

ART BOOK ❀ORLD

Story by **Kaiu Shirai**
Art by **Posuka Demizu**

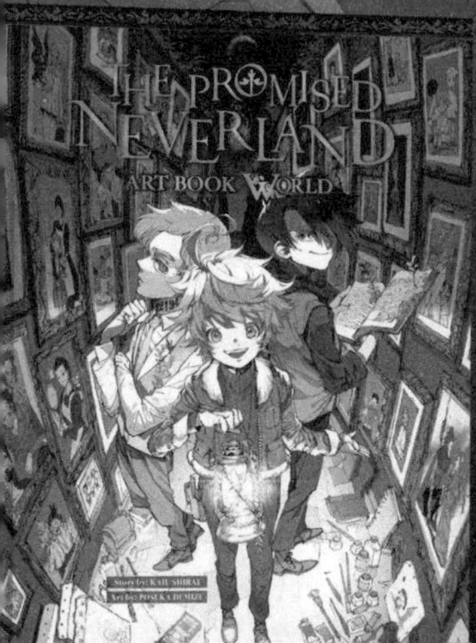

Featuring Posuka Demizu's incredible artwork,
as well as creator commentary and interviews,
The Promised Neverland: Art Book World is
a beautiful and haunting gaze into the art of one of
today's most popular Shonen Jump manga series.

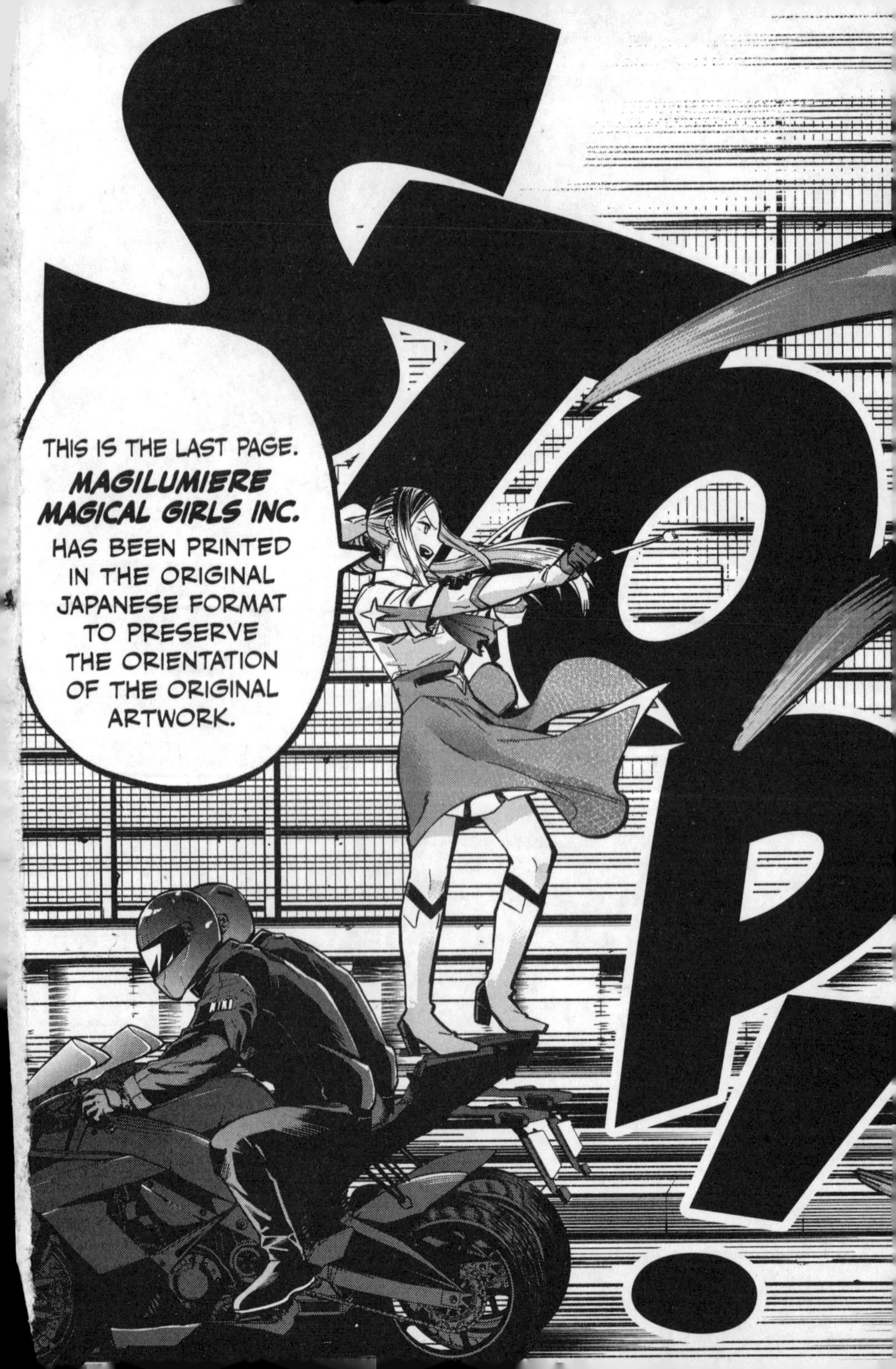
THIS IS THE LAST PAGE. MAGILUMIERE MAGICAL GIRLS INC. HAS BEEN PRINTED IN THE ORIGINAL JAPANESE FORMAT TO PRESERVE THE ORIENTATION OF THE ORIGINAL ARTWORK.